WHERE THE HOOD AT?

WHERE THE HOOD AT?

FIFTY YEARS OF CHANGE IN BLACK NEIGHBORHOODS

Michael C. Lens

Russell Sage Foundation • New York

The Russell Sage Foundation

The Russell Sage Foundation, one of the oldest of America's general purpose foundations, was established in 1907 by Mrs. Margaret Olivia Sage for "the improvement of social and living conditions in the United States." The foundation seeks to fulfill this mandate by fostering the development and dissemination of knowledge about the country's political, social, and economic problems. While the foundation endeavors to assure the accuracy and objectivity of each book it publishes, the conclusions and interpretations in Russell Sage Foundation publications are those of the authors and not of the foundation, its trustees, or its staff. Publication by Russell Sage, therefore, does not imply foundation endorsement.

ROR: https://ror.org/02yh9se80
DOI: https://doi.org/10.7758/tjvh5404

Library of Congress Cataloging in Publication Control Numbers:
2024027111 (print) / 2024027112 (ebook)
ISBN 9780871548184 (paperback) / ISBN 9781610449311 (ebook)

The paper used in this publication meets the minimum requirements of American National Standard for Information Sciences—Permanence of Paper for Printed Library Materials. ANSI Z39.48-1992.

Text design by Suzanne Nichols. Front matter DOI: https://doi.org/10.7758/tjvh5404.9047

RUSSELL SAGE FOUNDATION
112 East 64th Street, New York, New York 10065
10 9 8 7 6 5 4 3 2 1

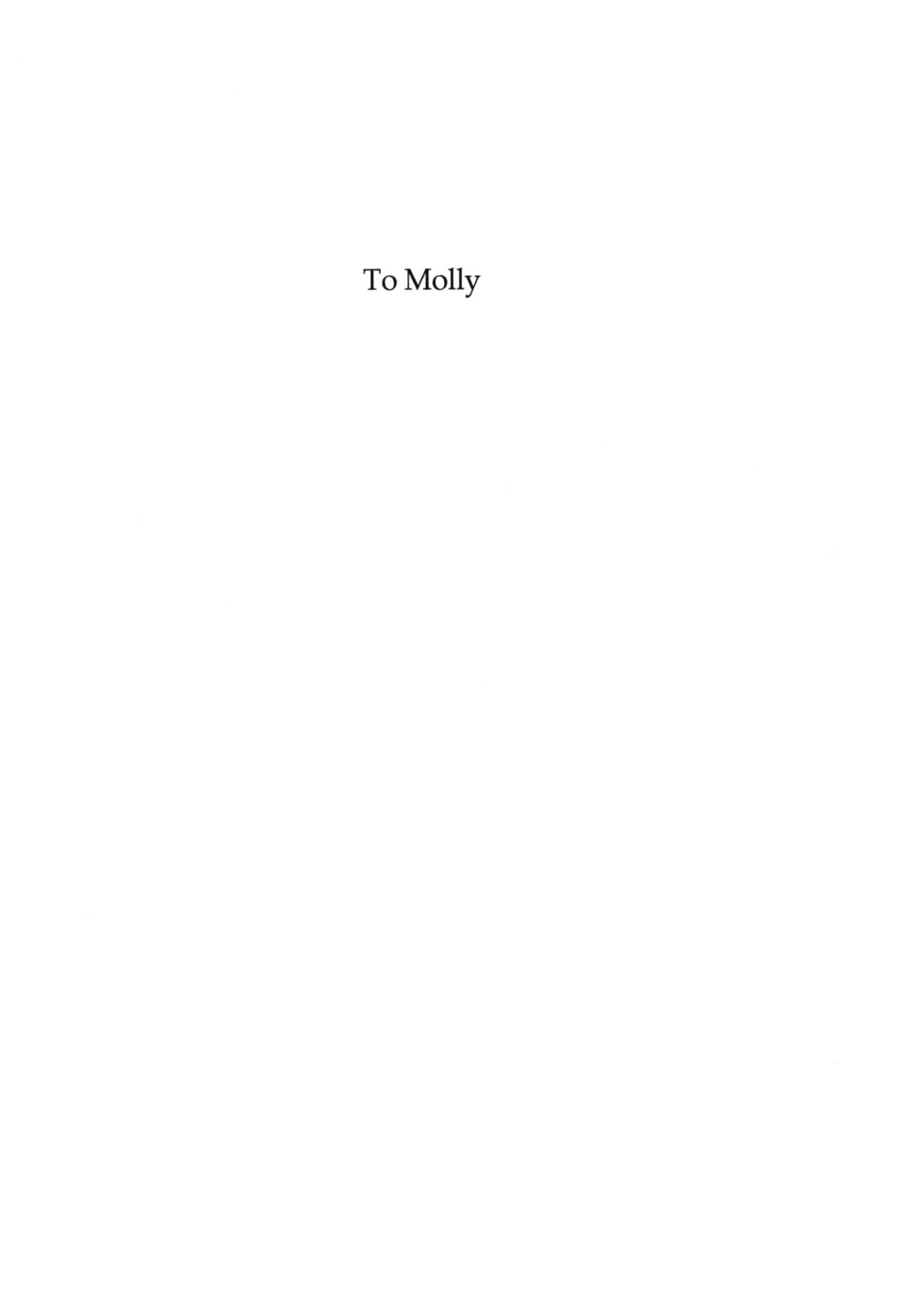

To Molly

Contents

Illustrations

Figures

Tables

About the Author

Michael C. Lens is professor of urban planning and public policy at the UCLA Luskin School of Public Affairs.

Acknowledgments

I am mindful of the many scholars who have never had their study of Black life supported by their institutions or fields. My experience has been very different and is probably the biggest reason why this book is now a reality. The University of California–Los Angeles and my colleagues in the Luskin School and Urban Planning Department have always made an inquiry like this feel possible. I can say the same about the broader field of urban planning, particularly my colleagues in the Planners of Color Interest Group.

Ingrid Gould Ellen, Kathy O'Regan, and the New York University Furman Center community that they created, along with Vicki Been and others, have been an ongoing academic support system and source of training and inspiration for over fifteen years. No housing panel at a conference can be lonely for a Furmaner.

I draw inspiration, wisdom, and knowledge from so many Black scholars that came before me and are still coming, including Charisma Acey, Lisa Bates, Raphael Bostic, Nisha Botchwey, Sheryll Cashin, Camille Zubrinsky Charles, Prentiss Dantzler, Sandy Darity, Jacob Faber, Lance Freeman, Tod Hamilton, Marcus Hunter, Rucker Johnson, Mark Joseph, Robin D. G. Kelley, Willow Lung-Amam, Kelly Lytle Hernandez, June Manning Thomas, Mary Pattillo, Andre Perry, Akira Drake Rodriguez, Catherine Ross, Rashad Shabazz, Sigmund Shipp, Mario Small, Michael Stoll, Forrest Stuart, Henry Taylor, Keeanga-Yamahtta Taylor, Isabel Wilkerson, and William Julius Wilson.

I began writing this book on sabbatical in London. I am thankful to Michael Storper and colleagues in the London School of Economics and Political Science Department of Geography and Environment for giving me an intellectual home away from home. The LSE library became indispensable when I realized I had moved away from UCLA's stacks to write a book. Friends old and new made our family's London experience something we will never forget.

I am indebted to Greg Preston, Xavier Kuai, Rasheed Shabazz, Lillian Liang, Bernadette Tropel, and Lee Guekguezian for outstanding research assistance. Greg spent years with me on this project and warrants special mention for not just doing exemplary data work but helping me think conceptually and addressing measurement challenges.

I can't make a table or chart look nice, so I was very lucky to have Charity Capili come onboard to provide amazing graphic design. Aaron Barrall did outstanding work making all of the maps in the book.

Mike Manville and Paavo Monkkonen took the first look at a very incoherent chapter and helped set me on a course when I was flailing about looking for purpose. Mike, the best writer I've known, closely edited chapters at a much later stage. He is still teaching me how to write.

This work would not have been possible without generous funding from the UCLA Bunche Center for African American Studies, the UCLA Lewis Center for Regional Policy Studies, the UCLA Office of the Vice Chancellor for Research's Racial and Social Justice Grant Program, and the Russell Sage Foundation.

Several people supported me through very early conversations about this idea: Ed Goetz, Hilary Malson, Marques Vestal, Richard Sander, Pat Sharkey, Andrew Greenlee, Elizabeth Delmelle, and Lois Takahashi. Lois is the most giving mentor I have known.

I learned a lot through opportunities to present early findings to several audiences at the LSE International Inequalities Institute, the UCLA Bunche Center, the UCLA Luskin Center for History and Policy, UCLA Lewis Center, the UCLA Department of Urban Planning's Community Economic Development and Housing Seminar, the Association of Collegiate Schools of Planning fall research conferences in 2022 and 2023, and the Russell Sage Foundation Pipeline Grants conference.

Three anonymous reviewers provided excellent feedback via the National Science Foundation on my proposal and methodology. I am incredibly thankful to two anonymous reviewers of the full manuscript, and to Karen Chapple, Trevon Logan, and George Galster, who reviewed the manuscript in whole or in part. George generously read two drafts of the book, was available to discuss several details between the two drafts, and provided in-depth feedback on every chapter and aspect of the book and analysis.

Suzanne Nichols, RSF's director of publications, has lent her support and guidance from the time I was granted funding by RSF over four years ago, and she is hugely responsible for any confidence I had that I could get this done. She also organized four extremely incisive reviews that dramatically improved the manuscript. It has also been incredibly rewarding to have Sheldon Danziger leading the foundation through its support of me, given that he has been my teacher and mentor for over twenty years.

This book is borne out of my family's joy and pain living in Black neighborhoods from Dixmoor, Illinois, to St. Paul, Minnesota, and in Black "neighborhoods" in the American penal system. The memories of those who passed too soon, particularly my father Cephas, are hard to think about, but they keep me motivated to study what I study.

My mother, Becky, never wavers in her support for what I do or in her love for who I am.

My sons, Carter and Lucien, fill my days with fun and challenges and ever-deepening relationships. Both helped update their old man on the twenty-first-century rap scene that makes appearances in chapters 4 and 7.

Molly, you know what you do.

Chapter 1

Introduction

Why must Earl Simmons swim in dirt?

—DMX

Earl Simmons was born in 1970. By his account, it was in Mount Vernon, New York. But other sources say Baltimore.[1] We do know that he moved to Yonkers, New York, when he was young. His parents were both teenagers and his father was rarely around; as young as his mother was when she had Earl (nineteen), he was already her second child. Given this parental youth and poverty, it is not entirely surprising that, in his telling, his childhood had significant hardships and, even worse, abuse. This is how Earl put it in his Grammy-nominated song "Who We Be":

My mother, my father, I love 'em, I hate 'em (uh)
Wish God, I didn't have 'em, but I'm glad that he made 'em (uh)

Earl was born two years after the Fair Housing Act was enacted. He was also born the same year the U.S. Census Bureau conducted a decennial census, providing in this case the first snapshot of the nation's residential living patterns in the aftermath of the landmark legislation. In principle, living patterns should have had little to do with race, because housing discrimination had become unlawful. But of course living patterns had everything to do with race, in part because such patterns change slowly under the best of circumstances, and America in 1970 was not the best of circumstances—as evidenced by the story of Earl Simmons. Growing up in public housing in Yonkers, Earl was unwittingly a major character in what would become one of the country's most prolonged fights for public housing integration.

Although far from the only site of intense backlash against housing desegregation, Yonkers—and surrounding Westchester County—featured the country's most sustained opposition to geographic dispersal of public housing. In the early 1970s, New York State's Urban Development

https://doi.org/10.7758/tjvh5404.5884

Corporation (UDC) developed the "Nine Towns" plan, which was intended to scatter a fair share of affordable housing across several jurisdictions in Westchester County.[2] The plan was vociferously opposed by local jurisdictions, and the state legislature subsequently stripped the UDC of the power to override local zoning ordinances.

In 1980, when Earl was ten, the federal government sued the Yonkers Board of Education, the City of Yonkers, and the Yonkers Community Development Agency for intentionally segregating public housing in southwest Yonkers, where Earl lived.[3] The suit described Yonkers as consisting of three broad areas, with southwest Yonkers housing about 38 percent of the total population yet over 80 percent of the city's Black and Hispanic population and serving as the site of virtually all of its public housing. Many such suits were brought against segregated schools in the 1970s, but the case against Yonkers was unique in alleging that school segregation stemmed from zoning and housing policy decisions. School segregation was a problem but also a symptom of another problem: a land use system designed to segregate its neighborhoods by race (and thus the schools as well). Judge Leonard B. Sand agreed, and he ordered the City of Yonkers to develop a plan to desegregate its public housing. The city appealed.

In 1987, weeks after a new mayor, Nick Wasicsko, was elected on a wave of opposition to desegregation, a federal appeals court upheld the original decision by Judge Sand. Two years later, Mayor Wasicsko would be defeated in his reelection bid, owing to his reluctant acquiescence to the court order. Given that the city was hemorrhaging cash from court fines, the mayor and city council had to give in and build subsidized homes on the White side of town. Three years later, in 1992, the opposition was represented by a pipe bomb that damaged one of the new subsidized townhomes under construction. Nobody yet lived there, so nobody was hurt, but the controversy did claim one life—in 1993, former mayor Wasicsko would die of suicide at the age of thirty-four.[4]

It is unclear how much young Earl Simmons knew about all of this. In his autobiography, he notes that his building and neighborhood at the School Street projects were all Black and Hispanic. But he also states that "the ghetto was in the best area of the city" because of its location near the waterfront separating New York and New Jersey.[5] By the time the controversy would have been widely discussed in Yonkers after Judge Sand's decision, Earl was fifteen years old and had lived in two different boys' homes. It was in one of those homes, Children's Village, that he got into rap music from listening to Mr. Magic's radio show. He practiced beat boxing well enough to come under the tutelage of an older rapper up from Brooklyn named Ready Ron. Taking on a moniker inspired by a drum machine called the DMX, Earl would go by DMX The Beat Box Enforcer.

While Yonkers was trying to delay the inevitable by appealing Judge Sand's decision, Earl was becoming the stereotype of what desegregation's opponents feared: a Black teenager robbing people near his segregated high school and neighborhood. By 1986 he was robbing not just to feed his hunger, or his growing interest in clothes and jewelry, but also his addiction to cocaine, introduced to him by Ready Ron. This life quickly caught up with him, and he wound up in a juvenile detention facility, until 1988. Fortunately, Earl's passion for music and the belief that it could earn him a way out of the hood inspired him to spend more time selling mixtapes than robbing people.

The southwest side of Yonkers in the early 1990s was not the right place or time for a lot of positive things—with the possible exception of breaking through in the rap game. This was the era before rap had ascended to the top of the music industry. To make it, you pretty much had to rise through the ranks in New York City or, in the case of some groundbreaking acts, Los Angeles, Oakland, or Houston. Earl's childhood home was less than two miles from the northern border of the Bronx, where rap was born. As a result of that proximity, he was battling legends like Lord Finesse by 1990 and a young unsigned artist named Jay-Z a few years later. After a couple of more years of hustling (in several ways), his connection to rising producer Irv Gotti got him a contract with the iconic rap label Def Jam. Earl was to be the East Coast's answer to the more violent themes coming out of L.A.'s Death Row Records.

In 1998, Earl—recording as DMX—released his first album with Def Jam, and it debuted at number one on the Billboard charts. He released another album that year that also debuted at number one; through 2003 he would release three more albums that debuted at number one. In the late 1990s and early 2000s, DMX was the biggest rap star on the planet. Some saw him as the logical heir to slain rapper and movie star Tupac Shakur. Both could rap with fierce energy and power, and each capitalized on the marketability of urban violence. They both even preached to their fans in ways that most MCs did not get away with. Raised by a mother who was a leader in the Black Panther Party, Tupac infused many of his songs with socially conscious messages. DMX was deeply religious and could put prayer front and center on an album seemingly without his relatively secular fanbase batting or rolling an eye. Both also displayed a raw vulnerability that made them seem accessible and real to legions of fans. In each case, unfortunately, that vulnerability was all too real. Tupac's mother battled drug addiction. DMX was battling drug addiction when he should have been graduating from high school. DMX's upbringing infused his music with a series of contradictions that made it compelling, if at times also repellent. His lyrics were not accessible to everyone. Even in the violent, misogynist, and homophobic lyrical landscape of 1990s rap, DMX stood out. His use of homophobic slurs in particular grates on ears listening now.[6]

The rawness and offensiveness of DMX's lyrics cannot be fully defended by his tragic upbringing, but neither can they be fully separated from it. That he would use such content to become one of the biggest music stars in the world raises uncomfortable questions about how race, violence, and misogyny intersect in our popular culture. But the tragedies more germane to this book are the racial segregation and concentrated disadvantage that shaped Earl Simmons's life. The neighborhood in Yonkers where he grew up was never majority-Black; it also had a few Whites, but fewer as time went on. Many immigrants from Mexico and Central America moved to southwest Yonkers as the White population was leaving. In 1970, according to the census, DMX's neighborhood on School Street was 79 percent White and had a poverty rate of 13 percent. Ten years later, nearly half as many Whites remained. This drop was in part artificial: before 1980, the census had never asked about Hispanic or Latino ethnicity, so many Latinos had been recorded as White. But much of the decrease was real: the neighborhood had experienced White flight as well as an influx of Blacks and Hispanics. By 2000, when DMX became a hit machine, the neighborhood was 11 percent White and had a poverty rate of 30 percent.

The forces that shape a person's success in life are often ambiguous, but some are fairly straightforward. Earl was born to two teenage parents who had little money. His father wasn't present in his life, and by Earl's account, his mother and other adults in his life were physically or emotionally abusive. It is easy to conclude that his family and household circumstances limited his social and behavioral development and his progress in school and led to the theft, violence, and incarceration in his teen and young adult years. But his neighborhood is likely to have played a role as well. One of his mother's parenting strategies was to lock Earl in his room, not only to punish him but also to keep him away from the influence of the streets, where drugs and violence were common. It's possible that his neighborhood environment contributed to his stunted social growth, or at the very least, that his familial and neighborhood environments interacted to create negative social outcomes. Further supporting this point, Earl's mother was part of a rapidly growing army of women running single-parent households in his neighborhood. When Earl was born, only 15 percent of his neighbors' households were run by women, according to the census. By the time he was ten, that figure had more than doubled, and it would triple by the time he was twenty. Earl and many of his peers lacked a father in the home, and the community overall had few father figures.

Earl's antisocial behavior had extreme consequences. In his autobiography, he openly confesses to frequently robbing people in his neighborhood. He would roam the streets of Yonkers with his beloved pit bull Blacky and take gold chains from peers and purses from old ladies. Even if Earl's neighborhood didn't cause his antisocial behavior, it doesn't seem to have worked against it. It's telling that his bold criminal activities could last as long as they did. In most neighborhoods in the United States—particularly the affluent ones—this behavior would meet a swift end. But in Earl's hood, criminal behavior was probably more commonplace and neighbors were often wary of going to the police; even when someone did go to them, the police were likely to have bigger concerns.

Despite his success as a rapper, Earl Simmons never quite escaped the challenges of the neighborhood he grew up in. He continued to use drugs for much of his life and was arrested several times well after he became famous; he went to jail and prison multiple times. Westchester County, for its part, took a long time to shake off the ghosts of desegregation. As late as 2009, the incumbent Democratic county executive, Andrew Spano, would lose his seat over fair housing politics.[7] The U.S. Department of Housing and Urban Development (HUD), under President Barack Obama, would reject all of the county's mandatory assessments of its fair housing processes. But in 2021 a federal monitor ruled in favor of Westchester County's fair housing efforts, signaling the probable end of the federal government's four decades–long push against the county. That April, Earl died of a cocaine-induced heart attack at the age of fifty.

This book is about Black neighborhoods in the United States. Not every Black neighborhood is like the place where Earl became DMX, and not every Black person who lives in such a neighborhood will share Earl's fate. Indeed, some features of Earl's neighborhood suggest that even "troubled" Black neighborhoods contain a lot more diversity than many people might assume. Yonkers is clearly different in some ways from the archetypical disadvantaged central-city Black neighborhood. First, it is suburban. Yet with its dense population of over two hundred thousand people, living mostly in multifamily housing, it has many urban characteristics. Second, its location within the New York City metropolitan area puts it in one of the most productive economic regions in the world; at the same time, it is located on the other side of New York's highest-poverty borough, the Bronx. The proximity of Yonkers to the Bronx probably also drives the fact that Blacks constituted the largest racial or ethnic group in Earl's neighborhood for only a short period of time; the neighborhood is now roughly 70 percent Hispanic or Latino. According to conventional wisdom, suburban neighborhoods offer greater opportunities for residents of all races, and Black neighborhoods tend not to change racial composition quickly. Southwest Yonkers counters this conventional wisdom in each of those ways. As time marched on after the Fair Housing Act was passed and other forces shaped residential segregation patterns, it is likely that many other Black neighborhoods now deviate from the stereotypes.

Motivations: Black Spaces

Gaps between Blacks and other racial and ethnic groups in the United States (most glaringly Whites) persist across several social and economic contexts. Black children score lower than White children on all types of standardized tests, and these gaps in test scores start early and persist throughout their educational careers.[8] The Black incarceration rate (in state prisons, which house the vast majority of American inmates) is a mind-boggling 1,408 per 100,000, compared to Whites' rate of 275 per 100,000.[9] Blacks live in neighborhoods with higher crime rates and more violence than is experienced by any other racial group.[10] As a result, Blacks are roughly six times as likely to be victimized by crime as Whites.[11] The unemployment rate for Blacks has been about twice that for Whites for over sixty years.[12] Accordingly, the Black-White labor income gap was even greater in 2016 than in 1962, when Blacks earned approximately 52 percent of what Whites earned.[13] In 2017, the homeownership rate for Blacks was 30 percentage points below that of Whites (71.9 to 41.9 percent).[14] This gap is so pervasive that Blacks with a bachelor's degree are less likely to own their own homes than Whites without a high school diploma.[15] At a time when urban renters are facing rising rent burdens, being less likely to own their homes leaves Black households more at risk of displacement and unable to capitalize on rising home values. These disparities interact with neighborhood location in important ways. Not only are crime rates, homeownership opportunities, rent burdens, and policing and schooling inputs often neighborhood-specific, but neighborhood-based disparities are one reason why these gaps persist. We know this from the strong evidence that neighborhoods affect life outcomes as well as from the substantial disparities in neighborhood attributes across races.

This book examines the characteristics and trajectories of Black neighborhoods over the fifty years since the Fair Housing Act. Although the gaps cited here also affect many Black people who live outside of Black neighborhoods, and this book is inevitably about individuals as well, I focus on Black spaces as the unit of analysis, for several reasons.

Disproportionate disadvantage in Black neighborhoods is chiefly the result of state-sanctioned violence and discrimination. U.S. history is riddled with several of these spatial configurations, ranging from the Italian American and Irish American slums of the nineteenth century to the Chinatowns of the late nineteenth and early twentieth centuries, the Mexican and Central American barrios, and the Native American reservations. All of these have been worthy objects of several studies, as have Black neighborhoods. But we lack a comprehensive picture of Black neighborhood conditions and advancement. This is a glaring omission in social science given the ubiquity and persistence of these neighborhoods in urban America. In the largest metropolitan areas, Black neighborhoods house over twenty-six million people, or over 10 percent of the total population in those areas. Black neighborhoods have existed in significant numbers since the Great Migration began in the early 1900s, and scores of Black neighborhoods have remained Black since the middle of that century, when racial transition from White to Black was well underway.

Although Black neighborhoods often persist as loci of concentrated disadvantage in U.S. urban areas, some Black neighborhoods are quite prosperous. In Los Angeles, Ladera Heights and Baldwin Hills are single-family enclaves atop lovely rolling hills. Prince George's County, Maryland, in suburban Washington, D.C., is filled with Black middle-class families and subdivisions. As Black people slowly become more affluent, some of their neighborhoods advance as well. Sometimes Black individuals leave Black neighborhoods behind. In *The Truly Disadvantaged,* William Julius Wilson highlights the heightened Black neighborhood disadvantage resulting from Black middle-class families' greater ability to move out.[16] Black individual and neighborhood advancement are not synonymous but intertwined, and they are not shaped by the same forces.

The study of Black individuals provides important insights into Black life, but we should recognize that Black neighborhoods are discriminated against in different ways than Black people are. Real estate agents steer people with means away from Black neighborhoods. Andre Perry, Jonathan Rothwell, and David Harshbarger find that people devalue not only housing in Black neighborhoods but retail establishments as well, not because of the race of the individuals who own those entities, but because they think it unwise to invest in Black *neighborhoods*.[17]

On the other hand, Black neighborhoods are changing as demand for central-city living rises. Rents are rising fast throughout urban areas, including in low-income areas that have traditionally had relatively cheap housing. Black renters tend to be the most rent-burdened because their incomes are lowest, and these burdens are now exacerbated by rising rents. Low homeownership rates pose an additional challenge for these neighborhoods as rising property values create many potential losers among incumbent residents and few winners.

Persistent violence against Black Americans at the hands of police highlights the gravity of the challenge to improve conditions in Black neighborhoods. Tensions have always been high between police and residents of Black neighborhoods. Riots in Black neighborhoods in the 1960s were often sparked by police violence. More recently, Tamir Rice was shot and killed by police in a Black neighborhood in Cleveland. As was Michael Brown in Ferguson, Missouri. Freddie Gray died in police custody after being picked up from a Black neighborhood in Baltimore. But the case of Ahmaud Arbery—who left the relative safety of his home in a Black neighborhood in Georgia and was killed while running through a White one—may shed some light on why the answer to Black neighborhood violence or police tensions is not necessarily to allow people to move out of Black neighborhoods, or to push for their integration.

One logical lesson from the death of Arbery is that Black people are likely to continue to live in Black neighborhoods in large numbers for a long time, in part because that is where some Black residents feel most comfortable. We have limited survey data on neighborhood residential preferences, but the data we have suggest that Black people value living near people of their own race. Black people know better than anyone that Black neighborhoods are generally the most disadvantaged neighborhoods in urban America. Yet the 2000 General Social Survey found that the average Black respondent prefers a neighborhood that is 42 percent Black.[18] This is right in line with the estimate by the Multi-City Study of Urban Inequality (MCSUI) that the average Black respondent in Los Angeles prefers a neighborhood that is 37 percent Black.[19] Looking deeper into the Los Angeles and Boston subsets of the MCSUI, we see that a tiny share of Black respondents (less than 3 percent) prefer a neighborhood that is all Black.[20] Black respondents overwhelmingly preferred two scenarios: neighborhoods that were half-Black, and neighborhoods that were about three-fourths Black. Black people's first preference is for integrated neighborhoods, but like other racial and ethnic groups, they would rather live among their own race in significant proportions. Nevertheless, the virtually all-Black (or more recently, all-Black-and-Brown) composition of many Black neighborhoods in the United States is not what they prefer.

The drive to provide low-income households with options to live in higher-opportunity neighborhoods seemingly conflicts with Black residential preferences, because those neighborhoods rarely have many Blacks in them. Since Black neighborhoods are typically disadvantaged, it is hard to meet Black demand for living in those neighborhoods while avoiding the negative impacts of living in disadvantaged neighborhoods. Black neighborhoods lag behind on many important indicators, but there is no immutable law mandating that these neighborhoods remain behind. By better understanding where Black neighborhoods flourish, we can provide insights into how to make more of these neighborhoods. It is important that Black neighborhoods advance economically, but that can be done without upending their racial characteristics. A better understanding of flourishing Black neighborhoods can help us get to a place where we are not trying to offer tickets out of these neighborhoods, but building them up and discarding the notion that there is a pathology of blackness or black spaces.

Hundreds of books, reports, journal articles, and studies interrogate the past and present of segregation and its causes and consequences, but there is no comprehensive, quantitative summary of the socioeconomic conditions of the thousands of Black neighborhoods in this country.

Researchers pay significant attention to Black neighborhoods in at least three areas of social science: quantitative research on the prevalence, causes, and consequences of segregation; studies of the effects of residential location on life outcomes (an area of research known as "neighborhood effects"); and ethnographic research on neighborhood life. None of these prolific research areas paints a comprehensive picture of the conditions of Black neighborhoods.

Similar to the first two areas of social science research, this book uses methods of analysis found in economics, sociology, and geography. However, I deviate from these established literatures in important ways, First, segregation scholars do a tremendous job at using quantitative data on neighborhoods to assess the extent to which people of different incomes and races live apart. There is also a robust scholarship measuring the extent to which neighborhoods remain stably integrated. Much of this research is motivated by the segregation of Black Americans. However, Black neighborhoods are implicit characters in segregation research, not the main story.

Neighborhood effects is another highly productive area of research that uses quantitative social science to assess when, how, and why neighborhoods affect life outcomes. The neighborhood effects literature is what lets us draw some tentative conclusions about the connections between where Earl Simmons grew up and how he ended up. This literature is dominated by the Moving to Opportunity demonstration program and is highly influential in housing policy. There is also an extensive literature on spatial mismatch, which examines the consequences of racially segregated neighborhoods being located away from areas of job growth in many U.S. metropolitan areas. While Black neighborhoods are frequently the disadvantaged neighborhoods hypothesized to exacerbate various racial disparities, Black neighborhoods are still implicit characters in this area of research.

The only area of research where Black neighborhoods take center stage is in neighborhood ethnographies, which are typically conducted by sociologists. There are several great investigations of individual Black neighborhoods in this tradition, but these studies typically tell us only about one neighborhood at one point in time.[21]

Given that there is no comprehensive quantitative survey, summary, or description of the universe of Black neighborhoods in the United States (or even a smaller representative sample of those neighborhoods), the story of Black neighborhoods is incomplete. Segregation research is important, but residents of Black neighborhoods are not defined by their separation from other races. As their daily experience is as a resident of a Black neighborhood, that site must be studied. And to know more about the conditions in these neighborhoods and where there are promising outcomes, we need a comprehensive picture of the data on them.

These motivations lead to several key questions that this book addresses. What are the typical socioeconomic conditions in Black neighborhoods, and how do they vary across time and space? How do these conditions compare to those in non-Black neighborhoods? What is the role of the significant changes in racial composition, both in Black neighborhoods and outside of them, in these comparisons and neighborhood trajectories? What metropolitan areas have the most-advantaged and most-disadvantaged Black neighborhoods? *Why?* As demand for urban living rises (evidenced by rapidly rising housing costs), is gentrification more common in Black neighborhoods than it used to be? What are some of the housing, economic, and community development policies that have been tried in Black neighborhoods, and what policy interventions are needed in the future?

The Approach

This book takes a quantitative approach to summarizing the socioeconomic characteristics of urban Black neighborhoods in the United States from 1970 to roughly 2020. This time period provides a sample of somewhere between three thousand and seven thousand neighborhoods, depending on the year. Beginning with U.S. census data in 1970, I define a Black neighborhood as one in which Black people constitute a plurality—that is, they are the largest racial or ethnic group. I focus on how these neighborhoods vary across time and space, looking at the key indicators of poverty and disadvantage and at housing characteristics. Although there is a lot of variation within metropolitan areas, the histories of Black migration, discrimination against (or political and economic gains of) those migrants, and regional economic differences make for substantial variation in Black neighborhoods across the country.

I then evaluate how those neighborhoods evolved over time. Neighborhood change is usually considered in the context of gentrification and displacement. The late twentieth-century experience in Black neighborhoods in the United States has more typically involved high or rising crime and unemployment, poor proximity to jobs and good schools, and low property values. This experience is unlikely to have changed rapidly enough in recent years to the point that gentrification in Black neighborhoods is as common as the discourse suggests. Accordingly, I test whether gentrification is a rising concern in Black neighborhoods and compare its prevalence to neighborhood stagnation and concentrated disadvantage. I also highlight how these neighborhood trajectories vary across the country.

Finally, I identify where Black neighborhood indicators are better or worse, interrogate some reasons why Black neighborhoods flourish, and discuss the role of public policy in Black neighborhood outcomes. Discrimination and segregation in housing (past and present) have shaped our segregated urban landscape and concentrated disadvantage in Black neighborhoods. Accordingly, I focus on housing indicators in addition to poverty and disadvantage, as already noted. In addition, I focus on housing policy given its potential for directly alleviating Black neighborhood disadvantage. Labor and macroeconomic policies also affect racial disparities in income and wealth and thus contribute to Black neighborhood disadvantage, but these effects are more indirect.

The Organization of the Book

Chapter 2 begins well before 1970 and outlines the forces that led to the development of the Black neighborhood and how it came to occupy the bottom of a spatial caste system in the United States. The scholarly focus on Black neighborhoods has been overwhelmingly centered on cities in the North, and in subsequent chapters I demonstrate how this focus limits our understanding of Black neighborhoods. Black neighborhoods are most numerous in the South, and over time those neighborhoods have become more affluent than their northern counterparts. But in this chapter, I demonstrate that the framework of residential racial discrimination that would so profoundly limit where Black people could live and what they could own was built and reproduced in the urban North, largely as a response to the Great Migration.[22] There are many causes for and culprits in American housing segregation and the resulting disadvantage in Black neighborhoods. But government agencies, more than any other actor, were at every level uniquely poised to combat discriminatory forces and chose instead to enable and reproduce them. These actions would guarantee that Black people's neighborhoods—and in fact their very presence in other neighborhoods—would be devalued in real estate markets and enshrine what Sheryll Cashin terms a "racial residential caste system."[23] The essence of this caste system is that it produces and reinforces the unequal distribution of resources across space by race.

Chapter 3 is the descriptive backbone of data on Black neighborhoods in the United States. I begin by quantitatively defining Black neighborhoods and then use census and American Community Survey (ACS) data to provide a comprehensive picture of what Black neighborhoods have looked like at the end of each decade since 1970. The story of these fifty years is one of limited convergence with non-Black neighborhoods. Poverty rates in Black neighborhoods have declined substantially, yet they remain far higher than outside those neighborhoods. Americans are far more likely to graduate from high school and attend college than ever before, and this is also true in Black neighborhoods. And home values, after taking a dive in the 1970s, have rebounded in Black neighborhoods, though the comeback from the Great Recession of 2007–2009 has been slower in Black neighborhoods.

The limited convergence observed in chapter 3 belies a great diversity in Black neighborhoods, which is the focus of chapter 4. We can see profound differences simply by dividing this complicated country into four regions. The most positive story comes out of the South, where we have the most Black neighborhoods, the fastest growth in their numbers, and the strongest socioeconomic indicators outside of the West (where Black neighborhoods are essentially disappearing). The Washington, D.C., and Atlanta metro areas stand out as centers of Black affluence. Accordingly, each of these cities has been referred to in the literature as a Black Mecca.[24] Rising southern areas of Black neighborhood affluence include Houston, Raleigh, Dallas, and Charlotte. The well-worn stories of neighborhood disadvantage in the Midwest are very apparent when looking at Black neighborhoods in the metro areas of the so-called Rust Belt, as it stretches along the Great Lakes, and into upstate New York.

Although Black neighborhoods are very heterogeneous, they feature a narrower range of socioeconomic conditions than do non-Black neighborhoods. This is inevitable when selecting on neighborhood race, but also indicative of a rather low ceiling for even the most-advantaged Black neighborhoods, which are no more advantaged than middle-class non-Black neighborhoods. Nevertheless, this is a substantial improvement. Through about 1990, the most-affluent Black neighborhoods were more like lower-class non-Black neighborhoods.

But the variation in Black neighborhoods from a large sample of metropolitan areas allows me to identify some characteristics of metropolitan areas that are strongly associated with better outcomes in Black neighborhoods. Throughout the chapter, it becomes clear that the most populous metros have better socioeconomic conditions in Black neighborhoods, and this holds when I run regression models that allow me to identify the metropolitan and neighborhood characteristics that are most strongly associated with lower metro-area Black neighborhood poverty rates. Metropolitan average family income and the share Black in a metropolitan area are strongly associated with lower Black neighborhood poverty rates, while income inequality and to a lesser extent income segregation are strongly associated with higher Black poverty rates. These findings make clear that factors outside of Black neighborhoods relate to conditions within them. That said, even controlling for these metropolitan factors, other socioeconomic conditions within Black neighborhoods—the share of residents without a high school degree, the share of female-headed households, and the unemployment rate—are strongly associated with higher levels of Black neighborhood poverty.

Chapter 5 summarizes the spatial landscape of Black neighborhoods, incorporating information on the spatial location of these neighborhoods in a number of ways. To this point in the book, I have equated neighborhoods with census tracts and also treated these census tracts as islands.

That is, I have not accounted for the extent to which Black neighborhoods (or more precisely, census tracts) are adjacent, nor have I examined the socioeconomic characteristics of neighboring census tracts. In this chapter, I account for the spatial locations of Black neighborhoods and census tracts by looking at both centrality and the spatial concentration of Black neighborhoods and how that has changed over time. The Great Migration was a flow of Blacks largely into central cities, and subsequent U.S. suburbanization dynamics often left Black people behind in these urban areas. By the twenty-first century, more and more Black people were suburbanizing, while higher-income and White populations were increasingly demanding central-city living. Given the assumptions that neighborhood conditions are better in suburban areas, I examine connections between socioeconomic disadvantage and the centrality of Black neighborhoods, looking at distance to a metro's central business district and location in a central city or suburb. Finally, given the histories and patterns of neighborhood racial change, I compare Black neighborhoods in the core of Black enclaves to those that border non-Black neighborhoods. Border neighborhoods tend to be more racially integrated.

A surprising finding in this chapter is that while Black border neighborhoods are indeed more racially integrated, they are similar across most socioeconomic characteristics to neighborhoods in the core of a Black neighborhood. There is a much bigger gap between the non-Black core and the non-Black border neighborhoods, suggesting that the demographic and housing market effects from proximity to Black neighborhoods are consistently baked in. A Black neighborhood is likely to be disadvantaged regardless of its spatial orientation, and a non-Black neighborhood located near a Black neighborhood is also likely to be disadvantaged. Less surprising is that centrality matters quite a lot. Black neighborhoods become more advantaged with distance from the metropolitan central business district, and Black neighborhoods in the suburbs are more advantaged than those in the central city. Interestingly, this latter gap is increasing over time—suburban and central-city Black neighborhoods used to be more similar.

Chapter 6 describes the arc of Black neighborhoods over the last fifty years. I focus on neighborhoods that have undergone one of three types of change: (1) ceasing to be a Black neighborhood; (2) becoming a Black neighborhood; or (3) undergoing socioeconomic changes on the level of gentrification. The pace of change is generally slow in Black neighborhoods, which tend to remain the same for several decades. Gentrification is also relatively uncommon in Black neighborhoods, but there is some evidence both that the pace of racial change is speeding up in Black neighborhoods and that gentrification is becoming more common in Black neighborhoods. The likelihood that Black neighborhood gentrification is increasing in frequency has a lot to do with the dynamics of central-city demand. There is little evidence that population is flowing to our densest and most centrally located urban areas as much as it is to suburban ones, but higher-income and White populations either appear to be remaining longer in central-city locations or are more likely to move there from other parts of metropolitan areas.

Chapter 7 focuses on the two metropolitan areas where Black neighborhood socioeconomic conditions are clearly the best: Atlanta and Washington, D.C. Each of these metro areas has some of the highest numbers of Black neighborhoods in the country, and those neighborhoods, on average, are in the top five of most meaningful indicators. Some of the features of the Atlanta and D.C. metro areas are very hard to replicate in other cities. Each city had early Black middle-class populations that exercised meaningful economic and political power before it was possible in other cities. Both Atlanta and D.C. are home to historically Black colleges and universities (HBCUs), which have trained countless members of the Black elite in every profession. More than anywhere else, Atlanta, the birthplace of Dr. Martin Luther King Jr. and the city of his pulpit, functioned as the headquarters of the Black civil rights movement. But history is not the whole story, as evidenced by the extraordinary ascent of this Black elite in recent decades in both Washington, D.C., and Atlanta. Prince George's County was not an established Black middle-class enclave until the 1980s. As Black middle-class neighborhoods grow in number and affluence in other southern metros, the optimist's perspective is that Atlanta and D.C. provide a glimpse into a more widely shared future of affluent southern Black neighborhoods.

Chapter 8 concludes with a discussion on policy implications and directions for future research. Recognizing that eliminating Black and White neighborhood disparities is a complicated feat, I have narrowed the top policy priorities down to three pillars: regional focus, inclusive development, and investment in people. A research agenda on Black neighborhoods not only enhances what we know about policy interventions that operationalize these three pillars but also evaluates the effects of living in Black neighborhoods compared to neighborhoods that are similar on nonracial dimensions.

Chapters 2 through 7 begin as the book began—with a discussion of how a region's rap success and culture reflects the development and conditions of the region's Black neighborhoods.[25] I draw a few lessons from making those connections. The extraordinary financial and cultural success of rap music is a tangible example of why Black neighborhoods (and their study) matter. The mysterious alchemy of musical and cultural influence is better understood by examining the places from which they come. More to the point, while Black places and people have consistently produced much of America's most popular and influential music and entertainment, rap's rise to the top of the music industry was unlikely without the Black neighborhood, and that rise has further influenced Black neighborhoods over the past fifty years. This approach echoes Marcus Anthony Hunter and Zandria Robinson in their book *Chocolate Cities,* which is similarly focused on Black geographic spaces.[26] Hunter and Robinson have woven stories about and quotes from musicians as diverse as Aretha Franklin, Erykah Badu, and Tupac Shakur. A core concept that Hunter and Robinson advance in their book is the need to correct simple narratives of the North and South in American racial discourse. "*Chocolate Cities* is built on a simple premise," they explain. "Our current maps of Black life are wrong. Instead of the neat if jarring linear progress of movement from the rural South to the urban North, we suggest that the history of Black life in modernity is a boomerang rather than a straight line of progress."[27]

Rap's massive cultural imprint influences Black neighborhoods throughout the country by peppering our subconscious with imagery, stories, and stereotypes about those places. This effect is more relevant to some cities than to others. NWA's explosion onto the scene and broadcasting of the commonplace violence of Compton and South Central Los Angeles in the late 1980s had at least two effects. First, NWA was playing the role of "Black America's CNN," as Public Enemy's Chuck D once called rap music.[28] NWA's focus on police brutality primed the public for the Rodney King beating, providing America with a foreshadowing text. The country couldn't say it wasn't warned. On the other hand, the hyperviolent lyrics, coupled with Hollywood's portrayal of Black Los Angeles in movies such as *Boyz n the Hood* and *Menace II Society* painted a picture of a community so violent that nobody would possibly want to live there. The real and perceived threat of violence contributed to rapid flight from South Central in the 1980s and 1990s. Fortunately, unlike most declining Black neighborhoods throughout the country, South Central was kept alive by immigrants arriving from Mexico and Central America.

Atlanta had become the most influential rap city by the 2010s, with important implications for the city's perception by Black and White alike. I argue that the dominance of southern rap makes it more likely that the South will continue to be a destination for Blacks in particular. Although Blacks have been moving south in larger numbers in recent decades, the region is often seen as a cultural backwater. With the South playing such a significant role in both rap and global culture, those stereotypes are likely to soften, removing barriers to migration southward for some.

It is well established that there are persistent, substantial gaps between Blacks and other racial groups—particularly Whites—in virtually all of the most consequential life outcomes. Although there is some debate on the role of neighborhoods, the literature strongly suggests that neighborhood location contributes to these gaps. The typical neighborhood in which Black Americans reside has been considerably lower in quality and opportunity than other neighborhoods. Further, the neighborhoods where Blacks are the predominant racial group are persistently the most disadvantaged areas of the country. Yet we do not have a comprehensive examination of what life is like in these neighborhoods, and how conditions in them evolved over time. The central motivation of this book is to contribute to contemporary policy debates on housing, segregation, neighborhood effects, and race by providing a better understanding of the places and conditions where Black neighborhoods have flourished and where they have failed.

Chapter 2

The Role of the State in Black Neighborhood Disadvantage

> Whenever the government provides opportunities and privileges for white people and rich people they call it "subsidies." When they do it for Negro and poor people they call it "welfare." The fact is that everybody in this country lives on welfare. Suburbia was built with federally subsidized credit. And the highways that take our white brothers out to the suburbs were built with federally subsidized money to the tune of ninety percent. Everybody is on welfare in this country. The problem is that we all too often have socialism for the rich and rugged free enterprise capitalism for the poor. That's the problem.
>
> —Martin Luther King Jr., "The Minister to the Valley," February 23, 1968

Berry Gordy II was a rarity: a successful Black plantation owner in Georgia in the early 1900s.[1] This success brought potential danger to him and his family from jealous Whites and the Ku Klux Klan. So in 1922 he boarded a train for Detroit, following his brother John. His wife and kids would soon join him. From 1900 to 1970, roughly six million other Blacks left the South for cities in the North and West. Most were extremely poor, unlike the Gordys. But the threat of violence and economic, social, and political oppression was nearly universal in the South, even for the successful Gordys. That drove the family to Detroit with many of the same intentions of fellow Blacks of the time: to live in a free society and pursue economic opportunities as they saw fit.

Upon arriving in Detroit, Berry Gordy II faced many of the same challenges that other Black migrants were facing. He was sold a dilapidated home at an inflated price on the west side of Detroit in what was becoming an all-Black district. This was a typical example of what we now know as a "dual" housing market. The effective ban of Blacks from living in large swaths of the Detroit metropolitan area caused the artificial inflation of prices for housing in Black neighborhoods. Housing in these neighborhoods was both scarce and old, but Blacks had little choice but to overpay

https://doi.org/10.7758/tjvh5404.7443

for it. On the other side of the dual housing market, Whites had more plentiful options.

Gordy was also subjected to a racially discriminatory labor market, exemplified by Detroit's booming auto industry. But he was dogged and sharp, and he came to Detroit with capital. Before too long, Gordy owned a couple of construction and retail businesses. His son, Berry Jr. (technically the third Berry in the family), was born in Detroit in 1929. As an adult, Berry Jr.'s passions initially lay not in entrepreneurship but in boxing and eventually music. Hard work was mandatory in the Gordy family, and Berry Jr. was no exception, yet among his eight siblings he was considered something of a slacker. As a result, he found it challenging to obtain seed money from the family when he felt ready to expand his fledgling music label.

Berry Gordy Jr.'s early success writing hits for Jackie Wilson did not yield much income. But from there his fortunes took another leap through the mentorship of a teenage songwriter and singer named William Robinson, known as Smokey. A key moment in Berry's music business was winning a victory against the big-city major labels trying to poach Smokey and his group, The Miracles. Black DJs throughout the country played a big role by threatening a boycott against the majors if they took the Miracles from this new Black label brewing in Detroit. It was an early and rare moment when the Black music infrastructure could flex its slowly growing muscle.

Keeping Smokey and the Miracles would prove to be a massive win for Berry Gordy Jr., and one that changed the arc of twentieth-century music. Not only did Smokey become one of the most prolific and groundbreaking songwriters of the century, but it was also his idea for Gordy to start a record company that would rival the White-owned giants on the East Coast. Gordy was constantly frustrated by his failure to bring in big revenues from the hits that he and Smokey were writing for artists like Marvin Johnson and The Marvelettes. Following Smokey's advice—and heeding a growing realization that if he didn't like paying a third party to do something, he should do it himself—Gordy formed Motown Records to nationally distribute the records they were making. That kept the money in-house.

Motown's success and influence are almost impossible to overstate. Stevie Wonder, Marvin Gaye, Diana Ross, and Michael Jackson are evidence enough of that. The company had an astounding 110 top-10 hits from 1961 to 1971. Gordy's team worked out of his home and studio at 2648 West Grand Boulevard. Dubbed Hitsville U.S.A. by Gordy, the studio was an innovator in developing an assembly line–like production process (right at home in the Motor City). The process was dependent on the exacting standards and driving management style of Gordy himself, who required writers, musicians, and producers to manage heavy workloads.[2]

Arguably Motown's greatest source of influence was in taking Black music mainstream. Before Gordy, Black musicians such as Little Richard, Chuck Berry, Ray Charles, and James Brown had success with White audiences. But until Motown, Black musicians were categorized in entirely different musical genres. In the early modern era, music from Black Americans was called "race records." Then it was "R&B," or rhythm and blues. Motown did not eliminate racial delineations in music; R&B is still with us, and more often than not it is still a racially loaded term. But because of Motown, Black music became synonymous with *popular* music. Motown's success made it hard for them to keep their talent, as major labels not only started signing new Black musicians but also poached some from Motown.[3]

It is hard to imagine Motown without the massive population movement of the Great Migration. A comparison between the blues and jazz is illustrative. Many Black musicians and innovators were involved in both genres, which were ascendant in the first half of the twentieth century. A key difference was that the blues was largely a rural form of music. Without population density, word of mouth and local performance circuits can take a performer only so far. Dizzy Gillespie and John Coltrane both moved from the Carolinas to Philadelphia during the Great Migration. Thelonious Monk moved from North Carolina to New York City when he was young. All of the other jazz greats were urbanites, with much of their activity and innovation concentrated in Harlem. The Harlem Renaissance, fed by the Great Migration, was responsible not only for musical innovation but for an explosion of Black art and literature.

We know more about the influence of the blues from the rock-and-roll musicians who came along later and reappropriated songs from the Mississippi Delta—both the so-called British Invasion by the Beatles, the Rolling Stones, Led Zeppelin, and the like, and the White American contemporaries of 1950s blues musicians who were something akin to facsimiles of Black musicians, like Elvis or Jerry Lee Lewis. Most of the Black blues musicians who broke through to success were from Mississippi but did not become famous until they moved to Memphis, Chicago, or Detroit. B. B. King, John Lee Hooker, Howlin' Wolf, and Albert King all fit this description. But whether they were Black blues guitarists, jazz legends, or crooners like Nat King Cole or Sam Cooke, pre-Motown Black musicians had a low economic ceiling and often a short shelf life. Gordy biographer Nelson George summarizes this plight: "Success for a black performer was characterized by sales of 45-rpm records in the 100,000 to 300,000 range, a lack of substantial album sales, headline status in a national network of ex-vaudeville houses in black neighborhoods (labeled the 'chitlin circuit') and a rapid rise and fall."[4]

Similar to jazz, Motown is an example of the unique and innovative musical alchemy created in urban America by the Great Migration.

Berry Gordy's Motown shattered the glass ceiling for Black musicians and kept money in Black hands. Urbanization played a key role in this transformation, but it is likely that segregation, with the resulting economic diversity of Black neighborhoods, played a part as well. The highly successful Gordys, had they been given the opportunity, might have lived in integrated, higher-income neighborhoods. Consequently, Berry might not have been as likely to connect with a much poorer young man like Smokey Robinson. And it was not entirely coincidental—but it was of course helpful—that Smokey counted Diana Ross and Aretha Franklin as neighbors at different points in his childhood. Racial segregation thus provided Berry with the benefit of proximity to talent. The cohesion of the Black community and the Gordys' privileged place within it would help him connect to the various ancillary services that a fast-growing operation needed. Eventually, Gordy would use this influence to create not only the first successful Black record label but also, at its height, the biggest Black-owned company in the country.

This is the rosier take on the role played by the Black neighborhood in midcentury urban America: that racial segregation led to economically integrated Black neighborhoods that provided a way for Black migrants to assimilate to urban areas. But the 1960s were also the period when persistent dissatisfaction over labor and housing discrimination, as well as mistreatment by the police, led to riots and an abandonment of Black neighborhoods by those who could afford to escape them. The latter stages and eventual decline of Motown follow this trajectory. Consistent with the latter stages of the Great Migration, when Black people moved west in greater numbers than in the early twentieth century, Berry Gordy moved Motown to Los Angeles in 1967, after the Detroit riots, and tried with limited success to expand Motown into the film industry. The Detroit neighborhood that Motown left behind would remain decimated over the next few decades. Hitsville U.S.A. still stands at an address that is now known as 2648 Berry Gordy Jr. Boulevard. The census tract containing it had a high poverty rate (28 percent) in 1970, around the time the label left for Los Angeles. Over the next ten years, two-thirds of the White population would leave. By 2000, the census tract was 93 percent Black, and by 2017 the poverty rate was an astounding 71 percent (see table 2.1).

In Detroit and elsewhere, Black neighborhoods existed well before 1970. Clearly, the forces that shaped Black neighborhood disadvantage during this book's focal period after 1970—and the varying manifestations of that disadvantage across the country—had been in play since far earlier. Entire books, including Richard Rothstein's *A Color of Law*, Lance Freeman's *A Haven and a Hell*, Isabel Wilkerson's *The Warmth of Other Suns*, and David M. P. Freund's *Colored Property*, have been written about this history, mostly focused on the pre-1970 forces that shaped racial exclusion and Black neighborhood disadvantage.[5] To set the table for subsequent

Table 2.1 Poverty and Racial Composition near Hitsville U.S.A., 1970–2017

	1970	1980	1990	2000	2010	2017
Poverty rate	28	26	49	42	62	71
Percent White	30	9	8	3	5	8
Percent Black	68	86	87	93	92	88

Source: Author's tabulation of U.S. 2010 Longitudinal Tract Database (Logan, Xu, and Stults 2014) and American Community Survey Five-Year Estimates (U.S. Census Bureau 2019).

chapters, I summarize some of that work and history in this chapter, making the argument that Black neighborhood disadvantage has its roots in a mix of factors that include both individual and place-based discrimination and public and private actors and practices. The wide-ranging causes of Black neighborhood disadvantage make it particularly challenging to equalize opportunity between Black and non-Black neighborhoods.

Black neighborhood disadvantage and segregation are not the same thing. Such disadvantage is not inevitable with high levels of residential segregation. Although a separate but equal doctrine in housing and residential location is as logically flawed as the doctrine that persisted in U.S. educational jurisprudence from *Plessy to Brown*,[6] segregation and inequality across outcomes are not synonymous. White supremacy ensured that segregation would contribute to such inequalities, but scale and degree matter. I argue that by 1970 inequality between Black and non-Black neighborhoods was out of scale with the inequality between individuals, and that place-based outcome gaps were exacerbated by place-based policy decisions. I conclude the chapter with a brief summary of how and why neighborhoods matter. Although equalizing opportunity across neighborhoods can help narrow racial gaps in a number of domains, it cannot narrow those gaps entirely. Notably, evidence suggests that neighborhood effects are not particularly critical (or, perhaps, solvable) for adults; for children, however, changing their neighborhood location or improving the environment of their current neighborhood has substantial benefits.

Origins

Hitsville U.S.A.'s neighborhood is an extreme version of the Black neighborhood stereotype: a highly impoverished enclave in a northern city that has experienced a mass exodus of jobs and White households. However, these northern neighborhoods are only part of the story. As the South urbanized, typically on a smaller scale and at a slower pace than in northern cities, Black neighborhoods became more common in southern cities than in northern ones, owing to the South being home to a larger share of the Black population. Even after the Great Migration, roughly 40 percent of

Black neighborhoods were in the South. In that region, Black neighborhoods are more likely than in the rest of the country to be scattered around smaller metropolitan areas, but roughly half of the largest twenty metropolitan areas in terms of the number of Black neighborhoods were located in the South in 1970. Black neighborhoods have always had a significant presence in southern U.S. cities, but compared to the attention given to northern Black neighborhoods in segregation research and studies of Black neighborhoods, they have been relatively ignored.

Although the scholarly focus on northern Black neighborhoods has been disproportionate to their numbers, the forces that shaped Black neighborhoods throughout the country were largely a response to the Great Migration to northern cities. The dramatic changes that ensued first reshaped New York, Chicago, and Washington, D.C., and later Detroit, Philadelphia, Los Angeles, and eventually virtually every other major city in the country. These changes were driven by real estate actors and policymakers. Contrary to the perception of the civil rights movement that a progressive federal government was pitted against recalcitrant southern governors, mayors, and law enforcement, twentieth-century urban policies highlight the racially discriminatory tendencies of U.S. government agencies at all levels. In housing, policies tended to make White property and comfort the highest priority, well above the goals of integrating Black Americans into a variety of neighborhoods or reducing their material deprivation. These policies reflected the preferences of Whites, the most powerful voting bloc, but also the dogged lobbying efforts of real estate agents. Government consent to these interests, and a failure to push for different racial possibilities, helped draw and reinforce boundaries around Black neighborhoods and ensure that they would become the most disadvantaged places in urban America.

This chapter briefly traces this history: the development of Black neighborhoods in the United States and the public and private processes and decisions that created a spatial caste system. By 1970, when the empirical section of the book begins, Black neighborhoods had reached a nadir—the point at which, Lance Freeman concludes, Black neighborhoods had largely ceased being a "haven" and more frequently functioned as a "hell."[7] There was—and always has been—diversity among Black neighborhoods, but the pervasive nature of White supremacist policy and ideology through much of the twentieth century produced many commonalities in Black neighborhoods, too many of them negative.

The government role in Black neighborhood disadvantage is complex, but significant. Richard Sander, Yana Kucheva, and Jonathan Zasloff conclude that "the practices of real estate developers, brokers, and bankers remained almost universally discriminatory in the 1950s."[8] Given this discrimination by individuals and collectives, governments could have an impact on Black neighborhoods in one of three ways. First, government could discriminate against Blacks, as many have demonstrated they did in the provision of public housing and mortgage insurance and underwriting. Second, government could allow discrimination by individuals and collectives—de facto discrimination or segregation. Third, government could push back against the discrimination practiced by these individuals and collectives.[9] Federal pushback of this type was particularly slow on housing, exemplified by the fact that the Fair Housing Act (included in the Civil Rights Act of 1968) was passed after the major civil rights bills on employment and voting and well after *Brown v. Board of Education*.[10] Further, the government needed to pass additional major pieces of housing legislation to keep chipping away at housing discrimination. In 1974, the Equal Credit Opportunity Act was passed to eliminate racial discrimination in lending. To monitor progress on this front, the Home Mortgage Disclosure Act was passed in the following year to collect and disclose data on banks' lending patterns. And in 1977 the Community Reinvestment Act was enacted to encourage financial institutions to lend in communities where they operated. Nevertheless, for much of the twentieth century, various levels of government were clearly hesitant to push back against housing discrimination or against what were believed to be the predominant racial preferences in housing for the White majority. Housing was the last stage of the fight for equal protection.

Many forces led to disadvantage becoming the norm in Black neighborhoods by 1970. Racial discrimination and White supremacy were basic facets of American life in and out of the public sector. But the public sector, from the federal government on down, is uniquely culpable as the entity that could have done the most to combat racial discrimination. Instead, the heavy hand of the federal government exerted its influence to restrict Black movement and devalue Black communities—with impacts, we now know, that are taking generations to mitigate.

The Great Migration

The force that made northern, urban Black neighborhoods possible more than any other was the Great Migration of over six million Black people from the South to northern destinations during the period from the early 1900s to around 1970. The story of this migration—whose impact on urban America is impossible to overstate—has been told by several scholars.[11] Figure 2.1 provides Black population totals for twelve U.S. cities from 1900 to 1970. The six on the left are the northern cities that received the most migrants during the Great Migration, and the six on the right are the largest centers of Black population growth in the South (or South-adjacent, depending on how we classify Baltimore and Washington, D.C.). Chicago and New York each gained over one million Black people in seventy years. Los Angeles, Detroit, and Philadelphia all gained over

Figure 2.1 Black Population in Selected U.S. Cities, 1900–1970

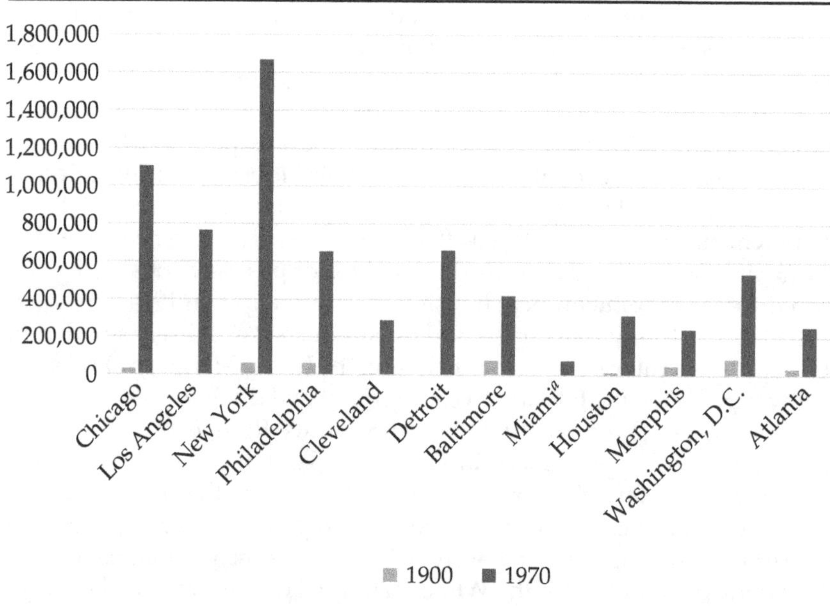

Source: Author's calculation of data from Gibson and Jung 2005.
[a] Miami data from 1910 and 1970.

half a million Black residents during that time. Such population flows would be impactful under any circumstances, but the nature of race in the United States multiplied the impact several-fold.

Black population growth was most robust in established metropolises in the Midwest and Northeast, such as Chicago, Detroit, New York, Philadelphia, and Washington, D.C.; Los Angeles would later be the destination of hundreds of thousands of Black migrants, largely from Texas and Louisiana. But the entire country was transformed by the Great Migration, including the South. Not only does figure 2.1 make clear that several southern cities saw substantial increases in their Black population, but it also shows that the South was shaped by the departure of Black migrants, largely from its rural areas. The South underwent a massive population change, inherent from any out-migration, and lost the anchor of its labor force, but at the same time the pace of political and social change may have been faster in the South as a result of the threat of further Black population losses.[12] In this telling, the Great Migration expedited the success of the civil rights movement.

Also clear from figure 2.1 is that Black migration flows varied significantly across the country. This figure greatly underestimates this variation, since it includes only a handpicked group of cities experiencing the largest gains in Black population during the time under study. The reactions by the recipient cities—legal and otherwise—varied as well. But there were commonalities in (1) the vitriolic reaction of majority-White cities outside of the South to the Great Migration; (2) the strong role of government in producing, shaping, and disadvantaging the Black neighborhood; and (3) the ways in which Black residents assimilated and grasped for power in cities within these constraints.

The Northern Response

The massive influx of Black Americans from the rural South met significant resistance in U.S. cities. Accordingly, the Great Migration is often considered the catalyst for intensified discrimination in housing by both public and private actors.[13] In fact, Black-White segregation was not particularly high at the beginning of the twentieth century—that is, before Blacks moved en masse to northern cities.[14]

Once the Great Migration was underway, there was undoubtedly enough racial animus in the general population to create widespread resistance to integrated neighborhoods. In housing, explicit and implicit racial boundaries became common in U.S. cities, especially as Blacks arrived in meaningful numbers. These boundaries were enforced through a variety of methods, including racially restrictive deeds and covenants, threats of violence, and discrimination by real estate agents and mortgage lenders (and the private and government institutions that established industry standards). Although many forces contributed to racial segregation and Black neighborhood disadvantage in urban America, two stand out for setting up the early legal frameworks that maintained racial purity in urban neighborhoods and set the stage for disadvantage in Black ones: restrictive racial covenants and exclusionary zoning.

Racial Covenants

Restrictions against the sale of property to non-Whites (typically Blacks in the early twentieth century) generally came in two flavors: restrictions on individual property deeds, or covenants that covered entire neighborhoods or new subdivisions. Blacks were not the only targets of these restrictions. The first racial covenant appeared in a case in 1892 in California that was designed to forbid sales to Chinese immigrants.[15] Some see the impetus for the rapid diffusion of racial covenants as the Supreme Court's striking down of racial zoning in 1917, with the *Buchanan v. Warley* decision.[16] But the chronology doesn't fit. More than ten years prior, racial covenants had made it to the other side of the country, appearing in many parts of the South. Importantly, racial covenants and racial zoning functioned side by side in the South. As the catalysts for racial covenants, Michael Jones-Correa cites the Great Migration and the race riots, which intensified racial competition and discrimination in northern cities, but this view probably underestimates the role of realtors.[17]

Gene Slater makes a strong case that real estate agents played a far greater role in the adoption, proliferation, and legality of racial covenants than is typically understood.[18] The realtors made their case for restricting property owners' rights by reframing the logic of freedom, shifting the focus away from housing rights for racial minorities and toward a property owner's freedom to discriminate as well as the rights of neighboring property owners to do the same. Slater argues that the realtors fiercely fanned the flames of a burgeoning conflict over the freedom *from* discrimination versus freedom *to* discriminate—with the latter increasingly winning out.

In this telling, the proliferation of restrictive covenants was tied to the professionalization of real estate brokers in early twentieth-century California. The story begins in Los Angeles, when a young metropolis was finding its way toward protecting White interests. Slater argues that realtors created racial exclusion virtually out of whole cloth. The real estate industry of the time was populated by confidence men and lacked standards and public trust. Pioneering realtors in Los Angeles, seeing a need to create local boards that would govern rules of conduct and exclude the shadier elements from the trade, founded the Los Angeles Realty Board (LARB), which would help establish the National Association of Real Estate Boards (NAREB).

These bodies organized several aspects of the real estate business, but perhaps none was more important than legitimating racial exclusion. The practice was given a jump-start by the realtor-developers Duncan McDuffie in Berkeley, California, and J. C. Nichols in Kansas City, Missouri, who sought to build and market luxury subdivisions. Roland Park in Baltimore had become a model for a subdivision with covenants that would restrict what people could and could not do with their properties. These covenants reassured buyers that the luxurious and orderly neighborhoods where they were buying a house would stay that way. The racial covenants that McDuffie and Nichols used were enforceable through another innovation: homeowners' associations.

Remarkably, McDuffie, Nichols, and their developer and realtor colleagues convinced White home buyers and sellers (as well as judges and state and federal regulatory agencies) that stripping away some individual property rights was necessary to protect the property values of the collective by using restrictive racial covenants to exclude Black people. As prewar cities and suburbs, developed under the influence of McDuffie and Nichols, became dotted with Whites-only subdivisions, the NAREB, with support from and influence on the federal government, enshrined a logic that uniformity was essential to protect housing investments. They convinced the public that introduction into a White subdivision of any residents of different races or any structure other than a single-family home would force property values to plummet. Slater convincingly shows that these claims had no basis in fact. Indeed, the little existing social science of the time suggested that excluding non-Whites from neighborhoods was actually detrimental to property values, because doing so reduced competition among buyers. But these market logics have a way of becoming self-reinforcing, and eventually policymakers would incorporate them into federal mortgage underwriting standards. Once the financial fear of integration was baked into property markets, Black people and Black spaces were consistently devalued by buyers and sellers alike, with devastating impacts on Black neighborhoods ever since.

Exclusionary Zoning

Planning practices such as zoning determine what can be built where, and they govern the size, shape, density, and use of residential buildings. Zoning proliferated in the United States near the beginning of the twentieth century. The earliest zoning laws were enacted before the Great Migration took off in earnest, and while unknowable, ubiquitous zoning was likely to take shape in some form even had Blacks never moved to the North in large numbers. However, there is substantial evidence that zoning took the form it did, and is practiced the way it is, in large part owing to the desire to exclude Black Americans from White neighborhoods. Zoning practices, which have been vital to the production of the Black neighborhood, are underdiscussed in the literature.

One piece of evidence that the presence of Black people influenced zoning practices is the fact that explicitly racial zoning first proliferated in southern U.S. cities before a critical mass of Blacks had moved to the North. Christopher Silver identifies the first such racial zoning law as one that was passed by Baltimore to restrict Blacks to very specific sections of the city.[19] Mayor J. Barry Mahool, who signed the zoning ordinance into law in 1910, is quoted as saying that "Blacks should be quarantined in isolated slums in order to reduce the incidents of civil disturbance, to prevent the spread of communicable disease into the nearby White neighborhoods, and to protect property values among the White majority."[20] Silver notes that after Baltimore's law was passed, such ordinances proliferated throughout the South, most famously in Louisville, Kentucky. The determination of government officials to contain Blacks within prescribed neighborhoods was exemplified by the proliferation of racial zoning ordinances even after *Buchanan v. Warley*. In 1917 alone, Atlanta, Indianapolis, Norfolk, Richmond, New Orleans, Winston-Salem, Dallas, Charleston (South Carolina), Dade County in Florida, and Birmingham all passed such ordinances.[21]

Eventually, *Buchanan* made cities change course and use more creative, less racially explicit tools to separate races and reinforce Black slums. Zoning ordinances were one tool among several used later, including, besides racial covenants, slum clearance, public housing siting, and redlining.

Zoning that restricts density (by mandating single-family housing or large lot sizes, for example) makes housing less plentiful and houses larger. Less plentiful and larger housing is more expensive, and Black households—particularly those of first- or second-generation sharecroppers arriving from the rural South—were much less likely to be able to afford such housing. Restrictions on housing production further constrained where Black households could live. One way for White jurisdictions and neighborhoods to exclude Black in-migration was to make it very difficult to build any housing at all.

There is ample evidence that such zoning tactics, commonly termed "exclusionary zoning," were a deliberate tool of racial exclusion, and an effective one. Rothstein argues that single-family zoning has not only had disproportionate impacts on the poor and racial minorities, but that this was commonly the intent all along.[22] He notes that St. Louis's influential planning engineer Harland Bartholomew stated explicitly that his goal was to prevent the encroachment of Blacks into all-White neighborhoods. The most protected neighborhoods in St. Louis were all-White and comprised largely of single-family housing with restrictive racial covenants that prohibited the construction of any multifamily dwellings. St. Louis also placed industrial zones near existing Black neighborhoods. Although many of the arguments for single-family zoning made at the time were economic, racial separation was accomplished through the same means, and zoning proponents were on record as being very much in favor of racially segregated cities.[23]

Although the Supreme Court ruled against racial zoning in 1917, it would uphold the constitutionality of broad zoning powers in *Euclid v. Ambler* in 1926.[24] In 1924, the Ambler Realty Company sued the village of Euclid, Ohio, over its zoning ordinance, which restricted land held by Ambler to residential use. Ambler bought the property intending to sell it for industrial use. In spite of the company's expressed intention, Justice George Sutherland included in his majority opinion a rant against multifamily dwellings and a defense of the detached single-family home:

> With particular reference to apartment houses, it is pointed out that the development of detached house sections is greatly retarded by the coming of apartment houses, which has sometimes resulted in destroying the entire section for private house purposes; that in such sections very often the apartment house is a mere parasite, constructed in order to take advantage of the open spaces and attractive surroundings created by the residential character of the district.[25]

Justice Sutherland went on to foreshadow many of the specious and overwrought arguments against multifamily housing that accompany neighborhood opposition to apartment buildings to this day, including issues over sunlight and shadows, noise, and parking and the assumption that they are bad for children.

Protecting single-family neighborhoods was not always explicitly race- or class-based, but zoning often functioned as a complement to racial covenants, or as another way to ensure neighborhood homogeneity (of home, class, and race) where such covenants were lacking. In a post-*Buchanan* environment, racial covenants were not always viewed as an adequate substitute for maintaining racially segregated neighborhoods.[26] Although racial covenants were widely used and legal until the 1948 *Shelley v. Kraemer* decision, they were limited by potential homeowner holdouts and incurred high administration costs.[27]

Sonia Hirt provides ample evidence that jurists, civil engineers, and public figures of the time clearly saw the potential for bans on density to also ban particular types of people from places and establish or replicate patterns of racial and economic segregation.[28] It is not only with the benefit of hindsight that we can evaluate single-family zoning as a contributor to economic and racial exclusion—decision-makers explicitly considered this impact at the time, and for some it was part of the appeal.

Recent empirical research confirms that zoning has long been an effective tool to reinforce segregation. Alexander Sahn has demonstrated that population flows from the Great Migration were strongly tied to restrictions on multifamily housing production.[29] Allison Shertzer, Tate Twinam, and Randall Walsh use historical quantitative data from Chicago to show that higher residential density was pushed into areas with a higher share of Blacks.[30] In a follow-up paper, they find that these zoning decisions entrenched and intensified racial segregation in Chicago for decades.[31] And there are many more studies that identify connections between contemporary zoning practices and racial and economic exclusion.[32]

Both racial covenants and zoning restrictions are local strategies to perpetuate segregation and concentrate disadvantage in Black neighborhoods. Though these strategies were locally employed and diverse in nature and scope, they were still very common across the country. But local laws have local impact. The federal government played a strong role in both allowing and disseminating these local segregating strategies and coming up with new ones of its own.

The Federal Role

In at least three direct ways, the federal government laid financial and physical infrastructure that would shape the Black neighborhood and constrain the housing possibilities of its residents: homeownership support, urban highway construction, and public housing. No government agency invented racial discrimination in housing markets. Before there was much housing policy infrastructure at all at the state, local, or federal level, there were Black ghettos in at least New York and Chicago.[33] But the federal government made segregation and Black neighborhood disadvantage far more widespread through its policies and its support for local and private discrimination. The federal government accelerated a negative feedback loop that devalued racial integration in housing markets and thus made integration an unstable and undesirable outcome. In turn, these neighborhoods decayed even more and so were further devalued. Blacks who sought to invest in these neighborhoods found credit difficult to come by because of federally regulated practices. These forces shaped the separation of Black and White neighborhoods, entrenched disadvantage in the Black ones, and suppressed Black ownership in neighborhoods of all types.

The Home Owners' Loan Corporation and the Federal Housing Administration

Unlike with zoning, the federal government led the way on homeownership support, beginning with the Home Owners' Loan Corporation (HOLC), which was created in 1933 as a response to the Great Depression, under the direction of the newly formed Federal Home Loan Bank Board (FHLBB).[34] HOLC's primary purpose was to rescue and refinance mortgages in danger of default and foreclosure.[35] Commonly, HOLC refinanced short-term mortgages into the kind of longer-term, fully amortized products that have been the standard ever since. In doing this, HOLC revolutionized home purchasing and mortgage lending.[36]

Longer-term, lower-interest loans required not only capital—which HOLC acquired by issuing bonds—but also stronger and standardized appraisal methods. Standard appraisal methods were essential to allow lenders to objectively value the properties they were underwriting and assess the likelihood that the loans could eventually be paid off. This is where race and decades of controversy (and injustice) enter the story. Between 1935 and 1940, in a massive effort to assess lending risk, HOLC produced "Residential Security Maps" for every major city across the country.[37] Neighborhoods were given grades from A (least risky) to D (most risky) (see figure 2.2). The maps were color-coded: A-rated neighborhoods were green, B-rated ones were blue, C-rated ones were yellow, and D-rated neighborhoods were red—thus giving us the term "redlining."

These maps have received considerable attention for the ways in which they produced or reinforced segregation. Ta-Nehisi Coates, in his widely discussed essay "The Case for Reparations," based much of his argument about the role of the federal government in excluding Blacks from homeownership and its potential for wealth building on these racially coded maps.[38] Public broadcasting networks have run stories on redlining maps.[39] And Richard Rothstein's recent book not only received a lot of academic and policy attention but made the long list for a National Book Award,

Figure 2.2 Los Angeles Home Owners' Loan Corporation Map

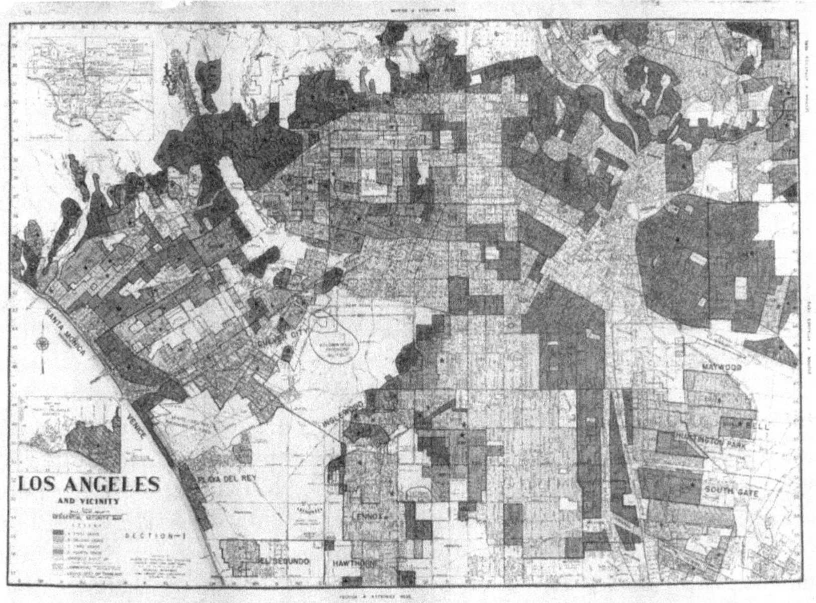

Source: City Survey Files, 1935–1940 at the National Archives.

with a redlining map of Newark, New Jersey, on its cover.[40] In the academic literature, HOLC is commonly blamed for institutionalizing redlining.[41] However, there is significant dispute over the extent to which HOLC's maps directed the flow of capital into particular neighborhoods, and therefore how responsible it was for the production and disadvantage of Black neighborhoods.

Race was undoubtedly a factor in these maps. The highest grade was given to neighborhoods that were "homogenous"—a reference to the people as well as the housing stock. Kenneth Jackson quotes a number of HOLC's City Survey Files that use explicit racial statements, including one justification for a top rating the fact that "not a single foreigner or negro" resided in the community.[42] Given the racial sentiments of the time—most likely shared by the appraisers doing the work—it is unsurprising that HOLC's appraisals would discriminate against Blacks and the places where they lived. HOLC did not invent considerations of race in housing and property value. And Blacks living in 1930s urban America were already likely to be living in neighborhoods with aging housing stock and other locational disadvantages. Further, there is plenty of evidence that HOLC did refinance mortgages in Black and red-colored neighborhoods, even if higher risk meant higher interest rates.[43] But HOLC put the federal seal of approval on the consideration of race in appraisal practices that were just beginning to set a national standard. Daniel Aaronson, Daniel Hartley, and Bhashkar Mazumder confirm that, controlling for other neighborhood factors, race was an important factor in neighborhood grades.[44] Louis Lee Woods emphasizes the role of HOLC's negative valuation of the poor and non-White in neighborhood risk valuation in the production of the widely used Federal Housing Administration (FHA) underwriting standards.[45] There is no doubt that HOLC played a substantive role in refinancing mortgages and rescuing the American mortgage system and homeowners while developing racially discriminatory methods that spread through the appraisal profession. But there is considerable doubt about the use of the widely discussed redlining maps themselves.

The smoking gun of the maps has been used as evidence that HOLC virtually eliminated the potential for lending in the disproportionately Black neighborhoods in the lowest categories. But according to Amy Hillier, it is actually highly unlikely that the HOLC maps played this role, and her case is persuasive.[46] First, she notes that lenders were already avoiding the lowest-category areas. Second, HOLC made a large percentage of its loans in areas in the C and D categories. Third, Hillier emphasizes the importance of distinguishing between discrimination against people and place-based discrimination. HOLC is likely to have engaged in racial steering—declining loans for Black people outside of Black neighborhoods—but was also probably willing to lend to Black people in Black neighborhoods. Finally, there is little evidence that HOLC's maps were disseminated widely enough to influence lending by a highly fragmented set of institutions spread across the country. The FHA and the FHLBB would have had access to the maps, but evidence suggests that they wished to keep them confidential so as to avoid further diminishing value in poor and risky areas.

Empirical research supports Hillier's archival interpretation that loans were often made with little attention to the HOLC maps. Price Fishback and his colleagues put together data on every loan issued by HOLC between 1933 and 1936 and by the FHA from 1935 to 1940 in Baltimore, Peoria, Illinois, and Greensboro, North Carolina.[47] When they geo-coded these sixteen thousand loans to neighborhoods eventually assigned by HOLC, they found no relationship between the pattern of lending by HOLC and the map designations. Since HOLC's maps were not created until after 1935, however, it is unreasonable to expect their initial loan activity to reflect those maps, as Todd Michney and LaDale Winling note.[48]

Additional recent empirical research nonetheless finds very strong impacts of HOLC maps on segregation and neighborhood disadvantage. This research provides compelling evidence that HOLC's maps seem to have affected the production and disadvantage of Black neighborhoods not only in the 1930s and 1940s but for many decades beyond. Scholars have been able to take advantage of two features of HOLC maps to study their effects in an unbiased way. First, the maps allow for comparisons between blocks on each side of HOLC map boundaries, so that, for example, D-rated blocks can be compared to adjacent C-rated blocks. Second, HOLC's "City Survey Files" program drew maps for over two hundred cities, using a population threshold of forty thousand, to determine which cities were mapped and which were not; thus, scholars can similarly detect if there are different outcomes for cities just above and below these thresholds. Using these methods shows that several outcomes appear to be affected by the maps: lower HOLC category neighborhoods had higher shares of Blacks and lower homeownership rates, house values, and rents than in higher-category neighborhoods. HOLC maps are also associated with greater segregation at the city level.[49] Subsequent research finds that individuals growing up in redlined neighborhoods *decades later* had lower incomes and credit scores, and that segregation levels in 2020 (roughly *seventy-five years later*) were eight to twelve percentage points higher in cities mapped by HOLC.[50]

These huge HOLC effects are difficult to explain, since it seems unlikely that these maps guided early lending policy. It is more likely that we have not fully uncovered the information transmitted between maps and mapmakers and the subsequent lending activity by the federal government and federally backed lending institutions. Michney and Winling emphasize that HOLC lent state support and a social scientific facade to existing discriminatory practices, thereby reinforcing beliefs that Black people and Black spaces were bad for property values.[51] The multigenerational effects have been severe. Blacks have been unable to build wealth at key points in the growth of the national housing sector. Further, Black property and Black places have been locked in a self-perpetuating downward spiral where they are devalued, capital fails to come, and Black people and their communities are blamed for deteriorating neighborhood environments.

Pinpointing the federal role in housing discrimination and residential segregation is complicated by the fact that there were multiple agencies supporting the complex process of mortgage lending. HOLC had a much shorter life and lesser impact than the FHA, about which Jackson claims: "No agency of the United States government has had a more pervasive and powerful impact on the American people over the past half-century."[52] Jackson bases that extraordinary claim on the remarkable volume of mortgage activity supported by the agency. The FHA's basic business is to insure lenders against mortgage default. Through 1972, the FHA had insured mortgages for purchase or renovation for over thirty million families.[53] It also implemented construction and underwriting standards. The FHA's 1938 underwriting manual—which was undoubtedly influential as underwriting standards proliferated at a crucial time—influenced segregation and the production of the Black neighborhood in racially explicit and implicit ways. The massive document does not dwell on race—depending on how one interprets the consistent focus on zoning and restrictive covenants. It does, however, include damning statements such as: "Areas surrounding a location are investigated to determine whether incompatible racial and social groups are present, for the purpose of making a prediction regarding the probability of the location being invaded by such groups."[54] The focus on the density and age of a neighborhood's homes was more prevalent throughout the document than racial composition; nevertheless, it had a similar impact on segregation and the production of Black neighborhoods. The FHA clearly held the adamant position that older neighborhoods could only get generally worse and less desirable. This assumption is of course wrong, and it disproportionately labeled Black neighborhoods as riskier even if race had nothing to do with it (it did). Further, the focus on density leaned heavily against multifamily housing production and almost certainly contributed to the widespread prevalence of single-family zoning and other low-density ordinances across the country.[55]

Sander, Kucheva, and Zasloff consider the FHA a racially progressive force at the time, since it financed tens of thousands of Black homebuyers in the first fifteen years and the Black homeownership rate rose substantially.[56] But even if much of the FHA's early activity was good for individual Black home-seekers (who, to be clear, were far less likely to receive FHA support than White home-seekers), Black neighborhoods suffered on net because of the FHA's segregating impacts and the huge disparities in lending between older Black neighborhoods and newer, low-density parts of metropolitan areas. As Fishback and his colleagues find in their empirical work, "The FHA largely excluded low income urban neighborhoods where the vast majority of Black mortgage borrowers lived, and instead targeted their insurance at areas with new construction and higher valued properties."[57] Michael Ebner's summary is succinct: "The policies of the respective agencies [HOLC and FHA] undermined the well-being of housing stock in the core, while enhancing circumstances on the periphery."[58]

One of the most infamous racial barriers in urban America undercuts the notion of a racially progressive FHA. In 1941, officials in the city of Detroit hoped to build an all-White subdivision in what was known as the Eight Mile–Wyoming neighborhood, located roughly eight miles north of downtown Detroit. HOLC gave the land proposed for development a D grade because it was too close to older housing largely occupied by Blacks on the other side of Eight Mile Road. As a result, the FHA would not fund the development. The compromise between the FHA and the developer was to build a physical wall along Eight Mile Road to separate the new all-White development and the Black enclave on the other side.[59] The Birwood Wall remains to this day.

FHA underwriting standards at times explicitly discriminated against Black people and neighborhoods, and they almost certainly had racially disparate impacts even when they were race-neutral. These underwriting standards made it much more likely that Black people would occupy older, less-desirable housing in majority-Black neighborhoods and that Whites would occupy newer, more-desirable housing in majority-White ones. This would further inscribe into housing markets the logic that integrated or Black neighborhoods were risky and of lower value.

Postwar Suburban Mortgage Originations

The skewing of HOLC and FHA underwriting criteria and lending activity toward newer housing and vacant tracts on the urban periphery subsidized and accelerated suburbanization, which came at the expense of limiting investment in the central-city neighborhoods disproportionately occupied by Blacks.[60]

The acceleration of suburban growth after World War II slowed housing production to a crawl, setting the stage for a housing boom in American suburbs when GIs returned from the war and formed new households. Further federal discrimination in favor of the suburbs and White suburban homebuyers came from the Veterans' Administration's mortgage support programs.[61]

For the broader (nonveteran) public, housing construction exploded in the postwar era. Jackson provides data showing that single-family housing starts were a meager 114,000 in 1944, 937,000 by 1946, and 1,692,000 by 1950.[62] However, the mortgages to fund the purchase of these newly built homes continued to disproportionately benefit White home-seekers in White neighborhoods.

Public Housing

Rothstein states that "the purposeful use of public housing by federal and local governments to herd African Americans into urban ghettos had as big an influence as any in the creation of our de jure system of segregation."[63] This assertion is almost certainly false. Although housing subsidies are a critical lifeline for the households that receive them and have done much to reproduce segregated living environments, they have had limited impact on the production of urban space and the development of Black neighborhoods. By 1968, after an era of particularly high growth in public housing production, the eight hundred thousand public housing units across the country represented only 1.2 percent of the overall housing stock.[64] At the same time, some Black census tracts have almost entirely consisted of massive public housing projects. For example, the four thousand units of the Robert Taylor Homes in Chicago (demolished in 2007) were nearly all-Black during their forty-five-year life span.[65]

But with all things public housing, Chicago is an extreme case. In more typical cities, often-segregated public housing projects reproduced segregated neighborhoods when they were built and reinforced segregated living spaces for decades to come. Thus, while most Black neighborhoods were devoid of public housing production, many were heavily influenced by it. A brief history of the role of race in public housing production is thus appropriate.

There are two government-guided mechanisms through which public housing contributed to the production of the Black neighborhood: (1) imposing racial restrictions on who could occupy particular public housing developments; and (2) basing the siting of public housing developments (in whole or in part) on the racial demographics of the surrounding neighborhoods. Public housing was more likely to segregate Blacks in Black neighborhoods because the occupants were often mandated to be people who matched neighborhood demographics. An additional mechanism toward the (re)production of segregation and Black neighborhoods was the potential for spillover effects, such as the presence of public housing (and/or its residents) prompting the exodus of White, higher-income households.

The Housing Acts of 1937 and 1949 shaped the federal role in public housing and its negative effects on Black neighborhoods. Given that Blacks were segregated in cities across the country prior to the introduction of public housing (and the FHA, HOLC, and other related government programs), and that public housing is a small fraction of any city's housing stock, it cannot be the case that federal public housing policy "caused" segregation. Further, as with any assessment of the federal role in segregation, it is not wise to make comparisons to a counterfactual of harmonious multiracial living. The median resident of a city in the pre–World War II United States was a White person who was highly unlikely to desire many Black neighbors. Segregationist federal policy largely followed the preferences of the time. Yet the federal government played a vital role as funder and developer and provided a clear signal to the real estate community that racial discrimination was good business. The federal government has often been portrayed as a leader and protector of Black interests as the civil rights movement gained steam. But this depiction is clearly contradicted by its record on housing from the New Deal through the War on Poverty.

The rhetoric in the Housing Act of 1937 centers on eliminating "unsafe and unsanitary housing conditions" and providing "decent, safe and sanitary dwellings."[66] What resulted was the first sustained effort to subsidize the construction of public housing in the country.[67]

The 1937 act put in place much of the architecture of U.S. public housing programming that stood for decades—for better or worse. Crucially, this included the U.S. Housing Authority and a funding stream to make public housing production essentially free for cities. The funding mechanism, through Treasury-backed bonds and an annual payment to local housing authorities, ensured that the subsidies were deep enough to make rents affordable to low-income families, and the subsidy was nearly guaranteed to be annually reauthorized by Congress.[68] But public housing would not be produced directly by the federal government; instead, it was constructed through a federal-local partnership. Local governments, which rarely had integrationist incentives, would have authority over site and tenant selection. The deep subsidies would have implications down the road as public housing fell into disrepair (in part because insufficient funds were authorized for maintenance) and became the housing of last resort. Market failure was the primary justification for the passage of the 1937 act, which mandated that programs avoid competing with the private market. This directive steered projects toward sites that would clear slums (where private housing provision had obviously failed) and away from more desirable and less segregated neighborhoods where private real estate interests held sway.

The act does not mention race or set parameters about site or tenant selection with race in mind, but the federal government had to explicitly deal with segregation in public housing siting and household composition, as Freeman notes.[69] Boundaries between Black and White neighborhoods were too stark and well known, and public housing could not quietly sneak into a neighborhood, as might be done with an FHA loan. Freeman argues that public housing could have been built in the urban periphery, where racial segregation had not taken hold because nobody yet lived there, but the real estate industry preferred slum clearance to reduce competition. Rothstein cites the U.S. Housing Authority manual as promoting segregation in its guidelines.[70]

Importantly, Blacks and Black institutions of the time appeared rather supportive of public housing, segregated or not. Freeman describes the implementation of the public housing portion of the 1937 act as a "separate but equal" policy that Blacks generally supported, even if such housing reinforced segregation patterns, because they stood to gain significant numbers of new and affordable housing units and the jobs to produce them.[71] Black newspapers such as the *Chicago Defender*, *Pittsburgh Courier*, *New York Amsterdam News*, and *Philadelphia Tribune* all wrote pieces in strong support of federal public housing projects, segregated or not. Freeman provides ample evidence that, for Blacks of the time, public housing was a significant step up in quality. Black support for segregated public housing stands in stark contrast to vociferous fights at the time against segregation in the armed forces and in public schools.

The 1949 Housing Act heralded a reemergence of public housing policy and production coming out of World War II. The 1949 act set a goal of providing "a decent home and a suitable living environment for every

American family."[72] While such a goal may sound like an entitlement, the 1949 act established no such thing. As with the 1937 act, the 1949 act relied on local initiative to create local housing authorities that would have the autonomy to decide where to site the housing and how much to build (within federal funding possibilities). These housing authorities had many incentives to build public housing in the least desirable places and to ensure that segregated neighborhood boundaries were left intact. More exclusive cities and towns could decide not to build public housing at all.

There is no comprehensive data source that allows for systematic measurement of segregation in public housing in the early to mid-twentieth century. We don't know the race of the people who lived in every unit, and we don't know the racial characteristics of the neighborhoods surrounding every building. But we have plenty of anecdotal information from the key public housing production years, which spanned roughly 1937 to 1973, when President Richard Nixon enacted a public housing moratorium. For example, Hunt estimates that nearly all of the 23,400 public housing units built by the Chicago Housing Authority between 1945 and 1966 were built in Black neighborhoods.[73] John Bauman, Norman Hummon, and Edward Muller write about Philadelphia's Richard Allen Homes, built exclusively for Black war workers and sited specifically using a neighborhood racial composition formula.[74]

Adam Bickford and Douglas Massey used the first national source of data on racial composition in public housing, produced in 1977, to analyze segregation in public housing at that time.[75] By the 1970s, the nation's public housing stock included scattered-site housing units and elderly housing; the authors disaggregate segregation indicators by those attributes and others. The data are far from perfect. Because it was a census of units, not individuals, the racial characteristics listed are unreliable and there are no other individual characteristics that the authors can control for. Such caveats aside, Bickford and Massey find considerable segregation in the nation's public housing in the vast majority of the metropolitan areas they studied. For the most part, Blacks were concentrated in family public housing and projects owned by housing authorities. Whites were more concentrated in elderly housing. Chicago was truly an outlier, with Black-White dissimilarity indices above 0.9 in some cases. (Out of 1.0, 0.6 is considered high.) In several metropolitan areas, however, public housing was more integrated than the overall population, suggesting that, by 1977 at least, public housing was not always a segregating influence.

The Detroit experience shows that attempts by public agencies to introduce integration into the public housing process could be doomed by local White resistance. Thomas Sugrue details the fight over the Sojourner Truth Homes, built in the early 1940s in a neighborhood still occupied by Whites, though adjacent to a Black neighborhood.[76] This was during a time when Blacks were finding very little success obtaining public housing in Detroit, as only one existing housing project in the city allowed them to live there. After the White backlash over Blacks being allowed to live in the Sojourner Truth Homes resulted in a riot, the Detroit Housing Commission promised residents that "public housing projects would 'not change the racial pattern of a neighborhood'"—wording similar to the language adopted by NAREB at the time.[77] Litigation over the siting of public housing would establish motives and outcomes of racial segregation, and the resulting racially disparate impacts, in San Francisco, Baltimore, Chicago, New Jersey, and Yonkers, New York, among other places.[78] Freeman and Rothstein provide further documentation that, in cities such as Los Angeles, Atlanta, Austin, Toledo, and Indianapolis, White residents were generally allowed to live only in public housing built in White neighborhoods and Black residents could live only in Black public housing neighborhoods.[79]

Although public housing did not create disadvantaged Black neighborhoods in any but the most extreme examples, it clearly helped perpetuate segregation through siting, discrimination, and spillover effects into adjacent Black neighborhoods. The 1949 Housing Act, which was focused much more on slum clearance, did little to combat the discrimination in public housing that would last well into the 1960s. By 1958, only eleven states forbade racial discrimination in public housing,[80] and even after a 1961 presidential order doing the same nationwide, localities continued to flout the law.[81] Public housing, in some cases, probably contributed to growing gaps between higher- and lower-income Black neighborhoods. The Black middle class, as it grew in U.S. cities, found ways to distance themselves from more disadvantaged Black districts, and public housing at times served as an indicator of such disadvantage. As Sander and his colleagues argue, the Supreme Court's 1948 *Shelley v. Kraemer* decision would help more advantaged Black Americans escape urban ghettos by invalidating racial covenants.[82] In turn, this would accelerate White flight to the suburbs.

Highways

In the mid-twentieth century, U.S. population movements out of cities and into the suburbs accelerated. Even though urban growth is not a zero-sum game, population losses in central cities—and particularly the loss of higher-income populations—shifted investment away from the urban cores where Black neighborhoods were located. Suburban growth was heavily subsidized by government (particularly the federal government), most glaringly in mortgage lending and the federal highway system.

The Federal Aid Highway Act of 1956 (more commonly known as the Interstate Highway Act) was the largest public works project in U.S. history.[83] It quickly created the world's greatest auto transportation network. There is little evidence that the U.S. Congress gave much consideration to the impact on urban neighborhoods.[84] For Black neighborhoods, the implications were both direct and indirect. Owing to the political economy of race, Black neighborhoods were often the places demolished for highway expansion. Indirectly, these highways allowed people to more freely drive away from the center of metropolitan areas where Black neighborhoods typically existed. This increased freedom for drivers facilitated depopulation in the urban centers where Black neighborhoods were located and reductions in investment and property values. The scale of American suburbanization, and its attendant negative effects on Black neighborhoods, would have been impossible without the world's greatest highway system.

The construction of the Interstate Highway System was in some ways similar to the effort to build public housing. In both cases, local governments had autonomy over the use of significant federal spending and, crucially, the siting of these public goods. But the impact of highways on urban form absolutely dwarfs the impact of public housing. By way of comparison, just the original outlay for the first ten years of highway construction was $26 billion. The U.S. government spent almost half that—only $13.5 billion—between 1953 and 1986 on slum clearance and urban redevelopment.[85] For public housing specifically, the 1949 Housing Act capped federal spending on operating costs (to cover what rent could not) at no more than $308 million annually, and it provided a revolving loan fund of $1.5 billion to state and local governments.

In addition to this massive spending gap, highways affected nearly as many housing units as the public housing program. Eric Avila estimates that the Interstate Highway Act demolished 37,000 units of housing per year between 1956 and 1966.[86] This is nearly half the total number of public housing units that were targeted to be built through the 1949 Housing Act (810,000). For both highways and public housing, the impact on the production of the Black neighborhood varies considerably across metropolitan areas. As with public housing, urban freeways had direct and unprecedented effects in some places on Black neighborhoods, and in other places the effect was negligible. Often, highway construction was used as an intentional tool of slum clearance and urban renewal.[87]

Ronald Bayor writes about the Black neighborhoods in Atlanta that I-20 and I-75 were routed through.[88] Kevin Kruse further describes how highway construction in Atlanta was used to protect White neighborhoods from potential encroachment from nearby Black residents of integrated neighborhoods.[89] Both the Lodge Freeway and the Edsel Ford Freeway cut through multiple Black neighborhoods in Detroit.[90] Christopher Silver describes the disproportionate impact of highway construction on Black neighborhoods in Virginia.[91] The Black Belt centered in West Oakland, California, was affected by the construction of four freeways from 1946 to 1985.[92] In Saint Paul, Interstate 94 ran straight through the Rondo neighborhood, into which racial covenants and other segregationist tactics had herded most of the city's Black population.[93] What had become a thriving Black neighborhood was decimated by the bisecting I-94.

This list could go on, and we can generalize about several long-lasting effects of highway construction on Black neighborhoods. First, the planning process perpetuated systems of Black powerlessness over their own urban spaces. Successful freeway revolts in places like New York and San Francisco were led by mostly White organizers, like Jane Jacobs. Very few urban neighbors wanted their homes or neighborhoods replaced by highways, but Black protesters were less likely to succeed in thwarting them. Second, Black home-seekers already had limited options because housing in White neighborhoods was often off-limits. When highways reduced the housing stock in Black neighborhoods, housing became even more scarce and costly. Third, highways fundamentally altered the accessibility benefits of central-city locations by shifting those benefits to the growing suburbs. When the Interstate Highway Act was passed, centrally located (and disproportionately Black) neighborhoods had superior accessibility. Highways leveled that playing field by making it easier for a commuter to live outside of the central city and commute back and forth. Centrally located Black neighborhoods tended to gain very few benefits from highway construction and often incurred devastating costs. In many cases, constructing a highway removed connections between neighborhoods, actually reducing local accessibility. The empirical evidence is strong that highways did lasting damage to urban neighborhoods. For example, Nathaniel Baum-Snow finds that highway construction had a lot to do with the decline in central-city population by 17 percent between 1950 to 1990, even as metropolitan population grew by 72 percent. He estimates that one new highway through a city reduced its population by nearly 18 percent on average.[94]

Urban Renewal

The history of urban renewal is intertwined with both highways and public housing. In the 1937 and 1949 acts that would establish the modern system of public housing, slum clearance and urban renewal were explicit goals, in part because they were political winners.[95] Many of the progressive reformers who pushed for public housing had been working for decades to address the unsafe and unsanitary conditions in low-income housing in many U.S. cities. And pairing public housing with urban renewal satisfied real estate interests as well. Urban renewal is also tied to the interstate highway system. Rothstein quotes the Highway Research Board in 1962 proudly proclaiming that "interstate highways were 'eating out slums' and 'reclaiming blighted areas.'"[96] Highways demolished thirty-seven thousand housing units per year for over a decade.

Empirical research on urban renewal complicates the common understanding that the practice bears so much responsibility for central-city disadvantage. These effects can be hard to study, but William Collins and Katharine Shester have a creative way to control for the fact that places with a particular need for economic development might be more likely to seek urban renewal projects in the first place.[97] They find substantial positive effects of urban renewal on median property values, median family income, and employment rates, and negative effects on poverty rates. Given that urban renewal is often thought to have ruined urban neighborhoods, these are surprising findings. Although some residents of Black neighborhoods surely lost out from some of these projects, the average Black neighborhood may have received a boost. Collins and Shester also find no evidence that Black people were more likely to be displaced through urban renewal. On the contrary, their models strongly suggest that urban renewal catalyzed change in urban neighborhoods (and sometimes in adjoining neighborhoods) that spurred investment and lasting economic benefits. Undoubtedly, many who left these neighborhoods did not share in these benefits, and many of these neighborhoods remained disadvantaged. Further, long-run increases in property values may have typically benefited landholders who did not live in urban renewal neighborhoods. And increases in property values from urban renewal could result in higher rents.[98] But this evidence complicates the conventional wisdom that urban renewal was a disaster for the targeted neighborhoods, many of which were Black. Ultimately, urban renewal may have had less effect than it's commonly said to have had. Wilson and Teaford both note that the conversation around urban renewal has often been louder than its actual influence on neighborhoods and urban form, particularly relative to game-changers like the FHA and highways.[99] Massey, on the other hand, gives renewal a starring role in the perpetuation of the Black ghetto: "Whenever black residential expansion threatened a favored district, a local urban renewal authority was established to gain control of the land using the power of eminent domain. Black neighborhoods were then razed for 'redevelopment' as a middle-class commercial or residential zone."[100]

Urban renewal on its own may be an overdiscussed factor in Black neighborhood disadvantage, but when paired with highways or public housing segregation, it was very consequential. It was also indicative of a top-down planning process that has always been applied more commonly to Black neighborhoods than anywhere else.

Other Factors

The Great Migration, mortgage lending, restrictive covenants, zoning, highways, and, to a lesser extent, urban renewal and public housing are probably the greatest contributing factors to Black neighborhood disadvantage. Unfortunately, there were more, from metropolitan fragmentation to the slow progress of the civil rights movement, violence toward and intimidation of Black home-seekers (and related state-supported violence from police), and an incoherent and incomplete urban policy apparatus.

Owing to FHA lending, urban renewal, White flight, and urban highway construction, the middle of the twentieth century saw robust population, income, and housing growth outside of central cities in metropolitan America. Such growth could have expanded central-city boundaries, but instead, in the vast majority of circumstances, new towns or "suburbs" were created out of whole cloth in what scholars have termed "metropolitan fragmentation."[101] This fragmentation allowed suburban jurisdictions to hoard resources by avoiding shared taxation and spending with the central cities that were arguably their only reason for existing.

The civil rights movement contributed to Black neighborhood disadvantage through the massive ramifications of its pace and limits for individual-level disadvantage in Black communities. Segregated schools continued to exist well past the 1954 *Brown v. Board of Education* decision, and it was not until the 1964 Civil Rights Act that employment discrimination was declared unlawful. School and employment discrimination continued to produce poor educational and earnings outcomes, thereby limiting Blacks' ability to escape disadvantaged Black neighborhoods, which themselves were disadvantaged because of these limitations placed on Black people. Further, these factors perpetuated disparities in ownership and wealth that persist to the present day.

The extreme rhetoric around race and property values combined with high levels of discrimination against Blacks to incite violence in opposition to Black movement into White areas, often with the tacit approval of local authorities. Examples abounded across the country, from Detroit to Chicago and Atlanta.[102] In Los Angeles, celebrity provided the means to buy homes in neighborhoods at the top of the heap. But in 1948, when Nat King Cole bought a home in Hancock Park, a tony neighborhood in Los Angeles, the local property association tried to buy him out rather than allow Cole and his family to move in. After the Coles refused, the singer's wild popularity failed to protect his family from violence and intimidation: "Vigilantes then burned a racial epithet into the Coles' lawn and poisoned their dog."[103]

Violence against Blacks was perpetrated not just by private citizens but also by those sworn to protect them. Differential treatment by the police is by now a well-known hazard of living in a Black neighborhood, and it has long historical roots. Freeman discusses the constant stress over police surveillance in Black ghettos in Philadelphia, Detroit, New York, Birmingham, and Los Angeles during the period leading up to 1970.[104] The riots of the late 1960s had many catalysts, but selective violence by police was undoubtedly one of them. Police involvement in violence made the suppression of urban unrest particularly difficult, given the tendency for police to heighten tensions in the Black community. The Watts riot began as a police stop with subsequent police brutality.[105] Freeman also cites complaints about police abuse as catalysts for riots in Buffalo, Newark, and Detroit. The Kerner Commission was sympathetic to the challenges of policing in disadvantaged Black communities, but its report was clear about the central role of poor police-community relations in urban unrest. The commission found that the key tension in Black communities was centered in routinely "abrasive" tactics and ghetto residents' feelings of not being adequately protected.[106] The tension in disadvantaged Black communities from being simultaneously overpoliced and underprotected remains to this day.[107]

Black neighborhood disadvantage was neither inevitable nor accidental. It is not an inevitable by-product of Black individual disadvantage—disadvantage that was exacerbated by segregation, housing policy, and the denial of Black wealth. The research on neighborhood effects that motivates this study tells us that individuals not only produce their neighborhood environments but are impacted by them.

Neighborhoods Matter

Housing locations determine the conditions that individuals face on the blocks where they live, which are nested within neighborhoods, within cities, within metropolitan areas. Each of these spaces has the potential to influence important outcomes for the individuals who live within them. George Galster defines the nested scales of a metro area as the "spatial opportunity structure" and notes that it affects individual socioeconomic outcomes along at least two pathways.[108] First, it shapes the kind of payoffs that people will receive from their human capital. For example, in metropolitan areas with lower unemployment and higher wages, people might earn more than they would elsewhere with the same skills. Second, the spatial opportunity structure shapes the very development of that human capital. This is most obvious in the context of school quality.

The study of neighborhood effects is a fertile research area in part because the connections are complicated. Neighborhoods have potential impacts on many outcomes (income, education, safety, social networks), at various spatial scales, through many mechanisms (neighborhood safety, poverty, and so on). This is also why some uncertainty remains about which individual outcomes are affected by which neighborhood attributes. But we have enough empirical evidence to conclude that neighborhoods do indeed matter.

Many excellent resources provide a review of empirical research on neighborhood effects.[109] These reviews summarize work in several social science domains on how various neighborhood characteristics affect key individual outcomes, including child and adult mental and physical health; education and future earnings for children; employment, earnings and social networks for adults; and children's risk behaviors and criminal victimization or involvement. Theoretically, neighborhoods are thought to affect outcomes for youth more than for adults. Neighborhood determines children's schools, the extent of crime and safety concerns, adult role models outside the home, and interactions with peers in school and near home. For adults, transportation networks, peer and social networks, and job locations can affect health and economic well-being. Empirically, the effects on children have been easier to find, particularly effects on children who spend more time in disadvantaged neighborhoods.[110]

Taken together, common sense and social science evidence tell us that neighborhoods do matter. But the evidence belies simple stories. Not everyone wishes to leave behind racially segregated or high-poverty neighborhoods, perhaps for good reason. For decades, as the Great Migration brought millions of Black Americans from the rural South to a rapidly urbanizing North, Black neighborhoods were a vital landing spot that could provide a way station to jobs and housing and help migrants assimilate into a new environment very different from what they were accustomed to. Black businesses and banks were formed, and in a more rigid caste system, Black professionals such as doctors, lawyers, and accountants were needed to serve Black people in Black neighborhoods. Freeman, analyzing data from the 1920 census, finds that "Blacks in predominantly Black neighborhoods in the North had the highest socioeconomic status among Blacks in the country, even slightly higher than northern Blacks living outside the ghetto."[111]

This book covers the entire country's Black neighborhoods over a period of nearly fifty years. It would be ideal to have data on all of the neighborhood characteristics that affected people's lives, but that is infeasible. Data on structural characteristics of neighborhoods, like school quality or the prevalence of crime and violence, are not systematically available. I focus on socioeconomic variables, leaning heavily on poverty rates, but I add a measure of disadvantage based on the share of adults with less than a high school degree, the poverty rate, the unemployment rate, the share of female-headed households, and the median household income. Because of discriminatory practices that bake racism into housing markets, I focus on neighborhood housing characteristics such as rents, home values, and vacancy rates.

1970 as an Inflection Point

The policy and legal shifts of the 1960s offer a paradox, specifically with respect to U.S. cities and Black neighborhoods and more generally with respect to race. On the one hand, these shifts were seismic; the gains of the civil rights movement were nothing short of a revolution. But this revolution fell short of righting past wrongs well enough to level the playing field in housing and rescue the Black neighborhood from the spiral of decay in which it was caught, precisely as the revolution was achieving its greatest successes.

The year 1970 marks a key inflection point in Black neighborhoods. The rights revolution of the 1960s had cemented the legal and policy frameworks that would shape Black individual and neighborhood well-being. With greater freedom of movement than ever before, the Black middle class was able to flee disadvantaged Black neighborhoods and either form their own enclaves or take up roots in previously White ones. Just as the Great Migration was coming to an end, changes in immigration complicated the Black-White paradigm that had dominated U.S. cities throughout the twentieth century, greatly diversifying Black neighborhoods where immigrants were concentrated.[112] The rights revolution and the War on Poverty put a new arsenal of tools at the disposal of the federal government and local jurisdictions that could be used to make swift and significant progress toward integrating urban America and elevating the status of Black neighborhoods. Unfortunately, the limited progress over the last fifty years strongly suggests that this path was not chosen.

This chapter has summarized several forces that had made disadvantage the norm for Black neighborhoods by 1970. Racial discrimination and White supremacy were basic facets of American life in and out of the public sector. Mortgage brokers, real estate agents, developers, landlords, and appraisers deployed racist preferences and incentives for containing Blacks in specific neighborhoods. But they could not have created the Black neighborhoods of 1970 on their own, without government support, legislation, and administration that ranged from poor enforcement of discrimination protections to seemingly racially neutral actions in the zoning code to racially explicit covenants. The public sector, from the federal government on down, is uniquely culpable as the entity that could have done the most to combat the varied forces of discrimination and instead too often wielded the heavy hand of the state to restrict Black movement and devalue Black communities. We now know that the tragic consequences are taking generations to undo.

The conditions in Black neighborhoods, and thus their probable effects on residents, have clearly changed over time. But these conditions are still evolving and likely very complex. Many Black neighborhoods have either retained their affluence or become even wealthier over time. Some have rebounded after declines in the middle or latter decades of the twentieth century. And many Black neighborhoods exist where they previously did not, or no longer exist where they were once plentiful. The data and narratives in the following chapters tell this story.

Chapter 3

The State of Black Neighborhoods, 1970–2017

Manhattan keeps on makin' it, Brooklyn keeps on takin' it
Bronx keeps creatin' it, and Queens keeps on fakin' it
—Boogie Down Productions, "The Bridge Is Over," 1987

The Birth of Hip-Hop

As big as Motown was, another Black neighborhood in the early 1970s—the South Bronx—would birth a new musical genre that is still the dominant form of music to this day.

Of several different ways to define the South Bronx, I define it as the eighty-five southernmost Bronx census tracts bounded entirely by major highways. These highways are the massive infrastructure projects of Robert Moses, chronicled in Robert Caro's classic biography *The Power Broker*.[1] The Cross-Bronx Expressway, the northern border of the South Bronx, was the last segment to fully encircle and isolate the area from the rest of the borough and city. The Cross-Bronx was infamously complex to build, from an engineering perspective, and incredibly costly, both in raw dollar figures and in terms of the massive amount of housing demolition and displacement that made it possible. As construction was carried out from 1948 to 1963 (the expressway would not be fully connected to surrounding interchanges and bridges until 1972), the Cross-Bronx expedited the exodus of the White population, many of whom were immigrants or descendants of immigrants who had first landed in the tenements of Manhattan's Lower East Side. According to the 1970 census, the eighty-five census tracts bounded by these expressways were 57 percent White and 40 percent Black, but it is very likely that many of those listed as White were actually Hispanic or Latino. We know this because by the 1980 census, when Hispanic or Latino identity was tabulated, nearly 50 percent of the neighborhood identified as such. At that time, Blacks were the largest racial or ethnic group in thirty-three of the eighty-five census tracts. In fifty-one

https://doi.org/10.7758/tjvh5404.2134

others, Hispanics were the largest racial or ethnic group. Although the South Bronx has been more Hispanic than Black over the past fifty years and by now has evolved into a Hispanic enclave, it was home to many smaller Black neighborhoods in the 1970s and 1980s and remains about 30 percent Black to this day.

Just across the Cross-Bronx Expressway, at 1520 Sedgwick Avenue, is what is now referred to as "the Birthplace of Hip-Hop." The origin story of a company turned cultural force like Motown is considerably simpler than the story for an entire musical genre, like rap or hip-hop.[2] DJ Kool Herc, who spun records at the party at 1520 Sedgwick Avenue in 1973 that is credited with being rap's foundational moment, was not the CEO of a music label. He was never even a popular musician. And it would be another seven years before a rap single reached the top forty (all the way down at number thirty-six). Herc earned his place as a founder of rap because of his innovation of sliding seamlessly back and forth between two copies of the same record, so that he could keep a key musical moment going as long as the dancing "B-Boys" and "B-Girls" needed it. This innovation would form the musical basis of backgrounds for rhymes and lyrics well into rap's ascendance to the top of the charts decades later. In the 1970s, the Bronx was home to many DJs who took Herc's methods and ran with them, most famously Afrika Bambaata, Grandmaster Flash, and Grand Wizzard Theodore.

Unfortunately, the Bronx in the 1970s was one of the most disadvantaged and dangerous places in urban America. The 1970 poverty rate of 14 percent in the census tract that included 1520 Sedgwick Avenue would explode to 33 percent by 1980. In the broader South Bronx neighborhood hemmed in by highways, the poverty rate was 29 percent in 1970 and 47 percent by 1980. The median household income during that decade dropped from $35,000 to just over $22,000. In *Can't Stop, Won't Stop: A History of the Hip-Hop Generation*, Jeff Chang rattles off a litany of indicators that the Bronx was falling off a cliff by the 1970s and throughout that decade.[3] He estimates that the neighborhood lost an astounding six hundred thousand manufacturing jobs during this time. The youth unemployment rate was upward of 60 percent.

But it was the vacancies and the fires that were the most infamous features of South Bronx life. In 1977, when the New York Yankees hosted the Los Angeles Dodgers at Yankee Stadium, located in the South Bronx, it would turn out to be a historic World Series, with America's two largest cities doing battle. Two of baseball's most decorated franchises, the Yankees and Dodgers, had been crosstown rivals when the Dodgers played in Brooklyn. In game 2 of this face-off—before the Yankees' highly paid and controversial new superstar, Reggie Jackson, eventually carried the Yankees to the title by hitting three consecutive home runs—the television audience would be shown vignettes of burning buildings throughout the neighborhood. The abandoned Public School 3 was on fire, as were multiple apartment buildings at Melrose and 158th Street. The startling images would inspire President Jimmy Carter to visit abandoned blocks and vacant, burned-out buildings in the neighborhood.

The vacant buildings and the fires were a result of cratering housing demand in the South Bronx, brought about by a combination of destructive highway development, White flight, and the end of the Great Migration. When property owners compared the insurance money they could receive if their buildings caught fire with the meager rent checks they could expect from a dwindling number of residents, buildings mysteriously started going up in flames.

Was the South Bronx Typical?

A key argument of this book is that we can be misled about Black (and Black-Hispanic) neighborhoods like the South Bronx in the 1970s. We are inundated with the negative imagery and stereotypes about Black neighborhoods that have shaped policy areas from public housing demolition to welfare reform. The fiftieth anniversary of Kool Herc's South Bronx party has recently been marked by a celebration of hip-hop's fiftieth birthday, replete with positive connotations of that time and place. But for the vast majority of the half-century since the birth of hip-hop, most Americans have been told that the typical Black neighborhood is poor, dangerous, and falling apart—if not as badly as 1977 South Bronx, then something close to it.

But just as the South Bronx provided a unique setting for the evolution of a musical genre that would eventually dominate the charts, the Black enclaves within the South Bronx are not representative of the diversity of Black neighborhoods across the country. Further, our perceptions of Black neighborhoods may be outdated. As concerns about concentrated poverty and crime have receded in some Black neighborhoods in favor of gentrification, the popular notion of widespread Black neighborhood disadvantage is probably even further out of date.

Table 3.1 makes clear that the South Bronx has been a different place from the typical Black neighborhood over the last fifty years. It is more Hispanic and less Black, and the poverty rate is much higher. The fourfold increase in home values is tempered by the fact that homeownership is extremely rare, rising only to 7 percent in recent decades. Its location in the New York metro area makes it typical in one sense, as nearly 15 percent of the nation's Black census tracts are located there. And contrary to New York's astronomical housing costs (and the expensive home values there), median rents in the South Bronx are in line with the rest of the country's Black neighborhoods.

Table 3.1 Socioeconomic Conditions in Eighty-Five South Bronx Neighborhoods, 1970–2017

	1970	1980	1990	2000	2010	2017
Poverty rate	31%	46%	47%	43%	40%	37%
Percent White	57	4	2	1	1	2
Percent Black	40	45	39	35	32	30
Percent Hispanic	NA	49	58	62	65	65
Percent Asian	1	1	1	1	1	1
Median rent	$535	$520	$599	$647	$863	$935
Median home value	$110,140	$116,066	$157,922	$222,380	$408,188	$403,121
Homeownership rate	3%	4%	5%	7%	7%	7%

Source: Author's tabulation of U.S. 2010 Longitudinal Tract Database (Logan, Xu, and Stults 2014) and American Community Survey Five-Year Estimates (U.S. Census Bureau 2019).

This chapter summarizes the economic and demographic characteristics of Black neighborhoods from 1970 to 2017 and sets the table for deeper dives into how these characteristics have varied across the country and evolved over time. Several key themes emerge from this broad, nearly fifty-year summary of data on Black neighborhoods. First, there has been some convergence in socioeconomic indicators between Black neighborhoods and non-Black neighborhoods. The 1970s were very challenging years for many Black neighborhoods, but on average they have rebounded since 1980; still, meaningful gaps persist. The rebound is tied to a decoupling of outcomes for Black individuals from Black neighborhoods, since Black people are less likely to live in Black neighborhoods than ever before. It is also relevant that comparison neighborhoods have become less White and more Hispanic/Latino and Asian. Even controlling for these changes, the convergence is real, but limited. Also, some indicators for Black households and individuals—particularly poverty rates and high school completion rates—have radically improved, at a greater pace than improvements to Black neighborhoods.

What Is a Black Neighborhood?

I define a Black neighborhood as a census tract in which the non-Hispanic/Latino Black population is the largest racial or ethnic group, constituting a plurality. My sample of census tracts is restricted to those in 172 of the largest combined statistical areas (CSAs), or core-based statistical areas (CBSAs), in the country as of the 2010 census.[4]

There are several key considerations when defining a neighborhood according to its racial composition. First, it is difficult to capture the social concept of a neighborhood through a consistent set of boundaries, and there have been several critiques of such limitations of census tracts as proxies for neighborhoods.[5] I dig deeper into these limitations and address some of them in chapter 5. But for the descriptions of Black neighborhood demographic, social, and economic characteristics in this chapter, I exclusively use census tracts.

The second geographic consideration is deciding which census tracts to include. The U.S. Black population is disproportionately urban, but Black census tracts do exist in non-urban areas, chiefly in the South. Rural Jasper County, Mississippi, for example, has four census tracts and three of them are majority-Black. Further, some non-urban census tracts include penal institutions where Blacks constitute a majority, owing to the racialized nature of mass incarceration in the United States. In fact, a recent analysis found that over half of the majority-Black census tracts in Wisconsin are majority-Black because they include a jail or a prison.[6] However, the goal of this study is to better understand the forces that shape *urban* Black neighborhoods. While I will miss non-urban Black communities, I restrict my sample of census tracts to those that in 1990 either are included in a CSA or, if not part of a CSA, are in a CBSA with a population over 100,000 and a Black population over 10,000. These criteria ensure that the Black neighborhoods in my sample are almost entirely in an urban context. My sample includes a total of 54,536 census tracts in 172 CSAs or CBSAs.[7] These metropolitan areas cover a huge share of the national population—over 76 percent in 2010—and an even larger share of the nation's Black population (90 percent in 2010).

Throughout the book, all analyses are conducted using the 1970, 1980, 1990, 2000, and 2010 decennial U.S. censuses and the 2015–2019 American Community Survey (ACS). For describing the socioeconomic characteristics of the nation's urban neighborhoods over this time period, census data are easily the best option, but they have several limitations. Data snapshots every ten years often hide changes that occur in the interim. Several variables of interest are not captured. We do not know, for instance, where people move to out of Black neighborhoods, how long they lived there, or where they lived before. We also lack some precision in income data. And though we no longer have to wait ten years for new data, owing to the recent change to annual data releases of the ACS, census tract–level estimates are reliable only when using the five-year waves of these surveys. The 2015–2019 ACS includes data collected in each of those five years, and the Census Bureau uses all five waves to estimate population, demographics, housing, and other characteristics for a given level of geography. Given that 2017 is the midpoint year, I often refer to neighborhood characteristics from the 2015–2019 ACS as "2017" data.[8]

A third decision is whether to consider the racial mix of the neighborhood beyond the primary racial group under analysis. Important work has been done on neighborhood racial and ethnic diversity, and I incorporate information about other racial and ethnic groups in many analyses.[9] But my sample of Black neighborhoods is solely defined by the presence of people who identify as Black, and whether that is the largest racial or ethnic group in the neighborhood.[10]

My final consideration is the threshold of the share of Black population to determine a neighborhood's racial identity.[11] A case could be made for at least three thresholds: a plurality (Blacks are the largest racial or ethnic group), a majority (Blacks are 50 percent or more), or a large majority (such as 90 percent Black or more). Given the tendency for American neighborhoods to include either very few or very many Blacks, plurality and majority are often synonymous when it comes to Black neighborhoods. The data bear this out quite clearly. In appendix table A.3.1, I provide counts and poverty rates for the three types of Black neighborhoods, using these thresholds. In 1970, Blacks were a plurality in 3,253 tracts. In just over 98 percent of those tracts, Blacks constituted a majority, which is startling. Black majority and Black plurality became more distinct over the years; by 2010, "only" 84 percent of Black-plurality census tracts were also Black-majority census tracts. A much smaller number of tracts were Black-dominant. Even in 1970, only 38 percent of Black-plurality tracts were also Black-dominant, and this share declined to 18 percent by 2017. But 90 percent Black neighborhoods were found in only sixty-six metropolitan areas, primarily in the South. Using a 90 percent threshold thus eliminates analysis in most metropolitan areas, limits statistical power, and throws out many places that locals would probably identify as Black. Further, the poverty rates in Black-plurality neighborhoods are similar to Black-majority and 90 percent Black neighborhoods, suggesting that Black-plurality neighborhoods share a lot of similarities with Black neighborhoods that are more racially segregated. Given the near-total overlap between Black-plurality and Black-majority census tracts, using the more expansive definition (a plurality) is a reasonable selection criterion. This results in 3,253 Black neighborhoods in 1970, which had expanded to 6,928 Black neighborhoods in 2017.

Where the Hood At? Concentrated in a Handful of Large Metros and the South

Even using the plurality threshold, Black neighborhoods are concentrated in a small number of metropolitan areas and the South. Some of this concentration is due to population: the New York and Los Angeles metro areas together account for over 10 percent of the nation's people. The Great Migration is another obvious factor for having established generations of Black households in metros like Chicago, Detroit, and Philadelphia. The concentration in a small number of large metros lessens over time, owing to several factors that changed the geography of race in U.S. metropolitan areas, including the migration of all racial and ethnic groups to the suburbs and the South as well as increased immigration from Asia, Mexico, and Central America. Table 3.2 shows the concentration of Black neighborhoods in U.S. metropolitan areas that were in the top six in Black population in 1970 or 2017—New York, Chicago, Washington, D.C., Los Angeles, Philadelphia, Detroit, and Atlanta. The share of the country's Black neighborhoods in these metros declined from 47 to 42 percent even though the number almost doubled (from 1,538 to 2,844) because the country's Black neighborhoods more than doubled. The main sources of change in this group were Los Angeles and Atlanta. Los Angeles lost over one-third of its Black neighborhoods during this time period, while Atlanta's increased sixfold. The top six metros did not change much, but Atlanta went from fifteenth to fifth, while Los Angeles went from fourth to twenty-second.

Although the largest numbers of Black census tracts, until recently, have been primarily located in the country's major population centers in the North and West, the U.S. cities and metropolitan areas with the highest

Table 3.2 Share of U.S. Black Neighborhoods, Top Six Metro Areas, 1970 and 2017

City	Share of U.S. Total in 1970	Share of U.S. Total in 2017
New York, N.Y.–N.J.–Conn.–Pa.	14%	11%
Chicago, Ill.–Ind.–Wisc.	8	7
Washington, D.C.–Baltimore, Md.–Va.–W.V.	7	8
Los Angeles, Calif.	7	1
Detroit, Mich.	4	6
Philadelphia, Pa.–N.J.	4	4
Atlanta, Ga.–Ala.	2	5
Share of U.S. total	47%	42%

Source: Author's tabulation of U.S. 2010 Longitudinal Tract Database (Logan, Xu, and Stults 2014) and American Community Survey Five-Year Estimates (U.S. Census Bureau 2019).

share of Blacks have always been in the South, and this share has generally increased as the Black population has continued to urbanize in the South (and migrate back to the South). While only 15 percent of New York's census tracts are Black neighborhoods, over half of Memphis's are.

Some Convergence after the 1970s

The trends in Black neighborhoods during the last half-century echo the changes for Black Americans more broadly. As with Black individuals, Black neighborhoods have only slowly caught up to the rest of the country across key indicators. The 1970s were a difficult period for Black neighborhoods in particular, but on average, the typical Black neighborhood has improved considerably along several socioeconomic indicators since the 1980s.[12] However, as with Black Americans, Black neighborhoods still lag well behind non-Black neighborhoods in every meaningful statistic, and in nearly every metropolitan area.

Poverty Convergence

Appendix Table 3.1 provides additional data on the poverty rates in the three types of Black neighborhoods, and table 3.3 provides the ratio between the poverty rates Black plurality neighborhoods and non-Black tracts in the metropolitan areas in the sample in the same period.[13] It is notable that regardless of how Black census tracts are defined, at least one-quarter of households in these neighborhoods lived in poverty, in all years, except Black-plurality tracts in the 2015–2019 ACS. Black-dominant census tracts, not surprisingly, had the highest poverty rates, followed by Black-majority census tracts. And the poverty rate declined less in

Table 3.3 Poverty Rates in Black and Non-Black Neighborhoods, 172 CSAs/CBSAs, 1970–2017

	1970	1980	1990	2000	2010	2017
Average poverty rate in Black neighborhoods	27%	28%	29%	25%	27%	23%
Average poverty rate in non-Black neighborhoods	9	9	10	10	13	12
Poverty rate ratio: Black to non-Black neighborhoods	3.09	3.02	2.79	2.40	2.04	2.00
Average poverty exposure for Black individuals	24%	24%	24%	20%	22%	20%
Poverty rate for Black households	35	30	30	25	26	23

Source: Author's tabulation of U.S. 2010 Longitudinal Tract Database (Logan, Xu, and Stults 2014) and American Community Survey Five-Year Estimates (U.S. Census Bureau 2019).

Black-majority (two percentage points) and 90 percent Black (one percentage point) census tracts. For Black-plurality census tracts, the poverty rates ranged from being 2.5 times as high as the poverty rates in non-Black census tracts in the same areas in 1970 to a low of 1.8 times the rate in 2017. The poverty rate in non-Black census tracts in these metros rose from 9 to 12 percent between 1970 and 2017, but declined four percentage points in Black-plurality census tracts over the same time period.

Also noteworthy is that the number of Black tracts grew much more quickly than the full sample of tracts. Although there was a small decrease between 2010 and 2015–2019, the number of Black tracts more than doubled between 1970 and 2010, while non-Black tracts in these CBSAs grew only 8 percent.

The glass half-full perspective notes a steady convergence and evidence for the decoupling of neighborhood disadvantage and race. In 1980, Black tracts were three times as impoverished as non-Black tracts, and that was down to a two-to-one ratio from 1970. Table 3.3 also provides the poverty rates for Black households, which plummeted from 35 percent to 23 percent during the same time—an even larger decline than for Black neighborhoods. The pessimist will note that the poverty rate in Black neighborhoods dropped only four percentage points in nearly fifty years and is still double the poverty rates outside of those neighborhoods.

More Racial Diversity Everywhere

Black neighborhoods are clearly more racially diverse now than they were in 1970. Not surprisingly, Black neighborhoods became less racially isolated with the loosening of de facto and de jure restrictions over where Blacks

Table 3.4 Racial and Ethnic Composition in Black and Non-Black Neighborhoods, 172 CSAs/CBSAs, 1970–2017

	1970	1980	1990	2000	2010	2017
Whites in Black neighborhoods	18%[a]	14%	15%	16%	16%	17%
Whites in non-Black neighborhoods	94[a]	85	80	72	65	62
Black individuals in Black neighborhoods	81[a]	79	76	73	69	66
Black individuals in non-Black neighborhoods	4[a]	5	7	8	9	8
Hispanics in Black neighborhoods	NA	5	7	8	11	12
Hispanics in non-Black neighborhoods	NA	7	10	14	18	20
Asians and Pacific Islanders in Black neighborhoods	1	1	1	2	3	3
Asians and Pacific Islanders in non-Black neighborhoods	1	2	3	5	7	7

Source: Author's tabulation of U.S. 2010 Longitudinal Tract Database (Logan, Xu, and Stults 2014) and American Community Survey Five-Year Estimates (U.S. Census Bureau 2019).

[a] In 1970, the U.S. census did not include categories for those identifying as Hispanic or Latino. The Asian, Black, and White populations are likely overestimated.

could live and the country's further diversification as a result of increased immigration. Table 3.4 summarizes the racial and ethnic composition of Black-plurality and non-Black census tracts, inclusive of four racial and ethnic groups—Whites, Hispanic/Latino, Asian, and Black. The census did not ask questions about Hispanic or Latino identification until 1980.

With four ethnoracial groups, the minimum share for a plurality is 25.1 percent (with a maximum of 100). From 1980 to 2017, the time period for which there are four groups—and a time during which the Black share of the population in these metro areas fluctuated only minimally (between 13 and 15 percent)—the average share of Black population in Black neighborhoods declined from 79 to 66 percent. In other words, Black neighborhood segregation went from extremely high (three times the minimum) down to very high. Another way to consider this is that Black neighborhoods went from being fifteen times as Black as non-Black neighborhoods in 1980 to eight times as Black in 2017. Blacks are still highly predominant where they comprise a plurality of a tract, but they are less predominant than they used to be. This change is almost entirely due to the substantial growth in the Hispanic and Asian populations in these tracts. Only 5 percent of people living in Black tracts in 1980 identified as Hispanic or Latino; this share more than doubled, to 12 percent, by the 2015–2019 ACS. Asians are less prevalent than Hispanics in Black tracts; their share grew from only 1 percent (1980) to 3 percent (2015–2019 ACS). Notably, over half of the decline in the share of Blacks in Black tracts was due to the increase in Hispanics and Latinos. However, both Asians and Hispanics/Latinos have become more prevalent, and at a faster rate, in non-Black tracts. Hispanics now make up 20 percent of the population outside of Black tracts (up from 7 percent in 1980), and Asians comprise 7 percent of the population outside of Black tracts (up from 2 percent in 1980).

What further stands out from this table is the substantial decline in the share of Whites in these CBSAs throughout the data period, and the contrasting stability of Whites in Black neighborhoods from the 1980 census through 2015–2019. Overall, the share of Whites in these metropolitan areas declined substantially as the share of Whites in non-Black tracts declined from 85 percent in 1980 to 62 percent. The share White in Black tracts increased slightly, from 14 percent in 1980 to 17 percent in 2017. Two forces collided to keep the share of Whites in Black neighborhoods constant from 1970 to 2017—the declining share of Whites overall was countered by the increased likelihood that Whites would locate in Black neighborhoods rather than non-Black metropolitan ones.

Although a lot of attention is paid in housing policy to the location decisions of racial minorities, White household decisions remain most impactful, since they are the largest population group. Thus, the very slow increase in the share of Whites living in Black tracts is a significant reason for the continued segregation of Black neighborhoods. Further, the recent attention to gentrification conflicts with the lack of change in the White presence in Black neighborhoods over the last twenty years. Nationally, the share of Whites in Black neighborhoods was essentially unchanged through the 2000 (16 percent) and 2010 (16 percent) censuses and 2015–2019 ACS (17 percent). This pattern held in some major metros where gentrification is more common. In New York, the share of Whites in Black neighborhoods rose only from 9 to 10 percent. In Washington, D.C.—the metropolitan area with the most rapid recent racial transition in Black neighborhoods—the White share grew from 13 to 15 percent. These are averages among a changing sample of neighborhoods that are Black plurality by definition, so they say nothing about neighborhoods that have ceased being Black plurality. And again, the share of Whites declined nationwide over this time, particularly in metro areas. I measure gentrification more directly in Black neighborhoods in chapter 6. Here I provide a more nuanced look at racial change in Black neighborhoods in figure 3.1.

Figure 3.1 displays the racial composition from 1980 to 2017 of what were Black neighborhoods in 1970. Over 88 percent of these neighborhoods were still Black plurality in 1990, and about 73 percent of them were Black plurality in 2017. Black neighborhoods tend to remain Black. However, the share of Blacks in these neighborhoods declined dramatically—from 84 to 57 percent by 2017. But the change that did occur in 1970 Black

Figure 3.1 Racial Composition of 1970 Black Neighborhoods, 1980–2017

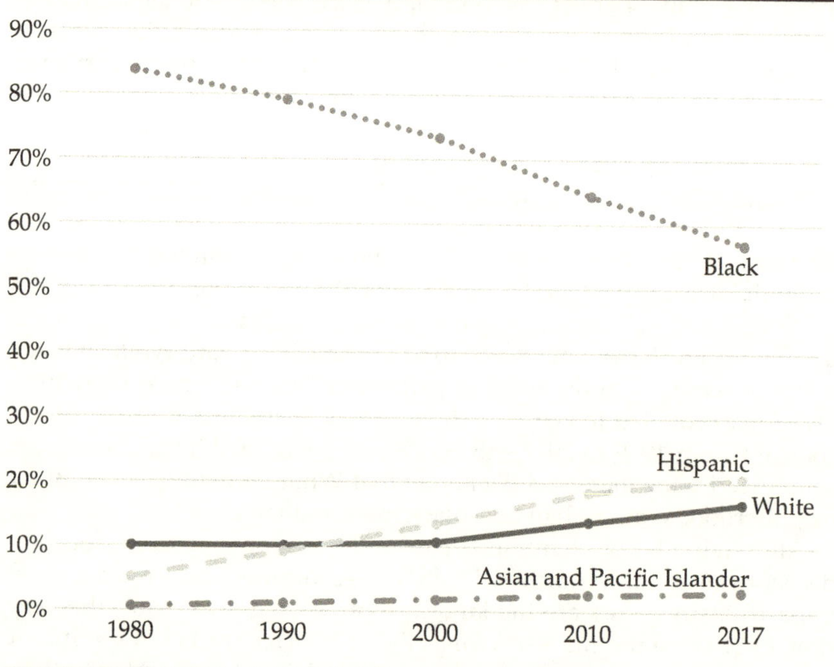

Source: Author's tabulation of U.S. 2010 Longitudinal Tract Database (Logan, Xu, and Stults 2014) and American Community Survey Five-Year Estimates (U.S. Census Bureau 2019).

neighborhoods was largely Black replacement by Hispanics. Represented by the dashed line in figure 3.1, the Hispanic population quadrupled from 5 to 21 percent. White households did replace Blacks, though to a lesser extent, rising in share from 10 to 17 percent.

White replacement of Blacks in Black neighborhoods looks a little more robust when we control for the changes in the overall racial composition of U.S. metropolitan areas. Figure 3.2 presents the ratio in racial composition between non-Black and Black tracts for 1970 Black neighborhoods over time, beginning in 1980, since we do not have Hispanic or Latino ethnicity data in 1970. In 1980, Whites were over eight times as likely to live outside of Black neighborhoods. Asian Americans were three times as likely, and Hispanics were one and a half times as likely to live outside of Black neighborhoods.

The coming decades saw two notable trends. First, Whites were far more likely to live in 1970 Black neighborhoods, relative to their overall share of the population: by 2017, they were just over three times as likely to live outside of these Black neighborhoods. Although Whites did not

Figure 3.2 Ratio of Racial Composition: 1980 Non-Black to Black Neighborhoods

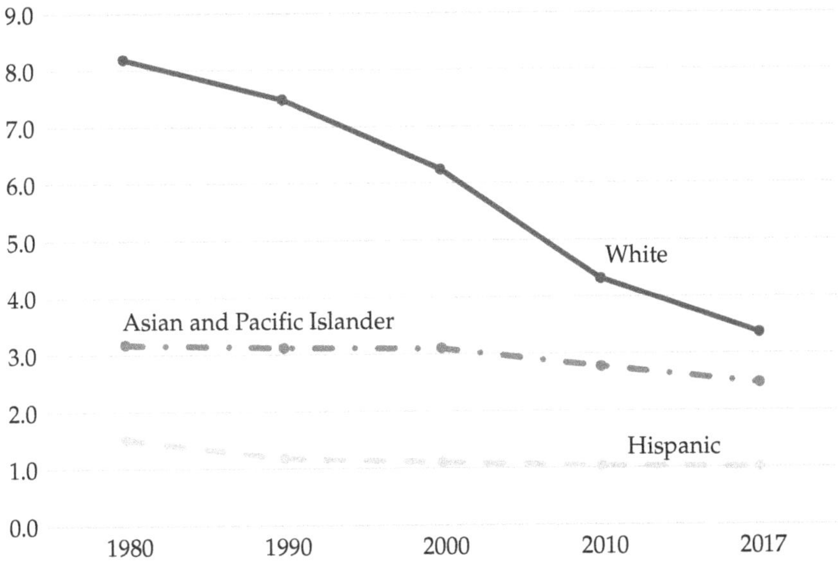

Source: Author's tabulation of U.S. 2010 Longitudinal Tract Database (Logan, Xu, and Stults 2014) and American Community Survey Five-Year Estimates (U.S. Census Bureau 2019).

replace Blacks in raw numbers in these neighborhoods, a White individual in a given metropolitan area was much more likely to live in a 1970 Black neighborhood over time. Much of that probability is due to Whites' substantial drop in population in non-Black neighborhoods, from 85 percent in 1980 to 62 percent in 2017. Second, Hispanics were equally likely to live inside or outside of 1970 Black neighborhoods by 2010.

Although some of these changes over time are predictable results from neighborhoods ceasing to be Black plurality, they are in fact anything but predictable, considering that these neighborhoods had extremely different trajectories from their status as 1970 Black neighborhoods: some maintained Black plurality, some did not, and some gained or lost Black population. Los Angeles is an outlier, notable for the extreme decline in the number of its Black neighborhoods (and its broader loss of Black population). But in contrast to the nation as a whole, Whites are almost nonexistent in 1970 Black neighborhoods in L.A., even now. In 2017, Whites were still over eight times as likely to live outside of 1970 Black census tracts in Los Angeles as in them (compared to three times as likely in the rest of the metro United States). Despite the Los Angeles metro being arguably the

Figure 3.3 Disadvantage Index, Black and Non-Black Neighborhoods, 1970–2017

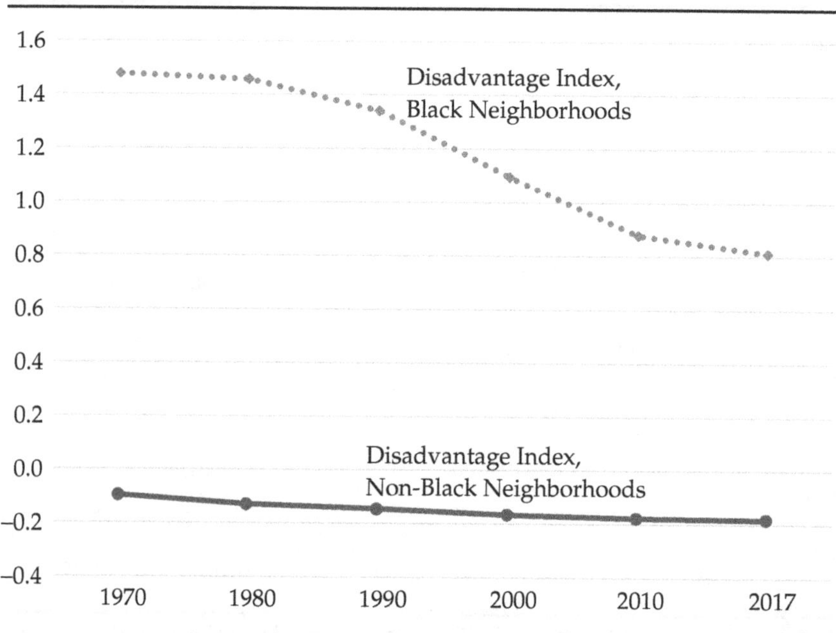

Source: Author's tabulation of U.S. 2010 Longitudinal Tract Database (Logan, Xu, and Stults 2014) and American Community Survey Five-Year Estimates (U.S. Census Bureau, 2019).

fastest-gentrifying in the country, White in-migration to Black and formerly Black neighborhoods is relatively nonexistent.[14]

Convergence in Some Indicators of Disadvantage

As noted in chapter 2, poverty and racial concentration are not the only indicators of neighborhood disadvantage or opportunity. I provide a more holistic measure, a "disadvantage index" based on five variables: the share of adults with less than a high school degree, the poverty rate, the unemployment rate, the share of female-headed households, and the median household income.[15]

Figure 3.3 displays the disadvantage index for Black and non-Black tracts from 1970 to 2017. This composite of five indicators shows substantial gains for Black tracts relative to non-Black tracts. Both types of tracts became less disadvantaged, but the drop in disadvantage was far greater for Black tracts.[16]

It is important, however, not to overstate this convergence. We know that declining poverty rates are playing a role in the decline of the disadvantage index in Black neighborhoods. The biggest factor is a dramatic decline in high school dropout rates—from 65 to 16 percent in Black neighborhoods compared to 43 to 12 percent outside of them. This decline mirrors drops in the percentage of Black individuals (in all neighborhoods) with less than a high school education, which dropped from 69 percent to 14 percent during this time period.

On the other hand, the share of female-headed households has risen everywhere, but dramatically so in Black neighborhoods. From 1970 to 1990, the percentage of female-headed households rose from 28 to 43 percent in Black neighborhoods, but never rose above 19 percent in non-Black neighborhoods. Unemployment rates and median household income gaps remained constant over time. Unemployment rates are more cyclical and dependent on broader macroeconomic factors. The sustained gaps in median household income suggest that even residents of the most-advantaged Black neighborhoods do not have extremely high incomes. Low poverty appears more common in Black neighborhoods than high wealth.

Convergence in Housing: Do We Still Have a "Dual Housing Market"?

Housing markets and the housing options they provide shape where people live, driving the presence and location of Black and non-Black neighborhoods. These markets are further shaped by critical factors such as racial discrimination, policy, information, and the permanence of the built environment. Like all housing markets, housing markets in Black neighborhoods are diverse across place and time. But a "dual housing market," even within U.S. metropolitan areas, has often been present, limiting housing options and outcomes for Black households and home-seekers.[17]

When this phrase was coined in the middle of the twentieth century, it spoke to the tendency of Black home-seekers to pay more to live in less-desirable neighborhoods, with older, lower-quality housing.[18] Blacks paid a considerable penalty for being constrained to specific neighborhoods because of (de facto and de jure) segregation, which always kept the supply of housing available to them artificially low. There were several reasons why low supply did not make Black neighborhoods of the 1950s and 1960s more desirable and housing values higher there than in non-Black neighborhoods. The housing was older and in worse shape; Black neighborhoods were more likely to experience higher crime rates, to have crowded schools, and to be closer to highways and industry; and racial discrimination devalued the homes where Blacks lived. The crux of the dual housing market was that Blacks had to pay more than the substandard housing would have been worth in the absence of discrimination.

Figure 3.4 Homeownership Rates and Share Multifamily Housing, Black and Non-Black Neighborhoods, 1970–2017

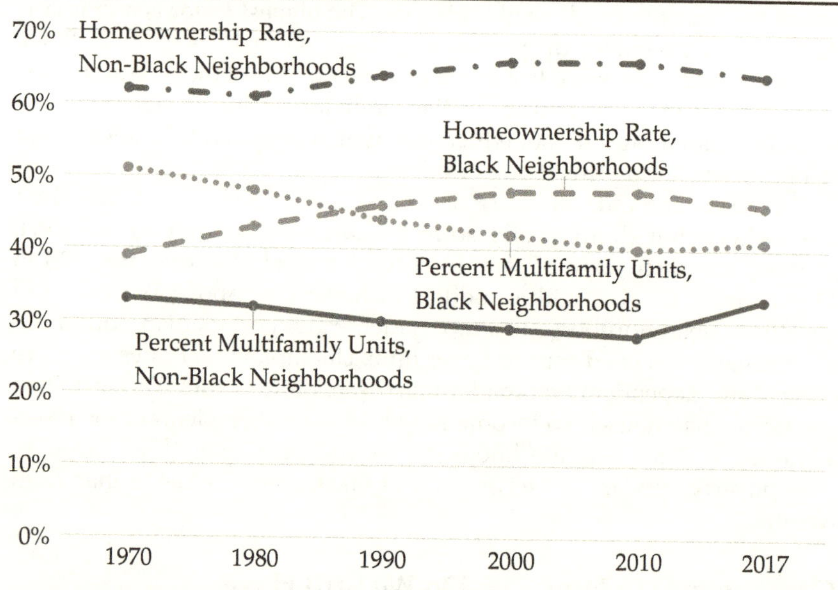

Source: Author's tabulation of U.S. 2010 Longitudinal Tract Database (Logan, Xu, and Stults 2014) and American Community Survey Five-Year Estimates (U.S. Census Bureau 2019).

To what extent do we still have a dual housing market? Figure 3.4 shows that substantial divergence in homeownership rates remains. Homeownership rates are always about 60 percent in non-Black tracts, but they never reach 50 percent in Black tracts. The gap narrowed from 23 percent in 1970 to 18 percent in 1980, but the gap has been stuck there ever since. Similarly, the homeownership rate has been remarkably steady (and low) for Black households: 42 percent owned their own home in 1970, and 42 percent owned their own home in 2017. This persistent gap is remarkably important in the context of the discriminatory policies that concentrated disadvantage in Black neighborhoods and as we contemplate what might work to alleviate that disadvantage. Given that concentrated disadvantage is coupled with low homeownership in Black neighborhoods, when that disadvantage is alleviated, rising property values in those neighborhoods benefit the many outsider home-seekers who are probably not Black. If ownership rates were high in those neighborhoods, rising wealth would be an uncontroversial good. Instead, renters fear that positive changes to their communities might price them out.

Since single-family housing is more frequently owner-occupied than multifamily housing, ownership rates are reflected in housing stock differentials.[19] Black neighborhoods have higher shares of multifamily units.

Figure 3.5 Share of Housing Units Built within the Last Ten Years and within the Last Thirty Years or More, Black and Non-Black Neighborhoods, 1970–2017

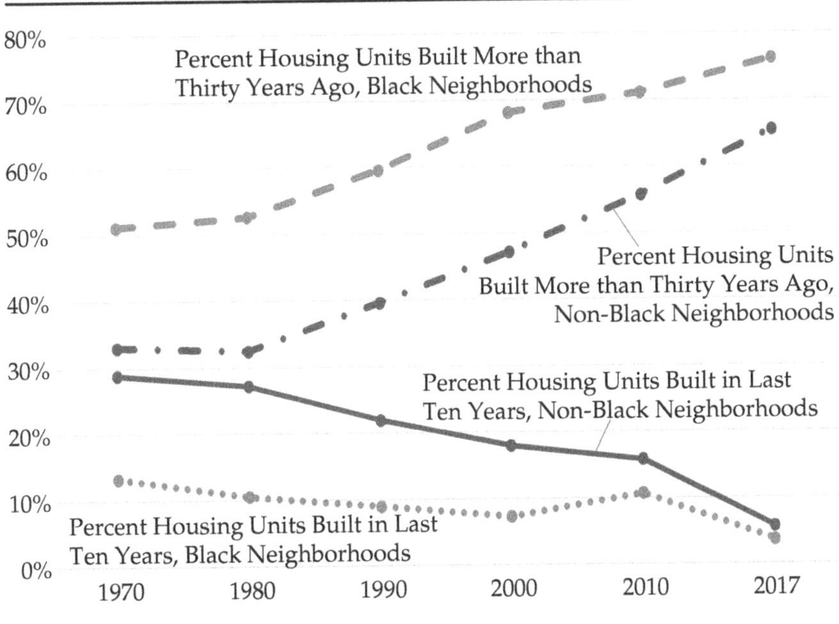

Source: Author's tabulation of U.S. 2010 Longitudinal Tract Database (Logan, Xu, and Stults 2014) and American Community Survey Five-Year Estimates (U.S. Census Bureau 2019).

This gap has narrowed more quickly, but mostly because the share of multifamily housing has gone down in Black tracts, from 51 percent in 1970 to 41 percent in 2017. The share of multifamily housing in non-Black tracts has held steady. Single-family zoning and other restrictions on density remain predominant and play a role in excluding people of color and lower-income families from living in a wider array of neighborhoods.[20] With some small convergence in both the type of housing stock and typical tenure (although homeownership rates in Black tracts have not bounced back from the Great Recession), the dual housing market is converging.

One way in which single-family zoning and other density restrictions exclude people of color is by slowing the pace of housing construction. In the 2015–2019 ACS, the median housing unit was built in 1972 in Black tracts and in 1978 in non-Black tracts. Housing in Black neighborhoods is persistently about five to nine years older than housing in non-Black tracts. In both types of neighborhood, housing is now about twice as old as it used to be.[21]

Figure 3.5 shows why housing aged in these neighborhoods—the reduced pace of home-building. The solid and dotted lines show the share

Figure 3.6 Median Rent, Black and Non-Black Neighborhoods, 1970–2017

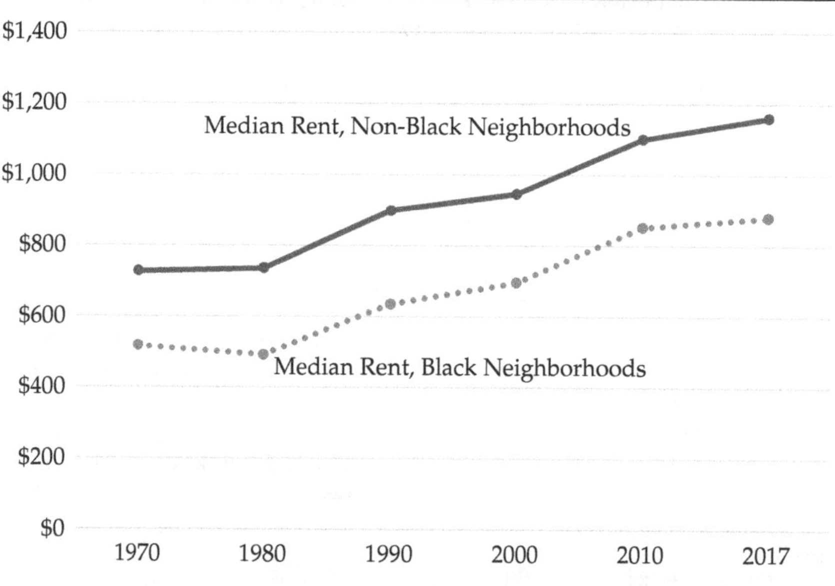

Source: Author's tabulation of U.S. 2010 Longitudinal Tract Database (Logan, Xu, and Stults 2014) and American Community Survey Five-Year Estimates (U.S. Census Bureau 2019).

of units in the last ten years, which has always been considerably lower in Black tracts. The dashed and dashed-dotted lines show the share of housing units built more than thirty years ago; there have always been more such housing units in Black tracts. In 1970, 13 percent of units in Black tracts and 29 percent of units in non-Black tracts had been built in the previous ten years; this share had declined to 4 and 6 percent, respectively, by 2015–2019. Conversely, 76 percent of housing units were built over thirty years ago in Black tracts (up from 50 percent), and in non-Black tracts the share of this older stock has risen from only 33 percent in 1970 to 65 percent in 2017. Housing in Black neighborhoods used to be much older than in non-Black neighborhoods, but by the 2010 census, housing production in non-Black tracts had become so slow that home-building proceeded at basically the same pace in Black and non-Black neighborhoods.

Not surprisingly, given the minimal home-building, rents and home values (pegged to 2010 dollars) have risen substantially over time in both types of neighborhood.[22] Rent trends are provided in figure 3.6. The median monthly rent was $725 in non-Black neighborhoods and $516 in Black neighborhoods in 1970, but those figures rose to $1,160 and $878,

Figure 3.7 **Median Home Values, Black and Non-Black Neighborhoods, 1970–2017**

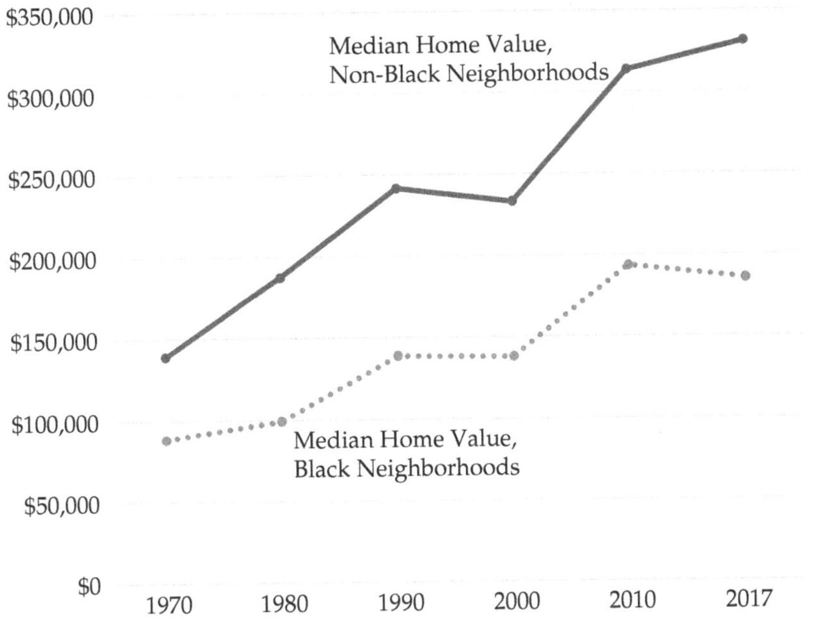

Source: Author's tabulation of U.S. 2010 Longitudinal Tract Database (Logan, Xu, and Stults 2014) and American Community Survey Five-Year Estimates (U.S. Census Bureau 2019).

respectively, by 2015–2019. The increases were a little higher in Black neighborhoods (a 70 percent increase compared to 60 percent).

Figure 3.7 shows median home values, which have exploded during the last half-century in both types of neighborhood: they were 2.3 times higher than 1970 in 2015–2019 in non-Black neighborhoods, and they almost exactly doubled in Black neighborhoods. Because of the similar rates of growth, the gap in housing values persists: median home values are about 83 percent higher in non-Black tracts than in Black ones. These gaps are similar to estimates by Perry, Rothwell, and Harshbarger, who find that majority-Black neighborhoods have home values roughly half as high as home values in neighborhoods where Blacks make up less than 1 percent of the population.[23]

In figure 3.7, the home value gap widened considerably in the 1970s, when it rose to almost 90 percent, a high that has decreased only slightly since. The gap narrowed considerably in the 2000s, but widened again in the 2010s. This trend confirms research by Elora Raymond, Kyungsoon Wang, and Dan Immergluck: in Atlanta, they find, the recovery from the Great Recession's housing bust has been the most sluggish in Black neighborhoods.[24] Further, the limited gains in housing value in Black neighborhoods are somewhat contrasted with the growth in rents in Black neighborhoods, which have risen consistently since 1980. Given the importance of house price growth to wealth-building and the disproportionately low incomes of renters, Black neighborhoods present significant housing cost problems. Owners do not tend to see good returns, but renters pay a lot—as reflected in the fact that 56 percent of renters in Black tracts spend 30 percent or more of their income on rent, compared to 47 percent of renters in non-Black neighborhoods.

So what happened in the 1970s? Sander, Kucheva, and Zasloff speak of the "inversion" of the dual housing market beginning around 1970.[25] The previous housing inflation in Black neighborhoods reversed, they observe, and by 1980 the forces of segregation were just as likely to deflate housing values and rents as to inflate them. As a result, house prices in Black neighborhoods began to decline relative to housing in non-Black neighborhoods. This decline was a by-product not only of White flight but also of the disappearance of the steady stream of demand flowing from the Great Migration. Once Blacks stopped moving from the South to northern cities en masse, housing demand often collapsed in Black neighborhoods. Sander, Kucheva, and Zasloff also cite the dramatic geographic expansion of Black neighborhoods in the 1950s and 1960s; blockbusting (intentional introduction of Black households into White neighborhoods to induce additional sales) and White flight freed up more land (and thus housing) where Black households could live.[26] Greater housing supply coupled with reduced demand from the Great Migration created a lot of slack in housing markets in Black neighborhoods in the 1970s.

Housing values have infamously gone boom and bust in the last twenty years across the country. Black neighborhoods experienced slightly faster growth in the 2000s (40 percent compared to 32 percent) and a slower recovery in the 2010s (–3 percent compared to 5 percent). The Great Recession (2007–2011) and differential recovery rates explain much of the slowdown in the 2010s. Notably, rent still increased in the 2010s (by 2 percent and 6 percent in Black and non-Black neighborhoods, respectively). These trends suggest that rents in Black neighborhoods are consistently trending upward, if not quite as quickly as in the rest of the country.

Housing discrimination has always hit the Black community with a double-punch: by targeting both Black individuals and Black neighborhoods, discrimination has both reduced the returns to homeownership in Black neighborhoods and made it less likely that Black individuals will own homes. This was particularly true in the middle of the twentieth century, when homeownership rates were rising dramatically for Whites, for whom those returns (outside of Black neighborhoods) were quite strong. Slowing demand in Black neighborhoods, particularly in the 1970s, further reduced the returns to homeownership in these neighborhoods, even as homeownership opportunities were expanding for Black individuals. Since the Great Recession, Black neighborhood home value growth has continued to lag behind growth outside of Black neighborhoods, though probably with considerable variation across regions and metropolitan areas. In chapter 4, I explore some of this variation. And in chapter 6, I more explicitly examine the neighborhood changes, such as gentrification, that capture the extent to which residents of twenty-first-century Black neighborhoods are being priced out by rising rents.

Wrapping up: Limited Progress

The South Bronx, the birthplace of hip-hop, is an outlier among traditionally Black neighborhoods. It is now majority-Hispanic, more impoverished, and more expensive than the typical Black neighborhood. Progress in the average Black neighborhood reflects the limited progress of the average Black household over the last fifty years. On the one hand, the gap between poverty rates in and outside of Black neighborhoods has narrowed substantially. On the other hand, Black neighborhood poverty rates have declined at a much slower pace than poverty rates for Black households. Poverty rates have remained high in Black neighborhoods to some extent because of immigrants moving into Black neighborhoods like the South Bronx, in search of relatively cheaper housing. Immigration has played this role in both Black and non-Black neighborhoods as neighborhoods have diversified throughout U.S. cities.

Poverty is not the only indicator of neighborhood disadvantage. Looking at other indicators, Black neighborhoods are less racially segregated than they used to be, housing values have rebounded somewhat, and gains in educational attainment have been large, although largely in line with the massive educational attainment gains across the country. I also create an index of neighborhood disadvantage informed by poverty rates, educational attainment, unemployment rates, female headship, and median household income. The gap between Black and non-Black neighborhood disadvantage was cut in half over the last fifty years.

Housing markets have also evolved in important ways. One of the most concerning trends in Black neighborhoods is that homeownership rates have not budged over those fifty years. In 1970, 42 percent of Black neighborhood residents owned their own homes, and 42 percent of Black neighborhood residents owned their own homes in 2017. Homeownership is not a perfect solution to housing affordability or neighborhood disadvantage, but these low homeownership rates greatly complicate efforts to increase value in Black neighborhoods. Demand for living in traditionally Black neighborhoods is slowly increasing, but the resulting gains in value are less likely to accrue to local homeowners, and the costs of this demand are more likely to price out the large number of renters. Median rents have increased at roughly the same pace in and outside of Black neighborhoods, adding dramatically to cost burdens for renters across the country. One of the clearest structural factors leading to rent increases is a failure to build homes in all neighborhoods. The gap between median home values in Black and non-Black neighborhoods is increasing. On the one hand, this makes it even less likely that residents of Black neighborhoods are benefiting from rising demand in their neighborhood. On the other hand, home purchasing options are more feasible for those looking to live in Black neighborhoods.

Black neighborhood conditions are essential indicators of progress toward racial equality. This chapter therefore began with snapshots of a cross-section of Black neighborhoods at six points in time. Chapter 6 looks more specifically at the evolution of neighborhoods as they ceased being Black, to give a better sense of why and how Black neighborhoods changed. This chapter also focuses on national averages, to capture the most broadly typical conditions. But there is substantial diversity across Black neighborhoods, even if there is a ceiling on how affluent and advantaged they appear in the data I examine. Chapter 4 focuses on this diversity.

Appendix

Table A.3.1 Poverty Rates in Black-Plurality, Black-Majority, and Black-Dominant Neighborhoods, 172 CSAs/CBSAs, 1970–2017

	1970	1980	1990	2000	2010	2017
Total neighborhoods	43,226	49,506	53,532	53,871	54,181	54,171
Number of Black plurality neighborhoods	3,253	4,619	5,461	6,503	6,989	6,928
Number of Black majority neighborhoods	3,197	4,292	4,979	5,675	5,845	5,539
Number of 90 percent Black neighborhoods	1,257	1,656	1,860	1,996	1,756	1,257
Average poverty rate, Black plurality neighborhoods	27%	28%	29%	25%	27%	23%
Average poverty rate, Black majority neighborhoods	27	29	29	25	28	25
Average poverty rate, 90 percent Black neighborhoods	30	32	33	29	32	30

Source: Author's tabulation of U.S. 2010 Longitudinal Tract Database (Logan, Xu, and Stults 2014) and American Community Survey Five-Year Estimates (U.S. Census Bureau 2019).

Table A.3.2 Poverty Rates Using Different Counterfactuals, 172 CSAs/CBSAs, 1970–2017

	1970	1980	1990	2000	2010	2017
Black plurality	27%	28%	29%	25%	26%	23%
White plurality	9	9	9	8	11	10
Ratio	3.07	3.27	3.22	2.98	2.37	2.31
Hispanic plurality	N/A	25%	26%	23%	23%	20%
Asian plurality	21%	17	15	14	13	11
Black majority	27	29	30	25	28	25
White majority	9	8	9	8	10	9
Ratio	3.07	3.42	3.39	3.14	2.63	2.62
Hispanic majority	N/A	26%	27%	25%	25%	21%
Asian majority	21%	19	17	12	12	10

Source: Author's tabulation of U.S. 2010 Longitudinal Tract Database (Logan, Xu, and Stults 2014) and American Community Survey Five-Year Estimates (U.S. Census Bureau 2019).

Table A.3.3 Poverty Exposure Rates for Black Individuals in Black-Plurality, Black-Majority, and Black-Dominant Neighborhoods, 172 CSAs/CBSAs, 1970–2017

	1970	1980	1990	2000	2010	2017
Black individual exposure to poverty, Black-plurality neighborhoods	28%	29%	30%	25%	27%	24%
Average poverty rate, Black-plurality neighborhoods	27	28	29	25	26	23
Black individual exposure to poverty, Black-majority neighborhoods	28	29	30	26	28	25
Average poverty rate, Black-majority neighborhoods	27	29	29	25	27	25
Black individual exposure to poverty, Black-dominant[a] neighborhoods	30	32	34	29	32	30
Average poverty rate, Black-dominant neighborhoods	30	32	33	29	32	29
Not Black plurality neighborhoods	17	15	16	14	17	15
Not Black majority neighborhoods	17	16	16	15	17	16
Not Black dominant neighborhoods	21	21	20	18	20	18

Source: Author's tabulation of U.S. 2010 Longitudinal Tract Database (Logan, Xu, and Stults 2014) and American Community Survey Five-Year Estimates (U.S. Census Bureau 2019).

[a] Black-dominant = 90 percent or more.

Chapter 4

Where Black Neighborhoods Thrive and Where They Struggle

You love to hear the story
Again and again
About these young brothers from the City of Wind.
—Common, "The Food," 2004 (featuring Kanye West)

In 1995, the Source Awards would fuel the raging regional battle in rap. *The Source* was the publication to go to for print journalism on hip-hop, and in its second year of hosting a live show in New York City, the Source Awards show was a hot ticket. The audience got testy when West Coast producer Suge Knight dissed New York's Sean "Puffy" Combs (producer for star rapper Notorious B.I.G., aka Biggie Smalls) in his acceptance speech for Motion Picture Soundtrack of the Year. When California's Dr. Dre won for Producer of the Year, he was booed, along with Snoop Dogg. In a harbinger of the geographic diversification of rap to come, the winner for New Group Artist of the Year was the Atlanta duo Outkast, who were largely ignored by the increasingly tense crowd, focused as it was on the fight for supremacy between west and east. The exchange of words that night between East and West Coast artists and fans would lead to a chain of events that claimed lives. Tupac Shakur, who had recently been shot and suspected that East Coast rappers were the perpetrators, subsequently recorded several songs directed at Combs and his Bad Boy Records labelmates, including Biggie. Just over a year later, Shakur was murdered in Las Vegas. Six months after that, Biggie was murdered in Los Angeles. Nobody has ever been arrested for Biggie's murder, and the first arrest was not made in Tupac's murder until 2023, almost thirty years later. East Coasters suspect West Coasters in Biggie's murder, and West Coasters suspect East Coasters in Tupac's murder.[1]

https://doi.org/10.7758/tjvh5404.5308

The 1995 Source Awards show is considered the key turning point in the rivalry between east and west in rap, and the catalyst for both murders.

Also in 1995, Keith Farrelle Cozart was born in Chicago. To that point, Chicago had been very quiet in hip-hop. Even considering the role of Los Angeles and New York as media and entertainment hubs, this is a perplexing absence. In 1990, Chicago had twice as many Black people as Los Angeles (although the massive total population of the L.A. metro area put it closer behind the Chicago metro), and this population was more concentrated in a smaller geography. Further, Chicago had played a significant role in other Black-dominated music genres, going back to the blues and jazz. And other cities with substantial Black populations had begun producing successful individual hip-hop acts in the early to mid-1990s. Massively successful rap production labels had been started in Houston, New Orleans, and Atlanta and remained active in those cities.[2] In the early 2000s, an entire rap subgenre, trap music, would come out of Atlanta, in addition to all of the other commercially and critically successful acts and producers from Outkast to Jermaine Dupri. By 1995, Chicago was home to successful individual MCs in Common, Da Brat, and Twista, and in the 2000s Atlanta-born but Chicago-raised Kanye West would become one of the most groundbreaking recording artists and producers in any genre. But a local rap scene of any import would elude Chicago until around the time Mr. Cozart became Chief Keef.

Many factors are likely to have contributed to Chicago's limited and late presence in rap, and we can't be certain which played the biggest role. But the slow development of rap infrastructure in a city with profound musical history and a massive Black population might have something to do with the particular devastation of Chicago's South Side and West Side Black neighborhoods. Other high-poverty cities and metros with substantial Black populations had similarly limited hip-hop scenes. In Philadelphia and Detroit, the most comparable to Chicago in terms of the size and poverty of their Black populations, the story is rather similar. Both Philadelphia and Detroit boast a meaningful list of MCs and rap acts. But like Chicago, each city lacks a local production machine that rivals those in New Orleans, Atlanta, and Houston, let alone the New York and Los Angeles rap industries.

When a local rap scene finally broke through in Chicago in the 2010s, it reflected this hypothesis. Rap as a genre is well versed in poverty, gangs, and the glorification of violence.[3] Chicago's rap subgenre, drill, took this to another level, as it was intimately connected to the city's ongoing gang wars in the 2010s. Forest Stuart provides an ethnographic account of drill rappers in Chicago in his book *Ballad of the Bullet*.[4] The story begins in the 1970s,[5] when the Black Belt was reeling from massive unemployment stemming from decades of lost manufacturing jobs. The drug industry picked up the slack in the labor market as a major employer providing substantial income to gangs and their foot soldiers. But by the 2000s, the drug business was considerably less lucrative. Successful prosecution of drug syndicates in these neighborhoods had eliminated many of the organizational structures necessary to provide local young men with entry into the business, which was also diffused by a diversification away from crack cocaine to meet demand for several other drugs. In short, gang-involved Black youth and young men had limited earning power. Enter drill music and social media—the "attention economy."

In 2012, Keith Cozart ("Chief Keef") posted a music video to YouTube for his song "I Don't Like." Keef grew up and was living in the Parkway Gardens housing development, and he recorded the video in his grandmother's living room. The census tract where Keef lived had a poverty rate of 18 percent in 1970 and was 99 percent Black. By 1980, the poverty rate had doubled, and it would rise to an astonishing 64 percent by 2010. The share Black in this tract has never budged below 98 percent. Eight additional census tracts form a neighborhood bridge between Parkway Gardens, which is hemmed in by Interstate 94 on the west, and the University of Chicago on the east, adding some of Woodlawn (one of Chicago's seventy-seven community areas) to Parkway Gardens.[6] Those nine census tracts had nearly fifty thousand people in 1970; their population is under seventeen thousand today. Similar to Parkway Gardens, the nine tracts' Black population has always been virtually 100 percent, and the poverty increase was less dramatic—though over twenty percentage points—between 1970 and 2010. The unemployment rate more than quadrupled, to 31 percent, during that time.

Parkway Gardens has a unique history. It is considered the first apartment complex to be cooperatively owned by Black residents, and Chief Keef is not the most famous person to have ever lived there—that honor surely goes to Michelle Obama. The complex shifted to HUD management in the 1970s and then back to private ownership in the 1980s.[7] The history of public housing in Chicago reveals it to have been the most glaring failure of public housing in the United States. The Chicago Housing Authority (CHA) was taken over by HUD in 1995, owing to excessive mismanagement and corruption that had compromised the city's ability to maintain its public housing stock and led to widespread deterioration of the city's stock of more than forty thousand units. In 2000, under Housing Opportunities for People Everywhere (HOPE VI), a federal public housing redevelopment program, HUD approved Chicago's "Plan for Transformation," which would be the country's most expensive and wide-reaching overhaul of a city's public housing stock.

On the one hand, Parkway Gardens provides an interesting privately held counterexample to the narrative that it was the "public" in public housing that made the disinvestment and deterioration of this stock inevitable. When a private developer took control of the property in 2011, the complex was reported by HUD to be in distress. A 2014 *Chicago Sun-Times* story reported that Parkway Gardens was responsible for more shootings than anywhere else in Chicago during the 2011–2014 period.[8] Chicago residents—and because of the growing popularity of drill, people all over the world—knew not to come near "O-Block," the name given to Parkway Gardens in honor of slain gang member Odee Perry.

On the other hand, there is good reason to lay some of the blame for the gang warfare in Parkway Gardens on the upheaval from nearby public housing demolition. A *Chicago Tribune* story alleges that the Black Disciples gang was headquartered in Randolph Towers, which was essentially adjacent to Parkway Gardens until it was demolished in 2006.[9] An additional CHA building next door to Randolph Towers was demolished in 1998. And about ten blocks north was the infamous Robert Taylor Homes, also demolished in the 2000s. Although people make tenuous links between public housing demolition, the resulting dispersal of public housing residents (the demolishing of the Robert Taylor Homes alone displaced residents from more than four thousand units), and crime, these links are probably valid in Chicago.[10] Owing in part to the desperate state of Chicago's public housing, several developments were under the control of Chicago's gangs and drug trade, and the dispersal of that population led to an unstable equilibrium as formerly solidified gang boundaries melted away and were redrawn through violence. Susan Popkin and her colleagues find evidence for these effects from public housing transformation in Atlanta and Chicago.[11] Neighborhoods where public housing was demolished saw declines in crime, but crime increased in neighborhoods that received high numbers of those displaced by demolitions.

Parkway Gardens now occupies a space between public and private. Bought by a major developer, Related Midwest, most of the funding for the $106 million project involved tax-exempt bonds and Low-Income Housing Tax Credits (LIHTC). Thus, the newly renovated property is covenanted for thirty years to remain affordable to those earning at or below 60 percent of the area median income. Parkway Gardens continues to house its tenants through a public-private partnership similar to those at the center of virtually every new subsidized housing project in the United States.

At age fifteen, Keef started making drill songs and videos with a group of friends from the South Side neighborhoods of Englewood, Grand Crossing, and Washington Park. In the absence of larger gang opportunities, they formed their own crew and called themselves GBE for Glory Boyz Entertainment. The video for "I Don't Like" became a viral sensation and launched Keef as the (still juvenile) godfather of drill music. The song and video are both incredibly sparse. The beats are ominous but heavy on a staccato drumbeat, mimicking gunfire. The video reflects the capabilities of nothing more than teenagers with smartphones, and in fact that is basically how it came to be. It is raw energy with more than an element of danger given what we have been conditioned to think of a group of Black teenagers boisterously smoking blunts, rapping, and gesticulating. The occasional flash of automatic weapons makes the implicit explicit. But the simplicity of the video and the song highlights how drill artists could become famous using only cheap twenty-first-century recording technologies that were available on virtually any computer. They had no need for the services of a local record label, and they didn't have to travel to New York or Los Angeles to make videos. They could just make homegrown music and go viral.

The drill scene in Chicago shares many similarities with gangster rap in the 1990s on both coasts and with trap music, which originated in Atlanta and chronicled life in the drug business, and the Chicago drill scene would go on to inspire a drill movement in the United Kingdom. What made drill unique was its use of social media as a vehicle for boasting about gang activity, including murder, and for frequent posting of songs and videos to advance conflict among local Chicago gangs. Not surprisingly, the artists themselves became targets. The 2012 murder of eighteen-year-old Joseph Coleman, an aspiring rapper going by Lil' Jojo, was a tragic example. In the months prior to being shot, Coleman had posted videos of himself and his friends posing with guns and driving through rival gang territory. He received many death threats and responded by posting his location on Twitter. Stuart claims that the retaliatory postings and shootings went on for years, and that law enforcement agencies in many jurisdictions have tracked social media to build cases against gangs and drill rappers who boast of their illegal activity online.[12]

The story of Chicago drill's late and violent entry into rap history illustrates how the extreme devastation and disadvantage of Chicago's core Black neighborhoods perhaps put musical innovation out of reach, until some desperate and creative teenagers clawed their way to a dangerously high profile through social media. But not all of Chicago's Black neighborhoods are poor. And New Orleans is quite poor, particularly its Black population, but punches well above its population weight in rap. There may be something to the difference in trajectory, however. Hollygrove, the neighborhood where Lil Wayne, New Orleans's most famous rapper, grew up, had a poverty rate of only 17 percent in 2010. That rose dramatically by the 2015–2019 ACS, to 32 percent, but by then New Orleans's rap scene was well established.

Rappers came from the Midwest and the East Coast outside of New York, but the rap *industry* did not take off in those locations. If New York and Los Angeles were the first and second capitals of rap, then the third was the South. Half of this chapter's story is about the rise of southern Black neighborhoods in number and affluence. The other half of the story is the extreme disadvantage of Black neighborhoods in the Midwest and smaller metro areas of the Northeast. Although Chicago's Black neighborhoods are relatively affluent (on average) compared to other metros in the pejoratively labeled Rust Belt, Black neighborhoods in this region of the country are typically much more disadvantaged than Black neighborhoods in the South and West.

Slow Convergence and Limited Diversity

Chapter 3 told a story of slow convergence between Black and non-Black neighborhoods. This chapter's examination of the diversity in Black neighborhoods makes clear that, while there are many Black neighborhoods that have become quite affluent, convergence has not happened everywhere. Black neighborhoods are generally less diverse across socioeconomic characteristics than non-Black neighborhoods. Because neighborhood race (and specifically the share Black) is quite determinant in U.S. neighborhoods, the gaps between the places with the highest and lowest socioeconomic status (SES) inevitably shrink. The clearest difference is that the most affluent Black neighborhoods are not remotely as affluent as their majority-White (or minority-Black) counterparts.

Still, conditions vary considerably in Black neighborhoods. Importantly, the convergence observed in chapter 3 does not apply to the many typical Black neighborhoods in the Midwest and Northeast that were left behind by manufacturing decline. On the other hand, the changing location of Black neighborhoods has probably sped up the pace of convergence. Specifically, the number of Black neighborhoods in the South compared to other regions is large and quickly increasing. Coupled with the relatively strong and improving conditions in many southern Black neighborhoods, this growth has contributed to improved conditions in Black neighborhoods in the aggregate. But the substantial loss of Black neighborhoods in metros of the West, such as Los Angeles, San Francisco–Oakland, and Seattle, has muted this convergence, as Black neighborhood conditions have always been comparatively good in those areas.

There have always been relatively affluent Black neighborhoods, and these neighborhoods have grown in number over time, but slowly. In 1980, only 8 percent of Black neighborhoods had a median income above the median of the surrounding metropolitan area. In 2017, that figure had increased to nearly 13 percent. However, though many Black neighborhoods are comfortably middle-class, there is an upper limit on income and housing value in particular in these neighborhoods that is far below the upper limits in non-Black neighborhoods.

In addition to capturing the diversity of Black neighborhoods, this chapter hopes to help shift the focus of the research literature on segregation and Black neighborhoods, which is largely centered on major post-industrial U.S. cities. Specifically, studies of Black neighborhoods are overwhelmingly set in cities in the North, such as New York, Chicago, Detroit, and Philadelphia.[13] The South has always contained more Black neighborhoods than any other part of the country, however, and Black neighborhoods have increased more in number in the South than anywhere else. Over half of the country's Black neighborhoods are now in the South. The West always contained the smallest share of Black neighborhoods, and West Coast Black neighborhoods have now all but disappeared. In the 2015–2019 ACS, only three metropolitan areas in the West had more than ten Black census tracts—Los Angeles, San Francisco–Oakland–San Jose, and Las Vegas. Phoenix, Denver, Sacramento, and Seattle all had fewer than eight Black neighborhoods.

Focusing on regional diversity also makes sense in the context of the Great Migration. Black migrant settlement patterns followed (and influenced) the growth of the manufacturing sector in primarily midwestern and northeastern cities. Later in the twentieth century, the collapse of that sector would depress the economies where Black people and neighborhoods were the most numerous.

The regional shifts in the last fifty years are well exemplified by three metropolitan areas: Los Angeles, New York, and Atlanta. The number of Black neighborhoods in Los Angeles has declined precipitously. New York's Black neighborhoods rose in number through 1990; now back down to 1970 numbers, the city's Black neighborhoods make up a much smaller share of the nation's total. Atlanta's Black neighborhoods, on the other hand, have grown significantly.

There is also significant diversity between metropolitan areas, as is apparent both in the gaps between Black and non-Black neighborhoods in these metropolitan areas and in how these gaps have changed over time. In some parts of the country—notably Washington, D.C., and Atlanta—the average Black neighborhood is as affluent as the typical non-Black neighborhoods in the country as a whole. For much of the country, however, there are still sizable gaps between the typical Black and typical non-Black neighborhood. In the South and West, the economic gaps between Black and non-Black neighborhoods are considerably smaller than they are in the Midwest and Northeast. In the Minneapolis–Saint Paul area, for example, poverty rates are over 3.6 times as high in Black neighborhoods as in non-Black neighborhoods. In Atlanta, the ratio is about half that. In Los Angeles, the ratio is 1.2 to 1.

Understanding this diversity is critical for evaluating neighborhood effects and the confluence between racial segregation and concentrated poverty. The integration goals commonly articulated through fair housing policies, for example, consider racial segregation to generally be equally problematic regardless of the underlying conditions in racially segregated neighborhoods. But the extent to which those neighborhoods are in fact policy problems varies across metropolitan areas. In metropolitan areas like Minneapolis, locational outcomes for Black households may be more critical because the Black neighborhoods where they are more likely to be located are so much worse off than the non-Black neighborhoods.

Black neighborhoods are comparatively thriving in the nation's largest metropolitan areas, metropolitan areas of nearly any size in North Carolina, and metropolitan areas with substantial public employment. Much of the debate about Black neighborhood disadvantage centers on whether it is primarily created by racial segregation, central-city joblessness, or metropolitan income generation and sorting processes.[14] In regression models, I find some evidence that highlights the importance of all three of these factors, but metropolitan income generation and sorting processes are much more important. Specifically, the share employed in manufacturing and average family income are persistently important in keeping Black neighborhood poverty rates lower. But I also find that metro areas with higher shares of Black residents have lower Black neighborhood poverty rates, suggesting that there is strength in numbers. Income segregation appears more critical than racial segregation, but high unemployment and a high share of female-headed households—factors that William Julius Wilson highlights as related to joblessness in Black neighborhoods—are strongly related to higher poverty rates in Black neighborhoods.[15]

The South Rises

At the 1995 Source Awards, Andre 3000 of Outkast, feeling ignored by the tense crowd, informed the audience, "The South got somethin' to say and that's all I got to say." This was a harbinger of the moving epicenter of hip-hop culture as well as of the shift in Black population and wealth back to the region. The South is a large region with the greatest number of the nation's census tracts overall (in 2017, 35 percent of the sample's census tracts were located in the South), but the South is still overrepresented by Black census tracts.[16] Further, this overrepresentation has been growing for four decades. As seen in figure 4.1, over 52 percent of the nation's Black census tracts are in the South. These numbers and trends make clear that the typical focus on Black neighborhoods in northeastern and midwestern metros in the academic and policy discussion in the scholarly literature is not fully representative.

There are many potential reasons for the slow improvement in conditions in Black neighborhoods over the last fifty years. One is that the geographic location of these neighborhoods has shifted to different parts of the country. Generally, conditions are better in Black neighborhoods in the West and the South than in the Midwest and Northeast (although there is a lot of variation in the Northeast). The big increase in Black neighborhoods in the South is likely moving the aggregate numbers, even if

Figure 4.1 Share of Black Neighborhoods by Census Region, 1970–2017

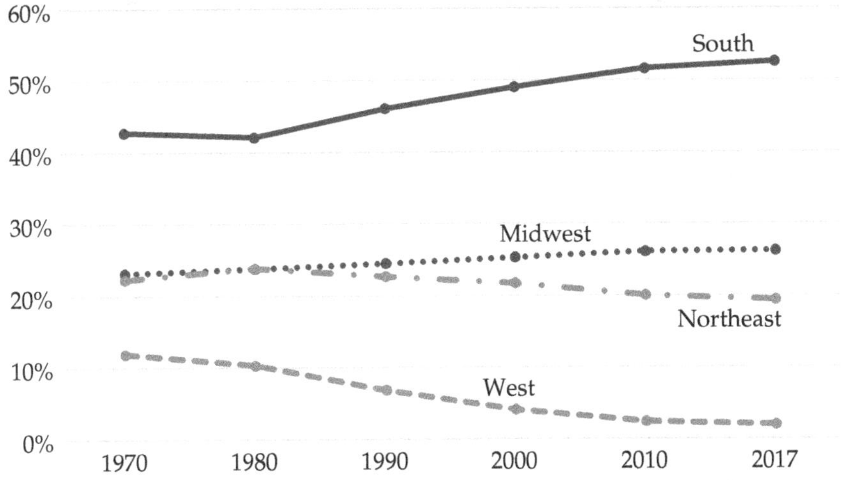

Source: Author's tabulation of U.S. 2010 Longitudinal Tract Database (Logan, Xu, and Stults 2014) and American Community Survey Five-Year Estimates (U.S. Census Bureau 2019).

this is somewhat offset by a decline in the share of Black neighborhoods in the West. The growth of southern economies has received considerable attention in the literature.[17] And the slow reversal of the Great Migration has also been noted.[18] Another dynamic is the reduction in Black neighborhoods in old Northeast and Midwest regions with declining economic conditions. Changes in shares between these large regions have contributed to improvements in conditions in Black neighborhoods, driven in part by the movement of Black Americans out of declining metros where Black neighborhood disadvantage has always been acutely high.

Whether or not these regional trends are driving the limited convergence between Black and non-Black neighborhoods, there is clear regional variation in how Black neighborhoods have been faring over time. Figure 4.2 shows poverty rates in Black and non-Black tracts by region, using data from the 2015–2019 ACS. While poverty rates are basically the same across regions in non-Black neighborhoods (roughly 11 or 12 percent), there is substantial variation in Black neighborhoods. In the Midwest, the average Black census tract has a poverty rate of 29 percent, compared to 18 percent in the West. In the Northeast and South, these poverty rates are about 22 percent. The good news is that the biggest growth of Black tracts is in the South, where the number of Black tracts is already the largest (and Black neighborhood poverty rates are relatively low). The bad news is that the Midwest is in second place, both in total Black

Figure 4.2 Poverty Rates by Census Region, Black and Non-Black Neighborhoods, 2017

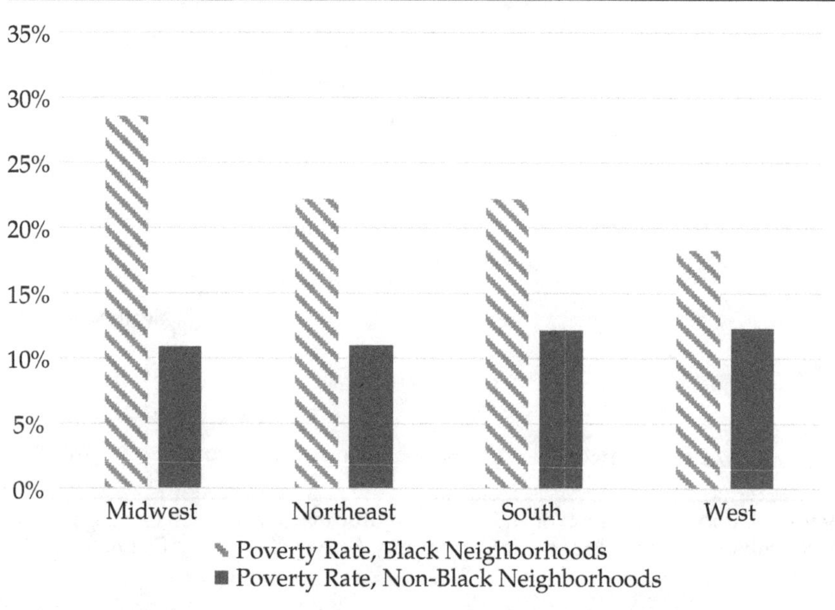

Source: Author's tabulation of American Community Survey Five-Year Estimates (U.S. Census Bureau 2019).

tracts and in rate of growth. More bad news is that in the West, where Black and non-Black poverty rates are only six percentage points apart (and Black neighborhood poverty rates are the lowest of the four regions), Black neighborhoods are virtually disappearing. In 2017 there were 6,940 Black census tracts, and only 137 of them were in the West. And half of those—69 tracts—were in the Los Angeles metro area. The disadvantage index (not pictured) tracks these poverty comparisons, with the exception that Black neighborhoods in the South are clearly less disadvantaged than Black neighborhoods in the Northeast.

Racial composition in and outside of Black neighborhoods varies significantly across these regions, but this does not explain why conditions in the West's Black neighborhoods are so much better. Black neighborhoods in the West have the lowest share Black of any region, and at 49 percent, it is not particularly close (the next closest is the Northeast with 64 percent). But Blacks in these western neighborhoods have been largely replaced by Hispanics and Latinos, whose poverty rates are similarly high.

Housing value differentials also highlight the gaps between Black and non-Black tracts in the Midwest. Figure 4.3 shows median home values in

Figure 4.3 Median Home Values, Black and Non-Black Neighborhoods, 2017

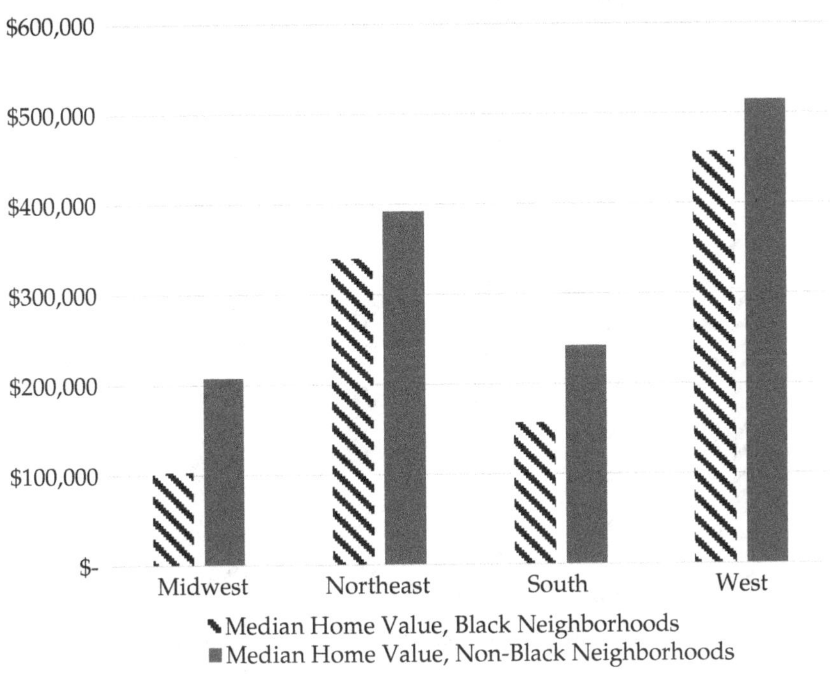

Source: Author's tabulation of American Community Survey Five-Year Estimates (U.S. Census Bureau 2019).
Note: These are population-weighted averages of census tract median home values.

Black and non-Black tracts by region, using the 2015–2019 ACS. Median home values are lowest in the Midwest and South and highest in the West. (Los Angeles again plays an outsized role in the numbers in the West.) Home values are 56 percent higher nationwide in non-Black tracts than in Black ones, and 15 and 13 percent higher in non-Black tracts in the Northeast and West, respectively. Considering the role of race in U.S. housing markets, this is a striking level of parity. In the Midwest, however, home values are twice as high in non-Black tracts as in Black ones.

Given that the South and Midwest have been the sites of growth in Black census tracts in recent decades, these two regions are worth a closer look, particularly given the divergent outcomes. The relative parity in the South between Black and non-Black tracts could be explained by the fact that even non-Black tracts in the South have relatively large Black populations. It would thus be possible that the parity comes from relatively disadvantaged non-Black tracts, in part because relatively disadvantaged

Figure 4.4 Poverty Rates in Black Neighborhoods in the Midwest and South, 1970–2017

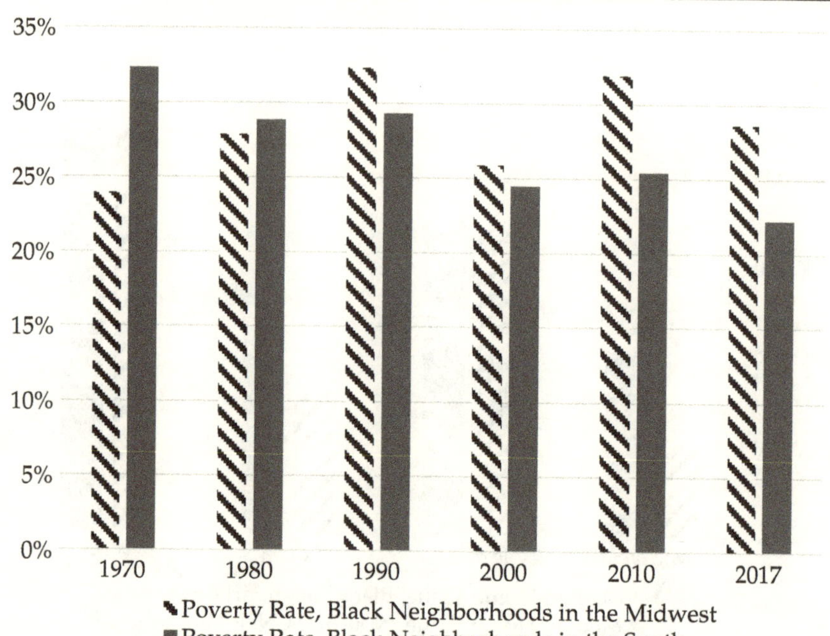

Source: Author's tabulation of U.S. 2010 Longitudinal Tract Database (Logan, Xu, and Stults 2014) and American Community Survey Five-Year Estimates (U.S. Census Bureau 2019).

Black people live there. But that is not the case. The poverty rates and disadvantage indexes in non-Black tracts are basically identical across the four regions. The clear takeaway is that Black tracts in the Midwest, and to a lesser extent those in the Northeast, are just extremely disadvantaged on average. As we have long known, the Midwest is also the most racially segregated: the share of Blacks in Black tracts is still 71 percent, compared to 65 percent in the South and just 49 percent in the West.

In figures 4.4, 4.5 and 4.6, we see that this is a relatively recent phenomenon. In 1970 the Black tracts of the South had considerably higher poverty rates than those in the Midwest, and the disadvantage index was basically the same. The higher poverty rates in southern Black tracts were due in small part to the higher overall poverty rate in the South, but there was no huge difference in non-Black tract poverty rates between the South (11 percent) and the Midwest (7 percent) (see figure 4.4). Poverty rates in southern Black tracts dipped below 25 percent for the first time in 2000,

Figure 4.5 Disadvantage Index in Black Neighborhoods in the Midwest and South, 1970–2017

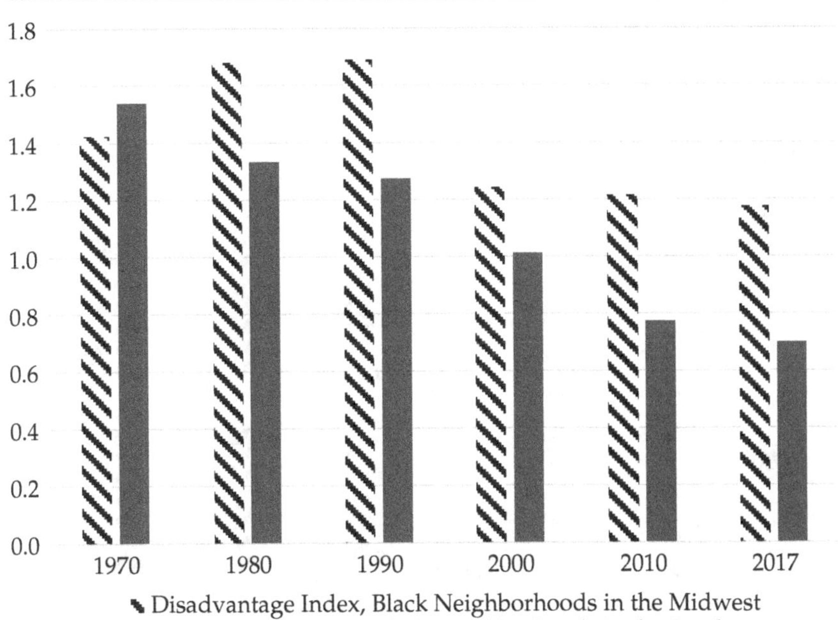

Source: Author's tabulation of U.S. 2010 Longitudinal Tract Database (Logan, Xu, and Stults 2014) and American Community Survey Five-Year Estimates (U.S. Census Bureau 2019).

rose slightly in 2010, and then went back down to 22 percent by 2017. In the Midwest, 1970 and 2000 had the lowest poverty rates for Black tracts—24 and 26 percent, respectively. But poverty rates in all other years during the period were considerably higher, including 32 percent in 2010 and 29 percent in 2017.

Disadvantage indexes declined even faster than poverty rates in southern tracts. The disadvantage index is calculated in a year-specific way in order to control for some big changes over time, such as the share of people with less than a high school degree, which drops precipitously over time. Thus, the 1970 disadvantage index is the level of disadvantage compared to tracts in 1970, and the 2017 disadvantage index is the level of disadvantage compared to tracts in 2017. In figure 4.5, the disadvantage index went up sharply in the Midwest between 1970 and 1980. It stayed that high through 1990 and then returned to levels below 1970 numbers in 2000, 2010, and 2017. But these tracts were still 1.2 standard deviations above

Figure 4.6 Median Home Values in Black Neighborhoods in the Midwest and South, 1970–2017

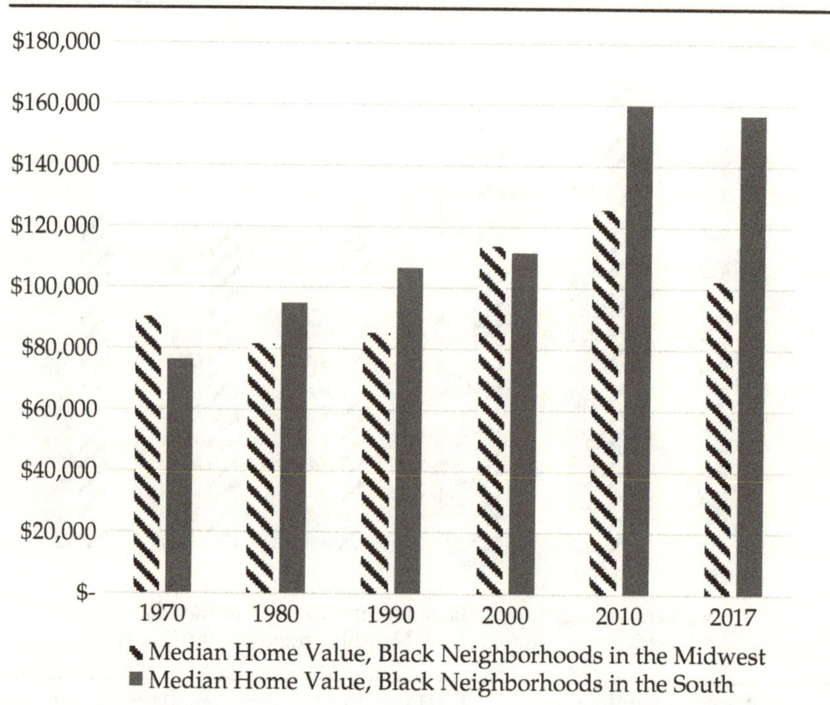

Source: Author's tabulation of U.S. 2010 Longitudinal Tract Database (Logan, Xu, and Stults 2014) and American Community Survey Five-Year Estimates (U.S. Census Bureau 2019).

the mean disadvantage index. Black neighborhoods in the South in 1970 were more disadvantaged than those in the Midwest but became consistently less so over time: the southern disadvantage index halved in less than fifty years, from 1.54 standard deviations above the mean to 0.7.

Median home values in Black neighborhoods follow a similar pattern: home values in midwestern Black tracts barely budged for twenty years. In fact, anyone who bought a home of median value in the average Black census tract in the Midwest in 1970 would have seen it drop in value by about $5,000 by 1990 (figure 4.6). And if they held on to the home through the 2015–2019 ACS, they would have owned a property that appreciated only by $12,000 *in nearly fifty years*. Home values in southern Black census tracts appreciated throughout the period, with the exception of a small drop from 2010 to 2017. Overall, median home values doubled during the period in southern Black neighborhoods.

Table 4.1 U.S. Regions' Black Neighborhoods in High- and Low-Poverty Quartiles, 2017

	Midwest	Northeast	South	West	Total
Lowest quartile among U.S. neighborhoods	2%	8%	5%	9%	5%
Highest quartile among U.S. neighborhoods	78	55	62	40	64
Lowest quartile among U.S. Black neighborhoods	0	30	30	100	26
Highest quartile among U.S. Black neighborhoods	37	30	22	0	26

Source: Author's tabulation of American Community Survey Five-Year Estimates (U.S. Census Bureau 2019).

Widespread Disadvantage in Midwestern Black Neighborhoods

Midwestern Black neighborhoods are comparatively disadvantaged on average in virtually all of the region's metropolitan areas. Even looking across the distribution, a Black neighborhood in the Midwest is highly unlikely to be advantaged, but particularly likely to be disadvantaged. Table 4.1 provides additional evidence that poverty is particularly high in the Midwest's Black tracts. And these data suggest that the problem in the Midwest is not just a high average poverty rate driven by a few neighborhoods or metros, but generally high poverty rates across the board. The first two rows use the poverty rate distribution of all of the country's urban census tracts and show the percentage of each region's Black tracts in the high and low quartiles of that distribution. In the 2015–2019 ACS, the threshold poverty rate for the nation's census tracts in the bottom quartile was 5.6 percent. This is obviously a very low poverty rate, but quite a few Black census tracts—340, or 5 percent of all Black tracts—actually met this criterion. (With poverty rates in excess of 19 percent, 64 percent of all Black tracts were in the highest quartile.) Only 2 percent of the Midwest's Black tracts—thirty-five, fifteen of them located in Chicago—were in the lowest quartile. Seventy-eight percent of the Midwest's Black tracts were in the highest quartile. The South fared worse, perhaps because there are many high-poverty Black neighborhoods that offset the low-poverty areas of Washington, D.C., and some other low-poverty southern metropolises (more on these to come). In the next two rows of table 4.1, I use the Black tract poverty distribution across all CSAs/CBSAs and estimate how many metro areas are in the highest and lowest Black tract poverty quartiles. Not a single midwestern metro was in the lowest quartile

Table 4.2 Top Fifteen CSAs/CBSAs by Black Neighborhood Poverty Rate, 2017

	Poverty Rate	Number of Black Neighborhoods	Region
Buffalo, N.Y.	37%	36	Northeast
Rochester, N.Y.	36	43	Northeast
Louisville, Ky.	32	32	South
Grand Rapids, Mich.	32	14	Midwest
Pittsburgh, Pa.	32	55	Northeast
Tulsa, Okla.	31	14	South
Albany, N.Y.	31	11	Northeast
Detroit, Mich.	31	382	Midwest
Cleveland, Ohio	31	197	Midwest
Cincinnati, Ohio–Ky.–Ind.	30	66	Midwest
Dayton, Ohio	30	39	Midwest
Minneapolis–St. Paul, Minn.–Wisc.	30	39	Midwest
Milwaukee, Wisc.	30	101	Midwest
Greensboro–Winston Salem, N.C.	30	66	South
Columbus, Ohio	28	76	Midwest

Source: Author's tabulation of American Community Survey Five-Year Estimates (U.S. Census Bureau 2019).

for Black neighborhood poverty rates, compared to 30 percent of metros in the Northeast and the South and all three of the West's metros with ten more Black tracts.

Table 4.2 lists the fifteen metro areas with the highest Black census tract poverty rate. Only three southern metros are in this group; among them, only the Greensboro, North Carolina, area has a particularly large number of Black neighborhoods. The two metro areas with the highest poverty rates are in the Northeast, Buffalo and Rochester; both are relatively old New York metros with declining economic fortunes. But only two other northeastern metros, Pittsburgh and Albany (another New York metro), are on the list. The remaining eight metros on the list are all in the Midwest. Three of them have over 100 Black census tracts (a very high number): Detroit (382), Cleveland (197), and Milwaukee (101).

On the flip side, table 4.3 lists the metro areas with the lowest Black neighborhood poverty rates. Washington, D.C., has the lowest poverty rate, at 14 percent. Roughly the same as the national average for the entire population, D.C.'s rate is about the same as the poverty rate in another metropolitan area with a large federal employment presence, Killeen-Temple–Fort Hood, Texas. Fort Hood is the most populated army base in the nation. Ten out of fifteen of the lowest-poverty metros are in the South,

Table 4.3 CSAs/CBSAs with the Lowest Average Poverty Rates in Black Neighborhoods, 2017

	Poverty Rate	Number of Black Neighborhoods	Region
Washington, D.C.–Baltimore, Md.–Va.–W.V.	14%	539	South
Killeen–Temple–Fort Hood, Tex.	14	17	South
Los Angeles, Calif.	17	68	West
Hartford, Conn.	17	23	Northeast
Charlotte, N.C.–S.C.	18	125	South
Atlanta, Ga.–Ala.	18	335	South
San Jose–San Francisco–Oakland, Calif.	18	37	West
New York, N.Y.–N.J.–Conn.–Pa.	19	778	Northeast
Dallas–Fort Worth, Tex.	19	140	South
Raleigh–Durham, N.C.	19	53	South
Houston, Tex.	19	131	South
Columbia, S.C.	20	61	South
Boston, Mass.–R.I.–N.H.	20	65	Northeast
Virginia Beach–Norfolk, Va.–N.C.	21	110	South
Richmond, Va.	21	83	South

Source: Author's tabulation of American Community Survey Five-Year Estimates (U.S. Census Bureau 2019).

and two out of the three western metros are on this list. Hartford, New York, and Boston represent the Northeast. None of the many midwestern metros made the list.

There are a number of ways to assess the extent to which the Black neighborhoods in the Midwest (and some Rust Belt northeastern metros) are particularly disadvantaged. They all come to the same conclusion. Black neighborhoods are disadvantaged on average and disadvantaged compared to non-Black census tracts in the same metros. They are highly unlikely to be advantaged and particularly likely to be disadvantaged. However, good news lies in the South.

Successful Southern Mega-regions: Washington, D.C., and Atlanta

Washington, D.C., and Atlanta have long included a disproportionate share of the nation's Black middle class, so these metropolitan areas stand out as having both very strong indicators in Black neighborhoods and a very large number of them. Poverty rates in Washington, D.C., are low everywhere, and just 7 percent in non-Black tracts. D.C.'s Black neighborhood poverty rate of 14 percent is the lowest poverty rate of any metropolitan area with ten or more Black tracts. Further, nearly one in five D.C. Black census tracts have poverty rates in the nation's bottom quartile (below 6 percent). Atlanta, whose 18 percent poverty rate is the sixth lowest, has more Black tracts than the metros ranked numbers two through five combined (table 4.3). For comparison, St. Louis has the lowest Black neighborhood poverty rate in the Midwest (for any metro with more than ten Black tracts) at 24 percent.

In the South, it is not just Atlanta and Washington, D.C., where Black neighborhood poverty is low. Other major southern metropolitan areas with Black neighborhood poverty rates below 20 percent include Charlotte, Dallas, Raleigh, and Houston. These four CSAs included 449 Black tracts as of the 2015–2019 ACS, or 6.5 percent of the nation's total. Adding D.C. and Atlanta, 19 percent of the nation's Black tracts in the 2015–2019 ACS had poverty rates below 20 percent. Nearly one-fifth of the nation's Black neighborhoods are in these six southern regions and are doing considerably better than in the rest of the country, where the average Black tract poverty rate is about 23 percent. Chapter 7 takes a deeper look at Washington, D.C., and Atlanta.

Black Middle-Class Neighborhoods

The Black middle class has been a feature of urban (and non-urban) life for many decades, and it grew substantially as explicit discrimination in education, labor markets, and other realms of American life declined as a result of civil rights gains. The study of Black middle-class neighborhoods has been dwarfed, however, by the study of disadvantaged Black neighborhoods. Mary Pattillo argues that even the small literature on Black middle-class neighborhoods is in fact about the movement of Black middle-class households out of areas of concentrated disadvantage.[19] Wilson, among others, argues that one of the forces that led to the decline of Black neighborhoods in the 1960s and 1970s was the exodus of Black middle-class households, leaving behind only the most impoverished Blacks.[20] Freeman emphasizes that racial discrimination in housing markets produced opportunities for Black professionals within earlier Black neighborhoods, where Black dentists, doctors, lawyers, and the like were employed.[21] The economic diversity of these neighborhoods was one beneficial upside to broader injustice.

Whether or not the benefits of Black neighborhoods exceed the costs of segregation, economic inequality between Black households and neighborhoods undoubtedly exists, as summarized in appendix table A.4.1.

Figure 4.7 Black Neighborhoods in the Best Quartile for Home Values, Poverty, and Disadvantage, 1970–2017

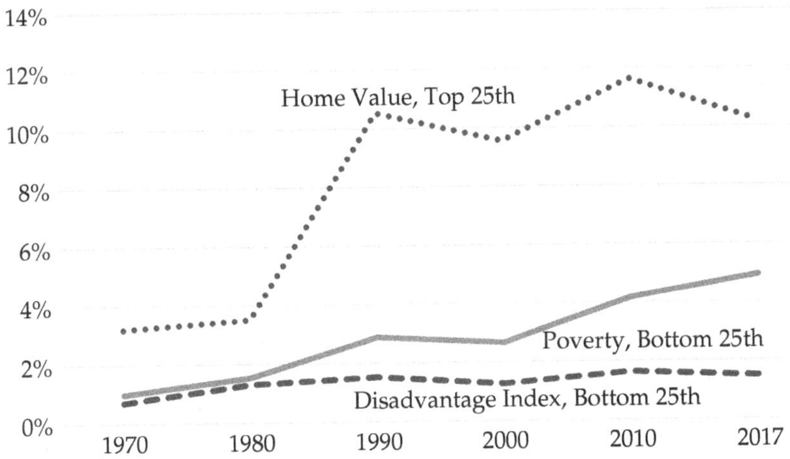

14%
12%
10%
8%
6%
4%
2%
0%
Home Value, Top 25th
Poverty, Bottom 25th
Disadvantage Index, Bottom 25th
1970 1980 1990 2000 2010 2017

Source: Author's tabulation of U.S. 2010 Longitudinal Tract Database (Logan, Xu, and Stults 2014) and American Community Survey Five-Year Estimates (U.S. Census Bureau 2019).

And while even the most advantaged Black neighborhoods are still not as advantaged as affluent non-Black neighborhoods, there are clearly some enclaves of Black wealth. These enclaves are most prominent in the Washington, D.C., metro, but are found in several other metros as well.

To measure the growth of Black middle-class neighborhoods over time, figure 4.7 shows the percentage of Black neighborhoods in the best quartile for median home values, poverty rates (bottom quartile), and the disadvantage index (bottom). First, it is striking how rare it is for a Black neighborhood to be in the highest quartile of the nation's census tracts for any of these indicators. In 2010, less than 2 percent of Black census tracts were in the bottom quartile for disadvantage. Home values looked better but were very regional: most of the Black census tracts in the top quartile of the nation's home value distribution were in Chicago, Los Angeles, New York, San Jose–San Francisco–Oakland, and Washington, D.C.

There is a general upward trend in the share of tracts in the best quartile for most indicators, but growth in Black middle-class neighborhoods is slow. Only 5 percent of Black tracts are in the bottom poverty quartile, up from less than 1 percent in 1970. However, the share of Black tracts in the highest quartile of the disadvantage index distribution has barely budged.

Strength in Large Metros

Although Washington, D.C., is an outlier for strong outcomes in Black neighborhoods, large metropolitan areas generally have stronger indicators in Black neighborhoods, as do places with substantial public-sector employment. And Atlanta and the three West metros have good indicators as well. In the Midwest, Black neighborhood disadvantage is widespread. Where else are conditions comparatively favorable or unfavorable in Black neighborhoods?

Looking at metropolitan areas at the high and low ends of the spectrum can better capture both what is typical in particular places and the diversity across Black neighborhoods. I conclude that conditions are generally best in the largest metropolitan areas (even accounting for higher incomes in large metros with a high cost of living) and worst in aging midsized metros in the Midwest and Northeast. Which particular metropolitan areas show up as the most and least disadvantaged places to live in a Black neighborhood show a lot of consistency. Again, larger and southern metros are clearly the most advantageous places to be living in a Black neighborhood, and older midwestern and northeastern metros the least advantageous. And the differences are big. Peoria's Black census tract unemployment rate is over three times that of six southern metros (Nashville, Beaumont, Dallas, Raleigh, Charleston, and Charlotte). The share of people with a BA degree in Washington, D.C.'s Black census tracts is over four times that share in Peoria. And that holds for San Francisco–San Jose–Oakland compared to Saginaw. Peoria is again the worst off when we look at the disadvantage index. The disadvantage index of 2.05 in Peoria, 1.95 in Youngstown, and 1.86 in Syracuse signifies that Black census tracts in those metro areas are roughly two standard deviations more disadvantaged than in the average U.S. census tract. Peoria's ten Black census tracts are uniformly impoverished, with poverty rates ranging from 24 to 68 percent. Peoria's poverty rates are 10 percent in non-Black tracts and 41 percent in Black tracts—an astonishing gap. The gap between large and midsized metros is even clearer when looking at lists of negative indicators, found largely in midsized metros or smaller. Detroit, Cleveland, and Pittsburgh are only occasional exceptions to this rule.

The emerging pattern is that the mega-regions, including Washington, D.C., New York, Los Angeles, Atlanta, Dallas, and San Francisco, are particularly good for Black neighborhoods. The million-dollar question for those metros is whether high and rising rents will make it more and more difficult for Black people to live there. Los Angeles and San Francisco are cautionary tales that those neighborhoods can disappear under the weight of rising housing costs.

The comparative flourishing of Black tracts in highly productive metropolitan areas suggests that incomes or education levels are just higher there. That would not take away from the fact that socioeconomic conditions are better in these neighborhoods, but a separate question is whether there is variation in the size of the gaps between Black and non-Black neighborhoods *within* metropolitan areas. Parity between Black and non-Black neighborhoods in a metropolitan area would suggest that there is something special about that area's Black neighborhoods that is not just a function of a high-performing economy.

Table 4.4 shows median home value ratios between Black and non-Black tracts. A list of top median home values for Black tracts would include only the most expensive metros, so looking at ratios makes more sense for home values. Three of the most expensive metros in the country—Boston, New York, and Los Angeles—are on the list for the greatest parity between Black and non-Black neighborhood home values. The ratios in these metros are remarkably close to 1.0, ranging from 1.1 in Boston to 1.14 in Los Angeles. One interpretation is that real estate is especially valuable in those metros no matter the predominant racial group. But that is likely too optimistic. Another explanation is that, particularly in New York and Los Angeles, the non-Black tracts are very likely to have significant populations of Hispanics and Latinos, and Asians or other large immigrant populations. In America's housing racial caste system, gaps between White and Black neighborhoods are likely to be much broader than gaps between non-White and Black neighborhoods.

It's not just large metropolitan areas where Black neighborhoods are more likely to thrive, but also areas with large public sectors. Some such metros that have flown under the radar thus far are located in North and South Carolina. Lumberton, Laurinberg, Rocky Mount, and Fayetteville in North Carolina and Columbia in South Carolina have home values that are very similar between Black and non-Black neighborhoods. All of these metros are anchored by cities with substantial Black populations (35 percent or more). Lumberton, Laurinberg, and Rocky Mount are all small cities, with less than fifty-five thousand people.[22] Fayetteville is home to Fort Bragg, the largest military base in the country (Fort Hood is second), and Lumberton, Laurinberg, and Rocky Mount are all within ninety minutes of Fayetteville. This is further support for the hypothesis that large centers of public employment buoy the economic fortunes of Black neighborhoods.

On the other side of the coin, Black neighborhoods continue to have negative outcomes in the Midwest and upstate New York regions. The top four metros with the greatest disparity between Black and non-Black neighborhood home values are in two states, Michigan and Ohio.

Table 4.4 Home Value Ratios between Black and Non-Black Neighborhoods, Top and Bottom Ten CSAs/CBSAs, 2017

Smallest Ratio CSAs	Housing Value Ratio	Average Median Housing Value (in Black Neighborhoods)	Largest Ratio CSAs	Housing Value Ratio	Average Median Housing Value (in Black Neighborhoods)
Boston, Mass.–R.I.–N.H.	1.10	$376,296	Youngstown–Warren, Ohio	3.62	$32,240
New York, N.Y.–N.J.–Conn.–Pa.	1.13	$467,783	Saginaw–Bay City, Mich.	3.32	$33,894
Lumberton–Laurinburg, N.C.	1.14	$ 76,131	Detroit, Mich.	2.91	$71,395
Los Angeles, Calif.	1.14	$497,625	Toledo, Ohio	2.62	$53,060
Killeen–Temple–Fort Hood, Tex.	1.15	$128,669	Peoria, Ill.	2.58	$56,249
Las Vegas, Nev.	1.17	$218,539	Milwaukee, Wisc.	2.55	$89,116
Rocky Mount, N.C.	1.25	$101,254	Buffalo, N.Y.	2.51	$63,589
Fayetteville, N.C.	1.30	$120,196	Rochester, N.Y.	2.49	$61,772
Columbia, S.C.	1.30	$134,567	Kansas City, Mo.–Kans.	2.47	$82,384
Beaumont–Port Arthur, Tex.	1.40	$ 92,462	Pittsburgh, Pa.	2.47	$69,725

Source: Author's tabulation of U.S. 2010 Longitudinal Tract Database (Logan, Xu, and Stults 2014) and American Community Survey Five-Year Estimates (U.S. Census Bureau 2019).

The remaining six metros with high disparity in these home values are split between the Midwest and the Northeast. Again, Black neighborhoods struggle considerably in upstate New York metros, specifically Buffalo and Rochester. Detroit is the largest metro on the list with the highest home value disparity between Black and non-Black tracts. Detroit is the twelfth-largest metro in the sample with a 2015–2019 ACS population of over five million. The next-largest metro on the list is Pittsburgh, the twenty-sixth most populous metro in the sample.

Whether looking at Black neighborhood poverty rates, disadvantage indexes, or home values in absolute terms or relative to non-Black neighborhoods in the same metropolitan areas, we find that the most advantaged Black neighborhoods are in the South and West and the most disadvantaged are in the Midwest. The most advantaged Black neighborhoods in absolute terms tend to be found in large metros such as Washington, D.C., Los Angeles, San Jose–Oakland–San Francisco, Boston, New York, Dallas, and Atlanta. But smaller southern metros, with or without a large military presence, such as Charlotte, Raleigh, and Killeen–Fort Hood, are similarly positioned.

The most relatively advantaged metros for Black neighborhoods are very concentrated in the South, and again, many are close to the major army bases of Fort Bragg and Fort Hood. Houston, Los Angeles, and Memphis are notable larger metros where Black neighborhoods are relatively advantaged. In Houston and Los Angeles, some of this advantage might be explained by the presence of high numbers of residents born outside of the United States, but that is less of a factor in Memphis.

Midwestern metros consistently contain the most disadvantaged Black neighborhoods, but Peoria, Illinois, which is over one-quarter Black, deserves particular scrutiny. Black neighborhoods in Peoria have an average poverty rate of 41 percent, and the disadvantage index is two standard deviations above the nation's average. The city of Peoria is home to Archer Daniels Midland, Bradley University, and, until very recently, Caterpillar, a major heavy equipment manufacturer. It has the fourth-highest Black-White dissimilarity index in the country after Milwaukee, Chicago, and New York. Black communities in Peoria appear to be almost entirely cut off from the economic benefits of major corporations and universities being located in the region. Midsized metros in Ohio, Michigan, and New York also consistently have very disadvantaged Black neighborhoods relative to other metros, especially Saginaw, Youngstown, Syracuse, Toledo, Rochester, and Buffalo.

It is clear that there is lot of diversity across metropolitan areas in how advantaged their Black neighborhoods are. Gaps between Black and non-Black tracts within metropolitan areas vary quite a lot as well. However, it is important to note that in no metropolitan area is the average Black neighborhood doing better than the average non-Black neighborhood on any indicator—educational attainment, household income, unemployment rates, poverty rates, disadvantage index, or home values. Inequality between Black and non-Black spaces is persistent and wide-ranging.

Although indicators for Black neighborhoods are considerably better in the South and the small number of Black neighborhoods in the West than in the Midwest and upstate New York, there is some evidence from these lists that the South has a bit of a bimodal distribution. Black neighborhoods are doing very well in many large southern metros, but there are a few, mostly smaller, southern metro areas with high poverty rates and other indicators of disadvantage in Black and non-Black neighborhoods. This reflects the role of metropolitan-area size and growth in promoting Black neighborhood advantage.

It is important to note that looking only at average characteristics hides variation both within Black neighborhoods and between neighborhoods within the same metropolitan areas. A deeper dive into the distribution of poverty rates and other characteristics in Black and non-Black neighborhoods (appendix table A.4.1) leads to two conclusions. First, looking at the differences between the top and bottom quintiles in socioeconomic characteristics, we see very large gaps between Black tracts at the top and bottom of the distribution, but these gaps are typically smaller than those in non-Black tracts. There is socioeconomic diversity between Black neighborhoods, but not as much as there is between non-Black neighborhoods. Second, despite the attention to the Black middle class moving away from disadvantaged Black neighborhoods over recent decades, the gaps between high- and low-performing Black neighborhoods did not change much over time.[23] This suggests that the slow convergence between Black and non-Black neighborhoods has more to do with gains across the Black neighborhood distribution. It does not seem to be the case that high-SES Black neighborhoods are pulling away from low-SES ones as quickly as all-Black neighborhoods along the distribution are slowly gaining status relative to non-Black neighborhoods.

Diversity among Black neighborhoods within metro areas is lower than in non-Black neighborhoods, depending on the indicator. But the socioeconomic conditions in the top quintile of Black neighborhoods highlights that there are some highly advantaged Black neighborhoods, as well as some metro areas where Black neighborhood advantage can really be quite high. This quantitative evidence for the presence of Black middle-class neighborhoods once again directs our attention to the Washington, D.C., metro.

Given the extent of inequality between Black and non-Black neighborhoods in the United States, Black neighborhoods in the best quartile for any of these indicators can reasonably be called a Black middle-class neighborhood. A higher bar is to be among the strongest on all three indicators—poverty rate, home values, and disadvantage index—and very few Black census tracts meet that bar.[24] In only *seventy-one* tract-years (out of over thirty-three thousand Black tract-years) did a Black census tract meet that threshold, and twenty-three of those tract-years were in Washington, D.C. The numbers grew slowly over time, but solidly middle-class Black neighborhoods are clearly quite rare. In 2017, less than 4 percent of Black neighborhoods were in the bottom half of the nation's tract poverty rate and disadvantage index or in the top half of the surrounding metro's home value distribution.

Why Might Some Black Neighborhoods Fare Better?

Variation in outcomes in Black neighborhoods allows me to identify some factors that may contribute to better conditions in them. Several scholars have studied the effect of the neighborhood and metropolitan factors that contribute to the higher levels of poverty (and other negative socioeconomic conditions) in Black neighborhoods. Most of the explanations for Black neighborhood poverty coming out of the early theoretical and empirical work evaluated several factors, including whether poverty was driven by manufacturing job loss or other metropolitan economic trends, or whether a culture of poverty had taken root in urban Black neighborhoods. Paul Jargowsky provides a convincing case, backed up by an empirical strategy, that drivers of neighborhood poverty in Black and Latino neighborhoods are (1) income processes generated at the metropolitan level; (2) income sorting within the metropolitan area; and (3) neighborhood sorting in the metropolitan area.[25] By adding a set of characteristics in Black neighborhoods within metropolitan areas, I contribute a fourth factor with which to assess the role of the culture of poverty, as explored by Galster and his colleagues in their research.[26]

With a sample of 172 metropolitan areas and six observations over time, I am able to run regression models to pinpoint some associations between metro-area characteristics and outcomes in Black neighborhoods.[27] To be clear, these are only associations and should not be interpreted as summarizing causal relationships.

Table 4.5 presents results from a regression model where the dependent variable is the CSA-level (or CBSA-level) average Black census tract poverty rate, on a sample of CSAs with at least ten Black census tracts in that year. The models are pooled cross-sections with controls for year effects, using 1970 as the reference year.[28] The first column includes income-generating processes: region of the country and the percentage of the population in professional and manufacturing occupations. All of the regions other than the Northeast had lower Black neighborhood poverty rates than the Midwest, and in all regions higher professional and manufacturing job shares are associated with lower Black poverty rates. This result suggests that the loss of manufacturing jobs has been a meaningful factor in Black neighborhood poverty to some extent.

Table 4.5 CSA/CBSA-Level Regression Models Predicting Black Neighborhood Poverty Rate

Variables	Income-Generating Processes	Income-Sorting Processes	Neighborhood Sorting Processes	Black Neighborhood Characteristics
Percent professional	–0.647***	–0.0255	–0.0399	0.258**
	(0.153)	(0.167)	(0.154)	(0.125)
Percent manufacturing	–0.248***	–0.157**	–0.133*	–0.166***
	(0.0836)	(0.0734)	(0.0700)	(0.0508)
Average family income (in thousands of dollars)		–0.00296***	–0.00312***	–0.00233***
		(0.000691)	(0.000718)	(0.000511)
Gini coefficient		0.446**	0.495**	0.302***
		(0.194)	(0.191)	(0.103)
Black neighborhood inequality		0.00730	0.00672	–0.00778
		(0.00981)	(0.00937)	(0.00696)
Percent Black			–0.0805**	–0.0877***
			(0.0398)	(0.0278)
Income segregation (H index)			0.143***	0.0410
			(0.0453)	(0.0332)
Black-White dissimilarity[a]			0.0422	0.0288
			(0.0530)	(0.0470)
Percent live in housing more than thirty years old (BN)				0.000702
				(0.0334)
Percent female-headed households (BN)				0.369***
				(0.0648)
Unemployment rate (BN[b])				0.520***
				(0.0676)
Percent less than high school diploma (not BN)				0.474***
				(0.0552)
Percent Hispanic (BN)				0.0147
				(0.0645)

Table 4.5 ***(Continued)***

Variables	Income-Generating Processes	Income-Sorting Processes	Neighborhood Sorting Processes	Black Neighborhood Characteristics
Percent Hispanic (not BN)				–0.155***
				(0.0455)
South	–0.0298**	–0.0536***	–0.0342**	–0.00001
	(0.0119)	(0.0129)	(0.0150)	(0.0117)
Northeast	–0.00494	–0.00654	0.000556	–0.0230*
	(0.0177)	(0.0164)	(0.0167)	(0.0116)
West	–0.0904***	–0.0916***	–0.0813***	0.00622
	(0.0173)	(0.0201)	(0.0237)	(0.0172)
Year 1980	–0.0314***	0.000491	0.0273*	
	(0.00861)	(0.0138)	(0.0160)	
Year 1990	0.00418	0.0747***	0.108***	0.0795***
	(0.0106)	(0.0227)	(0.0270)	(0.0149)
Year 2000	–0.00495	0.0870***	0.134***	0.108***
	(0.0162)	(0.0307)	(0.0370)	(0.0261)
Year 2010	0.0318	0.169***	0.208***	0.191***
	(0.0196)	(0.0402)	(0.0467)	(0.0383)
Year 2017	0.0198	0.188***	0.241***	0.255***
	(0.0220)	(0.0480)	(0.0555)	(0.0442)
Constant	0.548***	0.252***	0.147	–0.225***
	(0.0547)	(0.0879)	(0.105)	(0.0600)
Observations	454	454	454	400
R-squared	0.285	0.369	0.400	0.792

Source: Author's tabulation of U.S. 2010 Longitudinal Tract Database (Logan, Xu, and Stults 2014) and American Community Survey Five-Year Estimates (U.S. Census Bureau 2019).

Note: Robust standard errors in parentheses. Standard errors are clustered by the metropolitan area.

[a] The dissimilarity and isolation indices are the two most common ways in which we capture segregation at the city, county, or metropolitan area scale. The dissimilarity index captures the percentage of a group's population that would have to change neighborhoods (proxied here by census tracts) for each neighborhood to have the same percentage of that group as the metropolitan area (or city or county) overall. The isolation index is the extent to which minority members are exposed only to one another. The isolation index is sensitive to the percentage of that group in the metro overall.

[b] BN denotes average characteristics of the relevant variable in Black neighborhoods within the metropolitan area.

***$p < 0.01$; **$p < 0.05$; *$p < 0.10$

The second column adds income-sorting processes, which include the Gini coefficient as a measure of income inequality, average family income, and a measure of Black neighborhood inequality. Higher income is strongly associated with less Black neighborhood poverty, and more income inequality is associated with higher Black neighborhood poverty. The coefficient on professional occupation share is no longer significant, but otherwise nothing changes from column 1. When we add neighborhood sorting processes, the share Black in a metropolitan area is strongly associated with lower Black neighborhood poverty. More income segregation is associated with higher poverty in those neighborhoods, while the Black-White dissimilarity index is not related at all.

In the final column, I add metropolitan average socioeconomic characteristics in Black neighborhoods: age of housing and share Hispanic in Black neighborhoods (both unrelated to Black neighborhood poverty), in addition to the share of female-headed households, the unemployment rate, and the percentage with less than a high school diploma, all of which are strongly and positively correlated with higher Black neighborhood poverty rates. I also add the share Hispanic outside of Black neighborhoods, which is negatively associated with Black neighborhood poverty rates. Once I add these variables, most of the existing relationships hold. Also, controlling for these variables, the South and West are no longer as clearly low-poverty as the Northeast and Midwest. And the share professional is now associated with higher Black neighborhood poverty rates. But average family income, more manufacturing, and a higher share Black in a metro area are strongly associated with lower Black neighborhood poverty, with inequality being strongly associated with higher Black neighborhood poverty rates. These results lend more credibility to the notion that high-income southern regions such as Atlanta and Washington, D.C., are particularly strong metropolitan areas for Black neighborhoods. Interestingly, although Black neighborhood poverty rates have declined slowly over time, the time trend captured in these regressions suggests that 1970 was the lowest year for Black poverty rates. In other words, controlling for metropolitan-area fundamentals, Black neighborhood poverty rates were higher in later decades than in 1970. And the association rises over time: 2017 Black neighborhood poverty rates were higher than they were in 2010 (controlling for other factors), and so on.[29]

These four factors—income-generating, income-sorting, and neighborhood-sorting processes as well as Black neighborhood characteristics—explain the vast majority of variation in Black neighborhood poverty rates. The full model explains 79 percent of that variation. Nearly 30 percent is accounted for by income-generating processes. Income- and neighborhood-sorting processes together add only another 11 percent. Black neighborhood characteristics account for another 39 percent of variation in Black neighborhood poverty rates.

At first glance, these results suggest that policymakers should address Black neighborhood poverty through interventions that change other demographic characteristics in those neighborhoods. But it's important to reiterate that metropolitan-level characteristics are very important, particularly overall income and income inequality. So although poverty in Black neighborhoods is strongly correlated with other indicators of neighborhood disadvantage, Black neighborhood poverty rates reflect metropolitan-area conditions to a considerable extent.

Policymakers might like to know what characteristics are associated with *changes* in neighborhood poverty rates. In addition to Jargowsky, Galster and his colleagues offer strong examples of models that attempt to capture aspects of metropolitan areas and neighborhoods that influence Black neighborhood poverty rates.[30] Galster and Mincy estimate these models at the neighborhood level, while controlling for metropolitan-area characteristics.[31] They find that overall job availability in the metropolitan area is a strong predictor of lower Black neighborhood poverty rate growth. But most of the factors strongly related to Black neighborhood poverty rate growth were the demographic features of these neighborhoods at the beginning of the data period (1980). Given this, subsequent work by Galster and his colleagues, as well as the lower likelihood of predicting *changes* in neighborhood poverty at the metropolitan-area unit of analysis, I deviate from the previous models by estimating these models at the neighborhood level.[32]

Table 4.6 provides the results of a set of models predicting the changes in Black neighborhood poverty rates over five distinct decades of change. The variables in the first five rows are all measured as change over the same decade as the dependent variable, at the metropolitan level. The rest of the variables are measured at the neighborhood level at the start of the decade. At the metropolitan level, it is striking that the relationship between changes in family income and the number of families (a measure of population growth) is consistent and strong. Income inequality and Black-White segregation were related to these changes only in the first two decades.

The second notable finding is how strongly some indicators of disadvantage are related to growth in Black neighborhood poverty rates. Black neighborhoods with high shares of people without college degrees, renters, and female-headed households as well as high unemployment and vacancy rates consistently saw stronger growth in poverty rates. The share Black and poverty rates were negatively associated with poverty rate growth in Black neighborhoods, with the exception of the most recent time period, when the share Black was associated with faster growth in poverty. Between 2000 and 2017, new housing production was associated with slower growth in poverty rates. Although there are several statistically significant coefficients, the model explains only between 29 and

Table 4.6 Neighborhood-Level Regression Models Predicting Changes in Black Neighborhood Poverty Rate

	1970–1980	1980–1990	1990–2000	2000–2010	2010–2017
CSA/CBSA factors					
Change in percent low-income	0.0145 (0.0742)	0.207** (0.0805)	0.0265 (0.0749)	–0.339*** (0.0913)	0.0338 (0.145)
Change in average family income	–0.0102*** (0.000999)	–0.00723*** (0.000379)	–0.00336*** (0.000313)	–0.00436*** (0.000196)	–0.00525*** (0.000351)
Change in number of families	0.00878 (0.00651)	–0.0471*** (0.00884)	–0.0293** (0.0141)	0.0496*** (0.0174)	–0.0835** (0.0365)
Change in Gini coefficient	0.410*** (0.0862)	0.405*** (0.117)	–0.172* (0.0916)	0.0285 (0.103)	–0.167 (0.130)
Change in Black-White dissimilarity	0.0866** (0.0343)	–0.224*** (0.0409)	–0.00490 (0.0471)	–0.0150 (0.0546)	–0.0481 (0.0863)
Neighborhood factors[a]					
Percent Black	–0.0588*** (0.00487)	–0.0580*** (0.00622)	–0.0357*** (0.00456)	–0.100*** (0.0102)	0.0155** (0.00729)
Percent in poverty	–0.691*** (0.0229)	–0.498*** (0.0228)	–0.585*** (0.0161)	–0.661*** (0.0262)	–0.606*** (0.0155)
Percent with no high school diploma	0.110*** (0.0205)	0.143*** (0.0195)	0.105*** (0.0143)	0.119*** (0.0291)	0.147*** (0.0185)
Percent female-headed households	0.377*** (0.0288)	0.235*** (0.0247)	0.150*** (0.0152)	0.368*** (0.0338)	0.0724*** (0.0134)
Unemployment rate	0.344*** (0.0641)	0.235*** (0.0289)	0.0983*** (0.0244)	0.0629* (0.0355)	0.0828*** (0.0196)
Percent professional	–0.196*** (0.0250)	–0.0721*** (0.0249)	–0.0682*** (0.0177)	–0.0777*** (0.0229)	–0.0769*** (0.0132)
Vacancy rate	0.111*** (0.0401)	0.0242 (0.0239)	0.105*** (0.0170)	0.0634** (0.0257)	0.155*** (0.0197)
Percent renters	0.143*** (0.00759)	0.0995*** (0.00801)	0.0985*** (0.00607)	0.0396*** (0.0113)	0.121*** (0.00766)
Percent in housing units more than thirty years old	–0.0269*** (0.00673)	–0.0367*** (0.00568)	–0.00146 (0.00429)	–0.00889 (0.00830)	0.0107 (0.00761)
Percent in housing units less than ten years old	–0.00172 (0.00895)	–0.0136 (0.00937)	–0.0327*** (0.00768)	–0.0356** (0.0165)	0.0186 (0.0137)

Table 4.6 ***(Continued)***

	1970–1980	1980–1990	1990–2000	2000–2010	2010–2017
South	–0.0262***	–0.00737	0.0197***	–0.0190***	–0.0150***
	(0.00448)	(0.00482)	(0.00302)	(0.00426)	(0.00370)
Northeast	–0.0378***	–0.0202***	0.00741**	–0.0385***	–0.0123***
	(0.00447)	(0.00440)	(0.00325)	(0.00395)	(0.00369)
West	–0.0472***	–0.0108**	0.0245***	–0.0532***	0.00715
	(0.00485)	(0.00524)	(0.00529)	(0.00750)	(0.00943)
Constant	0.178***	0.176***	0.0943***	0.175***	0.107***
	(0.0192)	(0.0154)	(0.00943)	(0.0137)	(0.0123)
Observations	4,387	5,138	6,374	6,786	6,687
R-squared	0.449	0.385	0.441	0.287	0.310

Source: Author's tabulation of U.S. 2010 Longitudinal Tract Database (Logan, Xu, and Stults 2014) and American Community Survey Five-Year Estimates (U.S. Census Bureau 2019).
Note: Robust standard errors in parentheses. Standard errors are clustered by the neighborhood.
[a] Neighborhood-level variables are measured at the beginning of the decade.
$^{***}p < 0.01$; $^{**}p < 0.05$; $^{*}p < 0.10$

45 percent of the variation in poverty rate changes, so there are omitted variables that are unaccounted for.

Further, prior analyses of neighborhood poverty rates have emphasized that there is a nonlinear relationship between neighborhood poverty and downstream effects from concentrated poverty.[33] Specifically, increases in neighborhood poverty rates might not matter much when poverty rates are very low or very high. But increases across thresholds such as 20 or 30 percent can be indicative of a neighborhood going from relatively to severely disadvantaged. For simplicity, I estimated these models using linear regression without any tests for threshold or nonlinear effects, so I am unable to test for those.

Wrapping Up: Regional Variation, Baseline Disadvantage

Chapter 3 told a story of limited convergence between Black and non-Black neighborhoods. In this chapter, I find that the convergence is not due to a small number of Black middle-class neighborhoods taking off and leaving most of the others behind. On the one hand, the number of Black middle-class neighborhoods increased and they became more advantaged over time. But on the other hand, inequality among Black neighborhoods at the high and low ends of the distribution has not changed much since 1970 (see appendix A.4.1).

I also identify where Black neighborhoods are thriving, suggest a few hypotheses about why, and test them. First, there are substantial regional differences between Black neighborhoods in the South (where Black neighborhoods are growing and plentiful) and the West (where they are transitioning to something else) compared to Black neighborhoods in the Midwest and portions of the Northeast. This is not surprising given the substantial literature on economic decline in aging metros in the upper Midwest and Northeast. However, it is not just that all neighborhoods in these aging metros have fallen behind. The gaps between Black and non-Black neighborhoods are often much higher in the Rust Belt. These metropolitan areas are not uniformly disadvantaged: disadvantage is disproportionately concentrated in Black neighborhoods.

The well-worn narratives about the Rust Belt should not overshadow the substantial gains made in Black neighborhoods in the South, which has the highest concentrations of Black neighborhoods. The Washington, D.C.–Baltimore and Atlanta metropolitan areas are hubs of Black neighborhood advantage, reflecting long-standing Black middle-class populations in those metros. And the Houston, Raleigh, Dallas, and Charlotte metropolitan areas also have relatively strong Black neighborhood indicators, as do several smaller metros in North Carolina.

One explanation for some of these success stories is substantial public employment. It doesn't take a sophisticated regional economic analysis to notice that the nation's capital and its two most massive army bases anchor the metropolitan areas that have both a relatively large number of Black neighborhoods and very strong economic indicators in those neighborhoods. Federal employment has long provided opportunities for Black workers when they were shut out of other industries and occupations.[34] The long-established Black middle-class neighborhoods in these metro areas provide evidence that this pattern continues in the twenty-first century.

Although regression models cannot tell us definitively what aspects of metropolitan areas *cause* greater advantage in Black neighborhoods, they do uncover some meaningful associations. Black neighborhood poverty rates are clearly lower in metros with strong and growing economies. Also at the metropolitan level, a higher share of Blacks and manufacturing jobs are associated with lower Black neighborhood poverty, and poverty rates are higher in metros with greater income inequality. Black-White segregation is not correlated with Black neighborhood poverty rates, but income segregation is. Demographic characteristics associated with concentrated disadvantage—low educational attainment, high unemployment rates, and high shares of female-headed households—are strongly associated with Black neighborhood poverty and the growth in those rates, even accounting for the larger metropolitan-area processes that often shape such concentrations.

The descriptive results support the regression results in one key way: large metropolitan areas with strong population and economic growth tend to have the best Black neighborhood outcomes. Chicago has some of the strongest Black neighborhood indicators in the Midwest, and Los Angeles has some of the strongest Black neighborhood indicators in the country. New York and Boston stand out in the Northeast. And in the South, Washington, D.C., Dallas, Atlanta, and Houston have strong Black neighborhood indicators. Strong regional economies are essential for Black neighborhood advantage.

Appendix to Chapter 4: Is Widening Inequality between Black Neighborhoods Part of the Story?

Averages may mask inequality between Black neighborhoods themselves; in places with a few strong-performing middle-class neighborhoods, averages may be skewed by different levels of inequality between these neighborhoods. The extent of this inequality has ramifications for capturing the state of Black neighborhoods and how they have evolved in recent decades. If there is not a great deal of inequality between Black neighborhoods, then the small gains we have seen in these neighborhoods are more widespread. On the other hand, if inequality is high, or if it has increased in recent decades, then much of this improvement is likely to be just an artifact of improvements in more-advantaged Black tracts.

By looking at the higher and lower ends of the distribution, we are better able not only to capture the diversity of Black neighborhoods but also to specify how these neighborhoods have changed over time. Appendix table A.4.1 shows the values at the top and bottom quintiles (eightieth and twentieth percentiles) for several neighborhood characteristics in the 2015–2019 ACS. Values in the left two columns are in Black neighborhoods; on the right are values in non-Black neighborhoods.[35]

Because of persistent inequality across American neighborhoods, there are large gaps between the top and bottom quartiles for many variables. Poverty rates are about 2.8 times higher in the most impoverished Black tracts than in the least impoverished, and similar gaps exist for the percentage with a BA degree or higher, the unemployment rate, and the homeownership rate. Median rents and home values, percent Black, and percent with a high school diploma or less do not vary quite as much. The twentieth percentile tract has a poverty rate of about 13 percent on average, compared to 34 percent in the eightieth percentile tract. In other words, low-poverty Black neighborhoods are around the national average. High-poverty Black tracts are nearing the extreme poverty rate threshold of 40 percent. These percentages represent big differences in quality of life. The differences between high- and low-poverty non-Black tracts

Table A.4.1 Top- and Bottom-Quintile Neighborhood Characteristics, 2017

	Black Neighborhood, 20th Percentile	Black Neighborhood, 80th Percentile	Non-Black Neighborhood, 20th Percentile	Non-Black Neighborhood, 80th Percentile
Median rent	$687	$1,033	$855	$1,410
Median home value	$114,331	$230,717	$203,782	$428,135
Percent White	5%	28%	44%	81%
Percent Black	50	84	2	14
Percent Hispanic	4	17	7	30
Percent Asian	0	5	1	11
Poverty rate	13	34	5	18
Median household income	$31,703	$61,473	$52,418	$101,864
Unemployment rate	6%	14%	3%	7%
Percent with less than a high school diploma	9	22	4	18
Percent with a BA degree	12	30	18	53
Disadvantage index	0.2	1.4	–0.7	0.3

Source: Author's tabulation of U.S. 2010 Longitudinal Tract Database (Logan, Xu, and Stults 2014) and American Community Survey Five-Year Estimates (U.S. Census Bureau 2019).

(5 to 18 percent) are probably not as profound. Median income gaps are similar in Black and non-Black neighborhoods; at about two to one, these gaps correspond to a Black tract gap of $60,000 to $30,200 and about $100,000 to $50,000 in non-Black tracts. The unemployment rate is 14 percent in the eightieth percentile tract in Black neighborhoods, compared to 6 percent in lower-unemployment neighborhoods. There are huge education gaps between neighborhoods at the top and at the bottom in both types of neighborhood. The percentage with a BA degree or higher in low-education Black neighborhoods is only 12 percent, compared to 30 percent for higher-educated neighborhoods. This gap is even larger in non-Black neighborhoods—between 18 and 53 percent.

Racial composition is very different across the distribution of Black tracts. In the Black tracts with the highest share White, 28 percent of residents are White. These are very integrated neighborhoods; integration is about six times what is seen in Black tracts with the lowest share White. The eightieth percentile median home value in Black tracts is $230,000—just $27,000 above the twentieth percentile in non-Black neighborhoods.

The main takeaway from this look at 2017 disparities between the high and low quintiles for these characteristics is that while there are very large gaps between Black tracts at the top and bottom of the distribution, these gaps are often smaller than comparable gaps in non-Black tracts. And while the least disadvantaged Black tracts are usually in pretty good shape, they are not much more advantaged than the most disadvantaged non-Black tracts. In other words, the most advantaged Black neighborhoods are like middle-class neighborhoods across the United States. The most disadvantaged Black neighborhoods are in very bad shape, the most disadvantaged non-Black neighborhoods are basically middle-class, and the most advantaged non-Black tracts are some of the most desirable places to live in the country, if not the world.

The most disadvantaged Black census tracts have improved at the same pace as the most advantaged ones. I look at the change over time in two ways. Appendix table A.4.2 shows the neighborhood characteristics at the top and bottom quintiles in 1980, to see if the more advantaged Black neighborhoods used to compare differently to the least advantaged non-Black neighborhoods. Notably, in 1980, the median home value in the non-Black neighborhoods in the lowest quintile was slightly higher than the (average) median home value in the highest-quintile Black tracts. This is an example of the inversion of the dual housing market. Poverty rates in the lowest-poverty Black tracts were higher than the poverty rates in the highest-poverty non-Black tracts. Finally, the changes in the disadvantage index are especially illuminating. In 1980, the bottom-quintile Black tracts were twice as disadvantaged as the most disadvantaged non-Black tracts. In 2017, the Black tracts at the twentieth percentile had a slightly better disadvantage index than the eightieth percentile non-Black tracts.

Table A.4.2 Top- and Bottom-Quintile Neighborhood Characteristics, 1980

	Black Neighborhood, 20th Percentile	Black Neighborhood, 80th Percentile	Non-Black Neighborhood, 20th Percentile	Non-Black Neighborhood, 80th Percentile
Median rent	$391	$609	$554	$893
Median home value	$72,941	$128,340	$129,671	$233,979
Percent White	2%	25%	76%	95%
Percent Black	64	94	1	8
Percent Hispanic	2	9	2	11
Percent Asian	0	1	0	3
Poverty rate	16	39	4	13
Median household income	$25,439	$50,124	$46,136	$76,601
Unemployment rate	8%	16%	4%	8%
Percent with less than a high school diploma	36	60	16	42
Percent with a BA degree	3	12	8	28
Disadvantage index	0.66	2.20	–0.64	0.32

Source: Author's tabulation of U.S. 2010 Longitudinal Tract Database (Logan, Xu, and Stults 2014) and American Community Survey Five-Year Estimates (U.S. Census Bureau 2019).

Figure A.4.1 Ratios between the Top and Bottom Quartiles, Black Neighborhoods, 1970–2017

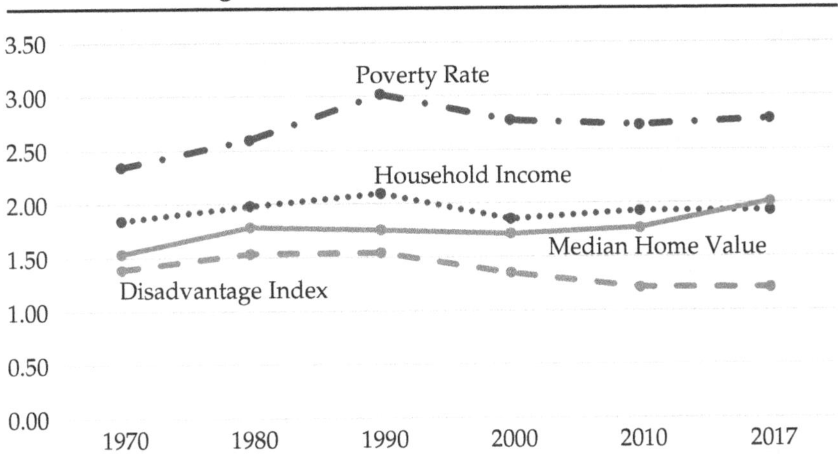

Source: Author's tabulation of U.S. 2010 Longitudinal Tract Database (Logan, Xu, and Stults 2014) and American Community Survey Five-Year Estimates (U.S. Census Bureau 2019).

Appendix figure A.4.1 shows the change over time in four key measures: poverty rate, household income, disadvantage index, and median home value. The gaps between the top and bottom quartiles grow for the poverty rate and median home value. The disadvantage index gap declines, and the household income gap rises and then falls. For all variables other than median home value, 1990 was the high-water mark, when inequality was highest between Black tracts. Taken together, the minimal changes over time in the relative position between high- and low-SES Black tracts suggest that the convergence we observed in chapter 3 has more to do with slow but steady gains across the Black neighborhood distribution. It does not seem to be the case that high-SES Black neighborhoods are pulling away from low-SES ones as quickly as all Black neighborhoods along the distribution are slowly gaining status relative to non-Black neighborhoods.

Appendix table A.4.3 further allays concerns that metropolitan areas with low average poverty rates are that way because of wide inequality between high- and low-poverty Black census tracts. The correlation between average and eightieth percentile rates is a very high 0.85, but it is identical to the correlation between the twentieth percentile poverty rate and the average poverty rate. In other words, a metro area is equally likely to have a low Black neighborhood poverty rate driven by the high

Table A.4.3 Correlation between High- and Low-Quartile Average Black Neighborhood Poverty, 2017

Variables	Bivariate Correlation
Average Black neighborhood poverty rate, 80th percentile Black tract poverty rate	0.85
Average Black neighborhood poverty rate, 20th percentile Black tract poverty rate	0.84
Average Black neighborhood poverty rate, 80/20 Black tract poverty ratio	–0.15

Source: Author's tabulation of U.S. 2010 Longitudinal Tract Database (Logan, Xu, and Stults 2014) and American Community Survey Five-Year Estimates (U.S. Census Bureau 2019).

end of the distribution as one driven by the low end. Additionally, the correlation between the top and bottom quintile ratio and the average poverty rate is actually negative (–0.15), suggesting that areas with higher inequality have lower poverty rates in Black neighborhoods. The simplest explanation is that inequality is driven by higher median incomes in the top quintile of census tracts.

Chapter 5

Race and Space

C-O-M-P-T-O-N and the city they call Long Beach / Puttin' the sh*t together
Like my ni**a D.O.C., no one can do it better

—Dr. Dre, "Nuthin' but a 'G' Thang," 1992
(Featuring Snoop Dogg)

The nation's second-largest population center and global capital of the entertainment industry was not going to sit on the sidelines of the hip-hop explosion for long. Southern California had been a late destination during the Great Migration for Black migrants from the South, but once word came back to family and relatives in Louisiana and Texas about the beautiful climate and lower racial tension, their migration to the West was well on by the 1940s. By 1970, over 760,000 Black people lived in the city of Los Angeles—the third-highest Black population of any city in the country. At its peak, however, L.A.'s Black population topped out at only 18 percent of the city's total; today it is down to 8 percent. In the vast Los Angeles metropolitan area, the Black population has never been over 9 percent (1980) and is roughly 6 percent at present.

This vast metropolitan area has always contained both a highly concentrated and relatively scattered Black population. The concentrated Black population is in the area that stretches south of downtown L.A. for several miles, known commonly as either South Central L.A., or, since that name fell out of fashion after the 1992 riots, South L.A. By 1970, the Black Belt of Los Angeles was an uninterrupted stretch of neighborhoods extending fifteen miles south from Interstate 10 down to where the 405 freeway heads east toward Orange County. East to west, this territory spanned about seven miles at its widest point. The territory was hemmed in by freeways and heavy manufacturing on all sides, with some of those noxious land uses cutting through the middle of it. But the location offered proximity to one of the nation's most productive manufacturing sectors. Unfortunately, that sector would decline rapidly as the Black population grew. Unemployment in South L.A. would rise from 9 percent in 1970 to 14 percent by 1990.[1]

https://doi.org/10.7758/tjvh5404.6015

Even then, the Black population of Los Angeles was scattered, unlike most metropolitan areas. While there were 760,000 Blacks in 1970 L.A., another 350,000 were located in the vast sprawl surrounding the city, heading into the desert. The Black Belt stretched into suburban Compton and then jumped into nearby Long Beach. There were also Black neighborhoods nearly fifty miles north of Long Beach, in Pacoima. Another twenty miles to the southeast from Pacoima was a long-standing Black community, redlined into an enclave in Pasadena. Then, another fifty-two miles to the east of Pasadena was a Black neighborhood in San Bernadino, in a separate county altogether. In recent decades, as the Black Belt has transformed into a brown one, Black neighborhoods have spread seventy miles north of the center of South L.A., into the high desert of Palmdale. Black settlement in Southern California is polycentric, matching the region's urban form.

In this context, the Los Angeles rap scene would develop a bit differently than in New York. The main actors who brought L.A. rap to the top of the charts were based out of South L.A., but the suburbanization of Black L.A. was a main ingredient as well. Most famously, the first rap album to go platinum from the Los Angeles album was titled *Straight Outta Compton*, by NWA, which featured an all-Compton lineup aside from South L.A.'s Ice Cube.

Los Angeles has never been alone in featuring Black suburbs. In many metro areas with large urban Black belts, those neighborhoods tend to spill across jurisdictional lines into adjacent suburbs. Reynolds Farley wrote about Black suburbs emerging in several metropolitan areas, focusing on New York and Chicago.[2] In Chicago, Farley documented robust Black population growth in suburban towns such as Harvey, to the south of Chicago's Black Belt. My Black grandparents migrated from Mississippi to the Chicago suburb of Dixmoor around 1950. New York's Black suburban population also grew, though not as swiftly. For example, Earl Simmons's hometown of Yonkers was one locus of Black suburban population growth on the East Coast. In L.A., Compton stands out as an extension of the South L.A. Black Belt. By 1980, nearly all of Compton's census tracts were Black. Similar to South L.A., racial succession would come to Compton: immigrants from Mexico and Central America—and their descendants—populated these Black neighborhoods as the Black population crested and declined. In Compton, the Hispanic/Latino population grew at a swift pace similar to South L.A.'s. By 2000, South L.A. and Compton were both majority-Hispanic. The large presence of Hispanics and Latinos during the formative years of L.A.'s rap scene would shape it as well.

Although Southern California's Black community was centered in Los Angeles proper, as were many of its most prominent early rap artists, it is telling that the album that put West Coast rap on the map is not called

Straight Outta L.A. Thanks to *Straight Outta Compton*—and Eazy E's highly coveted black Compton hat—Compton is probably the best-known suburb in the United States other than Beverly Hills. Unfortunately, given NWA's violent lyrical content, echoed by many of Compton's future rap artists, the city's high visibility has given it an extremely negative reputation. More unfortunately, this reputation has reflected (if inflated) reality, as Compton has often been one of the highest-crime cities in the country.[3]

Another way in which L.A.'s suburbanized, polycentric urban form affected the development of its rap culture was in the emphasis on the automobile. Dr. Dre, NWA's musical genius and arguably the most successful rap producer of all time, has said that he specifically recorded songs with attention to how they would sound on car stereo systems.[4] Such considerations were unlikely to be top of mind for New York's early rap innovators, given that they and their initial audiences were much more likely to travel by subway. This was just the latest connection between modes of transportation and contemporary music. The railway was an early inspiration for songwriters of the blues and early country.[5] Johnny Cash's "boom-chick-a-boom" rhythm made famous by "I Walk the Line" and "Folsom Prison Blues" was mimicking the sound of the train. The rock-and-roll explosion of the 1950s and 1960s was concurrent with the establishment of a car culture, and popular songs celebrated automobile makes and models, such as the Beach Boys' "Little Deuce Coupe" and Wilson Pickett's "Mustang Sally."[6] In this tradition, it was highly unlikely that even the most knowledgeable fans of 1980s rap based in New York would associate a particular car with the likes of LL Cool J, Run DMC, or the Beastie Boys.[7] But a clear indicator of whether someone was paying attention to West Coast rap in the 1990s is whether they could name the ride that Snoop Dogg and Dr. Dre made famous again (the 1964 Chevy Impala).

For pioneering MCs in L.A., cars were much less a topic of conversation than the elements of street life—gangs, violence, women, and the police. NWA was not the first rap act to center crime and violence in their music—Schooly D from Philadelphia and Boogie Down Productions are often credited with blazing that trail.[8] And with the braggadocio and machismo on display by most MCs, violence was never far from the topic of conversation. Prior to NWA's explosion onto the scene, L.A.'s Ice T used his criminal experiences as lyrical fodder for what would become a major-label career as a solo artist. NWA did not invent the idea of telling stories of Black youth caught up in drugs, gangs, and power struggles with police, but the incredible success they had established gangsta rap as marketable lyrical content and broadcast a particularly violent story of L.A. Black life to the world.[9]

Robin D. G. Kelley reminds us that rap is art, first and foremost.[10] As such, rap lyrics should not always be read as autobiography or as nonfictional stories about real life. But it was no accident that gangsta rap would flourish in Los Angeles. Alex Alonso connects the birth of the Crips and the Bloods in Los Angeles—two of the nation's first and most enduring modern urban gangs—to the demise of the Black Panther Party.[11] After the success of the FBI's COINTELPRO in infiltrating and ending the Los Angeles chapter of the party, the Crips filled an organizational void in the Black community. The new organization shifted its focus from protecting the community from police (a higher priority for the Panthers) to protecting the neighborhood from other street gangs. Over time, the Bloods would form as the primary counter to the Crips. The heroin- and later crack-fueled drug trade provided the financial incentive for the Crips and Bloods to engage in perpetual violence with one another. In response, most law enforcement agencies devised militant tactics in service of the War on Drugs; in this respect, the Los Angeles Police Department (LAPD) would stand out for its brutality and racism. The Watts and L.A. riots of 1965 and 1992 bookended this period to an extent. This is the world that NWA and subsequent Los Angeles MCs would describe.

The success of L.A. rap did not happen overnight. *Straight Outta Compton* portended massive success for NWA and some of its key members, but it was scarcely played on the radio and peaked at number thirty-seven on the Billboard 200. This was 1987, and radio was still segregated by genre and race; the cultural phenomenon MTV scarcely played Black musicians outside of Prince and Michael Jackson. Further, the profanity and subject matter of NWA and its peers were obviously not ideal for radio or MTV. But West Coast radio pushed these boundaries. KDAY in Los Angeles was on the AM dial but featured NWA's DJ Yella and Dr. Dre mixing records in one of the first regular rap radio shows in the country. Up the coast, KMEL in San Francisco was the first FM station with regular rap programming, which eventually took over the station. The wild success of KMEL provided proof of concept that rap was marketable not only to a Black audience but to young listeners of all races and ethnicities. This success in turn influenced Power 106 in LA to become a majority-rap station. Further, West Coast artists Tone Loc and MC Hammer would help remove MTV's rap barriers. By the early 1990s, as L.A.'s hard-core sound was in the ascendancy, rap music was beginning to be synonymous with pop music.

This popularity extended across all races and throughout all regions of the country, city and suburb. The widespread consumption of gangsta rap by White Americans in particular has come under scrutiny for some time.[12] Although there is a case to be made that gangsta rap carries a message in service of Black liberation, particularly with the attention it pays to police brutality, it is unclear whether the typical White fan is animated by that message. Consumers of violent rap probably enjoy the rush and the fantasy first. For all of the merits of gangsta rap—and I believe there are many—it undoubtedly helped solidify the connection between violence and Blackness in the minds of many Americans.

Given the role of the film industry in Los Angeles, the rap industry was not the only broadcast partner in presenting L.A. gang culture to the world. Films like *Boyz n the Hood* and *Menace II Society* would portray Los Angeles as besieged by gang violence. L.A.'s film industry has always had a way of portraying the region in apocalyptic terms. Movies such as *Falling Down*, the Terminator franchise, and *Blade Runner* are some of the many examples. But the racial implications of popularizing portrayals of gang violence led to massive reputational challenges for Black Los Angeles.

Neighborhoods Are Not Census Tracts, and They Are Not Islands

L.A.'s Black Belt, and the heart of its rap culture, was not a randomly scattered set of census tracts. Black South L.A. was a large, continuous land mass of over two hundred census tracts. To this point, I have treated census tracts as islands in urban space, but just as no person is an island, neither are census tracts. In urban areas, census tracts typically border several other census tracts and are often within a short drive or even walking distance of many more. The effects of neighborhoods on individual and family health and well-being are likely to extend beyond the borders of census tracts, which in very dense urban areas can be quite small.

Further, most Black neighborhoods developed as enclaves consisting of several census tracts. The Chicago metropolitan area, pictured in figure 5.1, has massive Black enclaves on its southern edge. As in Los Angeles, the typical Black census tract in the Chicago area is surrounded by many more, and the residents of core South Side neighborhoods such as Roseland would have to travel for miles to leave the Black enclave. In fact, heading south, one would leave the city of Chicago well before leaving this enclave. Chicago's southern suburbs are unlike the vast majority of U.S. suburbs in that they are predominantly occupied by Black households.

While Chicago and Detroit share some aspects of geography and histories of racial discrimination, segregation, and neighborhood succession, the spatial orientation of Black neighborhoods in the Detroit metropolitan area (figure 5.2) is quite different. First, the city of Detroit is effectively a large Black neighborhood, one almost entirely enclosed by the Detroit border, with the exception of the northwest corner bleeding into Southfield and Farmington. The relatively sharp distinction at Detroit's northern edge is a result of the infamous Birwood Wall, introduced in chapter 2.[13]

The Detroit metro's Black neighborhoods are unusually contained (and ubiquitous) within the city limits, but there are other enclaves in the

Figure 5.1 Spatial Location of Black Neighborhoods in Chicago, 2017

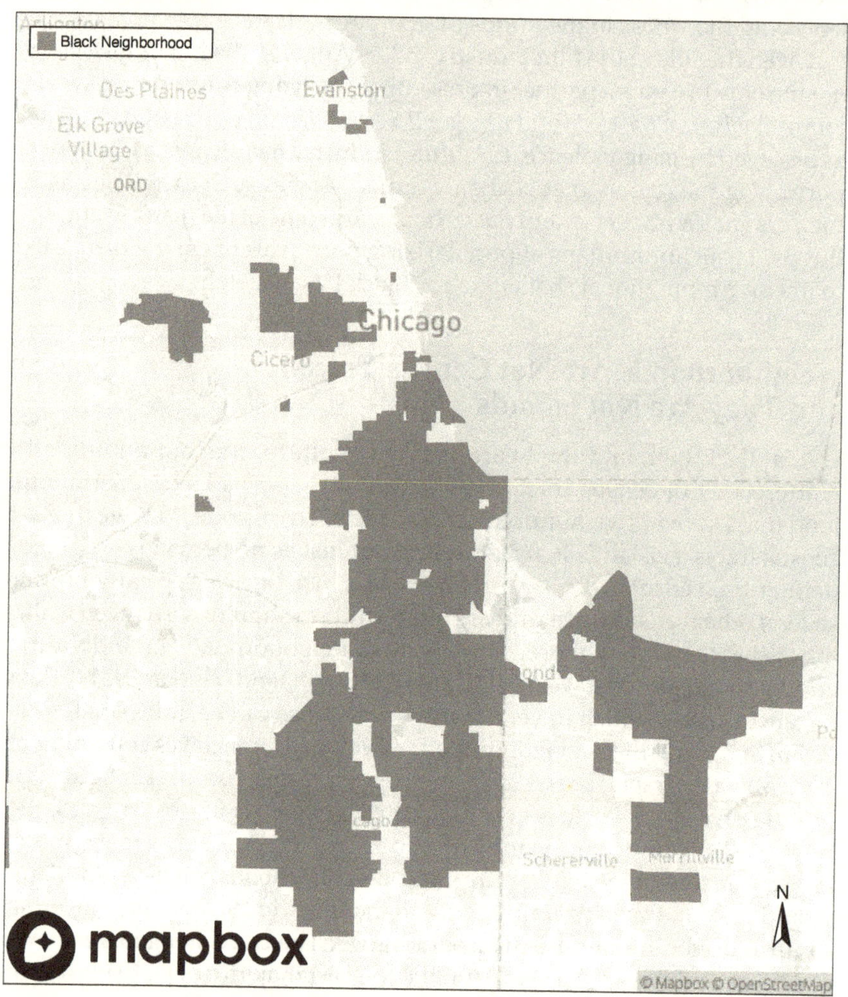

Source: Author's tabulation of American Community Survey Five-Year Estimates (U.S. Census Bureau 2019).

Figure 5.2 Spatial Location of Black Neighborhoods in Detroit, 2017

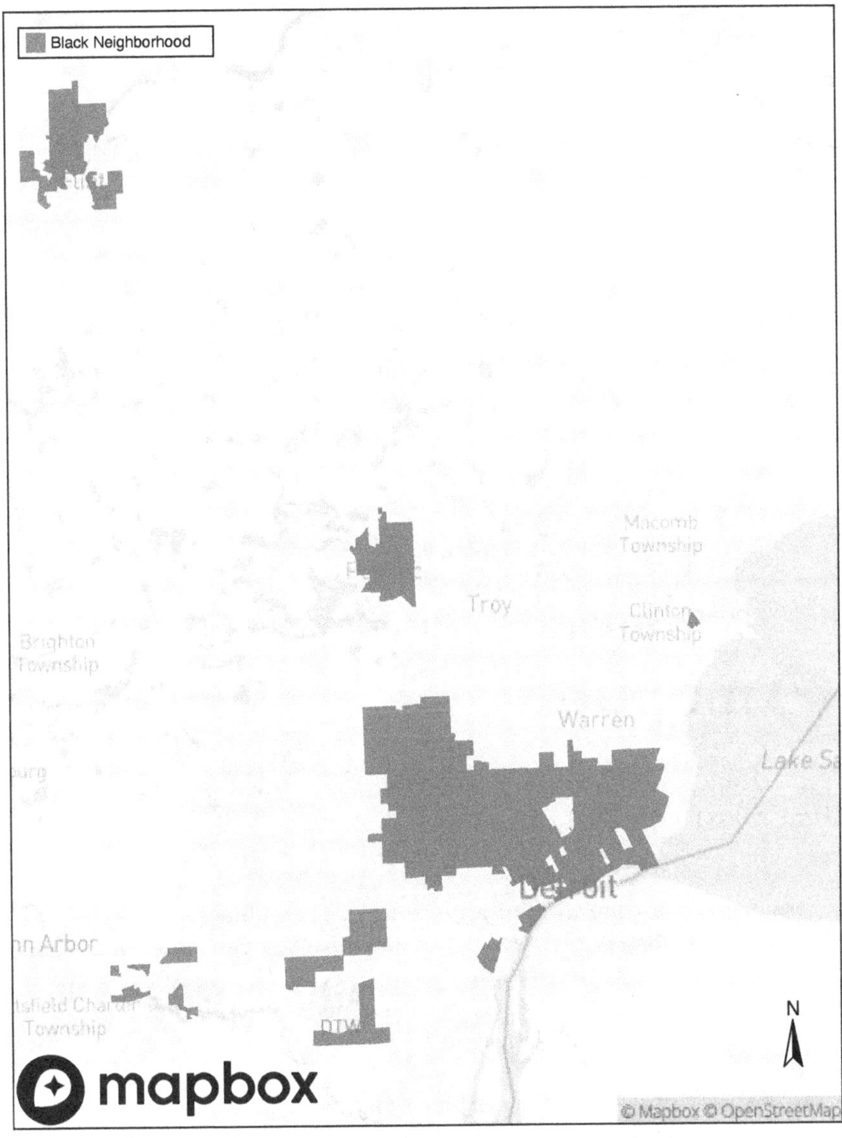

Source: Author's tabulation of American Community Survey Five-Year Estimates (U.S. Census Bureau 2019).

Figure 5.3 Spatial Location of Black Neighborhoods in Philadelphia, 2017

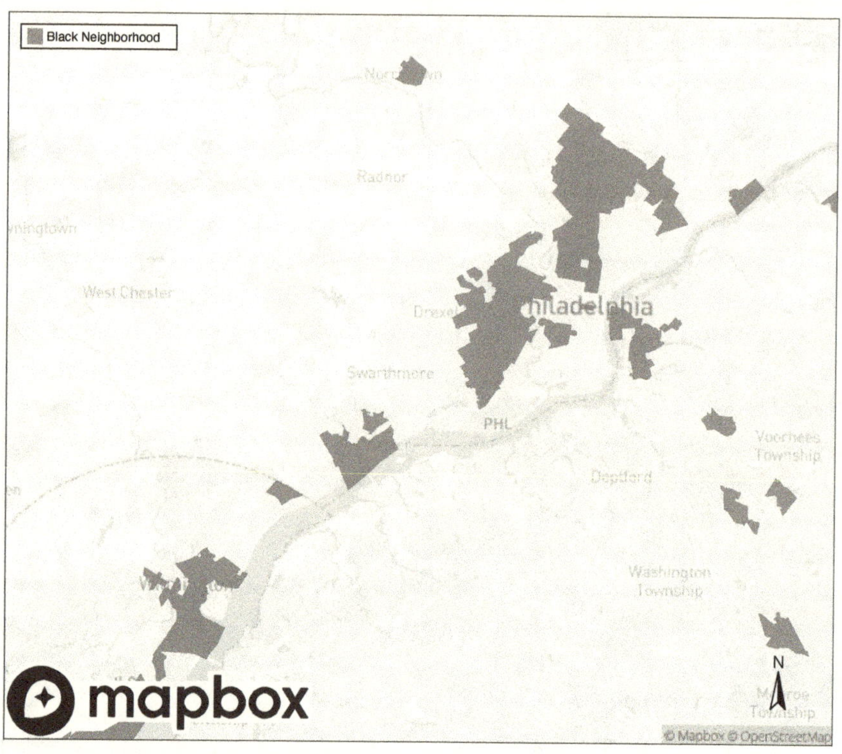

Source: Author's tabulation of American Community Survey Five-Year Estimates (U.S. Census Bureau 2019).

metro area, including in Flint and Pontiac. Those Black neighborhoods are also very urban enclaves that almost entirely cover these cities. (Flint is not considered a suburb, but Pontiac, population roughly sixty-one thousand, fits the description.) Otherwise, there are a few Black neighborhood "islands" between Detroit and Ann Arbor, home of the University of Michigan.

In Philadelphia, another northern city with many Black neighborhoods, those neighborhoods are located in a very different pattern than they are in Detroit and Chicago. Figure 5.3 shows that Black census tracts in Philadelphia are a little bit like islands, albeit large ones. There are two Black enclaves in the north of the city and in West Philadelphia, where the Fresh Prince was born and raised before he departed for Bel Air. But then there are sporadic and small Black enclaves moving southwest from the city, as well as isolated census tracts (or two to three census tracts to the southwest and northwest, in addition to one large census tract south of the city). These Black neighborhoods cross state lines, as many of them are in neighboring New Jersey and a couple are in Delaware.

Clearly, Black neighborhoods take different shapes in different metropolitan areas, and while not shown here, these shapes evolve over time. But more importantly for our purposes, census tracts might not capture the socioeconomic characteristics of the areas that surround people living in Black neighborhoods. Although census tracts clustered together often share similar characteristics—and Black census tracts in particular tend to share many similar characteristics—there is undoubtedly greater variation in the types of neighborhoods that surround Black neighborhoods than in those surrounding non-Black neighborhoods. Sharkey finds that even Black middle-class neighborhoods are more likely than other middle-class neighborhoods to be surrounded by relatively disadvantaged neighborhoods.[14] In this finding, what he terms "neighborhood spatial disadvantage" is underestimated when we look only at census tract characteristics.

Spatial Distinctions

Black neighborhoods were formed through explicitly spatial processes. In virtually every U.S. city in the late nineteenth century and through most of the twentieth, public and private actors erected physical and social barriers to confine Black neighborhoods to particular places. Generally, these locations were older and less desirable in several ways. As metropolitan areas sprawled and suburbanized with new housing, Black neighborhoods largely remained in central cities. But in recent years, demand for living in central cities has slowly increased, and in some cities the long-standing gap between demand for suburban and urban living has been inverted. This trend is often overstated, but it is real in some of the major metropolitan areas, particularly among higher-income White households. This shift in demand could influence the spatial location of Black neighborhoods, with implications for access to jobs, transit, and affordable housing in traditionally Black enclaves.

These concerns have to do with the *centrality* of Black neighborhoods, but their *concentration* may also be changing. The influx of Latino and Asian households into U.S. metropolitan areas is more predominant than a rise in central-city demand, and taking place over a longer time horizon. In Los Angeles, immigration has clearly diminished the size of Black enclaves in the expansive South L.A. region. A likely trend nationwide is the dispersal of Black neighborhoods (even where there is an equal number of such neighborhoods) to inner-ring suburbs and some former Black enclaves being broken up by neighborhoods consisting of other racial minorities.

More importantly, identifying the spatial location of Black neighborhoods can help us understand differences in indicators in these neighborhoods across location types. A major theme of fair housing fights over the last five decades has been the premise that Black households are missing out on something by being disproportionately excluded from suburban jurisdictions and neighborhoods. Black neighborhoods are not the only option for Black families, but to the extent that they already live in suburban neighborhoods, it is illuminating to know whether socioeconomic characteristics are stronger for Black neighborhoods in suburban jurisdictions. Given the sizable gaps between American suburban and urban neighborhoods across several indicators, this would seem obvious. And though the typical Black suburban neighborhood is likely to be more advantaged than the typical Black central-city neighborhood, the gaps may not be particularly large, for two reasons. First, suburban poverty and concentrated poverty are growing. Although central-city neighborhoods still have much higher rates of concentrated poverty, suburban neighborhood concentrated poverty is growing more quickly. From 2000 to the 2010–2014 ACS, the share of poor residents living in census tracts with poverty rates between 20 and 40 percent rose from 18 to 25.5 percent in central cities, but that share nearly doubled, from 4 to 7 percent, in suburban neighborhoods.[15] Both trends are concerning, but the suburban trajectory has been faster.

Another reason why suburban areas may not quite be a promised land for residents of Black neighborhoods is that, just as Black households have tended to live in the oldest neighborhoods and housing in central cities, the same is often true for the suburban neighborhoods where they can find housing. Many inner-ring suburban jurisdictions are between fifty and a hundred years old, and Black neighborhoods, when they exist in the suburbs at all, tend to be in these older jurisdictions where housing quality and other amenities have often deteriorated.

Another spatial distinction between different types of Black neighborhoods is a census tract's location in the "core" of the Black enclave or along the "border." Figure 5.4 shows the outline of the Black enclave in Cleveland, which comprises two prongs—one that rises northeast out of the city, along Lake Erie, and the other that moves southeast from the city. Several tracts form the border of Cleveland's Black enclave, and these neighborhoods probably differ from core Black neighborhoods in interesting ways. First, as Sander, Kucheva, and Zasloff and many others have demonstrated, neighborhoods along the border of Black neighborhoods in the twentieth century were inevitably the sites of the complex interplay between integration and racial tipping.[16] As Black enclaves expanded in size because of rising population and the failure by racial covenants (or in the post-*Shelley* environment, their unenforceability) and other forms of discrimination to stop integration, previously White

Figure 5.4 Spatial Location of Black Neighborhoods in Cleveland, 2017

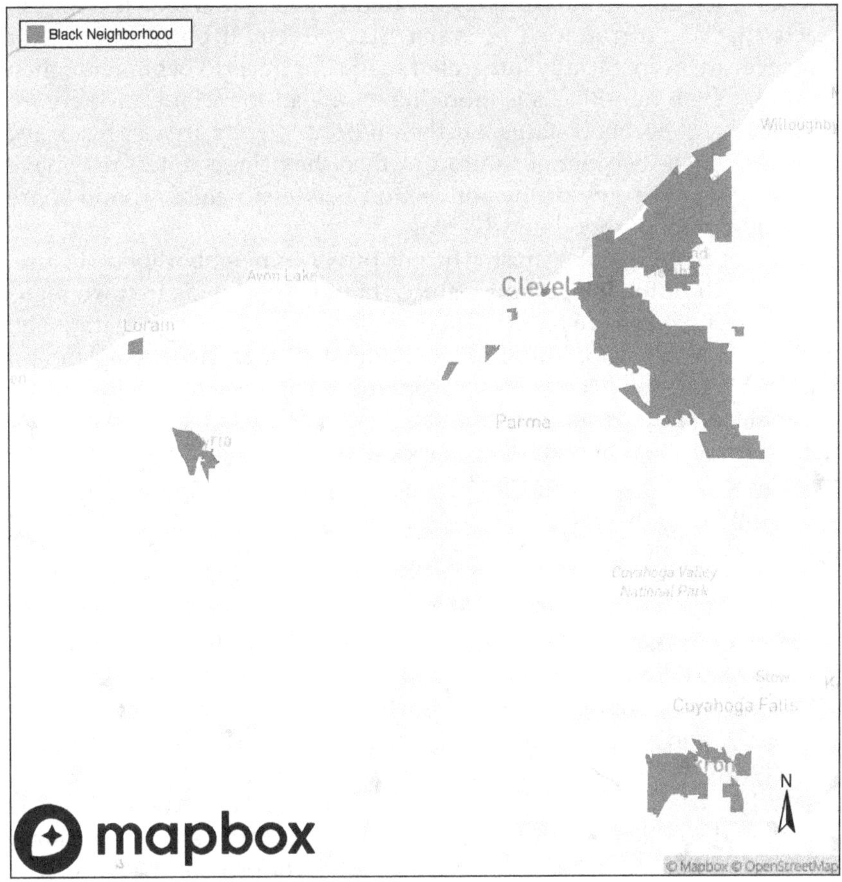

Source: Author's tabulation of American Community Survey Five-Year Estimates (U.S. Census Bureau 2019).

neighborhoods on the other side of these borders became Black neighborhoods. Although racial tipping often produced neighborhoods with a very high share of Black families, the process took time; thus, border neighborhoods tended to be more racially integrated, particularly during these transitions. Importantly (and fortunately), racial tipping has been less common in recent decades, and some metros may even be more likely to racially tip in the opposite direction—previously Black neighborhoods transitioning from Black to something else. These integrative (or in some cases, gentrifying) moves are more likely to occur along the border rather than in the core of a Black enclave.[17] We know from survey evidence that majority-Black neighborhoods are the least preferred, regardless of the race of the respondent.[18] Given this preference, integrative moves into border tracts are far more likely, as non-Blacks will avoid locating in tracts that are surrounded by other Black tracts. If border tracts, for instance, are more racially integrated than core tracts to begin with, then an influx from non-Blacks is more likely to lead to racial transition out of Black neighborhood status. Further, if border tracts are less Black *and* have higher socioeconomic indicators, then the prior chapters may have underestimated some of the connection between neighborhood share Black and neighborhood disadvantage.

Census tracts are the most efficient proxy in neighborhood studies. Virtually all of the interesting features of neighborhoods that we regularly collect data on are reported at the census tract level. Comparatively, a look back at figures 5.1 through 5.4 illuminates the challenges of defining a neighborhood conceptually and operationalizing that neighborhood in a dataset. Is each series of shaded shapes in Philadelphia one Black neighborhood? What about the shapes that border one another but that may be separated by a barrier? We cannot possibly know about all of these barriers and the social and spatial arrangements and relationships that define thousands of neighborhoods across 172 metropolitan areas. Even if we had information about all of these complexities, the mind boggles at how to operationalize that in a dataset with a consistent set of neighborhoods. Galster defines a neighborhood as "the bundle of spatially based attributes associated with a proximate cluster of occupied residences, sometimes in conjunction with other land uses."[19] It's a wonderful and succinct definition. Operationalizing it is another matter entirely. All of this is indicative of a long-standing issue in segregation research known as the modifiable areal unit problem (MAUP).[20] There is no optimal solution for the MAUP, although explicitly spatial measures for segregation have been developed.[21] The underlying logic of these measures informs what I do in this chapter, even if they are probably more complex than necessary for describing the sociospatial characteristics of Black neighborhoods.

Further, while census tracts may not be the correct size and shape for every situation, capturing the appropriate size and shape of the unit of analysis is only one issue. Regardless of how the unit is defined, there is always the question of what to do with the information in adjacent areas. For the purposes of understanding the neighborhood characteristics of Black neighborhoods, the key limitation of treating census tracts as islands is that we do not consider the characteristics of adjoining tracts, or how close census tracts with similar (or dissimilar) attributes are to one another. This has long been understood in segregation research as the "checkerboard" problem.[22] Given two types of neighborhoods, they can be arranged like the red and black squares on a checkerboard, with all the reds and blacks clustered together with similar squares, or in any way between those two extreme arrangements.

Core and Border Census Tracts

In this chapter, I address the checkerboard problem more directly than the MAUP, but I have some ways of mitigating the latter. I have two ways of addressing the checkerboard problem. First, I identify whether neighborhoods border Black or non-Black neighborhoods. There are several reasons to look at census tracts along the border of Black enclaves, where we can test the hypothesis that census tracts along the border might be different in some meaningful ways, owing either to the spatial dynamics of racial tipping or perhaps, as Camille Zubrinsky Charles discusses, the racial determinants of residential location decisions.[23]

Recent research also shows that gentrification is a spatial process that is likely to affect tracts along the border of enclaves of affluence as well. Veronica Guerrieri, Daniel Hartley, and Erik Hurst find that when city economies grow, the borders of affluent neighborhoods expand.[24] This expansion can lead adjacent neighborhoods to transition from relatively impoverished ones to greater affluence, thus serving as a source of racial transition from a Black neighborhood to a non-Black one. Given the spatial geography of race and affluence in American cities, racial transitions of this type would occur along the border of Black enclaves adjacent to an expanding affluent neighborhood.

My primary focus is on comparing border Black tracts to core tracts, but I also look at tracts along the non-Black border. Keeping in mind that there is wide variation in the number of census tracts that each tract (Black or not) can border, I created eight categories of census tracts in this analysis:[25]

1. Black core tracts: only border other Black tracts
2. Black border tracts: a Black census tract that borders at least one non-Black tract
3. Black census tracts that border two or more non-Black tracts
4. Black census tracts that border four or more non-Black tracts
5. Non-Black core tracts: only border other non-Black tracts
6. Non-Black border tracts: non-Black census tracts that border at least one Black tract
7. Non-Black census tracts that border two or more Black tracts
8. Non-Black census tracts that border four or more Black tracts[26]

I define Black and non-Black border tracts in multiple ways because there is likely to be variation in the length and nature of borders; defining

Figure 5.5 Black Core and Black Border Neighborhoods, by Year, 1970–2017

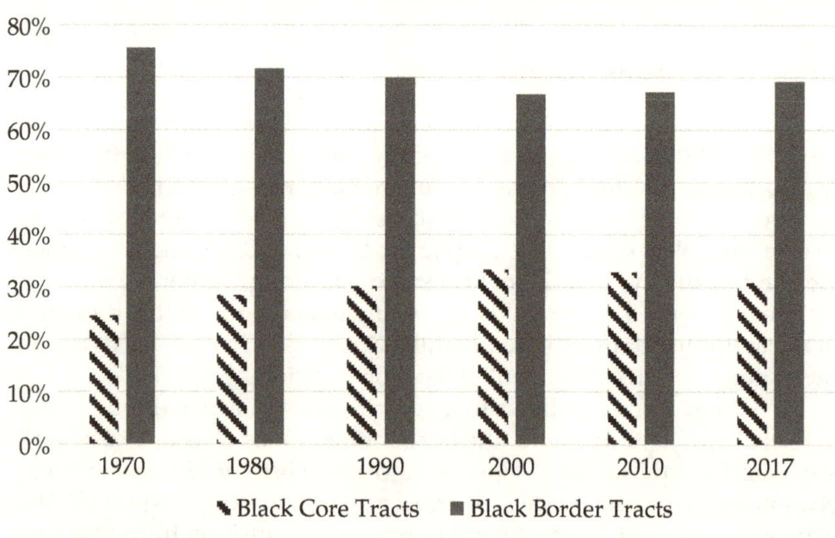

Source: Author's tabulation of U.S. 2010 Longitudinal Tract Database (Logan, Xu, and Stults 2014) and American Community Survey Five-Year Estimates (U.S. Census Bureau 2019).

them in only one way—for instance, as those that border tracts of the other type (such as Black bordering non-Black)—leaves out some nuance. Some Black tracts that border one non-Black tract may share a long border, some may share a very short border, and some of those borders might be entirely uninhabited. I chose two and four non-Black census tracts somewhat arbitrarily, but these numbers signify 25 percent and 50 percent, respectively, of the high end of the total number of bordering tracts for most census tracts. The vast majority of census tracts in the sample border eight or fewer census tracts.

Figure 5.5 displays the share of Black census tracts that are core and border (using the simplest definition of border), by year. The share of Black census tracts in the core (that do not border a non-Black census tract at all) rose from 25 to 33 percent from 1970 to 2010, and then declined a bit, to 31 percent, in the most recent ACS. The decline is likely to be a function of growth in the size of Black enclaves, which creates additional core tracts faster than border tracts are added. The share of Black tracts bordering at least two non-Black tracts declined from 61 percent in 1970 to 50 percent in 2010. Black tracts bordering at least four non-Black tracts declined from 32 to 22 percent. In other words, the majority of Black border tracts border more than one non-Black tract, but a minority border four or more.

Table 5.1 Poverty Rates for Core and Border Black Neighborhoods, 1970–2017

	1970	1980	1990	2000	2010	2017
Black core neighborhoods	25%	29%	29%	26%	30%	27%
Black border neighborhoods	28	28	29	26	29	26
Black neighborhoods bordering at least two non-Black neighborhoods	28	28	29	25	28	26
Black neighborhoods bordering at least four non-Black neighborhoods	28	27	29	25	27	25

Source: Author's tabulation of U.S. 2010 Longitudinal Tract Database (Logan, Xu, and Stults 2014) and American Community Survey Five-Year Estimates (U.S. Census Bureau 2019).

Table 5.1 looks at poverty rates in these four types of Black census tracts, between which there is a surprising lack of variation. The biggest gap in any year is actually the result of *lower* poverty rates in Black core tracts in 1970, but the gap is only three percentage points. In the last two years measured, poverty rates were highest in core tracts, and they were lower as Black tracts bordered more non-Black tracts, but there is only a two-percentage-point gap between Black core tracts and Black tracts bordering four or more non-Black tracts in 2017. These are surprisingly small differences. Poverty rates are high on average, regardless of core or border location.

For comparison's sake, the differences between core non-Black tracts and border non-Black tracts (bordering at least one Black tract) are also small, though larger than with Black census tracts. Core non-Black census tracts, which do not border Black census tracts, have considerably lower poverty rates than those along the border, but the gap shrinks over time (table 5.2). In 1970, the poverty rate in core tracts was less than half that of those that bordered at least four tracts, but by 2017 the poverty rate in core non-Black tracts had risen to 12 percent and the border tracts ranged from 17 to 19 percent. There is more evidence for relative disadvantage along the non-Black border than for advantage along the Black border.

Table 5.3 provides a fuller picture of demographic and housing characteristics in the most recent year of data, the 2015–2019 ACS. The biggest differences, by far, are in racial composition. Only 7 percent of residents of Black core census tracts were White, compared to 21 to 25 percent in border tracts, a share that rises with the number of non-Black border tracts. Core Black census tracts were 81 percent Black, compared to 51 percent of tracts that bordered four or more non-Black tracts. The share of Hispanics in census tracts with four or more non-Black border tracts was double that in core Black tracts (16 to 8 percent). The difference was also double for the share Asian, though that share was very low (between

Table 5.2 Poverty Rates for Core and Border Non-Black Neighborhoods, 1970–2017

	1970	1980	1990	2000	2010	2017
Non-Black core neighborhoods	8%	9%	9%	10%	13%	12%
Non-Black border neighborhoods	14	15	16	15	18	17
Non-Black neighborhoods bordering at least two Black neighborhoods	16	17	18	16	19	18
Non-Black neighborhoods bordering at least four Black neighborhoods	18	19	20	17	19	19

Source: Author's tabulation of U.S. 2010 Longitudinal Tract Database (Logan, Xu, and Stults 2014) and American Community Survey Five-Year Estimates (U.S. Census Bureau 2019).

2 and 4 percent) in all Black census tract types. Generally, border tracts are racially integrated. However, looking at this at one point in time could be deceiving, as not all racially integrated neighborhoods remain so for a long time.[27] The disadvantage index is considerably higher in core Black tracts, which are nearly one standard deviation more disadvantaged than the average tract in the sample, compared to two-thirds of a standard deviation for Black tracts with four non-Black borders.

Some counterintuitive differences appear in table 5.3 when comparing median rent and home value numbers. Black core census tracts have higher rents and home values than do border tracts, probably because very small Black enclaves are unlikely to have any "core" tracts at all—all of the Black census tracts are likely to border non-Black tracts. By contrast, very large Black enclaves will have many core Black census tracts. The metropolitan areas most likely to have large Black enclaves are the largest metropolitan areas, which have high-demand and high-cost housing. Metros such as New York, Washington, D.C., and, to a lesser extent, Los Angeles are likely to have a high number of core Black tracts as well as famously high housing costs and thus are probably skewing the housing cost averages in core Black tracts.

To better compare core and border housing costs, figure 5.6 presents median home values and median rents expressed as within-CSA percentiles. Here, the relationship is turned on its head and follows a more predictable pattern: as Black tracts gain more non-Black border tracts, median rents and home values increase. But these differences are still quite small. Core Black tracts are in the thirty-fourth and twenty-eighth median rent and home value percentiles, respectively, and that jumps to only thirty-ninth and thirty-first for all border tracts, which are effectively the same as Black tracts with two or four (or more) non-Black border tracts.

For comparison, table 5.4 provides a fuller set of demographic and housing variables for non-Black border tracts. There is less need to normalize these variables by using within-CSA percentiles because of the large number

Table 5.3 Demographic and Housing Characteristics of Core and Border Black Neighborhoods, 2017

	Black Core Neighborhoods	Black Border Neighborhoods	Black Neighborhood Borders, Two or More Non-Black Neighborhoods	Black Neighborhood Borders, Four or More Non-Black Neighborhoods
Percent White	7%	21%	23%	25%
Percent Black	81	60	56	51
Percent Hispanic	8	13	14	16
Percent Asian	2	3	4	4
Median rent	$904	$868	$873	$882
Median home value	$205,016	$178,299	$178,330	$185,963
Percent homeowner	48%	48%	48%	47%
Vacancy rate	14%	12%	12%	12%
Disadvantage index	0.97	0.75	0.71	0.66

Source: Author's tabulation of American Community Survey Five-Year Estimates (U.S. Census Bureau 2019).

Figure 5.6 Within-CSA/CBSA Median Home Value and Rent Percentiles, Black Core and Black Border Neighborhoods, 2017

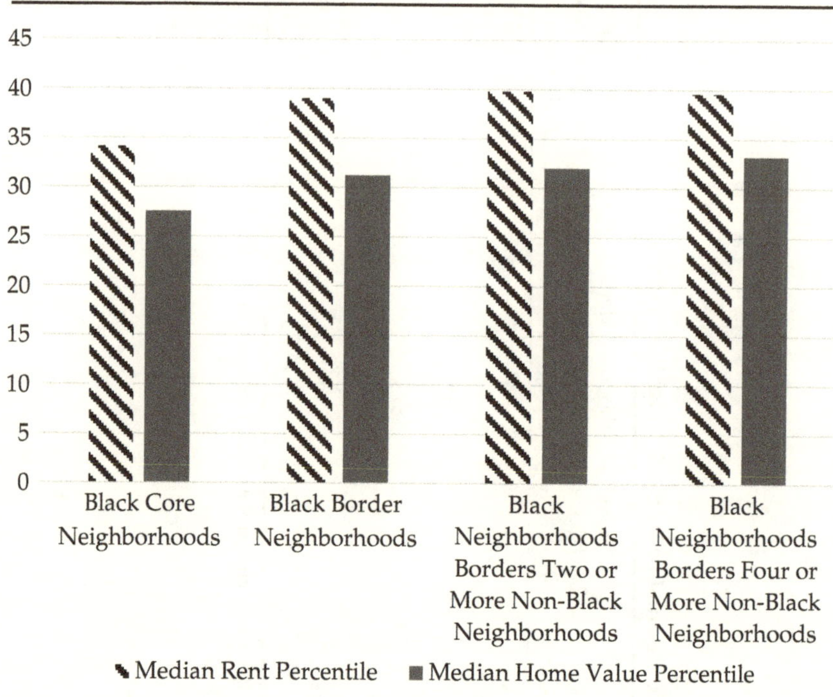

Source: Author's tabulation of U.S. 2010 Longitudinal Tract Database (Logan, Xu, and Stults 2014) and American Community Survey Five-Year Estimates (U.S. Census Bureau 2019).
Note: The medians are population-weighted averages of median census tract home values and rents.

of tracts in every metropolitan area. The differences between core non-Black tracts and border non-Black tracts are much more substantial. The simplest conclusion is that something about a non-Black census tract located along the border of a Black enclave is more different than a Black census tract located on the other side of that border. In other words, the demographic and housing market effects of being a Black neighborhood or *located near* a Black neighborhood are more consistently apparent in the socioeconomic conditions that the data represent. A Black neighborhood is likely to be disadvantaged in particular ways, regardless of its spatial orientation. A non-Black neighborhood located near a Black neighborhood is *also* likely to be disadvantaged in the same ways, if to a lesser extent. In non-Black census tracts that border four or more Black tracts, the median household income is 75 percent as high as in core non-Black tracts, and the share of Blacks is four

Table 5.4 Demographic and Housing Characteristics for Core and Border Non-Black Neighborhoods, 2017

	Non-Black Core Neighborhoods	Non-Black Border Neighborhoods	Non-Black, Borders Two or More Black Neighborhoods	Non-Black, Borders Four or More Black Neighborhoods
Poverty rates	12%	17%	18%	19%
Median household income	$81,233	$65,317	$63,177	$61,091
Percent White	63%	53%	50%	47%
Percent Black	6	20	24	29
Percent Hispanic	20	19	18	17
Percent Asian	7	5	5	4
Median rent	$1,189	$997	$968	$950
Median home value	$346,747	$238,520	$223,792	$211,798
Percent homeowner	66%	60%	59%	58%
Vacancy rate	8	10	11	11
Percent with less than a high school diploma	11	14	14	14
Percent with a BA degree or higher	36	32	31	31
Disadvantage index	–0.23	0.10	0.16	0.21

Source: Author's tabulation of American Community Survey Five-Year Estimates (U.S. Census Bureau 2019).

and a half times higher. Median rents are 80 percent as high and median home values are 60 percent as high. The gap in the disadvantage index is similar, however: about four-tenths of a standard deviation compared to one-third of a standard deviation between core and four-border Black tracts.

Central Cities and Suburbs

A less precise way of looking at how characteristics of Black neighborhoods differ across space is to identify whether the neighborhoods are located within central cities or suburbs. There are limitations to this dichotomy, as jurisdictional boundaries do not determine socioeconomic differences, but they are more determinant of inputs and amenities than census tract boundaries. As American suburbs age, the socioeconomic differences between urban and suburban areas are becoming less stark, but gaps in affluence between cities and suburbs are still quite large.

The census does not have a perfect way of determining whether a census tract is located in a central city or a suburb. I use a variable called the legal/statistical area description (LSAD).[28] Figure 5.7 shows change over time in the share of Black and non-Black neighborhoods located in the central city of the metropolitan area. In 1970, 83 percent of Black neighborhoods were located in the central city, but by 2017 that share was down to 67 percent. For non-Black neighborhoods, the share was steady—between 35 and 40 percent (the high in 1970).

Table 5.5 presents poverty rates for Black and non-Black neighborhoods in and outside of central cities from 1970 to 2017. For Black neighborhoods in central cities, poverty rates fluctuated between 27 and 31 percent and were at their lowest in the most recent decade. In the suburbs, Black neighborhood poverty rates declined considerably, from 26 to 18 percent. Outside of Black census tracts, poverty rates increased everywhere and at a similar rate—from 11 to 16 percent in central cities and from 7 to 10 percent in the suburbs. Perhaps the most interesting finding here is that Black neighborhoods in the suburbs have poverty rates almost as low as those for non-Black neighborhoods in central cities.

Table 5.6 provides a fuller picture of demographic and housing variables in central cities and suburbs for Black neighborhoods in 2017. Household income is considerably higher in suburban Black census tracts, although racial differences are rather small, in contrast to what we saw in comparing core and border Black census tracts. The disadvantage index is double in central cities, and homeowner rates are considerably higher in the suburbs, but education characteristics are not hugely different. Rents are lower and home values are higher in central cities. This contradicts the idea that landlords are compensated for renting in riskier neighborhoods, on the assumption that the age of the housing stock makes central-city neighborhoods riskier on average.

Figure 5.7 Share of Black and Non-Black Neighborhoods in Central-City Neighborhoods, 1970–2017

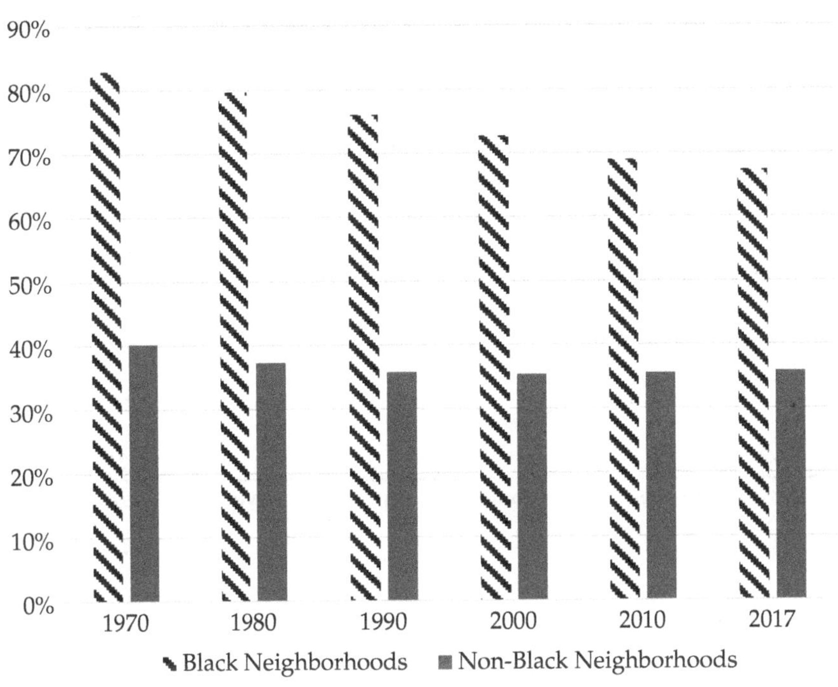

Source: Author's tabulation of U.S. 2010 Longitudinal Tract Database (Logan, Xu, and Stults 2014) and American Community Survey Five-Year Estimates (U.S. Census Bureau 2019).

Table 5.5 Poverty Rates in Black and Non-Black Neighborhoods in Central Cities and Suburbs, 1970–2017

	1970	1980	1990	2000	2010	2017
Black neighborhoods, central cities	28%	30%	31%	28%	30%	27%
Black neighborhoods, suburbs	26	22	21	18	20	18
Non-Black neighborhoods, central cities	11	12	14	15	18	16
Non-Black neighborhoods, suburbs	7	8	8	8	11	10

Source: Author's tabulation of U.S. 2010 Longitudinal Tract Database (Logan, Xu, and Stults 2014) and American Community Survey Five-Year Estimates (U.S. Census Bureau 2019).

Table 5.6 Demographic and Housing Characteristics in Black and Non-Black Neighborhoods in Central Cities and Suburbs, 2017

	Black Neighborhoods, Central Cities	Black Neighborhoods, Suburbs
Median household income	$41,515	$57,591
Percent White	15%	20%
Percent Black	68	62
Percent Hispanic	11	12
Percent Asian	3	3
Median rent	$808	$983
Median home value	$190,515	$178,398
Percent homeowner	42%	56%
Vacancy rate	15	11
Percent with less than a high school diploma	18	14
Percent with a BA degree or higher	20	24
Disadvantage index	1.05	0.46

Source: Author's tabulation of American Community Survey Five-Year Estimates (U.S. Census Bureau 2019).

Centrality

I assess the spatial location of Black neighborhoods in two additional ways: centrality and clustering. Owing to great heterogeneity across metropolitan areas in the number of political and economic centers, the connections between centrality and socioeconomic conditions, and other aspects of urban form, there is no perfect way to measure centrality or its relationship to socioeconomic characteristics in Black neighborhoods. I follow Matthew Holian in choosing a central point that is the imputed location of the central business district (CBD), then measure the distance of every census tract, and every Black census tract, from that central point.[29] The centrality of Black neighborhoods relates to the extent to which these neighborhoods are located in central cities versus suburbs. The farther the distance, the more likely the census tract is located in the suburbs.

Figure 5.8 shows the average distance from the city center for Black neighborhoods and non-Black neighborhoods from 1970 to 2017. Black census tracts have always been closer to the city center, on average, than non-Black tracts. But both types of neighborhoods have been located farther from the city center over time. In 1970 the average Black tract was 6.6 miles from the city center, whereas the average non-Black tract was 12.6 miles away. By 2017 those distances had increased to 10.7 miles and 16.4 miles, respectively.

A very low share of neighborhoods of any type (approximately 2 percent) are located within a mile of the CBD, reflecting largely commercial

Figure 5.8 **Average Number of Miles from the City Center, Black and Non-Black Neighborhoods, 1970–2017**

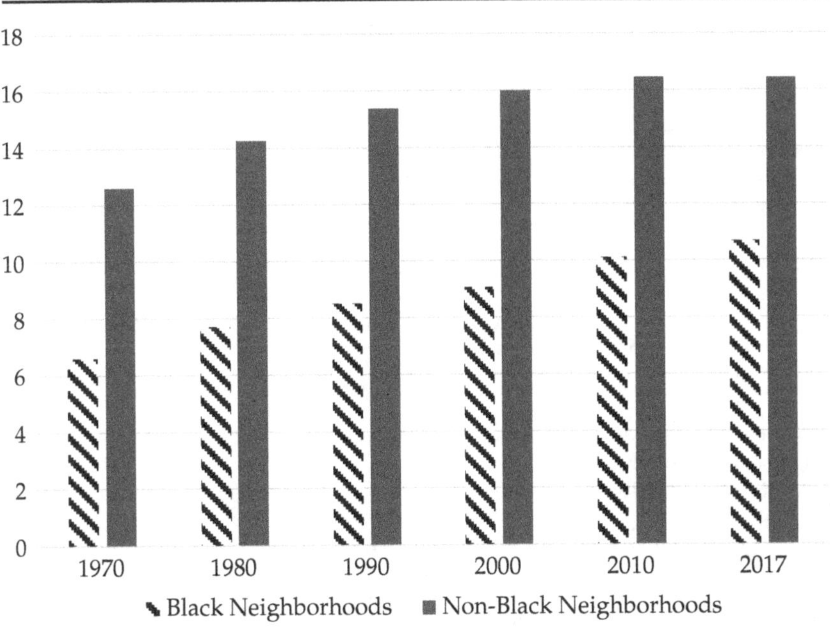

Source: Author's tabulation of U.S. 2010 Longitudinal Tract Database (Logan, Xu, and Stults 2014) and American Community Survey Five-Year Estimates (U.S. Census Bureau 2019).

uses for those areas. For that reason, I look at neighborhoods within and beyond five miles of the CBD. There are big differences between Black and non-Black neighborhoods within five miles of the CBD—over 43 percent of Black neighborhoods are within that distance, versus 19 percent of non-Black neighborhoods. The reverse is true for neighborhood locations greater than fifteen miles from the CBD—nearly 40 percent of non-Black neighborhoods and under 14 percent of Black neighborhoods are located that far from the CBD. And there are large differences in some key indicators between Black neighborhoods located within a short distance of the CBD versus those located beyond it. Table 5.7 presents key demographic indicators for Black neighborhoods located within the CBD and five miles beyond it. Poverty rates are eleven percentage points higher within five miles of the CBD, where they surpass 30 percent. Median household incomes are nearly $18,000 higher in Black neighborhoods more than five miles beyond the CBD. The differences in racial composition are scant, which is a result of selecting on race; we have seen before that Black

Table 5.7 Demographic Indicators for Black Neighborhoods Located within and beyond Five Miles of the Central Business District, 2017

	Black Neighborhoods Five Miles or Less from CBD	Black Neighborhoods More than Five Miles from CBD
Percent poverty	31%	20%
Median household income	$35,884	$53,568
Percent White	17%	17%
Percent Black	68	65
Percent Hispanic	10	13
Percent Asian	2	3
Median rent	$705	$963
Median home value	$162,131	$198,243
Percent homeowner	39%	51%
Vacancy rate	17	11
Percent with less than high school diploma	19	15
Percent with a BA degree or higher	18	23
Disadvantage index	1.26	0.61

Source: Author's tabulation of U.S. 2010 Longitudinal Tract Database (Logan, Xu, and Stults 2014) and American Community Survey Five-Year Estimates (U.S. Census Bureau 2019).

neighborhoods vary in racial composition, but not in this case. And that is an interesting contrast with the other indicators in table 5.7. Median rents and home values are substantially higher in Black neighborhoods farther away from the CBD, as are homeowner rates, and vacancy rates are much lower. Given the locational benefits of being closer to the CBD, it is particularly notable that rents and home values are so much higher in Black neighborhoods farther away. But given the history of centrally located Black neighborhoods and the aging housing stock typically found in those neighborhoods, it is not particularly surprising. The slightly higher educational attainment in Black neighborhoods farther away from the CBD contribute to the big gap between these types of neighborhoods in the disadvantage index, which is more than twice as high in Black neighborhoods within five miles of the CBD.

I also look at centrality at the CSA level, but a more accurate way to examine this is to look at the distance of the average *Black individual* from the CBD rather than Black neighborhoods. The weakness of looking at centrality from the perspective of the Black neighborhood is that there are so many CBSAs, and even CSAs, with very low numbers of Black neighborhoods. Although looking at the distance from the central point of the CBD of the average Black person is a departure from the key unit of

Table 5.8 Average Distance (in Miles) from the Central Business District, 2010

	Midwest ($N = 38$)	Northeast ($N = 15$)	South ($N = 92$)	West ($N = 7$)
Mean Black population–weighted distance between all neighborhoods and the CBD	5.8	6.8	8.7	11.9
Mean total population–weighted distance between all neighborhoods and the CBD	9.7	11.7	10.8	14.2

Source: Author's tabulation of U.S. 2010 Longitudinal Tract Database (Logan, Xu, and Stults 2014).

analysis of the book, it makes more sense than looking at the distance of the average Black neighborhood from the central point of the CBD.[30] And in so doing, I uncover some interesting patterns and associations.

In table 5.8, I present two population-weighted distances from census tracts to the central point in each CBSA. The first row presents the Black population–weighted distance and the second row is the total population, by region of the country, all in the 2010 census. Each metric essentially measures how far the census tract of the average Black person (first row) or person of any racial or ethnic background (second row) is from the central point of the CBSA. This coarse breakdown by region reveals some interesting differences. Midwestern populations are more centrally located regardless of race, and northeastern Black populations are much more centrally located than the general population. Importantly, the regions where the Black population is most centrally located (in total and in comparison to the population overall) are the regions where Black neighborhood disadvantage tends to be highest—in the Midwest and Northeast.

Concentration

Centrality is one way in which Black neighborhoods and populations can be dispersed (or not) across metropolitan space. Another is spatial concentration, which may have implications for whether Black neighborhoods are more or less disadvantaged. On the one hand, in metropolitan areas where Black neighborhoods are more spatially concentrated, individuals may be more cut off from resources or amenities, and Black sections of town may be more identifiable and marginalized. On the other hand, some concentrated Black enclaves may provide vital support for their predominantly Black residents. Prince George's County, Maryland, is an extremely affluent example.

I use a common measure of spatial concentration to assess the extent to which Black neighborhoods and the Black population are clustered

Table 5.9 Spatial Concentration of Black Individuals and Black Neighborhoods, 1970–2017

	1970	1980	1990	2000	2010	2017
Spatial concentration, percent Black	0.44	0.48	0.51	0.55	0.57	0.54
Spatial concentration, Black neighborhoods	0.31	0.32	0.33	0.37	0.35	0.34

Source: Author's tabulation of U.S. 2010 Longitudinal Tract Database (Logan, Xu, and Stults 2014) and American Community Survey Five-Year Estimates (U.S. Census Bureau 2019).

across space.[31] Specifically, it measures how much the value of a variable (such as percent Black, or whether it is a Black neighborhood) in one tract is correlated with the same variable in its neighboring census tract. The measure varies from –1 (no concentration or similarity to neighboring census tracts) to 1 (total similarity with its neighbors). The maps of Chicago, Detroit, and Philadelphia in figures 5.1 through 5.3 illustrate how this measure evaluates the spatial concentration of Black neighborhoods. In those maps, Detroit's Black neighborhoods look more concentrated than Chicago's, which look more concentrated than Philadelphia's. All three of their spatial concentration numbers are high, but Detroit's is highest (0.77), followed by Chicago's (0.73), and then Philadelphia (0.65).

Table 5.9 shows how the spatial concentration of the Black population and Black neighborhoods has evolved over time. For both the share Black in a census tract and the binary indicator of whether a neighborhood is predominantly Black, all of the values are above zero, indicating more spatial concentration than not. And despite recent decreases in isolation and dissimilarity indices for Blacks, the spatial concentration of the Black population and Black neighborhoods stayed steady or grew through at least 2000 (Black neighborhoods) or 2010 (percent Black).[32] Black neighborhood spatial concentration has always been lower than percent Black spatial concentration and did not increase after 1970 as the percent Black spatial concentration did.

To assess the strength of associations between the centrality and concentration of the Black population and neighborhoods and outcomes in Black neighborhoods, I ran regression models using the poverty rate in Black neighborhoods, at the CSA level, as the dependent variable. These models replicate those in chapter 4, adding the weighted average of the Black population's distance from the CBD and the measure for spatial concentration as independent variables. In the framework of chapter 4's models, these variables are neighborhood sorting processes similar to other measures of segregation by income and race.[33]

The results are summarized in table 5.10. The top three rows have the results of the key variables. The first two rows are measures of spatial

Table 5.10 Models Assessing the Association between Black Clustering, Centrality, and Poverty Rates in Black Neighborhoods

Variables				
Black spatial concentration	−0.0725* (0.0435)	−0.0731** (0.0293)		
Black neighborhood spatial concentration			−0.0781** (0.0334)	−0.0745*** (0.0202)
Black population average distance from CBD	0.000448 (0.00253)	0.00291* (0.00155)	0.000144 (0.00247)	0.00283* (0.00146)
Total population average distance from CBD	−0.00490* (0.00262)	−0.00372** (0.00149)	−0.00450* (0.00256)	−0.00361** (0.00139)
Black-White dissimilarity	0.164** (0.0628)	0.112** (0.0467)	0.173*** (0.0606)	0.108** (0.0433)
Percent professional	0.110 (0.170)	0.332*** (0.115)	0.0936 (0.157)	0.301*** (0.104)
Percent manufacturing	−0.131* (0.0692)	−0.172*** (0.0467)	−0.141** (0.0667)	−0.181*** (0.0437)
Average family income (in thousands of dollars)	−0.00255*** (0.000619)	−0.00211*** (0.000438)	−0.00256*** (0.000587)	−0.00206*** (0.000408)
Gini coefficient	0.585*** (0.170)	0.320*** (0.104)	0.576*** (0.168)	0.327*** (0.103)
Black neighborhood inequality	0.00454 (0.00910)	−0.00715 (0.00699)	0.00375 (0.00913)	−0.00790 (0.00694)
Percent Black	−0.109*** (0.0385)	−0.109*** (0.0297)	−0.102*** (0.0372)	−0.103*** (0.0286)
Income segregation (H index)	0.116** (0.0453)	0.0396 (0.0355)	0.126*** (0.0441)	0.0439 (0.0327)
Percent in housing more than thirty years old (BN)		0.00642 (0.0296)		0.0127 (0.0289)
Percent female-headed households (BN)		0.454*** (0.0564)		0.457*** (0.0563)
Unemployment rate (BN[a])		0.521*** (0.0602)		0.532*** (0.0608)
Percent with less than a high school diploma (not BN)		0.378*** (0.0543)		0.354*** (0.0550)
Percent Hispanic (BN)		0.0392 (0.0618)		0.0258 (0.0572)
Percent Hispanic (not BN)		−0.146*** (0.0540)		−0.134** (0.0520)
South	−0.0266* (0.0150)	0.00254 (0.0108)	−0.0253* (0.0146)	0.00379 (0.0104)

(Table continues on p. 136)

Table 5.10 ***(Continued)***

Variables				
Northeast	−0.00176	−0.0281**	−0.00119	−0.0271***
	(0.0158)	(0.0112)	(0.0152)	(0.0103)
West	−0.0794***	0.00170	−0.0826***	−0.00436
	(0.0224)	(0.0141)	(0.0212)	(0.0136)
Year 1980	0.0332**		0.0328**	
	(0.0161)		(0.0153)	
Year 1990	0.109***	0.0631***	0.108***	0.0579***
	(0.0257)	(0.0138)	(0.0244)	(0.0137)
Year 2000	0.115***	0.0734***	0.116***	0.0661**
	(0.0342)	(0.0256)	(0.0325)	(0.0252)
Year 2010	0.187***	0.142***	0.185***	0.129***
	(0.0425)	(0.0369)	(0.0405)	(0.0364)
Year 2017	0.204***	0.196***	0.204***	0.183***
	(0.0509)	(0.0436)	(0.0485)	(0.0426)
Constant	0.0848	−0.226***	0.0779	−0.222***
	(0.102)	(0.0568)	(0.100)	(0.0547)
Observations	448	394	448	394
R-squared	0.467	0.808	0.475	0.815

Source: Author's tabulation of U.S. 2010 Longitudinal Tract Database (Logan, Xu, and Stults 2014) and American Community Survey Five-Year Estimates (U.S. Census Bureau 2019).

Note: Robust standard errors in parentheses. Standard errors are clustered by the metropolitan area.

[a]BN denotes average characteristics of the relevant variable in Black neighborhoods within the metropolitan area.

***$p < 0.01$; **$p < 0.05$; *$p < 0.10$

concentration. The first two columns use a measure of spatial concentration based on the Black population, and the second two columns measure the spatial concentration of Black neighborhoods. The second and fourth models include neighborhood-level socioeconomic controls. The results are very similar. In three of the four models, spatial concentration is strongly, negatively associated with higher poverty rates in Black neighborhoods. The more concentrated these neighborhoods are, the lower the poverty. This runs counter to the expectation that increased segregation is bad for Black neighborhoods and suggests that there is a positive enclave effect from Black neighborhoods being more concentrated in the same residential space.

The third-row variable is the average distance of the Black population from the CBD, or its centrality. I include the distance from the CBD for the metro population as a control in the next row, to control for the geographic dispersion of the overall population. The association between

Black centrality and Black neighborhood poverty tests the hypothesis that a more suburbanized Black neighborhood is more likely to be less impoverished. The results in two models suggest the opposite relationship, albeit weakly—that metros with more suburbanized Black populations have higher Black neighborhood poverty rates. It's not quite that simple, however, because distance and suburbanization are not the same thing. In a sense, the findings on centrality and concentration concur with one another. Metropolitan areas with Black neighborhoods (and population) that are less concentrated are likely to also have less centralized Black neighborhoods, since concentrated Black neighborhoods tend to be in central cities. To be clear, these are only associations and should not be interpreted as summarizing causal relationships. Although these results do not allow us to conclude whether the spatial concentration or the centrality of Black people or neighborhoods is likely to be *causing* lower poverty rates in Black neighborhoods, they do suggest rather strong associations. Higher segregation levels that do not account for space—the commonly used dissimilarity index—correlate to higher Black neighborhood poverty rates in two of the four models, contrary to the null findings in chapter 4.

Spatial Disadvantage

Finally, I incorporate information from neighboring census tracts to construct a fuller picture of the socioeconomic conditions beyond the borders. Following Sharkey, I assess poverty rates and disadvantage spatially.[34] Specifically, in order to address the limitation of analyzing census tract characteristics as if they were islands in urban space, I identify all of the census tracts that border a focal census tract and average the poverty rate and disadvantage index values of the focal census tract and all of the bordering census tracts.[35]

I begin by assessing whether taking into account information from neighboring census tracts changes the comparative poverty rates or disadvantage index characteristics of Black and non-Black neighborhoods. Figure 5.9 shows poverty rates in Black and non-Black census tracts, in both standard and spatially weighted form. Figure 5.10 shows the same for the disadvantage index, which was the focus of Sharkey's analysis. My disadvantage index is slightly different from Sharkey's, but very similar.

There are a couple of ways to interpret these figures, but what you see is largely what you get: Black neighborhood poverty rates and disadvantage indices are lower when we account for characteristics from surrounding census tracts. We expect extreme poverty rates and disadvantage indices to decline some when we smooth out those characteristics over space, but that does not happen in non-Black neighborhoods.

Figure 5.9 Spatially Weighted and Unweighted Poverty Rates in Black and Non-Black Neighborhoods, 1970–2017

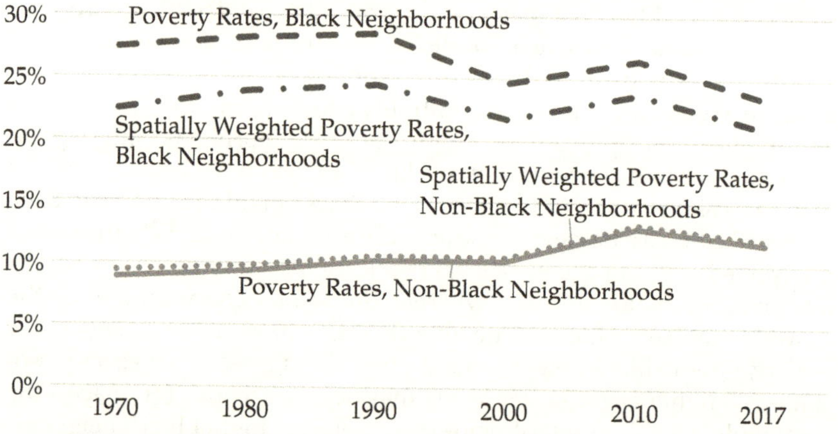

30%
25%
20%
15%
10%
5%
0%
Poverty Rates, Black Neighborhoods
Spatially Weighted Poverty Rates, Black Neighborhoods
Spatially Weighted Poverty Rates, Non-Black Neighborhoods
Poverty Rates, Non-Black Neighborhoods
1970 1980 1990 2000 2010 2017

Source: Author's tabulation of U.S. 2010 Longitudinal Tract Database (Logan, Xu, and Stults 2014) and American Community Survey Five-Year Estimates (U.S. Census Bureau 2019).

Figure 5.10 Spatially Weighted and Unweighted Disadvantage Index in Black and Non-Black Neighborhoods, 1970–2017

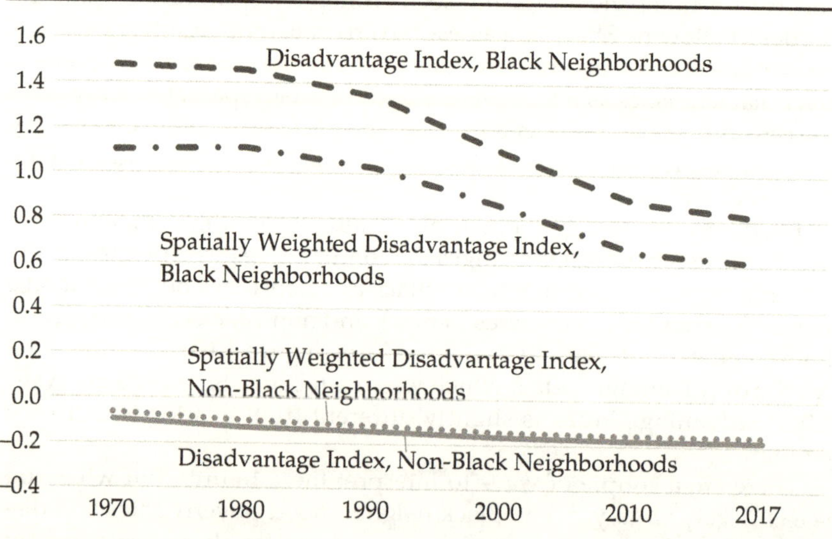

Source: Author's tabulation of U.S. 2010 Longitudinal Tract Database (Logan, Xu, and Stults 2014) and American Community Survey Five-Year Estimates (U.S. Census Bureau 2019).

Table 5.11 Spatially Weighted and Unweighted Advantage and Disadvantage, Black and Non-Black Neighborhoods, 2000 and 2017

	2000	2017
Black neighborhoods, advantaged	7%	11%
Non-Black neighborhoods, advantaged	66	64
Black neighborhoods, spatially advantaged	9	13
Non-Black neighborhoods, spatially advantaged	65	64
Black neighborhoods, spatially disadvantaged, conditional on being advantaged	40	42
Non-Black neighborhoods, spatially disadvantaged, conditional on being advantaged	12	15
Black neighborhoods, advantaged and spatially advantaged	5	6
Non-Black neighborhoods, advantaged and spatially advantaged	58	55

Source: Author's tabulation of U.S. 2010 Longitudinal Tract Database (Logan, Xu, and Stults 2014) and American Community Survey Five-Year Estimates (U.S. Census Bureau 2019).

The poverty rates and disadvantage indices are similar in non-Black neighborhoods whether we incorporate information from neighboring tracts or not.

In figure 5.9, poverty rates in Black tracts are consistently a little bit higher than the spatially weighted rates. The gap is stable, about two to five percentage points. But the gap does narrow over time, as poverty rates using both measures generally decline over time. In figure 5.10, the disadvantage index in Black neighborhoods is considerably lower when we account for surrounding census tracts, although this gap shrinks over time. In 1970, the gap was nearly 0.4 standard deviations, but that had declined to 0.2 standard deviations by 2017. In non-Black census tracts, the gap is basically nonexistent—roughly 0.02 or 0.03 standard deviations throughout the data period.

A key finding from Sharkey is that Black middle-class neighborhoods (or advantaged neighborhoods) are much more likely to be surrounded by disadvantage than non-Black middle-class neighborhoods.[36] This is plainly evident from table 5.11. Following Sharkey, I consider a middle-class neighborhood to be one where the disadvantage index is less than zero. In other words, the disadvantage index in that neighborhood is less than the nationwide mean.

We know that Black neighborhoods are far less likely than non-Black ones to be advantaged, and table 5.11 clearly shows this. In 2000 and 2017, only 7 and 11 percent, respectively, of Black census tracts were measured as advantaged. Although the growth in less than two decades is promising, the increased advantage in Black tracts is far lower than the 66 and 64 percent growth in non-Black tracts in those years. These numbers are nearly

Table 5.12 Spatially Weighted and Unweighted Advantage and Disadvantage, Black Neighborhoods, 1970–2017

	1970	1980	1990	2000	2010	2017
Percent of Black neighborhoods, advantaged and spatially advantaged	2%	3%	5%	5%	5%	6%
Percent of Black neighborhoods, advantaged and spatially disadvantaged	2	2	3	3	4	5
Percent of Black neighborhoods, disadvantaged and spatially advantaged	5	5	4	5	6	6
Percent of Black neighborhoods, disadvantaged and spatially disadvantaged	91	90	88	88	84	83

Source: Author's tabulation of U.S. 2010 Longitudinal Tract Database (Logan, Xu, and Stults 2014) and American Community Survey Five-Year Estimates (U.S. Census Bureau 2019).

identical (9 and 13 percent in Black tracts) when we measure advantage spatially. Where the spatial advantage measure picks up something interesting is when we look at the probability that a census tract is going to be spatially disadvantaged, conditional on being advantaged. Advantaged Black neighborhoods are roughly three times as likely to be spatially disadvantaged as advantaged non-Black neighborhoods.

Table 5.12 looks at concentrated advantage and spatial advantage over time in Black neighborhoods. It shows slow progress over time: the share of Black census tracts that are advantaged and spatially advantaged grew only from 2 to 6 percent from 1970 to 2017. By far the most typical experience for a Black neighborhood is to be disadvantaged and spatially disadvantaged, though this condition has declined in prevalence, from 91 percent in 1970 to 83 percent in 2017.

Wrapping Up: Space and Race Interactions

The goal of this chapter has been to more comprehensively capture variations in Black neighborhood characteristics across metropolitan space. I summarized distinctions between core and border Black census tracts, as well as between Black central-city census tracts and suburban ones. Surprisingly, given how race and space typically interact in U.S. metropolitan areas, differences between core and border Black census tracts were fairly minimal. In fact, differences were greater between core and border non-Black neighborhoods, suggesting that disadvantage along the non-Black border is more common than advantage along the Black border. Black border tracts do appear much more racially integrated than those in the core. The evidence suggests that the demographic and housing market effects of being a Black neighborhood *or* near a Black neighborhood are more consistently baked into the data; that is, a Black neighborhood is likely to be disadvantaged in particular ways, regardless of its spatial orientation. A non-Black neighborhood located near a Black neighborhood is *also* likely to be disadvantaged.

Black people and their neighborhoods are increasingly locating in suburban areas. The average Black neighborhood is located almost 11 miles from the central business district of the metropolitan area, up from 6.6 miles in 1970. Roughly two-thirds of Black neighborhoods are in central cities, down from 83 percent in 1970. Back in 1970, Black suburban and central-city poverty rates were about the same. Since then, Black neighborhood poverty rates have declined considerably in the suburbs, from 26 to 18 percent, but stayed flat in central cities. In regression models, I find that the centrality and the concentration of Black neighborhoods are correlated with lower poverty rates and disadvantage at the metropolitan level: where Black neighborhoods are more centrally located or concentrated, poverty rates and levels of disadvantage are higher. These results are a bit counterintuitive. Centrally located Black neighborhoods are what gave rise to the pejorative term "inner city," so to see more centrally located Black neighborhoods associated with lower poverty is surprising. It is possible that these models are overcontrolling for this relationship. The bivariate connection is clearly different: Black neighborhoods located less than five miles from the CBD have poverty rates of 31 percent, compared to 20 percent for those located more than five miles from the CBD.

Finally, I look at spatial disadvantage to determine whether incorporating data from neighboring census tracts changes the extent to which Black neighborhoods are disadvantaged. These measures largely confirm the nonspatial results. But while spatial and nonspatial disadvantage is basically the same in non-Black neighborhoods, spatial disadvantage is lower in Black ones. On the other hand, I find that advantaged Black neighborhoods are far more likely than advantaged non-Black neighborhoods to be surrounded by disadvantaged neighborhoods. This has not changed since Sharkey provided similar measures using data from the 2000 census.

Incorporating these measures matters because neighborhoods have different sizes and shapes, and census tracts are not islands. When we treat them as such, we assume that census tracts are randomly scattered across urban space, but Black census tracts never are. More consequential than measurement, however, is acquiring a better understanding of the relationships between space and Black neighborhood characteristics, which can shed light on where policy should direct its efforts to assist Black neighborhoods and their residents. Given that Black neighborhood conditions in the suburbs are better than in central cities, and that the gap is widening, efforts to open up suburban jurisdictions and neighborhoods to more housing, especially more affordable housing, should provide Black households with more opportunities to locate in more-advantaged neighborhoods.

Looking at spatial disadvantage complicates how we view relatively advantaged Black neighborhoods. Given that advantaged Black neighborhoods are more likely to be surrounded by disadvantaged neighborhoods than non-Black ones, Black neighborhood advantage may be more fleeting, because high poverty and disadvantaged neighborhoods are often nearby. This suggests the need for more sustained investments in Black neighborhoods to ensure that relatively advantaged outcomes in those neighborhoods do not recede because disadvantaged conditions from surrounding neighborhoods encroach on the advantaged ones.

Finally, looking at measures of concentration complicates the consistent findings that Blacks have become more integrated residentially with other races and ethnicities. Black neighborhoods are just as spatially concentrated in metropolitan areas, on average, as they used to be. Further, while Black neighborhoods have become more racially diverse, their spatial location is actually more concentrated over time.

On the whole, spatial measures largely confirm what we observed in the previous chapter: there is heterogeneity in Black neighborhoods, but they are more consistently disadvantaged and less heterogeneous than non-Black neighborhoods. The most surprising finding is probably that there is so much similarity in housing and socioeconomic characteristics between Black neighborhoods along the border and those in the core. There is something about living in a Black neighborhood—whether border or core—that portends relative disadvantage, giving more evidence that Blackness and spatial disadvantage are strongly interconnected. Border neighborhoods tend to be more racially integrated, and they certainly are in this case. But those racial differences do not also bring big changes in other socioeconomic characteristics. In particularly high-cost metropolitan areas, neighborhoods along the racial border are more likely to undergo racial transition and gentrification. This is the topic of the next chapter.

Chapter 6

Trajectories of Neighborhood Change

You! You can't hurt me
Why? I'm banned in D.C.

—Bad Brains, "Banned in D.C.," 1982

Let's hypothesize that the necessary ingredients for a robust hip-hop scene in the genre's early days were a critical mass of Black people, density, and metropolitan size, and some mix of poverty, crime, drugs, and conflict with the police to help make the lyrics colorful. Washington, D.C., is a very clear counterexample as a scene that never transpired. The most famous MC from the Washington, D.C.–Maryland-Virginia area (aka the DMV) is probably Wale, who, while successful, would be considered a second- or third-tier star in most major markets.

Wale's early career provides a hint about what might have kept D.C. from making significant contributions to rap. He is a rapper, but his early work was a crossover between rap and go-go music. Go-go, a close relative of funk, has been as intertwined with D.C. Black culture since the 1970s as rap has been with South L.A. or South Bronx Black (and Latino) culture. Although the DMV's Black population is diverse and large enough to supply a diverse array of musicians, the go-go scene has probably crowded out the production of hip-hop to some extent, as local Black musicians have long aspired to be the next Chuck Brown rather than Chuck D.[1]

Brown is considered the godfather of go-go, but go-go has produced neither individual stars nor famous bands, songs, or albums.[2] Go-go is a live experience. Kip Lornell and Charles Stephenson describe the musical elements of go-go as a heavy emphasis on percussion and a distinguishing sound coming from congas and timbales.[3] They give credit to the D.C. public schools, where intense marching band rivalries had formed

https://doi.org/10.7758/tjvh5404.9966

by the 1960s, creating a well-trained group of percussionists accustomed to playing as a group of drummers and using multiple types of drums.

Another key element is call-and-response between the lead emcee (often a rapper or an R&B singer) and the crowd. Frequent attendees of a go-go band's shows might know to interject with a particular chant or callout as the band begins a song, even before the emcee gets into it. The centrality of the live experience has kept go-go music distinctly local. While hip-hop is a global behemoth and wealth generator, go-go is provincial. Natalie Hopkinson makes the comparison:

> Go-go took such a wildly different trajectory to hip-hop that it could be seen as a counterdiscourse to this standardization of youth culture. Both art forms have roots in urban youth culture, and their origins are both a byproduct of the urban centers' sociopolitical outlook following the collapse of the industrial economy in the 1970s. . . . Three decades after Black and Latino youth created it in the Bronx, the face of hip-hop remains dominated by Black urban imagery. Yet hip-hop no longer constitutes a uniquely Black public sphere; rather, it has become a global commodity whose profits rarely go to the communities the music ostensibly reflects. . . . Go-go, with its live, heavily percussive instrumentation and discursive, non-linear narrative forms, remains aesthetically faithful to a long history of uniquely Black public spheres. . . . [The recordings' content is] aggressively zoned toward individuals and neighborhoods otherwise ignored by mainstream news media. The lyrical content is not devoid of the negative influences that exist in all communities. However, the individuals both calling and responding to the messages reflect on Black life in a way that is not distorted by multinational profit motives or the international gaze.[4]

Hopkinson's point may be fairly straightforward: the massive growth of hip-hop has left it inevitably shaped by commercial interests, for better or worse, and go-go's small-time success leaves it more strictly under the ownership of its musicians and fans. But it's a particularly critical point with respect to the Black musical tradition. First, Black music, from jazz to the blues to early rock and roll, has consistently been co-opted by non-Black financial interests. Second, and perhaps more importantly, the global hip-hop fanbase has often elevated the artists and content that emphasize the most dysfunctional aspects of Black life—as the prior chapter's discussion of gangsta rap makes clear.

Given D.C.'s status as the nation's "murder capital," go-go could not avoid violent connections and episodes. Go-go's physical epicenter was the same as the center of the D.C. Black community. Shaw and the U Street corridor, which has long served as something like D.C.'s Harlem, were first settled by escaped Black slaves in the early Civil War.[5] In April 1968, visitors to the city were anticipating the arrival of Dr. Martin Luther King Jr. for the Poor People's March on Washington, but then he was gunned down in Memphis. The subsequent riots began on U Street. In the 1980s, U Street was effectively an open-air drug market where prostitution was also rampant.[6] At night, many of the clubs had the hottest go-go bands playing, and fights with and without weapons would break out in the clubs and outside their doors. By the 2000s, the rapidly changing demographics of the neighborhood contributed to a crackdown against go-go by the D.C. government. In 2005, Washington's Alcoholic Beverage Control Board voted to rescind the liquor license for Club U, one of the most popular go-go spots on the U Street corridor.[7] Through ethnographic studies of gentrification in the Shaw–U Street area, both Derek Hyra and Brandi Summers have documented the steady disappearance of go-go music from the area as Black residents left, to be largely replaced by higher-income White transplants.[8]

The racial succession of Shaw–U Street is unprecedented. South Los Angeles transitioned rapidly from a Black belt to a brown one, and while the geographic and time scale of that change was also unprecedented, neighborhood racial succession from Black to Hispanic and Latino was more common across the country than transition to White and tended to come with much less change in a neighborhood's economic characteristics. Such changes in the Black core of D.C. are striking. The neighborhoods known as Shaw and the U Street corridor comprise roughly eighteen census tracts. From 1970 to 2000, at least sixteen of them were Black neighborhoods. In 2010, four of them were no longer Black, and by 2017 five more were no longer Black. At that point, only seven of the original seventeen Black neighborhoods remained. The ten Black neighborhoods that transitioned at some point between 1970 and 2017 were 87 percent Black and 11 percent White in 1970. They were still 56 percent Black and only 20 percent White in 2000. Just a decade later, however, the Black population was an astonishing twenty-three percentage points lower and Whites had gained an almost identical twenty-four percentage points. In the 2015–2019 ACS conducted a few years later, Whites had gained eight more percentage points and Blacks had lost another eight. There are a handful of smaller cases—in Chicago, San Francisco, Atlanta, Philadelphia, Charleston, and Brooklyn—of a cluster of census tracts undergoing similar transitions from Black to White. But the size and historical import of the Shaw–U Street neighborhood transformation makes this a unique case.

The Shaw–U Street neighborhood has accordingly undergone massive socioeconomic change. The poverty rate has gone from 27 to 14 percent in less than five decades. In 1970, the disadvantage index was almost exactly equal to the nation's average for Black neighborhoods; now it is better than average for a non-Black neighborhood. The inflation-adjusted median rent is almost four times as high as it was in 1970, and the median home value has risen over half a million dollars, from $110,000 to nearly

$630,000. The neighborhood has been entirely transformed. Whether the Shaw–U Street transition will be replicated in other Black neighborhoods remains to be seen.

Is There Rising Demand for Living in Black Neighborhoods?

Washington, D.C., has one of the nation's strongest economies, and the city's drop in violence has helped usher in higher demand in the traditionally Black urban core. Whether we can expect Black neighborhoods to racially transition largely depends on whether there is rising demand for living in them. This chapter looks at the pace and nature of change in Black neighborhoods. I first examine racial transitions such as those observed in D.C. and L.A., where Black neighborhoods transitioned from predominantly Black to no longer so and non-Black neighborhoods transitioned into Black ones. After measuring the frequency with which these transitions occur, I look at the characteristics associated with Black neighborhood racial transition. Specifically, I look at the neighborhood indicators of Black neighborhoods that cease being Black neighborhoods, both before and after they racially transition.

We would expect the neighborhoods that were plurality Black throughout the period from 1970 to 2017 to differ in meaningful ways from neighborhoods that "exit" (transition out of being a Black neighborhood). Most obviously, exiting neighborhoods are likely to have lower shares of Black households, since it takes a smaller racial transition for these neighborhoods to change status. Second, they are likely to be in particular metropolitan areas. Not only are Black neighborhoods highly concentrated in a handful of metropolitan areas, but racial change varies across the country. An extreme case is Los Angeles, where immigration helped precipitate the racial transition of the region's Black neighborhoods. Finally, Black neighborhoods that exit Black neighborhood status are likely to be in different locations within metropolitan areas; perhaps they buffer neighborhoods that abut more integrated (and/or less-Black) neighborhoods on the other side of a Black enclave. Particularly in light of contemporary concerns over gentrification and the erasure of Black culture and communities from some cities, it is important to identify where and when this is happening. Further we need to understand the types of economic and housing changes that these neighborhoods undergo while they transition out of Black neighborhood status, and we can observe whether such changes in recent decades are materially different from changes in the past.

Neighborhood change is not only a frequent topic of study but a frequent cause of concern among residents and urban observers. Black people have long struggled to exert power and ownership over their neighborhoods, and with this lack of power comes a legitimate fear that a community can be irreparably changed without community benefit or control. All urban residents lack individual control over neighborhood and city dynamics, but Black and Hispanic/Latino residents in the United States in particular are less likely to own their homes and businesses, less likely to have sufficient political influence to shape urban change, and more likely to live in neighborhoods that are themselves shaped by histories of disinvestment, dispossession, and racial discrimination.

For Black neighborhoods in the United States, however, the empirical fact is that the more common condition is a lack of change, not an abundance of it. As discussed in chapter 3, the significantly older housing in Black neighborhoods is indicative of limited investment in the built environment of those neighborhoods. We also observed, however, that the typical non-Black urban neighborhood has been aging significantly over recent decades as housing production has slowed to a trickle. So while there has long been an age gap between Black and non-Black neighborhoods that contributes to lower demand for living in Black neighborhoods, the shrinking of that gap over time probably makes Black neighborhoods more desirable now than in the past.

Relatedly, living in the more central parts of metropolitan areas—where Black neighborhoods are often located—appears to be more attractive in recent years than at any point since the middle of the twentieth century. The extent to which traditionally Black neighborhoods are likely to experience rapid change hinges in large part on the extent of central-city demand. This is a complicated picture, particularly as we are still learning what impact the recent global COVID-19 pandemic and associated rise in remote work will have on urban population growth.

In terms of raw population, American metropolitan growth continues to be at the fringes. Less dense portions of metropolitan areas, specifically in the Sunbelt, have been the fastest-growing parts of urban America for several decades. Jed Kolko has calculated population densities for all census tracts in the country and put them in eight categories, based on their density.[9] Rural neighborhoods had population density from 0 to 101 people per square mile, four suburban categories ranged from 102 to 2,212, and three urban categories ranged from 2,213 to over 10,000. Population growth from 1990 to 2014 was highest in the four types of suburban neighborhoods, and population declined in all three urban neighborhoods (with the three highest population densities). As of 2014, the "back to the city" movement was hard to uncover in terms of raw population growth. Although Black neighborhoods are most numerous in the South, where population growth is robust, they are rarely located in the fast-growing, low-density fringes of metro areas.

Importantly for questions of gentrification, however, even if people are not urbanizing, money appears to be. Kolko finds that the poorest one-tenth of households were 12 percent less likely to live in urban neighborhoods in 2014 compared with 2000. The richest one-tenth of households were 12 percent more likely to live in higher-density urban neighborhoods and were only 1 percent less urban overall in 2014 than in 2000. The top four income deciles were all more likely to live in higher-density neighborhoods in 2014 than in 2000, while none of the bottom six deciles were.

In an update using recently released decennial census data, Kolko again finds that growth has been most robust in the lowest-density suburbs.[10] Specifically, growth from 2010 to 2020 was 15.5 percent in the lowest-density suburbs and 10.5 percent in the next-densest suburban category. However, the two densest categories (five thousand to ten thousand people per square mile and ten thousand people or more) had the third- and fourth-highest population growth (9.1 and 8.5 percent, respectively). This was a clear rebound of population growth rates in the densest areas from the 1990–2014 rates reported in Kolko's previous analysis. To be sure, only a fraction of these highest-density urban neighborhoods are likely to be Black neighborhoods, but Black neighborhoods are considerably more centrally located and denser than their surrounding metropolitan areas. If demand for dense living continues to rise in U.S. metro areas, demand for living in traditionally Black neighborhoods is likely to rise along with it. In some metros, this rise in demand has surely already occurred.

Famously, there are many definitions of gentrification. For the purposes of this chapter and what is measurable on a broad scale, I follow Jackelyn Hwang and Jeffrey Lin and refer to a "process in which neighborhoods with low SES [socioeconomic status] experience increased investment and an influx of new residents of higher SES."[11] Even when observing changes in income, education, and racial characteristics at the neighborhood level, it is not always clear whether those changes derive from the exodus of lower-SES residents, an avoidance of potential lower-SES residents due to rising rents, or the "influx of new residents of higher SES." Gentrification and displacement are not synonymous under this definition.

Hwang and Lin are also helpful in assessing the extent to which gentrification (as defined here) is increasing in U.S. metro areas, consistent with the growing chorus around the issue.[12] Looking at the 168 largest CBSAs, they estimate the connection between urban spatial structure and neighborhood socioeconomic status (SES) from 1880 to 2010 by graphing neighborhood SES percentile rank (within the metro area) against the distance from the city center. In 1980, the highest-SES neighborhoods were those closest to the city center, and neighborhood SES declined with distance. That relationship has been reversed in all decades since the middle of the twentieth century. But in each successive decade since 1970, the SES of the most central neighborhoods (Hwang and Lin call them "downtown" tracts or neighborhoods) has risen, and SES took a big leap in the neighborhoods closest to the city center between 2000 and 2010. It's complicated, because even in 2010 the neighborhoods farthest from the city center were still the most advantaged, but the most centrally located neighborhoods have been catching up. Hwang and Lin further document that gentrification, as defined, is more common than it used to be but is still relatively rare. In the nation's metros with one million people or more, 1 percent of downtown tracts saw a two-quartile increase in SES. By 2010 that increase was nearly 8 percent, but over a fifty-year span. That left 92 percent of tracts that did *not* experience such a large increase in SES. That said, many more metros are experiencing gentrification. By 2010, more than half of all large metros and 15 percent of small metros had at least one downtown census tract that had experienced a two-quartile jump in SES.

Hwang and Sampson provide evidence that gentrification has been less common in traditionally Black neighborhoods.[13] Looking at the pace of gentrification (measured through field observations and socioeconomic data) in Chicago neighborhoods from 2007 to 2009, they find that the share of Blacks in these neighborhoods in 1980, 1990, and 2000 was negatively associated with the likelihood that neighborhoods would gentrify during that time. Although these findings are from a short period of time and a particular city—and a city where Black neighborhoods are often very disadvantaged, as seen in chapter 4—they suggest that we cannot automatically assume that Black neighborhoods are experiencing a rapid uptick in demand or gentrification.

William Stancil provides further evidence that gentrification is unlikely to be the typical experience for Black neighborhoods—certainly not in the recent past, and probably not for the foreseeable future.[14] He uses the 2000 census and 2012–2016 ACS to classify all census tracts by the neighborhood change they experienced between the two surveys. First, a neighborhood could be economically expanding (where the number of non-low-income individuals increased by more than 10 percent and the share of low-income individuals declined by more than five percentage points) or economically declining (where that number did not change at all). Second, a neighborhood could have low-income population growth or decline. Neighborhoods that are experiencing gentrification and displacement are likely to be those that are economically expanding while the low-income population is in decline. By far, the most common type of neighborhood change is not an influx of higher-income people into low-income neighborhoods, and not a loss of low-income individuals from low-income neighborhoods, but rather a further concentration of low-income individuals. Gentrification is not typical for a low-income neighborhood—further poverty concentration is. But this varies considerably across regions; in two metropolitan areas, Los Angeles and Washington, D.C., a larger

Table 6.1 Share of 1970 Black-Plurality Neighborhoods That Were Also Black-Plurality in Later Decades

	1980	1990	2000	2010	2017
Number and percent that sustained Black plurality through that decade	3,078 (95%)	2,907 (90%)	2,745 (84%)	2,499 (77%)	2,337 (72%)

Source: Author's tabulation of U.S. 2010 Longitudinal Tract Database (Logan, Xu, and Stults 2014) and American Community Survey Five-Year Estimates (U.S. Census Bureau 2019).
Note: In 1970, 3,228 Black-plurality tracts were included in this analysis.

share of residents live in economically expanding low-income areas than in economically declining ones. As I have discussed in this book, these are precisely the metropolitan areas with the most dramatic recent racial transitions of Black neighborhoods.

The way that urban America has sorted itself across urban space has evolved since 1970. Some patterns still hold, such as population growth being most robust (among all racial groups) at the suburban fringe. But the rate of population growth in the country's densest and/or most centrally located neighborhoods is starting to catch up with suburban America. Further, White and higher-income households are undoubtedly more likely to settle or remain in these dense and centrally located areas. Although far from all of these neighborhoods are Black (or ever were), increased demand for central-city living—whether driven by lower crime rates, amenities such as restaurants and nightlife, delayed household formation, reduced racial discrimination by house seekers, or for other reasons—will inevitably make it more likely that Black neighborhoods change as a result.[15] This chapter assesses the extent to which Black neighborhoods transitioned from Black to non-Black ones in different metropolitan areas, and what we can learn from those transitions.

Racial Stability in Black Neighborhoods

Black neighborhoods tend to remain so for multiple decades. There were 3,228 Black-plurality tracts in 1970.[16] Table 6.1 shows how many of them were Black plurality tracts in future decades. Black neighborhoods are stably Black. In some ways, their stability is the flip side of a substantial body of research that assesses the extent to which neighborhoods are stably integrated in the United States. In the early 1970s, Thomas Schelling demonstrated that racial tipping—a neighborhood flipping from White to Black—was inevitable when race was a salient factor in residential location for at least some Whites, and that Whites had heterogeneous preferences for their neighborhood's racial makeup.[17] Later, Ellen countered with a more optimistic take on American segregation by looking at the growing phenomenon of integrated neighborhoods and the prospects for such neighborhoods remaining integrated for long periods of time.[18] She found that nearly 20 percent of neighborhoods were racially mixed in 1990. Further, she reports, over three-quarters of neighborhoods that were integrated in the 1980s remained so ten years later.

A set of recent papers update Ellen's work in both time and methodology, particularly regarding neighborhood diversity (or integration) and changes in racial composition.[19] These authors are more pessimistic than Ellen about both the prevalence and persistence of stably integrated neighborhoods. Steven Holloway, Richard Wright, and Mark Ellis contend that segregation and diversity are growing simultaneously in U.S. metro areas.[20] With immigration, chiefly from Mexico, Central America, and several countries in Asia, U.S. metros and many neighborhoods within them are diversifying. However, the most common type of neighborhood in the United States, as recently as 2010, is a low-diversity, White-dominant (White share 80 percent or more) neighborhood. Wright and his colleagues look at not only how frequently neighborhoods are highly diverse, but also at how many of them remain so for three consecutive decades.[21] Although they define diverse neighborhoods conservatively—in short, only neighborhoods in which no racial group was dominant qualified—a tiny number were found. In 1990, almost 200 of the nation's more than 65,000 tracts were highly diverse, and that number had increased to nearly 1,000 (or roughly 1.5 percent of the total) by 2010. From 1990 to 2000, 104 out of 197 tracts remained highly diverse. From 2000 to 2010, 471 out of 868 remained so. In other words, after ten years, almost half had ceased to be highly diverse.

Table 6.1 makes clear that Black neighborhoods evolve much more slowly than highly diverse neighborhoods. By 2017, 72 percent of Black neighborhoods in 1970 had remained Black through every decade. The pace of racial change is very slow in Black neighborhoods, making clear how anomalous are the rapid changes occurring in D.C. and L.A. Given heightened demand for living in urban neighborhoods, it is possible that Black neighborhoods have been racially transitioning more often in recent decades. There is mild evidence for this. Using the numbers in table 6.1, I calculated that the share of the previous decade's Black neighborhoods that remained that way until the following decade had fallen from 95 percent in the 1970–1980 decade to 91 percent in both 2000–2010 and the truncated 2010–2017. The fact that the most recent period is only seven years (not precisely, because of the 2015–2019 ACS) and has the smallest retention rate is suggestive that Black neighborhoods are a bit more likely to exit that status now than ever before. One clear explanation for this is that the average Black population is smaller in today's Black neighborhoods than in 1970 (down from 81 percent to 66 percent in 1970). Relatedly, immigration

Figure 6.1 Poverty Rates for 1970 and 1980 Black Neighborhoods, 1970–2017

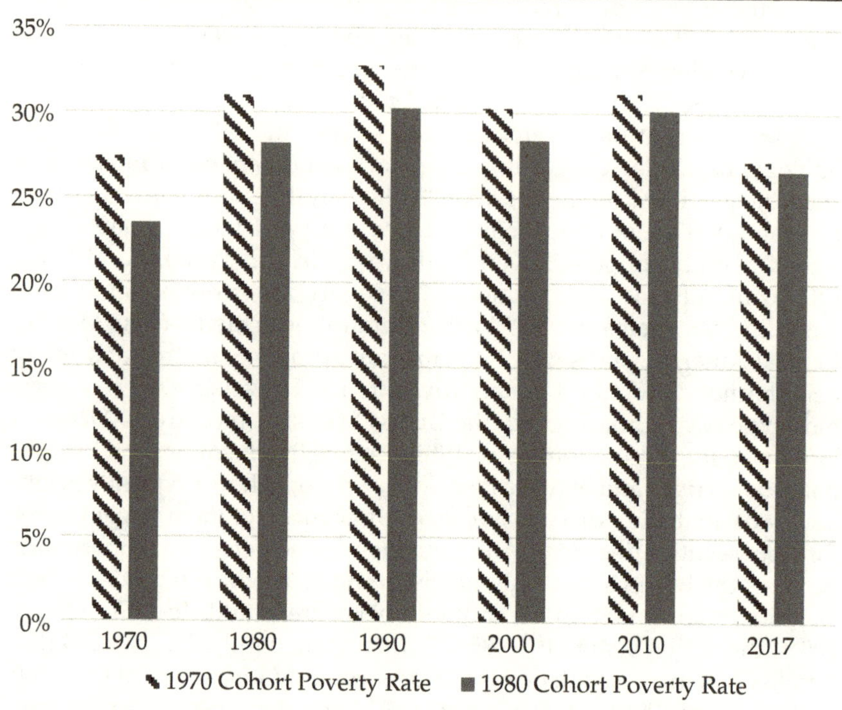

Source: Author's tabulation of U.S. 2010 Longitudinal Tract Database (Logan, Xu, and Stults 2014) and American Community Survey Five-Year Estimates (U.S. Census Bureau 2019).

makes it more likely that other non-White groups will become a plurality in existing Black neighborhoods, as seen with Hispanics and Latinos in many formerly Black neighborhoods in the West.[22] However, the growth of Black neighborhoods has far outpaced the decline, as the total number of Black tracts has more than doubled since 1970.

In chapters 3 and 4, I looked at the characteristics of Black neighborhoods over time and place, but the samples of neighborhoods were a moving target. The group of Black neighborhoods from 1970 to 2017 changed over time, from decade to decade. Here I examine the changes within a consistent sample of neighborhoods in order to speak to the nature of demographic change in the typical Black neighborhood over time. I begin with the 1970 and 1980 cohorts of Black neighborhoods.

The poverty rates of the 1970 and 1980 cohorts (figure 6.1) vary between six and seven percentage points over time. The 1970 cohort poverty rate

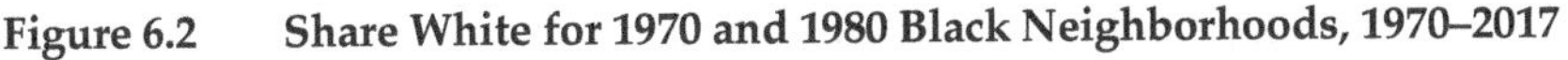

Figure 6.2 Share White for 1970 and 1980 Black Neighborhoods, 1970–2017

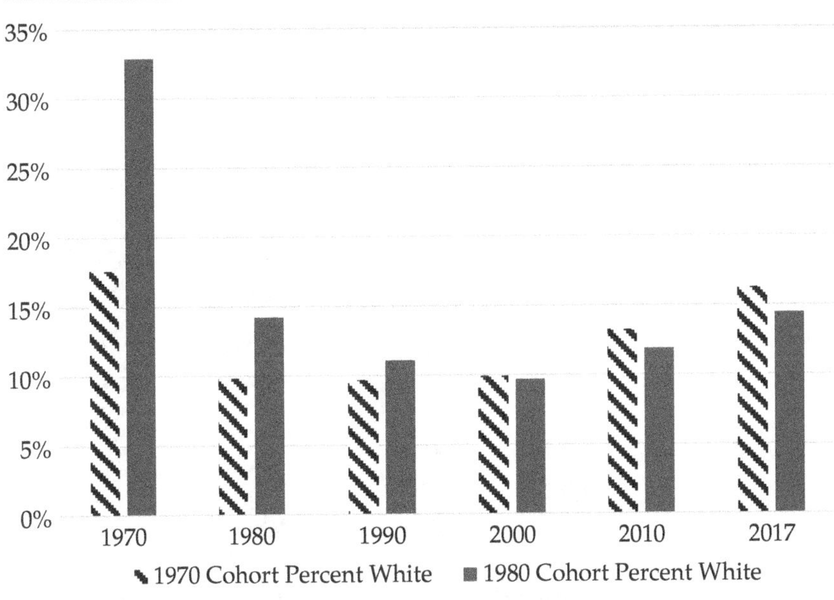

Source: Author's tabulation of U.S. 2010 Longitudinal Tract Database (Logan, Xu, and Stults 2014) and American Community Survey Five-Year Estimates (U.S. Census Bureau 2019).

ranges from 27 to 33 percent, and the 1980 cohort rate ranges from 23 to 30 percent. Both neighborhood groups' poverty rates peaked in 1990 (and again in 2010 for the 1980 cohort), although the nation's poverty rates were highest in 2010.

Racial change has been more dramatic over time in these neighborhoods. The share Black declined over time, owing in part most likely to regression to the mean. Figures 6.2 and 6.3 show the replacement of Black individuals by Whites and Hispanics, but with very different trajectories over time. Figure 6.2 shows that the 1970s were still marked by White flight from Black neighborhoods—the White share declined from 1970 to 1980 in 1970 Black neighborhoods. That share remained around 10 percent until 2010, when it increased a couple of percentage points and continued to rise, to 16 percent, by 2017. These are very small increases, but as noted in chapter 3, they occurred over a period of consistent decline in the share of Whites in metropolitan neighborhoods. The metropolitan areas as a whole were 90 percent White in 1970 but 57 percent White in 2017. The larger change is in 1980 Black neighborhoods, which followed almost a U-shaped pattern. White flight was substantial in these

Figure 6.3 Share Hispanic in 1970 and 1980 Black Neighborhoods, 1980–2017

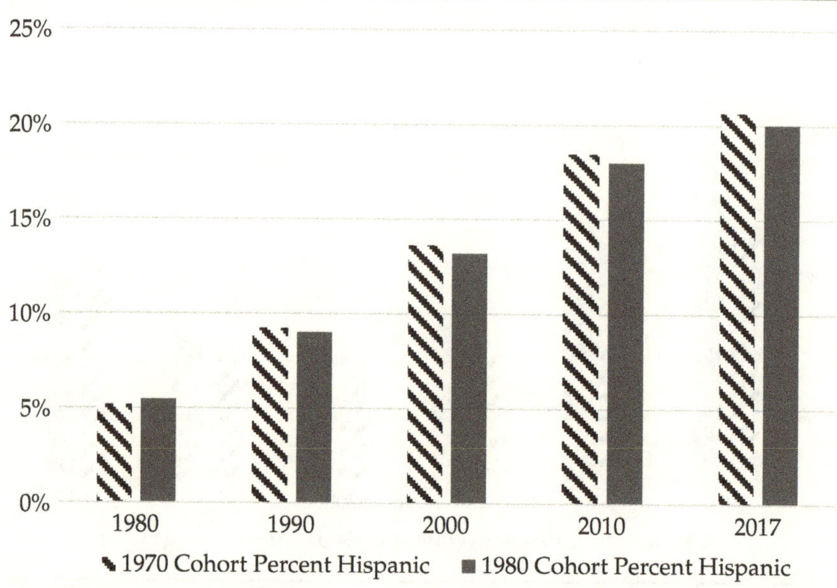

Source: Author's tabulation of U.S. 2010 Longitudinal Tract Database (Logan, Xu, and Stults 2014) and American Community Survey Five-Year Estimates (U.S. Census Bureau 2019).

neighborhoods during the 1970s, when they went from 33 percent White in 1970 to 14 percent White in 1980. As with 1970 Black neighborhoods, the 1980 cohort bottomed out at 10 percent White in 2000, then rose to 14 percent by 2017. The recent rise in White share in 1970 and 1980 Black neighborhoods is a deviation from the historical trend in all urban neighborhoods, including Black ones. This is some additional evidence that White demand for living in traditionally Black spaces is rising.

Hispanics and Latinos were not counted by the U.S. census until 1980. Figure 6.3 thus begins in that year. The share Hispanic in 1970 and 1980 Black neighborhoods climbed steadily from 5 percent in 1980 to roughly 20 percent in 2017. This increase is similar to the overall growth in the Hispanic population in these metropolitan areas, which went from 7 percent in 1980 to 17 percent in 2017.

Figures 6.4 and 6.5 look at what happened to the housing markets in the 1970 and 1980 Black neighborhood cohorts. Both median rents and home values were rather flat for both the 1970 and 1980 cohorts until 2010, when both took a significant jump. From 1970 to 2017, rents rose 79 and 64 percent for the 1970 and 1980 cohorts, which was only slightly higher

Figure 6.4 Average Median Rents for 1970 and 1980 Black Neighborhoods, 1970–2017

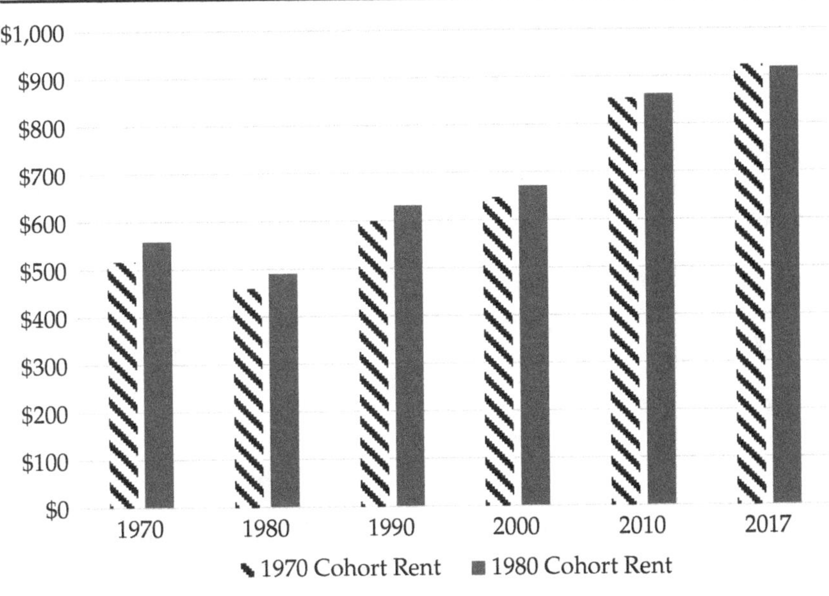

Source: Author's tabulation of U.S. 2010 Longitudinal Tract Database (Logan, Xu, and Stults 2014) and American Community Survey Five-Year Estimates (U.S. Census Bureau 2019).

than the 60 percent increase for all tracts in these metros. However, from 2000 to 2010, rents rose about 30 percent—twice as high as the national average—in these Black neighborhood cohorts. The difference is more pronounced with median home values, which more than tripled in the 1970 Black neighborhood cohort through 2017, including a 64 percent increase from 2000 to 2010, when the country was in the middle of a massive correction to the housing market.

Studying how the 1970 and 1980 cohorts of Black neighborhoods evolved over time is important for several reasons. First, these cohorts remained Black neighborhoods through 2017 at a high rate—72 percent of 1970 Black neighborhoods were still Black in 2017. Second, evaluating neighborhood change requires a stable sample of neighborhoods. And what we learn about these neighborhoods is that indicators generally improved over time, albeit at a slow rate. Interestingly, there is some evidence that the pace of change has picked up in the twenty-first century, which would fit with an increased pace in urban gentrification that has been identified in other studies.[23]

Figure 6.5 Average Median Home Values for 1970 and 1980 Black Neighborhoods, 1970–2017

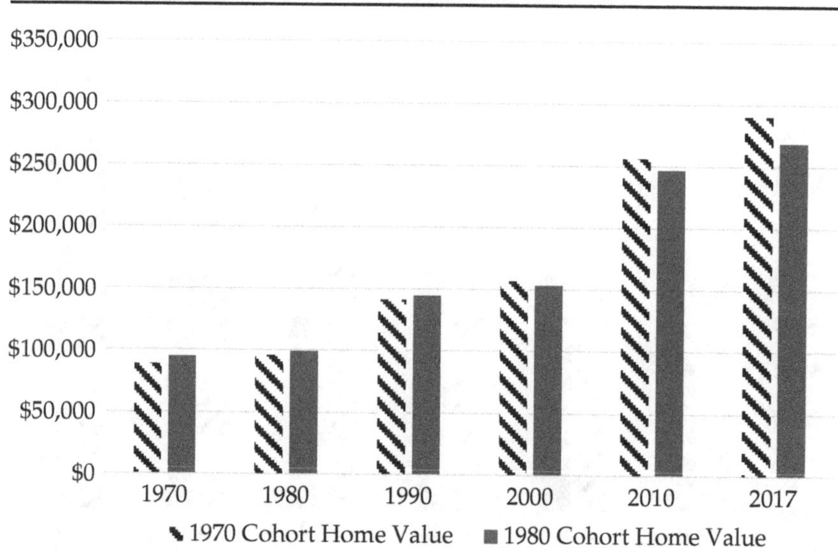

Source: Author's tabulation of U.S. 2010 Longitudinal Tract Database (Logan, Xu, and Stults 2014) and American Community Survey Five-Year Estimates (U.S. Census Bureau 2019).

Formerly Black Neighborhoods

One aspect of gentrification is economic—rising rents and home values either displace lower-income households or exclude them from entering a neighborhood in the first place. A second aspect is racial—whether or not, through these economic forces, neighborhoods that were once racial or ethnic enclaves lose a meaningful share of those residents. In this section, I analyze whether these changes happen in tandem by focusing on Black neighborhoods that I call "exiters": a neighborhood in which another racial group has overtaken Blacks as the most numerous and the neighborhood has thus "exited" Black status.

As noted, the share of Black tracts exiting each decade grows only slowly over time. There are two ways to interpret this. On the one hand, the consistent pace of neighborhoods losing their Black status (from 5 to 8 percent of remaining neighborhoods in each decade, whether looking at the 1970 or 1980 cohorts) suggests that this is not a fast-growing indicator of increasing racial gentrification in the twenty-first century. On the other hand, the 2000s had easily the largest number of exiting 1970 cohort tracts (8 percent) after three decades of exiting had already occurred, so the denominator is lower. An additional case that the pace of exiting Black

Figure 6.6 **Exiting Black Neighborhoods within-CSA/CBSA Share White Percentile, 1970–2017**

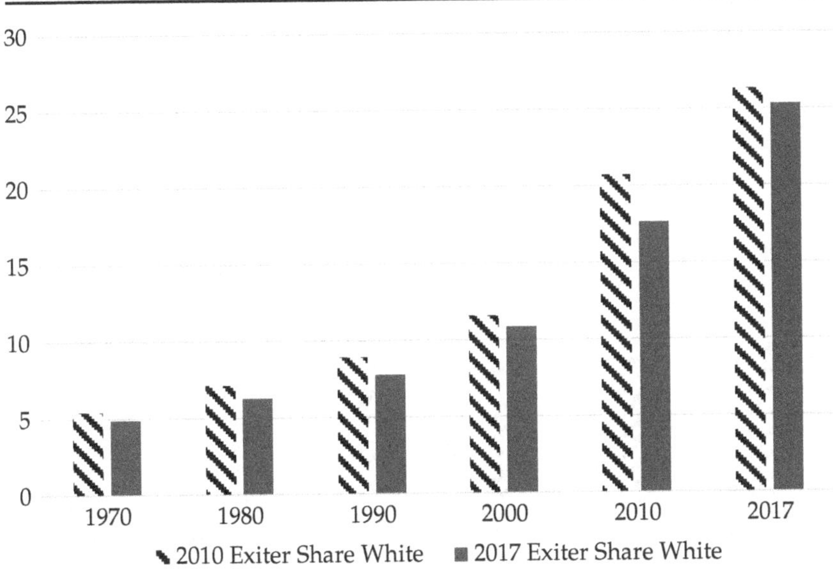

Source: Author's tabulation of U.S. 2010 Longitudinal Tract Database (Logan, Xu, and Stults 2014) and American Community Survey Five-Year Estimates (U.S. Census Bureau 2019).

neighborhoods is on the rise can be made by noting how much of the activity in the earlier decades was in Los Angeles, which accounted for 107 out of 317 exiting Black neighborhoods in the 1980s and 70 out of 270 in the 1990s. If we remove Los Angeles from the equation, the recent pace of racial transition is clearly faster than in the past (although much of that recent transition is concentrated in the Washington, D.C., area).

If the racial and economic processes of gentrification were merged in Black neighborhoods in recent decades, we might expect to see a marked change in these neighborhoods' socioeconomic indicators just as they were transitioning out of Black status. In the upcoming set of figures, I measure characteristics in these neighborhoods according to the percentile rank of each neighborhood within its metropolitan area. Following the literature on gentrification, measuring neighborhoods against other neighborhoods in the same metropolitan area is a more precise measure of gentrification.[24] This method is particularly important when we lump together several metros, since change occurring in a handful of metropolitan areas can be overweighted.[25]

Figure 6.6 shows the within–metropolitan area percentile ranks of neighborhoods that exited Black status in 2010 and 2017, from 1970 to

Figure 6.7 Exiting Black Neighborhoods within-CSA/CBSA Median Income Percentile, 1970–2017

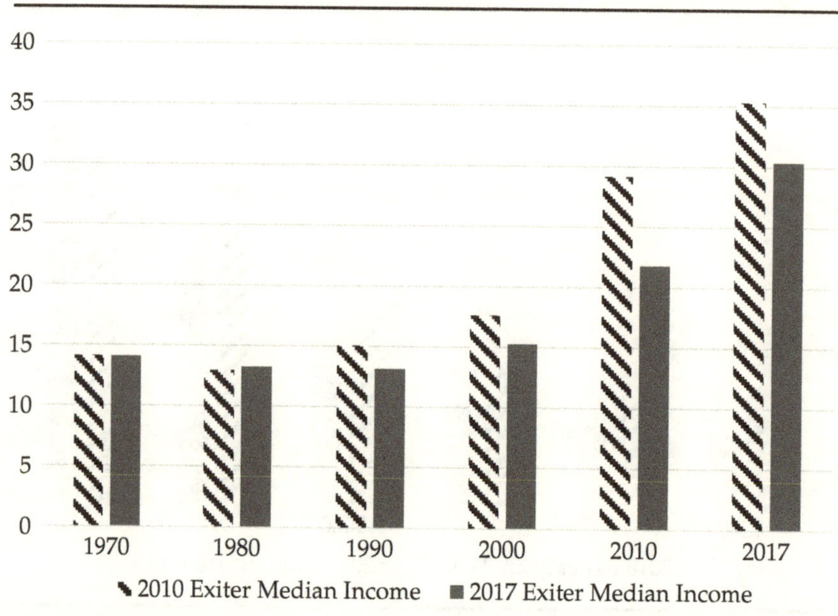

Source: Author's tabulation of U.S. 2010 Longitudinal Tract Database (Logan, Xu, and Stults 2014) and American Community Survey Five-Year Estimates (U.S. Census Bureau 2019).

2017. In 1970, both cohorts were, on average, in the fifth percentile in White share, and this increased very slowly through 2000, when the cohorts were at about the eleventh percentile. The 2010 cohort jumped to the twentieth percentile by 2010, and both were just above the twenty-fifth percentile by 2017. Although these were noticeably large jumps in 2010 and 2017, they were not particularly surprising, as exiting Black neighborhoods had to have some increase in non-Black racial groups, by definition.

In figure 6.7, which looks at neighborhood median income, we see that these percentiles show that it is not just race that is abruptly changing in these neighborhoods as they exit Black status. After holding steady through 2000, median income jumped to the thirtieth percentile in 2010 just as the 2010 exiters were leaving Black status. There was a smaller jump in 2010 for the 2017 cohort; they made it to the thirtieth percentile by 2017. The same figure for the share of households with a BA degree—another common indicator of gentrification—displays a similar trajectory (not shown).

Negative indicators tend to decrease as Black neighborhoods exit Black status, but the changes are not dramatic. This is exemplified by

Figure 6.8 Exiting Black Neighborhoods within-CSA/CBSA Poverty Rate Percentile, 1970–2017

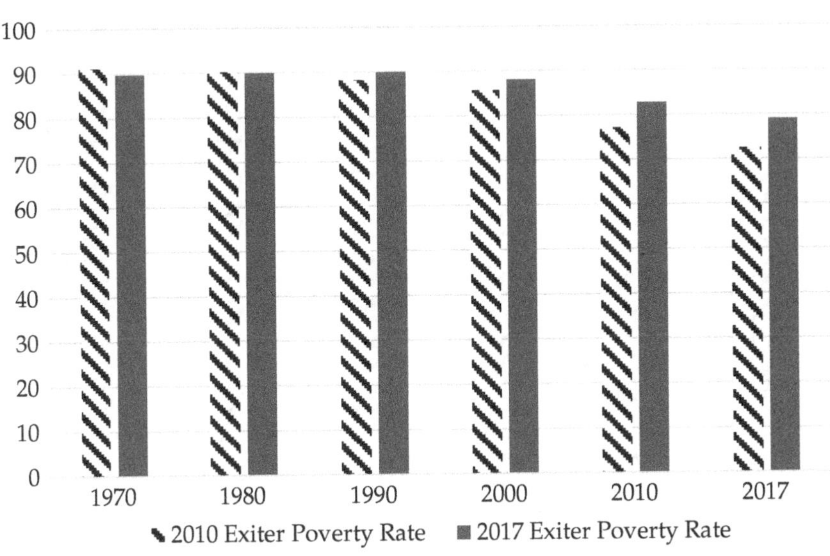

Source: Author's tabulation of U.S. 2010 Longitudinal Tract Database (Logan, Xu, and Stults 2014) and American Community Survey Five-Year Estimates (U.S. Census Bureau 2019).

changes in the poverty rate over time (figure 6.8). The smaller changes in the relative poverty rates in exiting Black neighborhoods suggest that people in poverty were moving out of these neighborhoods more slowly than higher-income households were moving in.

Housing affordability is likely to influence both the pace at which Black neighborhoods exit and the extent to which those exits coincide with other socioeconomic changes in Black neighborhoods, such as lower poverty rates and higher incomes. One way to evaluate this potential connection is to look at the median rent and home value percentiles of exiting Black neighborhoods. Figures 6.9 and 6.10 provide this for neighborhoods that exited in 2010 and 2017. In figure 6.9, we see that rents did not change much until the year in which the two neighborhood cohorts exited, and then they jumped. Figure 6.10 provides median home value percentiles, which have a similar trajectory.

In figure 6.11, I look at median rent and home value percentiles in the decade prior to exiting for all exiting cohorts, 1980 to 2017. Prior-decade home values remain at the twentieth percentile for the 1980 through 2017 exiter cohorts. But the 2010 exiter cohorts had home values above the

Figure 6.9 **Exiting Black Neighborhoods within-CSA/CBSA Median Rent Percentile, 1970–2017**

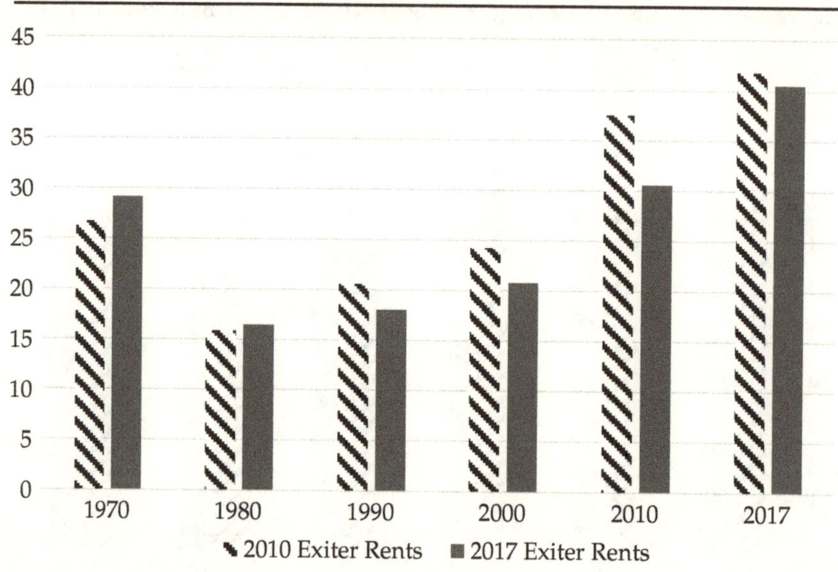

Source: Author's tabulation of U.S. 2010 Longitudinal Tract Database (Logan, Xu, and Stults 2014) and American Community Survey Five-Year Estimates (U.S. Census Bureau 2019).

Figure 6.10 **Exiting Black Neighborhoods within-CSA/CBSA Median Home Value Percentile, 1970–2017**

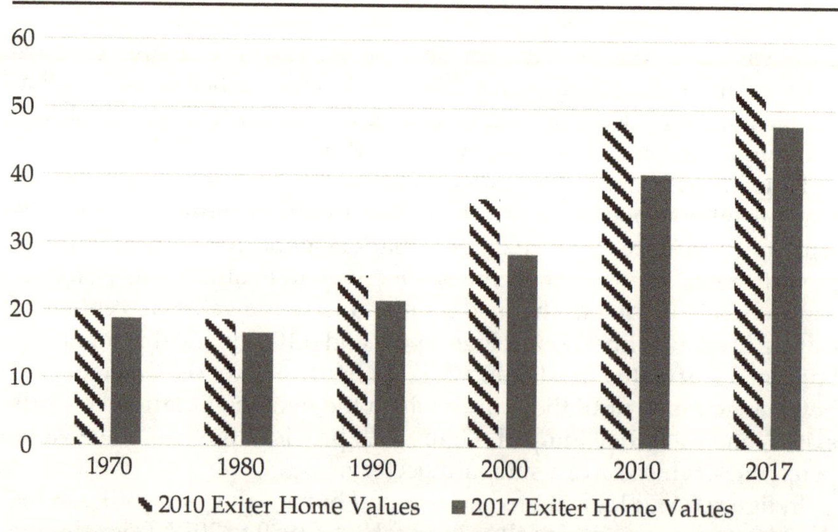

Source: Author's tabulation of U.S. 2010 Longitudinal Tract Database (Logan, Xu, and Stults 2014) and American Community Survey Five-Year Estimates (U.S. Census Bureau 2019).

Figure 6.11 Within-CSA/CBSA Median Rent and Home Value Percentiles One Time Period Prior to Black Neighborhood Exits, 1970–2017

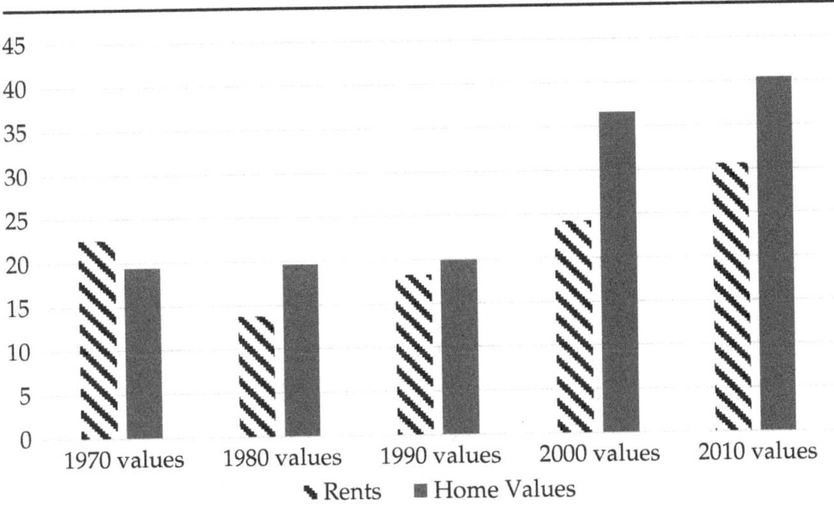

Source: Author's tabulation of U.S. 2010 Longitudinal Tract Database (Logan, Xu, and Stults 2014) and American Community Survey Five-Year Estimates (U.S. Census Bureau 2019).

thirty-fifth percentile in 2000 and the 2017 exiter cohorts had home values in the fortieth percentile in 2010. This coupled with the rises in prior-decade rents for the 2010 and 2017 exiter cohorts, is strong evidence that the rising cost of housing is more likely to contribute to Black neighborhood loss in recent decades.

New Black Neighborhoods

Given that there were more than twice as many Black neighborhoods in 2017 as there were in 1970, new Black tracts are much more numerous than former Black tracts. As figure 6.12 shows, this growth is strongest in the South.

Accordingly, the growth in the South portends better indicators for Black neighborhoods as a group, even if conditions in many individual Black neighborhoods are not changing for the better. Figure 6.13, which shows the poverty rate percentiles for 2010 and 2017 in new Black neighborhoods from 1970 to 2017, is indicative of these better conditions. On the one hand, poverty rates grew over time as these neighborhoods were becoming Black. On the other hand, the worst percentile was the sixty-second. This is considerably better than the typical Black neighborhood, where average percentiles range from the seventy-second to the

Figure 6.12 New Black Neighborhoods by Region, 1980–2017

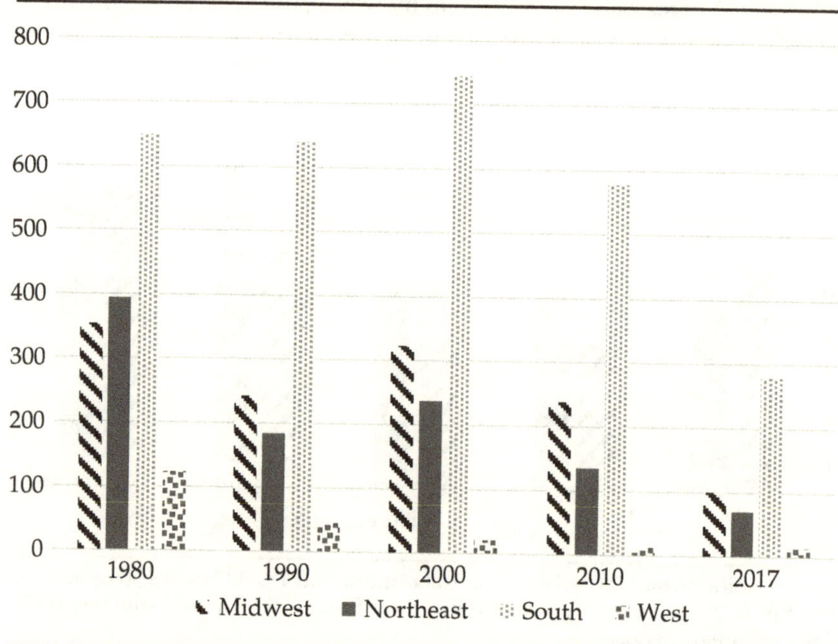

Source: Author's tabulation of U.S. 2010 Longitudinal Tract Database (Logan, Xu, and Stults 2014) and American Community Survey Five-Year Estimates (U.S. Census Bureau 2019).

eighty-ninth over the same time period. These numbers suggest not only that many of the new Black neighborhoods are akin to Black middle-class neighborhoods but also that mobile Black populations are residing in more advantaged areas than Black residents who remain in place.

Gentrification in Black Neighborhoods

Formal definitions of gentrification vary widely. Rapid changes in key demographics—such as the share of neighborhood residents who have a bachelor's degree, who are White, and/or who have higher incomes—are one indicator of gentrification. Such changes tend to be concurrent with rises in rents, changes in neighborhood amenities, and potential displacement of incumbent residents who cannot afford to remain or who feel less connected to their changing neighborhood environment.

Neighborhoods change in many ways and all the time. Absolute changes in neighborhood environment that are strongly felt by residents can result from changes in the metropolitan area that are less about the

Figure 6.13 Poverty Rate Percentiles in New Black Neighborhoods, 1970–2017

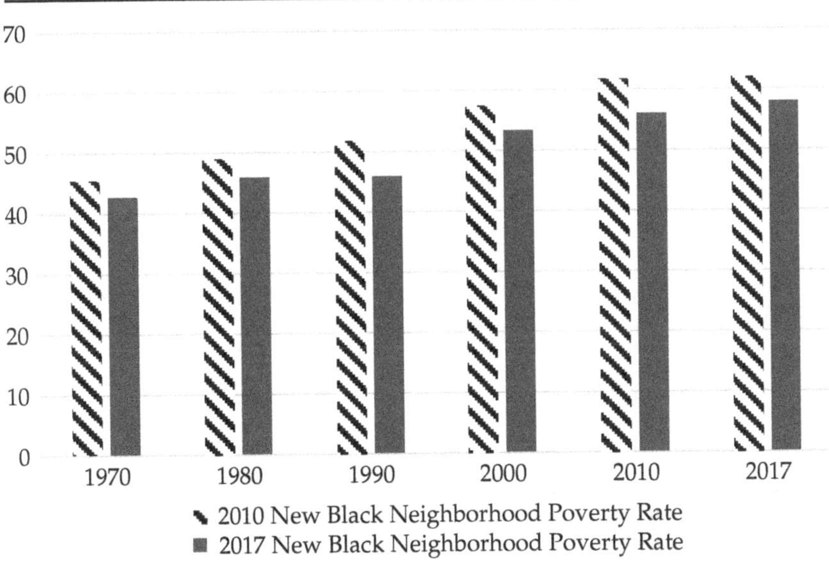

Source: Author's tabulation of U.S. 2010 Longitudinal Tract Database (Logan, Xu, and Stults 2014) and American Community Survey Five-Year Estimates (U.S. Census Bureau 2019).

spatial arrangement of people, resources, and amenities than about the metro's fortunes. For example, since incomes in Washington, D.C., have risen roughly 60 percent since 1970 (in 2010 dollars), incomes in many D.C. neighborhoods have risen as well. Absolute rises in income can feel like gentrification. But to measure processes that relate to local government decision-making and localized housing markets, looking at within–metropolitan area percentiles (as in the previous section) can more accurately capture gentrification.

Following Baum-Snow and Hartley, and Hwang and Lin, I rank each neighborhood individually according to its percentile in three variables: the share with a BA or higher, median household income, and the share White.[26] I then average the three percentiles to arrive at a variable that ranges from one to ninety-nine, with one reflecting the lowest percentiles or income levels in a metropolitan area in that year. In 2017, the average Black neighborhood was in the twenty-second percentile, while the average non-Black neighborhood was in the fifty-fourth. I then considered a neighborhood to have gentrified from one decade to the next if it had risen ten percentile points or more during that time. Figure 6.14 shows the prevalence of neighborhoods meeting this threshold from 1980 to

Figure 6.14 Number of Gentrified Neighborhoods, Full Sample, 1980–2017

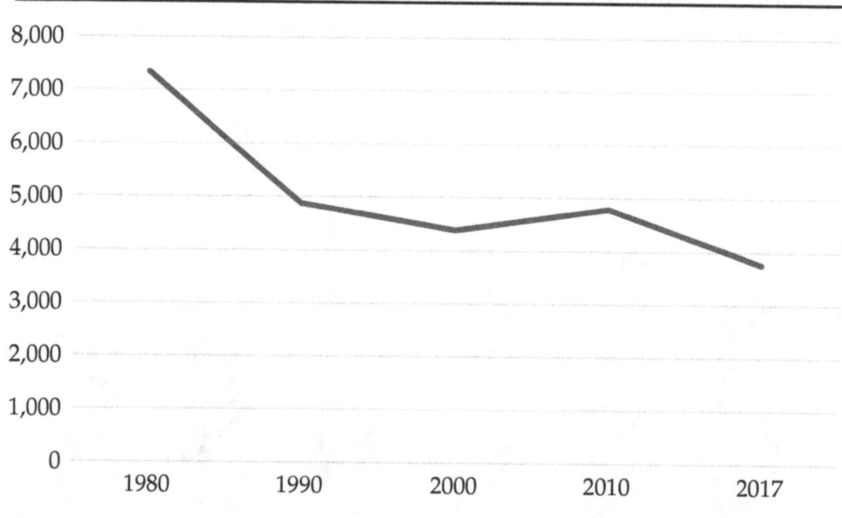

Source: Author's tabulation of U.S. 2010 Longitudinal Tract Database (Logan, Xu, and Stults 2014) and American Community Survey Five-Year Estimates (U.S. Census Bureau 2019).

2017. The number ranges from 7,340 in the 1970s to 3,760 in the 2010s. But there were many more high-poverty neighborhoods in 1970 that were more likely to undergo such large changes, and the 2010s are a truncated decade in our data.

Figure 6.15 shows the share of Black, Hispanic, and high-poverty (20 percent or higher) neighborhoods undergoing gentrification. As in Black neighborhoods, Hispanic neighborhoods are those where Hispanics and Latinos form a plurality of the population. For all three groups, the neighborhood status (Black, Hispanic, or high-poverty) reflects the prior decade. For example, the 1990 gentrification rates in figure 6.15 are expressed as a share of the number of Black, Hispanic, or high-poverty neighborhoods as of 1980. As figure 6.15 shows, the share of Black neighborhoods undergoing gentrification has been rather steady, although there is evidence for increased gentrification presence in the last two decades, given the sharp rise from 4 to 10 percent of Black neighborhoods from 2000 to 2010 and the fact that the shortened 2010s decade has a gentrification share of over 8 percent for Black neighborhoods. Trends are similar in Hispanic and high-poverty neighborhoods. The latter have gentrification rates that meet or exceed those in Black and Hispanic neighborhoods in every decade observed. Contrary to findings from Hwang and Sampson in Chicago, Black neighborhoods are typically gentrifying as frequently as Hispanic ones.[27]

Figure 6.15 Gentrification Rates for Black, Hispanic, and High-Poverty Neighborhoods, 1980–2017

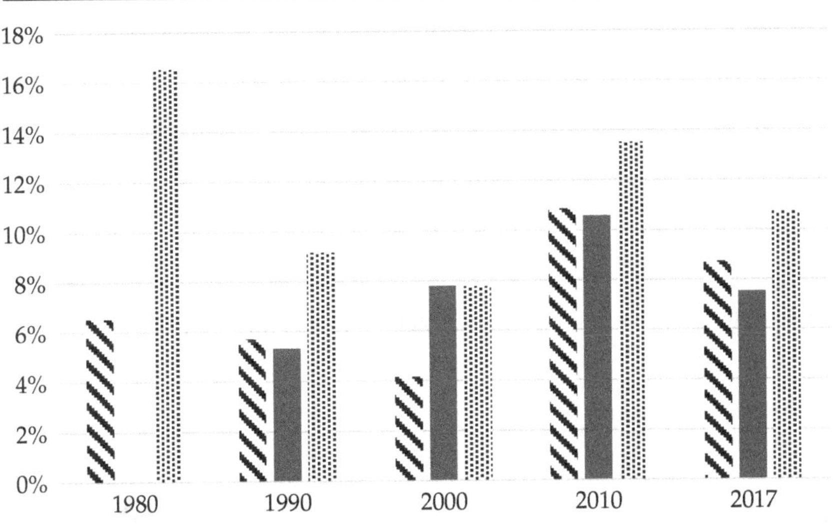

Source: Author's tabulation of U.S. 2010 Longitudinal Tract Database (Logan, Xu, and Stults 2014) and American Community Survey Five-Year Estimates (U.S. Census Bureau 2019).

Given that one of the variables used to determine gentrification is the share White in a census tract, racial change and gentrification overlap, by definition. That said, the disappearance of Black neighborhoods in some metros and its connection to gentrification are worth exploring further. I do this by looking at the confluence of exiting Black status and gentrification. Table 6.2 displays the share of gentrifying Black neighborhoods that also exited Black status and the share of exiting Black neighborhoods that also gentrified, from 1990 to 2017. Not surprisingly, there is substantial overlap between Black neighborhoods that gentrified and exited Black status over the same decade. From 1980 to 1990, 26 percent of Black neighborhoods that gentrified also exited Black status. That proportion never dipped below 17 percent, which happened in 2017. By comparison, only between 6 and 8 percent of Black neighborhoods overall exited Black status in any of the decades between 1990 and 2017. The bottom row of table 6.2 shows the share of exiting Black neighborhoods that also gentrified in that decade. That ranges from 14 to 41 percent, which, again, is much higher than the range of 4 to 11 percent of all Black neighborhoods that gentrified

Table 6.2 Gentrification Rates in Exiting Black Neighborhoods and Exiting Rates in Gentrifying Neighborhoods, 1990–2017

	1990	2000	2010	2017
Proportion of gentrifying Black neighborhoods that also exited Black status in that decade	26%	21%	24%	17%
Proportion of exiting Black neighborhoods that also gentrified in that decade	22%	14%	41%	31%

Source: Author's tabulation of U.S. 2010 Longitudinal Tract Database (Logan, Xu, and Stults 2014) and American Community Survey Five-Year Estimates (U.S. Census Bureau 2019).

Figure 6.16 Black Neighborhood Gentrification Rates by Region, 2010–2017

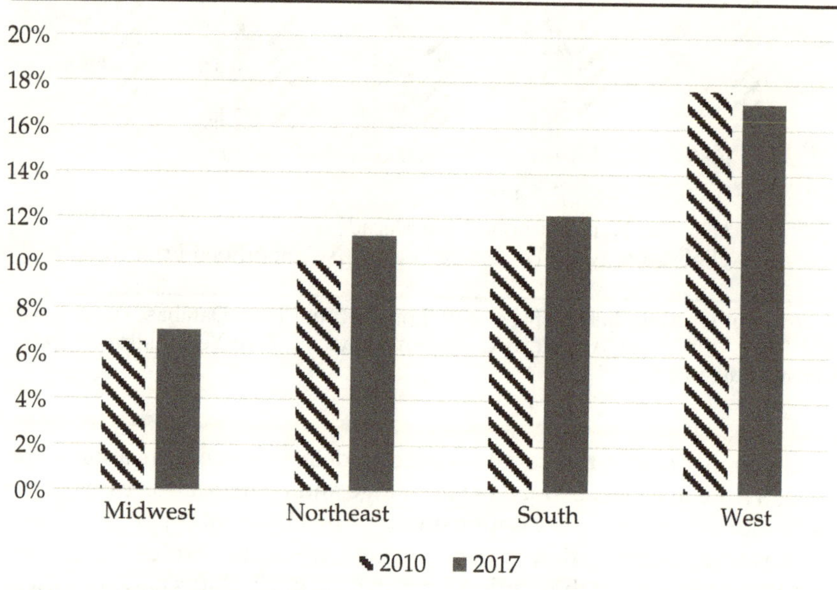

Source: Author's tabulation of U.S. 2010 Longitudinal Tract Database (Logan, Xu, and Stults 2014) and American Community Survey Five-Year Estimates (U.S. Census Bureau 2019).

in any one decade. Notably, gentrification rates for exiting Black neighborhoods rose substantially in 2010 and remained high in 2017.

Black neighborhoods have been gentrifying at a typical pace compared to neighborhoods they can reasonably be compared to; gentrification also appears to be happening more frequently in recent decades, but this trend is not obvious. Where is Black neighborhood gentrification most likely to occur? Figure 6.16 suggests that, since 2000, it is most common in the West and least likely in the Midwest.

Table 6.3 Black Neighborhoods Gentrifying in 2010 and 2017 Combined, Sorted by Total Number of Gentrifying Black Neighborhoods

	Not Gentrified	Gentrified	Total Black Neighborhoods	Percent	Percent of U.S. Total
New York, N.Y.–N.J.–Conn.–Pa.	1,485	210	1,695	12%	16%
Washington, D.C.–Baltimore, Md–Va.–W.V.	882	121	1,003	12	9
Atlanta, Ga.–Ala.	467	68	535	13	5
Chicago, Ill.–Ind.–Wisc.	832	62	894	7	5
New Orleans, La.	251	52	303	17	4
Detroit, Mich.	677	42	719	6	3
Philadelphia, Pa.–N.J.	484	36	520	7	3
San Jose–San Francisco–Oakland, Calif.	104	34	138	25	3
Miami, Fla.	349	33	382	9	3
Houston, Tex.	224	30	254	12	2

Source: Author's tabulation of U.S. 2010 Longitudinal Tract Database (Logan, Xu, and Stults 2014) and American Community Survey Five-Year Estimates (U.S. Census Bureau 2019).

Tables 6.3 and 6.4 list the top ten metros in Black neighborhood gentrification frequency. Table 6.3 sorts the country's metropolitan areas by the number of gentrifying Black neighborhoods in 2010 and 2017, combined. The list is not particularly surprising, as it is largely the list of the metros with the most numerous Black neighborhoods. However, there is substantial variation on this list in the share of Black neighborhoods in these large metros that are gentrifying. Black neighborhood gentrification was rare in Detroit, Chicago, Philadelphia, and Miami, where less than 10 percent of neighborhoods gentrified. By contrast, 25 percent of Black neighborhoods in the San Jose–San Francisco–Oakland metro gentrified during that time, while the next closest gentrification rate was 17 percent in New Orleans.

In table 6.4, the San Jose–San Francisco–Oakland area has the highest Black neighborhood gentrification rate. Three other metros—Nashville, Charleston, and Lake Charles, Louisiana—saw 20 percent or more of their Black neighborhoods gentrifying during this time. At least 16 percent of Black neighborhoods in ten metros met these gentrification thresholds, suggesting that in some Black neighborhoods throughout the country change has been rapid.

Table 6.4 Black Neighborhoods Gentrifying in 2010 and 2017 Combined, Sorted by Share of Black Neighborhoods Gentrifying

	Not Gentrified	Gentrified	Total Black Neighborhoods	Percent	Percent of Total
San Jose–San Francisco–Oakland, Calif.	104	34	138	25%	3%
Nashville–Davidson, Tenn.	56	17	73	23	1
Charleston, S.C.	55	14	69	20	1
Lake Charles, La.	16	4	20	20	0
Saginaw–Bay City, Mich.	17	4	21	19	0
Sumter, S.C.	17	4	21	19	0
Savannah, Ga.	61	14	75	19	1
Chattanooga, Tenn.	27	6	33	18	0
Fayetteville, N.C.	41	9	50	18	1
New Orleans, La.	251	52	303	17	4

Source: Author's tabulation of U.S. 2010 Longitudinal Tract Database (Logan, Xu, and Stults 2014) and American Community Survey Five-Year Estimates (U.S. Census Bureau 2019).

Gentrification is a spatial process. Previous work finds that poorer neighborhoods are more likely to gentrify when they border higher-income ones, because when higher-income residents leave, they often migrate into adjacent neighborhoods.[28] To test whether Black neighborhoods along the border are more likely to gentrify, I calculated gentrification rates, by year, for core and border Black neighborhoods. The results (shown in table 6.5) support the notion that census tracts in the Black core are less likely to experience rapid socioeconomic change in a decade. As recently as 2000, border Black tracts were more than twice as likely to experience gentrification as Black core tracts. All types of Black tracts have become more likely to experience gentrification over time, but the Black core rose to only an 8 percent gentrification rate by 2010—still a few percentage points behind the border tracts.

Table 6.5 Gentrification Rates in Black Core and Border Neighborhoods, 1980–2017

	1980	1990	2000	2010	2017
Black core neighborhoods	3%	3%	2%	8%	7%
Black border neighborhoods	8	7	5	12	10
Black tracts bordering at least two non-Black neighborhoods	8	7	6	13	10
Black tracts bordering at least four non-Black neighborhoods	8	9	8	14	10

Source: Author's tabulation of U.S. 2010 Longitudinal Tract Database (Logan, Xu, and Stults 2014) and American Community Survey Five-Year Estimates (U.S. Census Bureau 2019).

Table 6.6 Exiting Rates in Black Core and Border Neighborhoods, 2010 and 2017

	2010	2017
Black core neighborhoods	1%	1%
Black border neighborhoods	12	11
Black tracts bordering at least two non-Black neighborhoods	16	15
Black tracts bordering at least four non-Black neighborhoods	22	22

Source: Author's tabulation of U.S. 2010 Longitudinal Tract Database (Logan, Xu, and Stults 2014) and American Community Survey Five-Year Estimates (U.S. Census Bureau 2019).

Racial change in Black neighborhoods is even more of a spatialized process. In chapter 5, we observed that in the 2015–2019 ACS, Black neighborhoods in the core were 81 percent Black, while border Black neighborhoods ranged from 51 to 60 percent Black. The share Black was strongly tied to the number of non-Black tracts bordered. Accordingly, table 6.6 shows that exiting Black neighborhood status is very strongly tied to whether a Black tract is in the core or along the border. I calculated Black exiter rates in 2010 for neighborhoods that were in the core or along the border in 2000, and exiter rates in 2017 for neighborhoods that were in the core or along the border in 2010. Exiting Black neighborhood status almost never happens in the core (less than 1 percent of the time). And it happens up to 22 percent of the time for Black tracts that border at least four non-Black tracts.

Many studies have attempted to explain what causes gentrification (or displacement of vulnerable residents from neighborhoods that are gentrifying). Identifying those causes involves daunting identification challenges that are difficult to solve with the data at my disposal. With a national-scale dataset, I am unable to control for several factors that

Table 6.7 Average Characteristics of Gentrifying and Nongentrifying Neighborhoods, 2010 and 2017

	Gentrified	Did Not Gentrify	Gentrified	Did Not Gentrify
	2010 (*N* = 690)	2010 (*N* = 5,672)	2017 (*N* = 589)	2017 (*N* = 6,174)
Percent Black	71%	75%	70%	73%
Percent White	18	15	18	15
Percent Asian	2	2	2	2
Percent Hispanic	8	8	9	10
Median home value	$169,182.60	$130,839.20	$263,839.30	$179,155.30
Median rent	$642.50	$677.10	$810.20	$803.80
Vacancy rate	13%	10%	16%	14%
Percent renter	54	45	49	45
Percent with less than a high school diploma	33	31	21	21
Percent with a BA degree or higher	16	13	20	17
Poverty rate	30	26	31	29
Unemployment rate	13	13	17	18
Median household income	$39,499.50	$45,608.40	$40,179.30	$43,446.80
Distance from CBD (miles)	6.6	8.6	6.7	9.0

Source: Author's tabulation of U.S. 2010 Longitudinal Tract Database (Logan, Xu, and Stults 2014) and American Community Survey Five-Year Estimates (U.S. Census Bureau 2019).
Note: All characteristics are measured at the start of the previous decade.

may catalyze neighborhood change, be they changes in job access, public investments in amenities such as parks and transit, charter school growth, consumption amenities such as theaters, museums, and restaurants, or falling crime rates.[29]

For these reasons, rather than estimating regression models, I compare means of key variables in gentrifying and nongentrifying neighborhoods. Table 6.7 provides these comparisons for the full sample of Black neighborhoods across the country. Racial characteristics are very similar, as are poverty, unemployment, and education characteristics. The biggest differences are in housing markets. Home values were higher, while rents were about the same, if not a little lower, in 2010. Renter rates were higher in 2010, and the distance to the CBD was much shorter for gentrified neighborhoods.

Although the gentrification measures are metro area–specific, these averages are probably influenced by the concentration of gentrifying neighborhoods in particular metropolitan areas. Table 6.8 looks at the metropolitan areas of the nation's three largest cities for neighborhoods that gentrified in either 2010 or 2017 compared to neighborhoods that gentrified in neither 2010 nor 2017. Racial differences are still quite minimal—only in Los Angeles are the neighborhoods meaningfully less Black (and more White) than in nongentrifying neighborhoods. In New York and Chicago, home values are much higher. That median rents are a bit lower in New York and a lot lower in Chicago is some evidence that a rent gap is associated with gentrification in Black neighborhoods in these metros. The rent gap hypothesis contends that neighborhoods gentrify when the potential for rents well exceeds the actual rents that landlords obtain in the existing market.[30] Relatively high home values and relatively low rents, as we see in some of these comparisons between gentrifying and nongentrifying Black neighborhoods, suggest that such rent gaps are playing a role. Relatedly, the significantly higher renter rates in gentrifying neighborhoods in New York and Chicago are likely to facilitate more neighborhood change akin to gentrification. Interestingly, poverty rates are a lot higher in Chicago's gentrifying Black neighborhoods, where incomes are also quite low. Gentrification is typically occurring in central cities, not in the suburbs, as we see in these three metros, where gentrifying neighborhoods are considerably closer to the central business district.

Wrapping Up: Black Neighborhoods Rarely Gentrify, but Gentrification Is on the Rise

Black neighborhoods generally change less than other types of neighborhoods. The vast majority of 1970 and 1980 Black neighborhoods are still Black neighborhoods today. And the rapid neighborhood change associated with gentrification is not particularly common in Black neighborhoods.

But there are some signs that gentrification is becoming more common in Black neighborhoods, and that it may occur more often in the future. Although population growth is still robust in suburban areas where Black neighborhoods are not typically located, Whiter and higher-income populations are living in central cities more now than in previous decades. If this trend continues, centrally located Black neighborhoods are likely to change more often and more rapidly as a result of this increased demand.

Crime and violence have persistently plagued Black neighborhoods and been a major impediment to integration in Black neighborhoods. A likely reason for increased demand for central-city living over recent years has been the precipitous drop in crime across U.S. cities. Although crime did not decline in all Black neighborhoods during this period—and crime rates rose some during the COVID-19 pandemic to spark concern that those

Table 6.8 **Average Characteristics of Gentrifying and Nongentrifying Neighborhoods in New York, Los Angeles, and Chicago, 2010 and 2017 Combined**

	Gentrified 2010 or 2017 (*N* = 210)	Gentrified in neither 2010 nor 2017 (*N* = 1,485)	Gentrified 2010 or 2017 (*N* = 21)	Gentrified in neither 2010 nor 2017 (*N* = 182)	Gentrified 2010 or 2017 (*N* = 62)	Gentrified in neither 2010 nor 2017 (*N* = 832)
	New York Metro		Los Angeles Metro		Chicago Metro	
Percent Black	74%	71%	56%	63%	83%	85%
Percent White	8	8	12	6	9	7
Percent Asian	3	3	7	4	3	1
Percent Hispanic	15	17	24	26	4	7
Median home value	$445,421.10	$342,320.40	$371,647.90	$322,239.50	$246,682.70	$169,823.80
Median rent	$988.00	$1,047.50	$1,076.20	$1,001.40	$670.40	$793.10
Vacancy rate	10%	8%	6%	5%	19%	13%
Percent renter	68	56	51	49	58	46
Percent with less than a high school diploma	27	25	22	25	30	24
Percent with a BA degree or higher	20	18	23	19	17	15
Poverty rate	25	21	20	22	38	29
Unemployment rate	14	13	12	14	22	20
Median household income	$46,923.60	$58,043.00	$53,068.20	$55,752.30	$36,503.00	$45,075.40
Distance from CBD (miles)	6.9	11.0	7.1	8.6	6.8	12.4

Source: Author's tabulation of U.S. 2010 Longitudinal Tract Database (Logan, Xu, and Stults 2014) and American Community Survey Five-Year Estimates (U.S. Census Bureau 2019).
Note: All characteristics are measured at the start of the previous decade.

trends might be reversed—an increase in safety in Black neighborhoods could increase demand for moving there and fuel some gentrification. Rising crime rates were partly responsible for high rates of White flight in the 1980s, and a decline in crime rates is likely to have played a role in urban population growth in the 1990s and gentrification in the 2000s.[31] If Black neighborhoods continue to become safer, racial change may accelerate.

Of course, one person's gentrification may look like integration to another. Crime declines are good, and rising demand for living in Black neighborhoods probably is as well. It is a little odd for people to be gravely concerned about rising demand in these neighborhoods, when segregation and discrimination against Black neighborhoods has been arguably the greatest injustice of urban America over the last century. Yet these concerns are real and justified, in part because many of the properties in these neighborhoods are owned by others and rarely by Black residents, so the rising cost of living has great potential to squeeze people out. Moreover, recent research unfortunately suggests that gentrification is probably not a path to integration. Ingrid Gould Ellen and Gerard Torrats-Espinosa find that around 30 percent of predominantly minority neighborhoods that gentrified in the 2000s became racially integrated (rather than predominantly White or minority); this number has risen considerably since the 1990s, when it was just under 7 percent.[32] A very minority of Black neighborhoods have been gentrifying, and a minority of those have become racially integrated. Gentrification is a very uncommon pathway to either racial integration or increased socioeconomic stability for Black neighborhoods.

Chapter 7

The Rise of Black Middle-Class Neighborhoods in Washington, D.C., and Atlanta

The South got something to say and that's all I got to say.

—Andre 3000, 1995 Source Awards

As rap music became pop music, the fight between the East and West Coasts for supremacy overshadowed the proliferation of talented MCs and producers throughout the South. Atlanta is the biggest producer of rap talent and influence from the South and at this point is arguably the biggest anywhere. Memphis, Houston, and New Orleans have all had a major impact as well. Just as urban scholars focused on segregation and Black life often overlook the South, East and West Coast record industry insiders took for granted that the future of rap would always be centered in New York and L.A. They were wrong.

Kenneth French provides a simple metric for the rise of southern hip-hop generally, and in Atlanta specifically.[1] He identified the hometowns of 1,124 rappers from 1979 to 2015 (based on their debut album dates) to analyze the genre's geographic distribution. New York dominated the 1980s: nearly 60 percent of the country's rappers called the Big Apple home. Philadelphia's Schooly D was the first non–New York rapper to release an album, in 1985. New York and Los Angeles dominated the 1990s, together accounting for almost exactly half of the 440 new rappers in the decade. But the South came alive in the 1990s with sixty-eight new rappers. Then, from 2000 to 2015, Atlanta's ascendancy was the story. While New York still had the most new rappers during this time (seventy-two), Atlanta, in second with forty-five, was punching well above its weight. Per capita, Atlanta had ten times the number of rappers as New York.

https://doi.org/10.7758/tjvh5404.8607

Rapper counts tell us only so much about hip-hop hegemony. Album sales and cultural influence are more indicative. Although influence is hard to measure, Atlanta is currently the center of the rap world, even if that world is much more geographically dispersed than it was in the 1980s and 1990s.[2] In chapter 4, I discussed Chicago's late contribution to the genre, with drill music. The far more financially successful predecessor to drill was Atlanta's trap music. "The trap" is a common phrase for being stuck in a hustle, a frequent version of that being drug sales.[3] Trap music thus tends to tell tales of that life.

T.I.'s 2003 album, conveniently titled *Trap Musik,* is a foundational trap text, but it owes something to the Atlanta sound that came before it and sounds quite different than the hit trap-influenced albums of the last decade from rappers like Lil' Baby and Future, and the group Migos.[4] One respect in which T.I. is set apart from many Atlanta acts, besides having been a relatively early star for the city, is his stylistic similarity to the more fluid New York rappers like Jay-Z.[5] Lil' Baby, Future, and the Migos tend to drop phrases, utterances, or melodies (often with Atlanta slang and or twang to it) to produce lyrical moments that are quite distinct from the flow and storytelling that dominated rap until trap took over. Gucci Mane and Young Jeezy, also pioneers of trap, rap at a far more southern pace than their East and West Coast counterparts. T.I. is similarly not in a New York hurry to get through a verse.

Trap music was not Atlanta's first major rap music statement. That was Outkast, the duo formed by Andre Benjamin (Andre 3000) and Antwan Patton (Big Boi). Their 1994 debut album, *Southernplayalisticadillacmusik,* was the first major foray into rap of Atlanta's LaFace Records. The record company run by Babyface and LA Reid had big R&B stars such as Toni Braxton and Usher and crossover act TLC, and it had garnered a reputation as the "Motown of the South."[6] Outkast combined southern soul with New York and Los Angeles rap influences and frequently name-checked Atlanta neighborhoods and features, making it clear where they came from. Outkast's production group, Organized Noize, played a role in developing the trap sound, which is heavy on high-speed synthesized high-hat sounds made by the Roland TR-808.[7] The combination of Outkast and Organized Noize's innovative style and sound and LaFace Records' hitmaking prowess put Atlanta rap on the map and facilitated the later dominance of trap music.[8]

Atlanta's rap takeover was somewhat improbable. Darren Grem notes that southern Blacks have always had to fight against the perception of being "country" or unsophisticated in ways that long dampened the region's ability to rise to the top of music and fashion.[9] As southern rap became more mainstream, rap titans Nas and Jay-Z took shots at the synthesized and singsong style of much of the music from the region. However, some obvious preconditions for rap ascension were present in

Atlanta. It had one of the country's largest Black populations, a robust drug trade for lyrical fodder, and a successful recording industry (the "Motown of the South"). And then came an unexpected one . . . Freaknik.

Joe Coscarelli calls Freaknik the "Big Bang" moment of Atlanta rap.[10] The festival's origins are contested, but it grew from an HBCU-centered picnic in the 1980s to something like a Black combination of Southern California's Coachella and Austin's South by Southwest in the 1990s. College students and other young people flocked annually to Atlanta for Freaknik from all over the South and from up the coast, particularly D.C. Coscarelli estimates that by 1994, two hundred thousand people were attending the loosely connected shows and events associated with Freaknik. Local authorities were predisposed to assume the worst about hordes of rap fans, and Freaknik's informality and the questionable decision-making of young music fans provoked a predictable response. Further, the looming 1996 Summer Olympics had given police a broader mandate to clamp down on the massive party. By the time Freaknik petered out, around 1999, it had done more than enough to show Atlanta and the rap world that the city had something special going on.

Freaknik was an early flex of Atlanta's cultural and musical muscle that helped lay the foundation for its later dominance of the twenty-first-century music industry. Slowly but surely, the success of early trap pioneers Jeezy, Gucci Mane, and T.I. set the stage for the popularity of Lil' Baby, the Migos, and Future in the 2010s. The real indicator of Atlanta's reach, however, was the influence of the trap sound, style, and slang on the likes of Beyoncé and Ariana Grande. This reach has important implications for the future prospects of southern Black neighborhoods. As the ascendance of southern rap has raised the cultural cachet of the South, the region should become a more desirable destination for migrants. Atlanta has always been known to Black people, but for many northern Blacks, the South is a cultural backwater and a hotbed of White racism. Now that the South has begun to play such a substantial role in Black and global youth culture, however, some people's eyes have probably been opened to the benefits of making a home there.

Unfortunately, Atlanta's rap scene has also blazed some trails in the level of connection of some of its native sons to the drug trade. Jeffrey Lamar Williams, aka Young Thug, possibly laid his intentions a bit too bare with his choice of moniker. Williams was already legendary in the Atlanta rap scene for his mixtapes and guest appearances on major recordings before his debut studio album opened at number one on the Billboard 200 in 2019. After Williams founded the YSL (Young Stoner Life) record label in 2016, the Fulton County district attorney, Fani Willis, alleged that YSL was a criminal drug syndicate called Young Slime Life, an Atlanta chapter of the Bloods gang and one of the most murderous entities in the state. Williams has been behind bars since May 2022, and he and dozens of his YSL compatriots face fifty-six counts related to racketeering, murder and attempted murder, and drug distribution.

The role of Atlanta's drug trade in its ascension to the top of the rap game might suggest that Atlanta Black neighborhood life is a lot harsher than the findings in this book suggest. In some sections of Black Atlanta, that is undoubtedly true. But the fuller picture is a diverse one in this city with so many Black neighborhoods that they inevitably include rich, poor, and everything in between. Atlanta super-producer Jermaine Dupri put it well: "You go to other cities and it's a white section. Ain't no white section in Atlanta. If it's some big-ass houses over there, and ten white people live there, you can best believe there's two or three Black people in that same neighborhood, I swear to God."[11]

That New York and Los Angeles faded while Atlanta rose to the top of the geographic rap hierarchy tells us that Atlanta will not stay there forever. Musical tastes and trends are more fleeting than regional economic strength and neighborhood inequalities; nevertheless, changes in rap ascendancy hold lessons for Black neighborhoods. Right now, D.C. and Atlanta offer a greater combination of abundant and affluent Black neighborhoods than anywhere else does, but things will change. D.C.'s skyrocketing housing costs could expand the scope of the city's already devastating Black displacement and make its Black middle-class neighborhoods even more exclusive than they already are. In Atlanta, a surge in drug violence could further disadvantage the Black neighborhoods that broadcast trap life to the masses. More optimistically, other cities in the South or elsewhere may ascend to the top of the rap game—and eventually another music genre will supplant rap. Or some other metro may wrestle away some of D.C.'s and Atlanta's regional economic strength or the two cities' Black middle class.

How Different Are Black Neighborhoods in the Atlanta and Washington, D.C., Metro Areas?

Atlanta and Washington, D.C., are not perfect places for Black people by any means. They still have too many high-poverty Black neighborhoods, and the benefits of having affluent Black neighborhoods do not flow into the high-poverty ones. In Washington, D.C., the extremely affluent Black enclaves of Prince George's County (and adjoining, but smaller, Charles County) are not geographically far from Black ghettos in southeast Washington, but they are worlds apart in other ways. Further, residents of D.C.'s urban Black neighborhoods face rapidly rising housing costs, and because of their low homeownership rates, they will have to pay more to stay as their neighborhoods gentrify and will not reap the financial rewards of escalating property values. Atlanta, similarly, has a much more affluent Black population in the suburbs than in the central city, but that affluence is not quite as high as Black affluence in the Washington, D.C., area. Gentrification has been much slower in coming to Black neighborhoods in Atlanta.

These caveats aside, in the aggregate, the D.C. metro and, to a lesser extent, the Atlanta metro contain a greater combination of plentiful and affluent Black neighborhoods than other parts of the country. Their first source of strength is in the numbers. Because Atlanta and Washington, D.C., have always had such substantial Black populations, political power came relatively early to Blacks in both cities, although political power did not mean much in D.C. until home rule was established in the 1960s.[12] As Atlanta and Washington, D.C., expanded into sprawling metropolises, strong regional economies combined with a long-established Black elite to set the conditions for Black affluence that is relatively unparalleled anywhere else in the country. The uniqueness in these ways of Atlanta and D.C. makes them unsuitable as models for replicating such affluent and sizable Black enclaves elsewhere, but other metro areas in the South have some similar characteristics and could be logical destinations for Black migrants seeking to move to prosperity. The Charlotte metropolitan area has the same Black neighborhood poverty rate as Atlanta and a similar share Black as Washington, D.C. In addition to Charlotte, Raleigh-Durham, Dallas, and Houston all offer different mixes of higher education institutions, large and highly productive regional economies, low unemployment, large Black populations, and low poverty rates in Black neighborhoods. The smaller metros of Columbia, South Carolina, and Virginia Beach and Richmond in Virginia have similar combinations of high Black shares and low poverty rates in Black neighborhoods. It might take a generation or two of economic growth and Black middle-class advancement to replicate the affluent Black suburbs of Atlanta and Washington, D.C., but there are reasonable facsimiles elsewhere on which to build, primarily in the South.

Right now, Black neighborhoods in the Atlanta and Washington, D.C., metro areas are considerably more advantaged, on average, than elsewhere. The stronger socioeconomic characteristics of these neighborhoods, coupled with the substantial numbers of Black neighborhoods (and by extension, Black residents) in these metropolitan areas, have created the largest Black middle-class areas in the country.

The Washington, D.C., metro area had the lowest average Black neighborhood poverty rate of all eighty-six U.S. metropolitan areas with at least ten Black-plurality census tracts in 2017.[13] With the second-most Black-plurality census tracts, the D.C. metro also boasts an unequaled combination of quantity and affluence in Black neighborhoods. The average Black neighborhood poverty rate in the D.C. metro is only 14 percent, which is roughly equal to the national average, regardless of race. By the same metric, Atlanta, at 18 percent, is tied for fifth nationwide in the average

Figure 7.1 Poverty Rates in Washington, D.C., and Atlanta Black Neighborhoods, 1970–2017

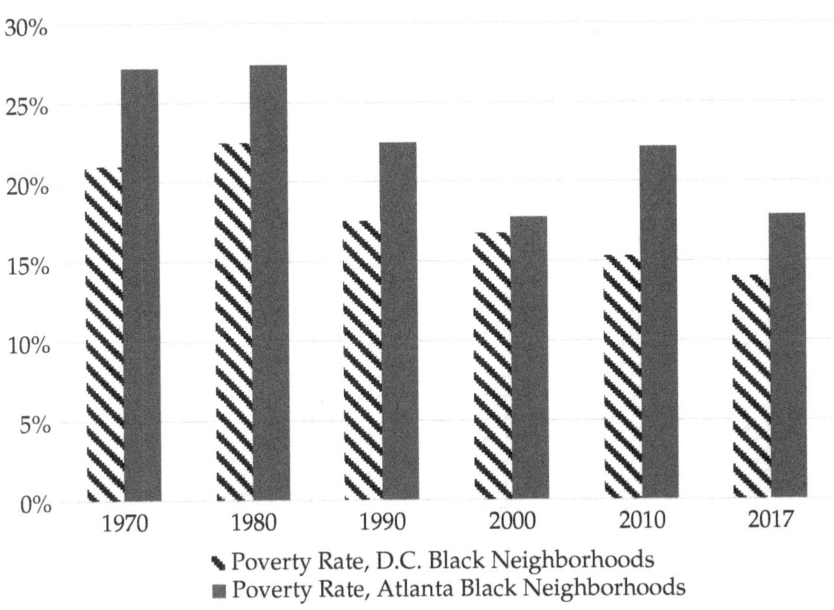

Source: Author's tabulation of U.S. 2010 Longitudinal Tract Database (Logan, Xu, and Stults 2014) and American Community Survey Five-Year Estimates (U.S. Census Bureau 2019).

Black neighborhood poverty rate, and it is also fifth in the country in the number of Black neighborhoods. There are over two million Black people in the Atlanta metro, more than in any other metropolitan area aside from New York.[14]

Figure 7.1 shows steady declines in Black neighborhood poverty rates in each of these metros over time. One caveat is that the Great Recession appeared to be much worse for Black neighborhoods in Atlanta, where Black neighborhood poverty rates increased in 2010 and in 2017 remained basically equal to the 2000 average poverty rate of 18 percent.

Figures 7.1, 7.2, and 7.3 emphasize that in spite of their long histories of being home to Black elites, Atlanta and Washington, D.C., are recent success stories for Black neighborhoods. The disadvantage index declined in Black census tracts in these two metro areas in nearly every decade, the sole exception being D.C. in the 1970s. Median home values have skyrocketed in D.C.'s Black tracts, and they have steadily risen in Atlanta's.[15] Remarkably, the two cities had about equal median home values in 1970 and were essentially equal to the Midwest average. Yet by 2017, D.C.'s home

Figure 7.2 Disadvantage Index in Washington, D.C., and Atlanta Black Neighborhoods, 1970–2017

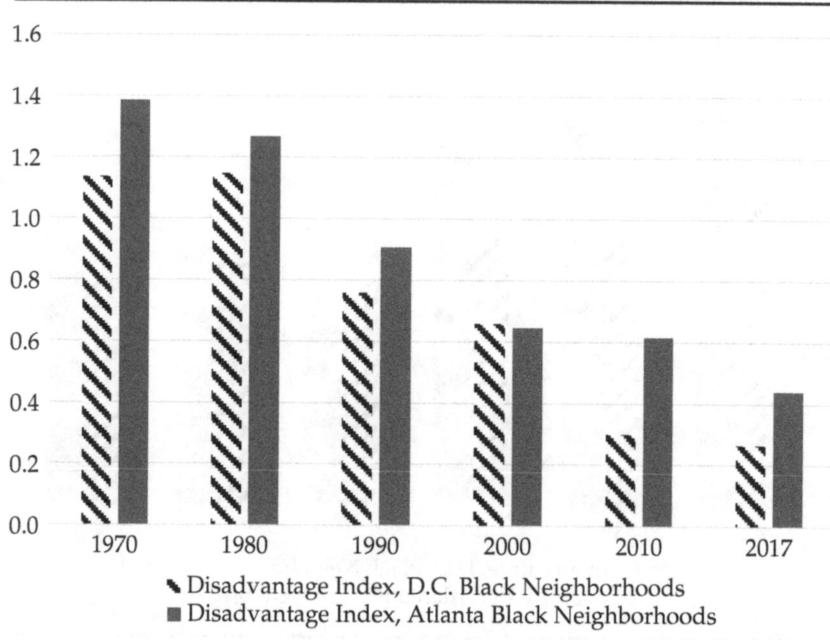

Source: Author's tabulation of U.S. 2010 Longitudinal Tract Database (Logan, Xu, and Stults 2014) and American Community Survey Five-Year Estimates (U.S. Census Bureau 2019).

values had tripled, were twice Atlanta's, and were nearly triple the Midwest's average. This dramatic increase is not without a downside: D.C. is a very expensive place to live—rents there are now double what they were in 1970—and Black neighborhoods have undergone rapid change and gentrification in recent years.

Although Black neighborhoods in the Atlanta and Washington, D.C., metro areas have made great strides in both absolute terms and in comparison to local non-Black neighborhoods, a pessimist could reasonably point out that neither metro is a "Black Mecca" so much as simply one of the most affluent metros in the country. The Washington, D.C., metro area has the country's highest median incomes and lowest poverty rates in both Black and non-Black neighborhoods. Median incomes and poverty rates in non-Black neighborhoods in the Atlanta metro are less of an outlier than the area's Black neighborhoods are, but they are still good. This being the case, is there actually anything special about Black neighborhoods in Washington, D.C., and Atlanta?

Figure 7.3 Median Home Values in Washington, D.C., and Atlanta Black Neighborhoods, 1970–2017

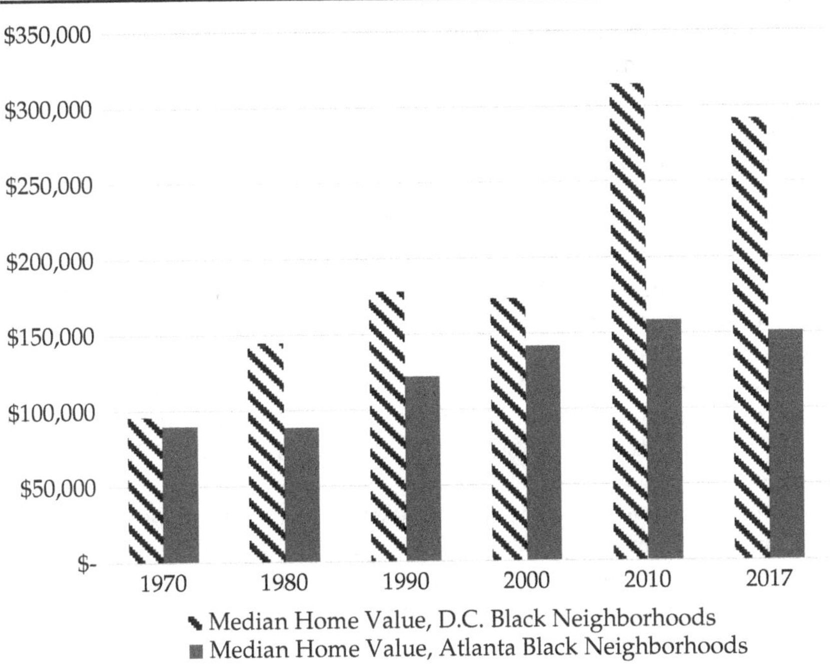

Source: Author's tabulation of U.S. 2010 Longitudinal Tract Database (Logan, Xu, and Stults 2014) and American Community Survey Five-Year Estimates (U.S. Census Bureau 2019).

Yes. Because race is so strongly correlated with affluence in this country, we would expect metro areas with large Black populations to have lower incomes and higher poverty rates. The Washington, D.C., metro area is over 25 percent Black, and the Atlanta metro is over 32 percent Black. They are the most populous metro areas in the country with such a high share of Black people, and yet they still have the some of the strongest socioeconomic indicators in the country. And that the average indicators in these metros' Black neighborhoods are so strong means that there is something different about Atlanta and Washington, D.C. An astounding 40 percent of Black census tracts in the Washington, D.C., have poverty rates of 10 percent or lower.

Atlanta and Washington, D.C., both have reputations for having a large Black middle class. In chapter 4, I highlighted Washington, D.C.'s position as an extreme outlier in its number of very affluent Black neighborhoods. I find that in only 66 tract-years (out of over 33,000) is a Black census tract in the best quartile for median income, poverty rate, percent with a BA degree or higher, unemployment rate, and disadvantage index. A startling 48 of those times were in the Washington, D.C., metro area. To find some more examples, I relaxed the condition to being in the top quartile for only median income, poverty rate, and percent with a BA or higher. There were only 208 tract-years (again, out of over 33,000) when a Black census tract met that standard. Twenty-two were in New York, 18 were in Detroit, 13 were in Atlanta—and more than half (114) were in Washington, D.C.

Although Black neighborhoods in Washington, D.C., and Atlanta have very high average socioeconomic characteristics, averages across a large number of neighborhoods can obscure whether those metro areas also have a large number of high-poverty Black neighborhoods. Much has been written about class divides among Blacks in Atlanta and Washington, D.C., and about concentrated disadvantage in Black neighborhoods in those metros.[16] In fact, Atlanta and D.C. do have significant numbers of high-poverty Black neighborhoods, but they still have a relatively low share of high-poverty neighborhoods.

Table 7.1 provides four ways of looking at the highest-poverty Black neighborhoods in comparable metro areas. The four indicators are the seventy-fifth- and ninetieth-percentile Black neighborhood poverty rates and the percent of high-poverty (30 percent or more) and extremely high-poverty (40 percent or more) neighborhoods. I chose the comparison metro areas because they are large and higher-income, and they have a large number of Black neighborhoods.[17]

Among these metros, Washington, D.C., has the lowest seventy-fifth percentile Black neighborhood poverty rate, but that poverty rate rises quickly up to the ninetieth-percentile threshold. Boston and Los Angeles have a lower share of high-poverty Black neighborhoods. But each of those metro areas has fewer Black neighborhoods. Atlanta's numbers are similar to Washington, D.C.'s, though not quite as low.

Washington, D.C., is disadvantaged in some of these metrics by the fact that we are looking at the consolidated statistical area, which also includes Baltimore. As shown in table 7.2, there are many high-poverty Black neighborhoods in Washington, D.C., proper, but several more in the city of Baltimore.

It is clear from table 7.2 that there is a spatial pattern to high-poverty Black neighborhoods in the D.C. metro area. There are 237 Black census tracts in Baltimore or Washington, D.C., and 300 more are located elsewhere in the metro area. Thirty-four percent of the Black census tracts in the cities of Baltimore and Washington, D.C., have high poverty rates, but of the 300 Black census tracts located in the mostly suburban areas outside of those two cities, *none* have poverty rates above 30 percent. In the 141 Black census tracts in Prince George's County, the average poverty rate is very low—7.5 percent.

Table 7.1 High-Poverty Black Neighborhoods in Atlanta, Washington, D.C., and Comparison CSAs, 2017

Metropolitan Area	75th Percentile Black Neighborhood Poverty Rate	90th Percentile Black Neighborhood Poverty Rate	Percent of Black Neighborhoods with Poverty Rate above 30 percent	Percent of Black Neighborhoods with Poverty Rate above 40 percent
Atlanta, Ga.–Ala.	23%	31%	19%	7%
Washington, D.C.–Baltimore, Md–Va.–W.V.	18	30	15	6
Los Angeles, Calif.	23	28	12	9
San Jose–San Francisco–Oakland, Calif.	24	33	19	3
Houston, Tex.	24	37	29	12
Boston, Mass–R.I.–N.H.	25	29	11	6
New York, N.Y.–N.J.–Conn.–Pa.	26	35	18	7
Dallas–Fort Worth, Tex.	27	34	24	7
Chicago, Ill.–Ind.–Wisc.	33	42	40	19
New Orleans, La.	35	44	43	15

Source: Author's tabulation of American Community Survey Five-Year Estimates (U.S. Census Bureau 2019).

Table 7.2 High-Poverty Black Neighborhoods in the Cities of Washington, D.C., and Baltimore, 2017

	Number of High-Poverty Black Neighborhoods	Total Number of Black Neighborhoods	Percent of City's Black Neighborhoods
Baltimore City	54	141	38%
District of Columbia	27	96	28%

Source: Author's tabulation of American Community Survey Five-Year Estimates (U.S. Census Bureau 2019).

Figure 7.4 confirms this spatial pattern. The Washington, D.C., boundary forms a line of demarcation between high- and low- to mid-poverty Black census tracts in the metropolitan area.

Black affluence in Prince George's County is both relatively recent and unique in comparison to all other Black enclaves in the country. The Black middle-class exodus to Prince George's County began in the 1970s, when the county's Black population tripled.[18] Resistance by the majority-White population culminated in school desegregation fights and rapid White flight.

Figures 7.5 and 7.6 capture the movement of the Black population from the core of Washington, D.C., into Prince George's County from 1980 to 2017. In 1980, Prince George's County had a Black belt concentrated in the center. By 2017, all but a few census tracts in Prince George's County were majority-Black, and some had Black populations comprising more than 30 percent. Most of the census tracts in Prince George's County with a lower Black population are located northeast of Washington, D.C., in the vicinity of the University of Maryland–College Park, whose student population is only about 12 percent Black.[19]

Prince George's County, the nation's largest Black middle-class enclave, has long been more affluent than most enclaves, but it is far larger and more affluent today. In 1980, it was one of four counties in the country with at least ten Black census tracts whose median incomes were in the nation's top quartile. The other three counties were Queens (New York), Cook (Chicago), and Los Angeles, which are far more populous, then and now. In *Blue-Chip Black*, Karyn Lacy studied Prince George's County's Black middle class.[20] She describes one of her study sites, Sherwood Park, as a recently built subdivision that is 85 percent Black and 90 percent college-educated professionals. By 2017, Prince George's County had almost one-quarter of the nation's Black census tracts in the top income quartile, with sixty-nine, compared to thirty-nine in Queens, the next-closest concentration of such census tracts.[21] Notably, Washington, D.C.,

Figure 7.4 **Poverty Rates in Washington, D.C., and Prince George's County, Maryland Black Neighborhoods, 2017**

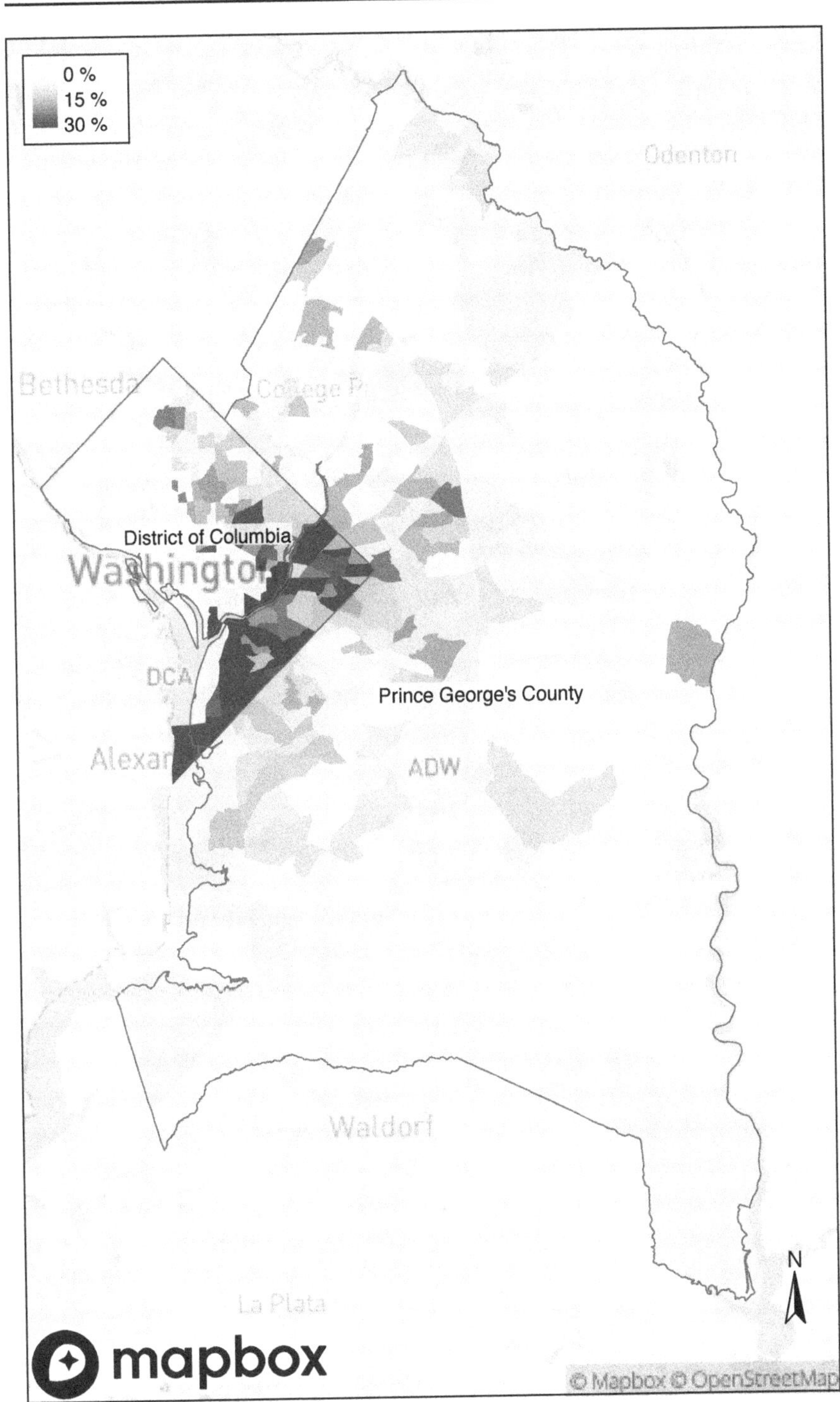

Source: Author's tabulation of American Community Survey Five-Year Estimates (U.S. Census Bureau 2019).

Figure 7.5 **Percent Black in Washington, D.C., and Prince George's County, 1980**

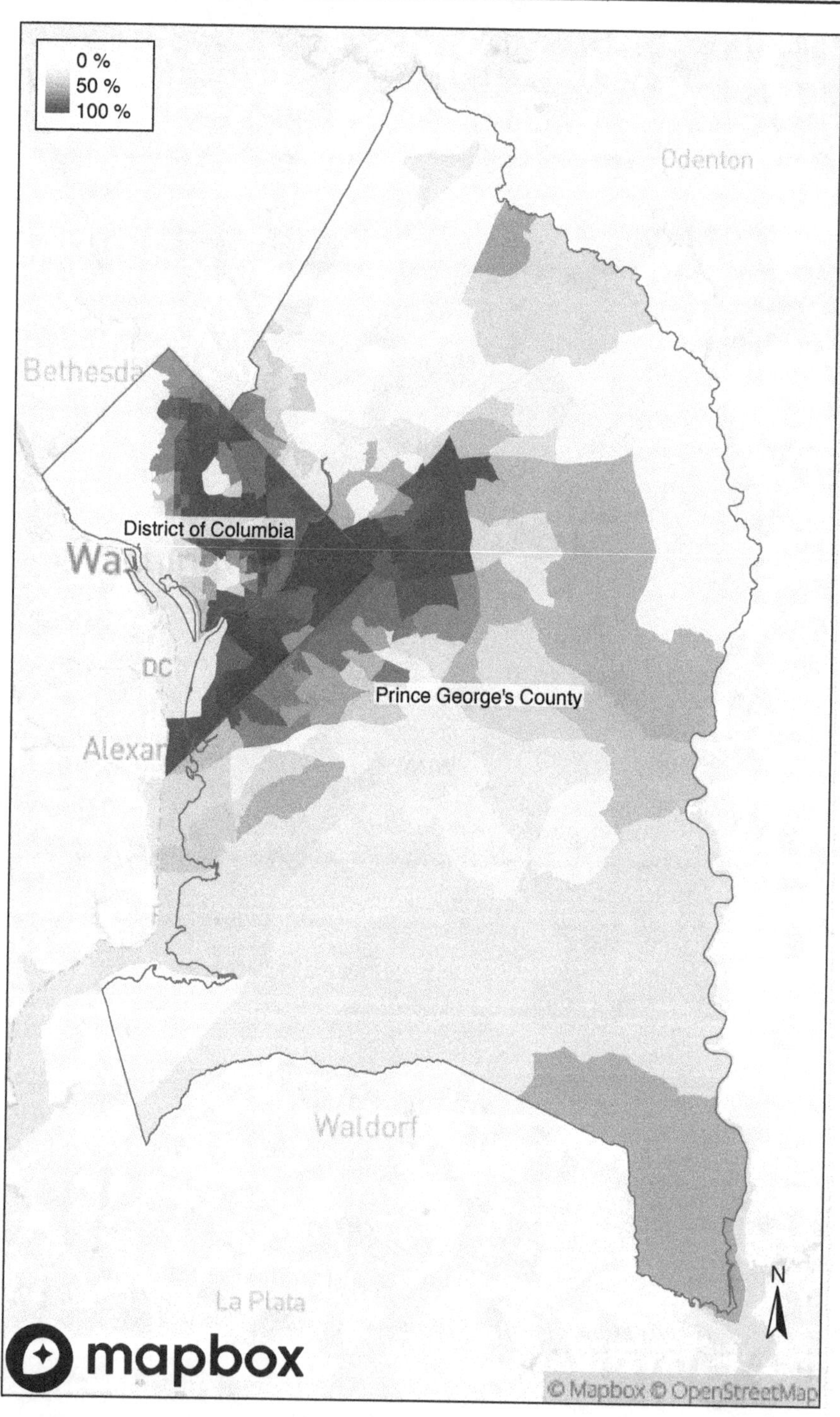

Source: Author's tabulation of U.S. 2010 Longitudinal Tract Database (Logan, Xu, and Stults 2014).

Figure 7.6 **Percent Black in Washington, D.C., and Prince George's County, 2017**

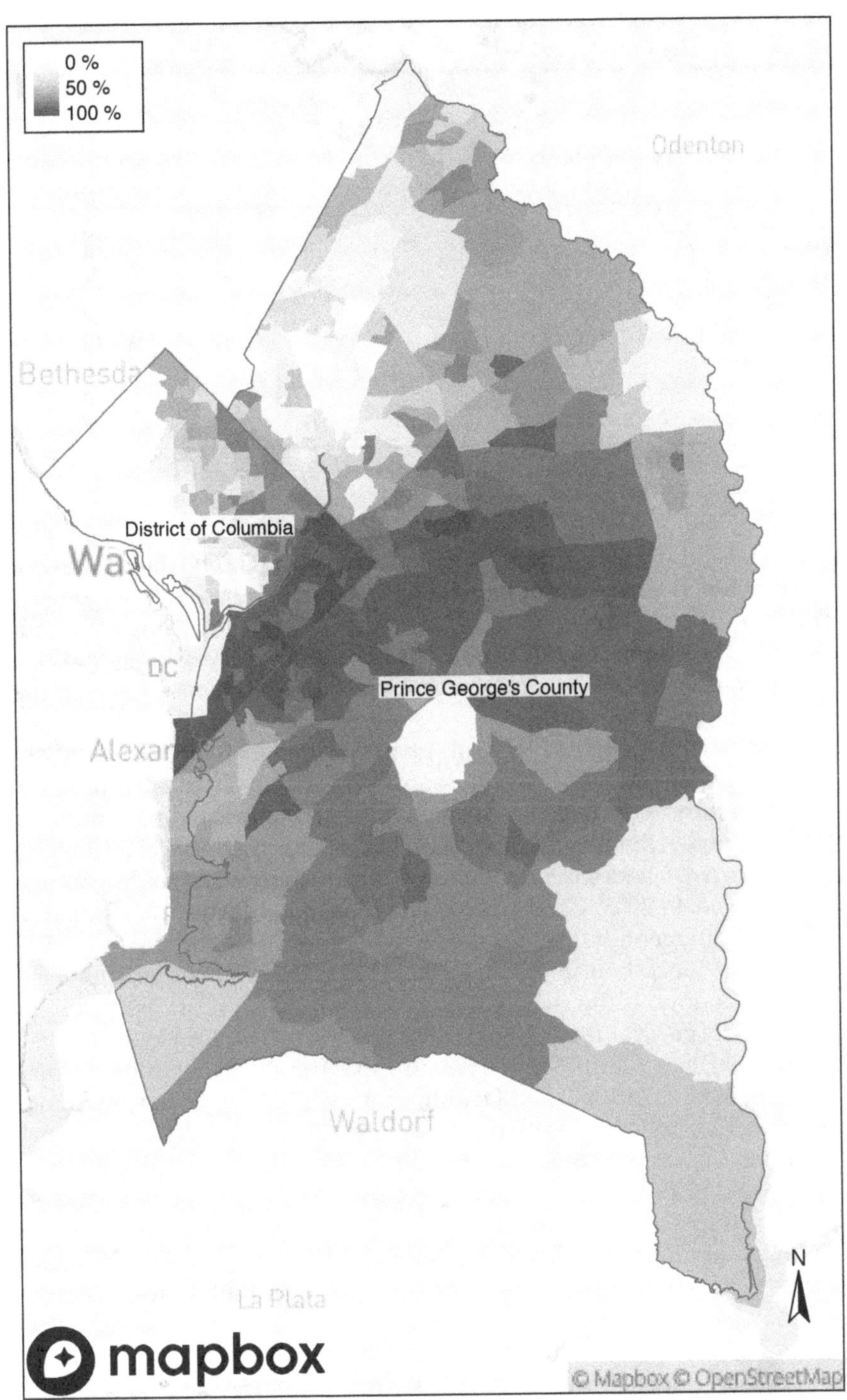

Source: Author's tabulation of American Community Survey Five-Year Estimates (U.S. Census Bureau 2019).

Table 7.3 High-Poverty Black Neighborhoods in the Atlanta CSA, by County, 2017

Atlanta Metro County	Number of Black Neighborhoods	Number of High-Poverty Black Neighborhoods	Percent of County's Black Neighborhoods
Clayton	48	4	8%
Cobb	28	0	0
DeKalb	73	10	14
Douglas	10	0	0
Fulton	95	43	45
Gwinnett	29	0	0
Henry	12	0	0
Rockdale	10	0	0

Source: Author's tabulation of American Community Survey Five-Year Estimates (U.S. Census Bureau 2019).

proper was third in the country with twenty-three; other counties in the Washington, D.C., metro (Anne Arundel, Baltimore, Charles, Montgomery, and Howard Counties in Maryland and Fairfax and Prince William Counties in Virginia) added another forty-eight. The Washington, D.C., metro area thus accounts for 49 percent of all Black census tracts in the nation's top income quartile.

The spatial patterns of Black suburban D.C. continue to evolve. Charles County borders Prince George's County and is much smaller, with fewer than two hundred thousand people compared to nearly one million in Prince George's. But a significant racial shift is happening as Prince George's diversifies and Charles County rapidly becomes more Black while retaining its affluence. In 2005, Charles County's Black population was estimated at only 34 percent, but it is just over 50 percent now. In the 2010s, the number of Black households earning $200,000 or more quadrupled in Charles County. If the richest Black county in the country is no longer Prince George's County, then it is neighboring Charles County.[22] The only other Black counties in the country that compare are Fulton County (median income $80,000) and DeKalb County ($64,000), which are found, not coincidentally, in the Atlanta metro area.

Fulton County is home to Atlanta and is one of the most affluent Black-plurality counties in the country, but it also has the kind of concentrated poverty that you see in many urban Black enclaves. In 2017, Fulton County had ninety-five Black census tracts, and forty-three of them had poverty rates higher than 30 percent (table 7.3). DeKalb County is more suburban and has a much lower prevalence of high-poverty Black census tracts. In chapter 5, I estimated that across the country, the Black neighborhood poverty rate was 27 percent in central cities but 18 percent in the suburbs. In the Atlanta metro area, the central-city Black neighborhood

Figure 7.7 **Percent Black by Neighborhood in the Atlanta Metropolitan Area, 1980**

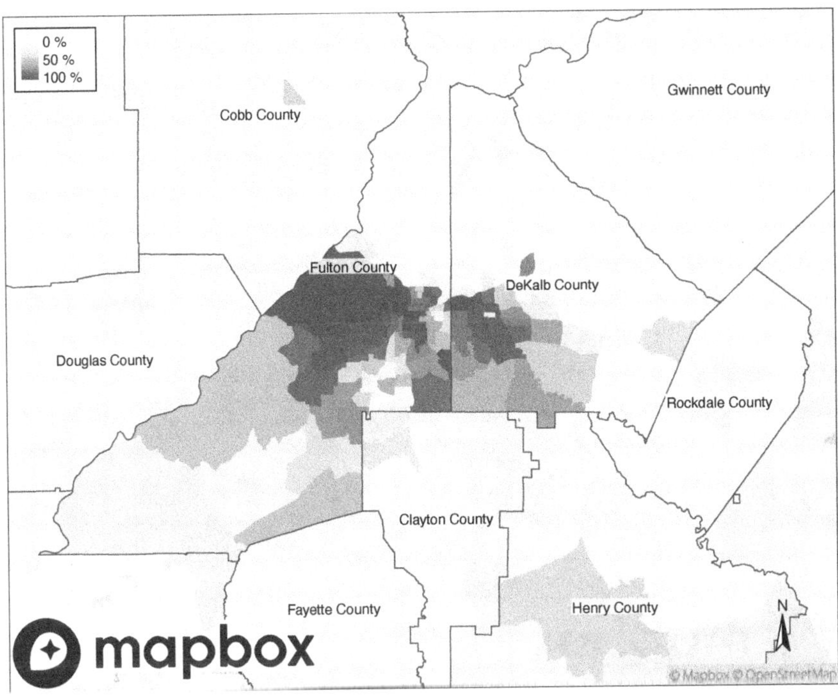

Source: Author's tabulation of U.S. 2010 Longitudinal Tract Database (Logan, Xu, and Stults 2014).

poverty rate is 31 percent and the suburban poverty rate is 16 percent. In the Washington, D.C., metro area, those numbers are 23 and 8 percent.

Similar to the suburbanization of Blacks in the Washington, D.C., area, Black Atlanta suburbanized rapidly from 1980 to 2017, as seen in figures 7.7 and 7.8. The Black population moved south into southern Fulton County and into Clayton County, as well as into the eastern part of DeKalb County. These migration patterns greatly expanded the geographic reach of Atlanta's Black enclave, which now encompasses all of Clayton County and more than half of DeKalb and Fulton Counties.

Mapping the Black neighborhood poverty rates in the Atlanta metropolitan area makes it clear that high-poverty Black neighborhoods are more diffuse there than in the Washington, D.C., metro area. They are still centrally concentrated in and around Atlanta, but several are many miles from the center of the metropolitan area (figures 7.9 and 7.10). Once more, the suburbanization of Black Atlanta appears more connected to the suburbanization of poverty as mid- and high-poverty neighborhoods diffused

Figure 7.8 Percent Black by Neighborhood in the Atlanta Metropolitan Area, 2017

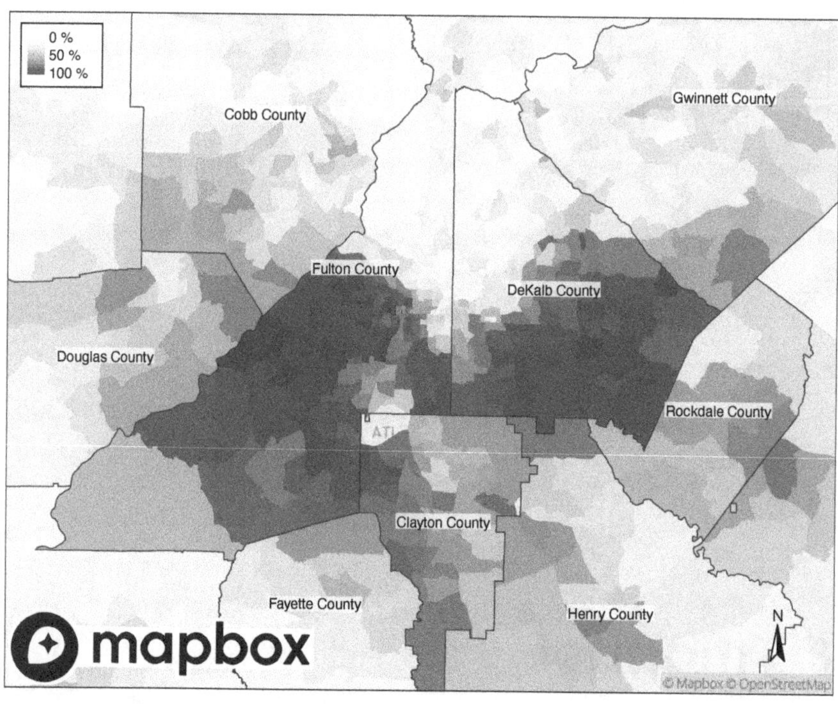

Source: Author's tabulation of American Community Survey Five-Year Estimates (U.S. Census Bureau 2019).

out into the suburbs. From 1980 to 2017, median household income changed in very different ways in the three predominantly Black counties in the Atlanta metro area (table 7.4). Similar to the income trend in Prince George's County, Fulton County's median incomes nearly doubled. DeKalb County's incomes were flat, and median income in Clayton County, which was not very integrated in 1980 and then became almost entirely comprised of majority-Black census tracts, fell from over $63,000 to a little more than $50,000. In 1980, Clayton County had no Black census tracts. In 2017, forty-eight out of forty-nine were.

Clearly Washington, D.C., has the most affluent Black neighborhoods in the country. The Atlanta metro area is behind D.C. but ahead of all other U.S. metro areas in Black affluence. Like any American metropolis, Washington, D.C., and Atlanta have concentrated poverty in Black neighborhoods, and poverty is particularly concentrated in the central cities (Washington, D.C., and Atlanta but also Baltimore) of these areas.

Figure 7.9 Black Neighborhood Poverty Rates in the Atlanta Metropolitan Area, 1980

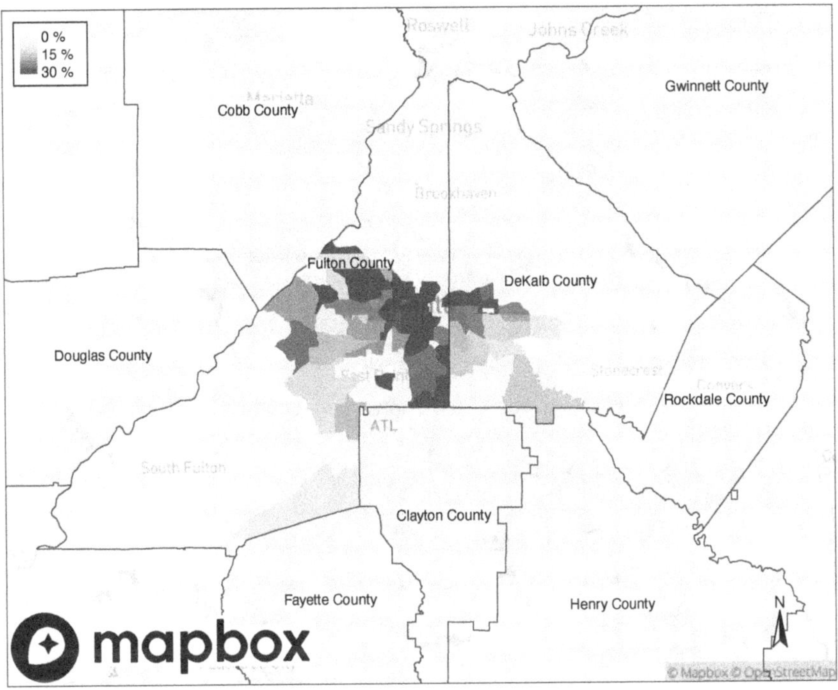

Source: Author's tabulation of U.S. 2010 Longitudinal Tract Database (Logan, Xu, and Stults 2014).

But neither metro area has enough concentrated disadvantage in Black neighborhoods to offset the affluence at the top of the Black neighborhood spectrum. In other words, Black neighborhood advantage in Washington, D.C., and Atlanta is exemplary, while Black neighborhood disadvantage in these metro areas is somewhere between typical and mild.

But there are challenges ahead for both metros. In chapter 6, I made the case that gentrification is still not the typical concern for Black neighborhoods in this country, but that gentrification prevalence depends a lot on the metro area. I also noted several reasons to believe that gentrification is becoming more common in Black neighborhoods, a trend that may continue in the future. Unfortunately, gentrification is much more common in the Washington, D.C., and Atlanta metro areas than in most others. The historic Black center of Washington, D.C., Shaw–U Street, is now majority-White.

Although gentrification has its downsides, prosperity is good. Incomes and wealth have risen rapidly in both Atlanta and Washington, D.C.;

Figure 7.10 Black Neighborhood Poverty Rates in the Atlanta Metropolitan Area, 2017

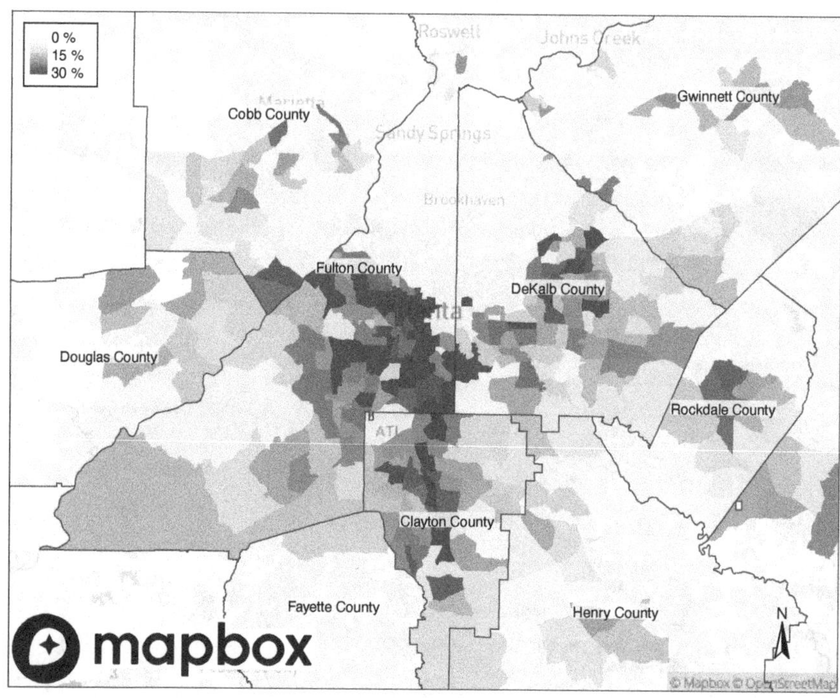

Source: Author's tabulation of American Community Survey Five-Year Estimates (U.S. Census Bureau, 2019).

Table 7.4 Neighborhood Population–Weighted Average Median Household Incomes, Atlanta Metro Area Counties, 1980 and 2017

County	1980	2017
Fulton	$49,665	$83,487
DeKalb	$65,938	$69,942
Clayton	$63,600	$50,675
Prince George's (D.C.)	$74,930	$90,180

Source: Author's tabulation of American Community Survey Five-Year Estimates (U.S. Census Bureau 2019).

though very large disparities do still exist, many Black families and neighborhoods have benefited from that prosperity in recent decades. There are some similarities and some differences in how these metropolitan areas became national epicenters of the Black middle class. The path of Atlanta's Black middle class has arguably been longer, while Washington's has risen since the 1960s.

Black Beginnings in Atlanta

The "Chocolate City"—one where Blacks are the majority or the most prevalent racial or ethnic group across an entire city—is an exception to the rule in the United States. George Clinton named few such cities in his song (and album) of the same name, and while his anticipation of trends in Atlanta would come to fruition, he had poor intelligence on Los Angeles. In 2020, Atlanta was almost exactly 50 percent Black, making it the fourth-largest majority-Black city in the United States, behind Detroit, Memphis, and Baltimore. At nearly half a million people, Atlanta is significantly larger than the other U.S. chocolate cities of New Orleans, Cleveland, and Newark. The share Black in Atlanta, however, is not substantially higher than in two other larger cities: Philadelphia (42 percent Black; 1.6 million people) and Washington, D.C. (44 percent Black and falling; 690,000 people). The contrast between Atlanta and other majority-Black cities, however, is striking. Each of those cities is well known as a site of Black disadvantage, while Atlanta, like Washington, D.C., an economic power, has earned the moniker "Black Mecca." What sets Atlanta apart as a hub for the Black middle class? What inconvenient truths and inequities contrast with the ideal of Black Mecca?

Atlanta's initial raison d'être was providing transportation access to the Southeast, but it developed as a transportation hub later than many other major American cities, as transportation in the region was predicated on rail access rather than water.[23] In the early twentieth century, Georgia's cotton industry declined rapidly, precipitating robust population growth in Atlanta through subsequent decades.[24] Black and White alike moved to Atlanta in large numbers, and the population more than doubled between 1900 and 1920. The Black share of the population grew fastest in the postwar decades; the city was majority-Black by the 1970 census, owing to this growth and White flight to the suburbs.[25]

The persistently high share of the Black population in Atlanta fundamentally shaped race relations in Atlanta and created conditions ripe for the development of a Black middle class in the region. Table 7.5 shows the robust growth in the total Atlanta population through the postwar period. Blacks made up at least 31 percent of the population throughout the twentieth century. Unlike major metropolitan areas in the North, the Black population was not a new phenomenon at any point in the city's

Table 7.5 Total and Black Population, Atlanta, 1900–1980

Year	Total Population	Black Population	Percent Black
1900	89,872	35,727	40%
1910	154,839	51,902	34
1920	200,616	62,796	31
1930	270,366	90,075	33
1940	302,288	104,533	35
1950	331,314	121,416	37
1960	487,455	186,820	38
1970	496,973	255,051	51
1980	425,022	283,158	67

Source: Data from Bayor 1996; author's calculations from U.S. census data.

development, and its share stayed relatively steady through the latter half of the century. For context, while Atlanta was 35 percent Black in 1940, it was 8 and 9 percent Black in Chicago and Detroit, respectively.[26] That Atlanta's Blacks remained a minority as long as they did was due in part to a massive annexation that the city undertook in 1952 under its "Plan for Improvement," which expanded the city square mileage from 39 to 118. Majority-White areas were intentionally brought inside the city boundaries to keep Black political power in check, but the move actually helped solidify a coalition of relatively moderate, higher-income Whites with the growing Black population.[27] Without this annexation, Atlanta probably would have attained Black-majority status well before 1970.

Since the postwar period, Atlanta has been an economic dynamo and a global city rivaled only by Houston and Dallas in the South, cities with smaller Black populations (23 percent in Houston, 24 percent in Dallas). Its combination of economic strength and an established Black population has profoundly affected power-sharing between Black and White coalitions, the sociospatial structure of the region, and the development of Black middle-class enclaves.

Politics: The Community Power Structure

Observers of postwar Atlanta politics emphasize its relative racial progressivism in service of economic growth. Mayor William Hartsfield lorded over the city from 1936 to 1962 and famously labeled Atlanta "the city too busy to hate."[28] This oft-repeated phrase shrouded widespread discrimination and heavily discounted the scale of the civil rights struggle in Atlanta, but it is telling for the image that the city's leaders wished to portray to the world. Like all southern U.S. cities (and in many ways northern ones as well), post–World War II Atlanta operated under the rules of a rigid racial caste system that evolved slowly until the gains of the civil rights movement afforded Black Atlantans more robust legal protections. In Atlanta, this system was more flexible than in other parts of the South, and Atlanta embraced relatively more progressive race relations in both the public and private spheres. The most common explanations offered for this racial progressivism are the city's reification of business interests (which viewed racial moderation as good for its bottom line) and the relatively early exercise of the voting franchise by Black Atlantans.

In the 1940s, two keys to Black voter enfranchisement raised the bar for Black political power in Atlanta. In 1944, the U.S. Supreme Court ruled in *Smith v. Allwright* that political parties could no longer set their primary rules for the purposes of discrimination.[29] Georgia's dominant Democratic Party had closed its primaries to Blacks until this point, but in 1945 Georgia's all-White primary was invalidated. Also in that year, the state legislature eliminated the poll tax, a strategic mistake by segregationists who believed that the state's Blacks would not vote unless encouraged by outsider agitators.[30] In response, the National Association for the Advancement of Colored People (NAACP), an organization with strong ties to Atlanta, intensified its ongoing voter registration campaigns in Georgia and radically increased the number of registered Black Atlantans in short time. Ronald Bayor reports that the number of Black registered voters more than tripled between February and May 1946, by which point they comprised over 27 percent of the city total.[31] Astutely seeing the inherent power in the Black vote, Mayor Hartsfield quickly changed his tune on the hiring of Black police officers in 1947.[32]

This set the stage for a solidifying coalition between the Black and White power elite in Atlanta. As Floyd Hunter described Atlanta at this time, the city was governed by a cabal of leaders disproportionately drawn from the business community; these leaders consulted with a subgroup of Black leaders, also heavily in business in addition to clergy and academics.[33] This "community power structure," as Hunter termed it, was really two power structures: a predominantly White one and a Black one that was considered a junior partner. Both sought openings for racial progressivism, chiefly in service to economic progress, but of course Black elites, besides being attuned to the economic strength of the region and the Black community, also had a stronger orientation to racial justice as an end in itself. Although race overshadowed everything in Atlanta politics and Blacks were still clearly a subjugated class, their political clout was taken seriously at the ballot box and in backroom negotiations.

As Blacks gained population and vote share and discrimination in voting, schools, housing, employment, and public places became less tenable in Atlanta owing to civil rights gains, the Black elite challenged its junior status in the community power structure. To the consternation of Hartsfield and his more racially progressive successor, Ivan Allen Jr.,

Black politicians started gaining seats on the board of aldermen by 1965; then the biracial coalition splintered in 1969 in a dispute over who to back in the upcoming mayoral election. A White (Jewish) candidate was elected in Sam Massell, but then the next election, in 1974, brought the first Black mayor, Maynard Jackson, into office. Atlanta's mayors have been Black ever since.

On the surface, the junior partner status of the Black elite in the post-war period and the relatively early ascension of Black leaders to the highest levels of city power demonstrate great achievement on the part of Black Atlanta and relative moderation by the White power structure. It surely could have gone worse, as evidenced by events in other southern cities of the time. However, many scholars have noted that the Black power structure sacrificed the needs of lower-class Blacks in exchange for its junior partner status.[34] Sometimes this was probably a necessary trade-off, but it also represented an ideology of racial uplift that had been a frequent undercurrent in Atlanta's Black leadership. Associated with W.E.B. DuBois, uplift ideology prioritized the gains of Black elites in the hope that their gains would help lift up the poorer masses of Blacks, who were seen as ignorant and unprepared for modern life.

Rodriguez frames the early production of public housing in Atlanta as reflecting this uplift ideology.[35] She argues that Atlanta's early and productive entry into the nation's public housing program was a form of "spatial uplift" that was intended to help poor Black Atlantans to learn how to navigate urban life.[36] Rodriguez further stresses that public housing tenant associations were a key platform for Black political organizing from the 1930s until the city bulldozed much of its public housing stock. Until then, the city had been a prolific builder of public housing, which accounted for as much as 10 percent of Atlanta's housing stock by 1978.[37] But when the run-up to the 1996 Olympics coincided with the federal HOPE VI public housing redevelopment program, Atlanta, along with Chicago, became one of the most active cities by far in public housing demolition. Although the most vital consequence was lost housing opportunities for many of the city's most disadvantaged, the Black political power base was also compromised by redevelopment because a key pillar of that power base had been the organizers based in public housing.

Maurice Hobson similarly frames Atlanta's pursuit of the 1996 Olympics as the Black political elite forsaking the needs of the city's Black poor to satisfy the desires of the White business establishment.[38] For cities, gaining the approval of the International Olympic Committee (IOC) has long been fraught with overspending on sport infrastructure of limited public value that can crowd out spending on more mundane but essential city services and public infrastructure. It is likely that Black elites chased Olympic dollars at the expense of public investments that would have benefited lower-income households.

Political and economic inequality within the Black community is inevitable and occurs everywhere. However, the Atlanta Black political establishment stands out for how early it rose to exert influence and then ultimately take over power in Atlanta. And rigorous observers of Atlanta's racial history repeatedly emphasize that this political establishment tended to curry favor with the White elite at the expense of the less-connected Black masses.[39] That Atlanta boasts such a precociously powerful Black political elite almost certainly contributes to its abnormally strong Black neighborhood indicators, even decades later. However, the Black political elite disproportionately favors the Black economic elite, and as we would see anywhere else, it is also beholden to non-Black economic and political interests.

Atlanta's Critical, Unique Role in the Civil Rights Movement

Atlantans made unparalleled contributions to the intellectual and organizing leadership of the civil rights movement. This involvement reflected a broader Black intellectual tradition exemplified by the city's historically Black colleges and universities (HBCUs), church leadership, and Black newspapers. Atlanta is home to four HBCUs, the Morehouse School of Medicine, and a consortium of historically Black theological seminaries. There is no other American city with such a concentration of HBCUs, and Spelman, Morehouse, and Clark Atlanta University are elite institutions that educate large numbers of the nation's Black middle class. In addition to these HBCUs, the Atlanta metro area has other strong institutions of higher education, such as Georgia Tech, Georgia State, and Emory. Jonathan Grant notes that Atlanta's Georgia State University, while not an HBCU, awards more bachelor's degrees to Blacks than any other nonprofit college or university.[40] It is undoubtedly the case that Atlanta has the greatest concentration of Black higher education institutions, students, and faculty in the country.

These institutions make Atlanta a unique home for Black intellectuals. They live and work in Atlanta in part because an ambitious Black elite has existed in Atlanta for a very long time. Two former slaves, James Tate and Grandison B. Daniels Clark, founded Atlanta University in 1865 as the first HBCU in the country. William Jefferson White, Tate's half-brother, founded Morehouse two years later. The country's most prominent Black intellectual of the early twentieth century, W.E.B. Du Bois, began his post-graduate academic career as a professor at (Clark) Atlanta University. Although the other famous Black intellectual leader at the turn of the twentieth century, Booker T. Washington, spent his career at the Tuskegee Institute in Alabama, his most (in)famous speech was made in Atlanta. His message to Blacks (or more directly to Whites with a keen ear) urging them to focus on industrial skills and commerce rather than access to voting and equal treatment under the law was pejoratively dubbed "the Atlanta Compromise" by Du Bois.

The success of its Black newspapers was another indicator of the rich intellectual and commercial life of Black Atlanta. Black newspapers served incredibly important roles in many U.S. cities throughout much of the twentieth century. The *California Daily Eagle* was instrumental in fighting housing discrimination in Los Angeles, and papers such as the *Pittsburgh Courier*, the *Chicago Defender*, and the *New York Amsterdam News* were a vital source of information on Black people and interests. Black newspapers were more widespread in the North, where it was safer to operate, but they had arisen in many southern cities by the 1930s. Leonard Ray Teel reports that by 1933 there was a southern newspaper syndicate that included forty-one Black newspapers, covering most major southern cities.[41] The *Atlanta World*, however, stood alone as the only daily Black newspaper in the South publishing with such frequency by 1932. Hundreds of Black newspapers had been started in the United States during the heyday of 1917–1934, but only thirty-three survived into the 1960s.[42] The *World*, now the *Atlanta Daily World*, continues publication to this day. Atlanta has actually had three Black newspapers with a significant readership over an extended period of time. In addition to the *World*, there was its precursor, the *Atlanta Independent*, and the *Atlanta Inquirer* has operated from 1960 to the present day. The *Inquirer* began as a more outspoken alternative to the *World*, which was hesitant to support civil rights demonstrations in the city, fearing an exodus by its advertisers.[43] That both papers reached such circulation at the same time speaks to the clout of Black Atlanta and the need for media that could speak to a diverse population.

Given the size of the Black population in Atlanta and the city's intellectual and institutional heft, it was no surprise that the civil rights pioneers of the mid-twentieth century were often headquartered and active in Atlanta. Prior to Rosa Parks's refusal to sit in the back of a Montgomery, Alabama, bus and the subsequent Montgomery Bus Boycott, Black ministers in Atlanta refused to sit in the back of the city's buses and successfully pushed for the end of segregation on Atlanta's public transportation.

Dr. Martin Luther King Jr. requires very little introduction, nor do his ties to Atlanta need much explanation. King's focus was national, but the fact that the country's preeminent civil rights leader was born and raised in Atlanta and returned there to become copastor (with his father) of Ebenezer Baptist Church reflects the strength of the Black church in Atlanta and its indelible imprint on the civil rights movement. What were arguably the two largest civil rights organizations of the 1950s and 1960s, the Southern Christian Leadership Conference (SCLC, cofounded by King) and the Student Nonviolent Coordinating Committee (SNCC), were headquartered in Atlanta for much of their existence. Andrew Young led the SCLC, served as the second Black mayor of Atlanta, and then represented an Atlanta congressional district in the U.S. House of Representatives. John Lewis led SNCC from 1963 to 1966 and then held Young's congressional seat from 1987 to 2020. Kruse adds to this incredible roster of Atlanta civil rights heroes and institutions in noting that James Weldon Johnson, Walter White, Ralph Abernathy, Whitney Young, Julian Bond, and Vernon Jordan also counted Atlanta home for all or some of their lives, as did the Commission on Interracial Cooperation and the Southern Regional Council.[44] Unfortunately, in struggles for justice as in physics, an action often precipitates an equal and opposite reaction. Thus, White supremacist leadership has also been heavily concentrated in Georgia. The Ku Klux Klan's headquarters were in Atlanta in the 1920s and 1930s, and the Columbians, the nation's first neo-Nazi organization, was founded in Atlanta in 1946.[45]

Perhaps more than anything else, Atlanta's Black intellectual leadership—in the academic and civil rights spheres in particular—set the city apart. Neither this leadership nor the previously discussed political leadership brought forth full citizenship or equal protection for Black Atlantans until the Civil Rights Act of 1964 and subsequent legislation, along with continued struggle. However, in part because of Black intellectual leadership and the key role of the Black elite in politics, Atlanta was not as fraught for Blacks as was the case in other southern cities. The University of Georgia in nearby Athens desegregated less violently and publicly than the University of Alabama, and the fight over integrating Little Rock's Central High School was much more intense than the integration of Atlanta's public schools. But the integration of schools unsettled White Atlantans to a significant degree and was intertwined with their unwillingness to share residential neighborhoods with Black Atlantans. The fight over housing had local characteristics, as all housing struggles do, but it also shared many of the same tactics and aspects as other housing fights across the country.

Housing Discrimination

Atlanta's late population growth, early Black presence, and location in the South had particular ramifications for housing discrimination and spatial segregation. First, northern cities did not often find it necessary to draw explicit racial boundaries until after the dust settled on the 1917 *Buchanan v. Warley* decision, which made it clear that such boundaries were unconstitutional.[46] Blacks and Whites had lived together in Atlanta in large numbers ever since there was much of a city to speak of, and well in advance of *Buchanan*, so Atlanta engaged in several efforts to enshrine racial boundaries into its zoning code, both before and after the Supreme

Court's decision. Another difference was that racially restrictive covenants did not gain a foothold in Atlanta until a late attempt to thwart Black home-seekers in a racial covenant drive in the 1940s. This effort came too late, for two reasons. First, cities like Los Angeles were highly successful in spreading racial covenants because they were applied en masse to new subdivisions.[47] The effort in Atlanta required a costly process of going door to door to convince individual homeowners to add covenants to existing deeds in established neighborhoods. Second, the Court struck down the enforcement of racially restrictive covenants in 1948 in the *Shelley v. Kraemer* decision.[48] Thus, as Atlanta's White homeowners were attempting to organize one another to expand the coverage of restrictive covenants, these covenants were increasingly difficult to enforce.

Otherwise, Atlanta shares many similarities with other U.S. cities when it comes to enforcement of racial segregation and the production of Black neighborhoods. Public housing segregation played a significant role in the segregation of the city. Atlanta built the first public housing development in the country, the Techwood Homes, set aside for Whites only. As in many other U.S. cities, many of Atlanta's numerous (by U.S. standards) public housing units and Atlanta's notorious highways were constructed through slum clearance and urban renewal projects. And the city used zoning and urban renewal to reinforce race and class boundaries, most famously by engaging in racial planning through the annexation spelled out in the 1952 "Plan for Improvement."

As in many cities across the country, residential segregation in Atlanta was enforced by violence. In September 1906, White mobs, inflamed by politicians and newspapers alleging that multiple White women had been sexually assaulted by Black men, indiscriminately attacked Black Atlantans over the course of three days.[49] Estimates of the dead vary, but it is likely that scores of Blacks were killed in the 1906 Atlanta race riots.

The moderate Atlanta political and business establishment largely shunned explicit racial attacks (verbal or physical) through World War II, but that changed when White and Black veterans returned to a city that had not built much housing at all in their absence.[50] Black neighborhoods, particularly those to the immediate west of downtown, were bursting at the seams. And a burgeoning Black middle class sought housing in transitioning and White neighborhoods. As a response, a potent White supremacist force arose as defenders of White neighborhoods.

A key battleground was the potential expansion of the Black district along Ashby Street to the west of downtown. Two major and violent organizations came to the fore. First, the neo-Nazi Columbians began patrolling the area with guns and other weapons. They intimidated potential Black homebuyers, engaged in several acts of violence, and assaulted Blacks who entered the area. The Columbians were short-lived, however, as the city and state cracked down on the organization to try to steer the housing fight in a more nonviolent direction. Meanwhile, the fight over housing in Atlanta spawned the rebirth of the Ku Klux Klan, which had been dormant for many years in the United States.

Although the KKK was also met with an official crackdown, its new membership would find an outlet through the newly formed West End Cooperative Corporation.[51] The WECC, led by KKK member Joe Wallace, operated as a more respectable group organizing White Westside homeowners, but it was the likely culprit in multiple bombings of homes purchased by Blacks. Kruse argues that while political leadership did not favor violence and intimidation, neighborhood groups were very effective in organizing against Black realtors attempting to make sales and banks interested in making loans in neighborhoods with potential for racial transition. By the 1950s, White homeowners had learned a lesson: they expunged radical, violent elements from the WECC and worked to make White resistance to integrated neighborhoods more respectable.

The most remarkable and Atlanta-style aspect to managing neighborhood racial transition was the move by Mayor Hartsfield in 1952 to create a biracial planning committee that would focus on issues of racial transition on the city's Westside.[52] The West Side Mutual Development Committee (WSMDC) included three Black leaders as well as representatives of local White homeowners' associations. The WSMDC, charged with investigating complaints about neighborhood racial change, became an important driver and representative of official city policy on neighborhood racial transition. Kruse describes how this process typically worked:

> With such information in hand, the WSMDC would generally call White homeowners' groups and black real-estate agents together to see if some sort of compromise—a boundary line, a program of repurchasing homes already sold to blacks, an alternate site for black homes, and so forth—could be voluntarily worked out. Once such a "gentleman's agreement" had been achieved, the WSMDC used the information to advise and influence property buyers and sellers, realty and home finance firms, and city departments about the neighborhood.[53]

While other city mayors also probably tried to engage in backroom deals to minimize the dissatisfaction on all sides from neighborhood racial transition, the WSMDC reflected a particularly Atlanta model: including Blacks as a junior partner and giving racial conflict an air of respectability and cooperation. The WSMDC managed several major neighborhood racial transitions and participated in reorienting highways and major arterials as well as other urban renewal projects to establish boundaries when necessary, in addition to making deals as described by Kruse. The WSMDC acted like an informal racial zoning board. But of course, when determining which neighborhoods were "a lost cause" (to Black succession) and which could still be saved, its judgments were far from scientific and were undoubtedly made with limited information and from a deeply flawed worldview. But, Kruse claims, "most Atlantans recognized that 'unofficial' recommendations of the WSMDC were, in fact, the official word on race and residence."[54]

Ultimately, however, Atlanta's population dynamics went in the same direction as most U.S. cities in the late twentieth century. School integration interacted with neighborhood racial transition, but in Atlanta it deviated from how White flight transpired in northern cities. Prior to *Brown v. Board of Education*, Atlanta's public schools were entirely segregated.[55] Thus, Blacks were moving into previously White residential space just as Atlanta's schools were forced to integrate. This undoubtedly accelerated White flight to the suburbs and out of the Atlanta public school system. Perhaps not coincidentally, in 1962, the city built roadblocks between an existing line of demarcation between Black and White neighborhoods on the Westside, which became the Peyton Wall. Although the wall was removed after persistent protests (on both sides), Whites rapidly fled the surrounding neighborhood, Peyton Forest. Kruse estimates that in the 1960s around sixty thousand Whites left Atlanta, and that one hundred thousand more would leave in the 1970s.[56] Further, Atlanta's White flight was not just a population migration—it also contributed to the political realignment of the Republican Party. Feeling that activist judges and politicians had violated their "freedom of association" (with one another only), Whites retreating from Atlanta to the surrounding suburbs became more mistrustful of government. This mistrust caused White Atlantans to retreat from public spaces as well and to defund public services that they saw benefiting Black Atlanta. The same dichotomy between suburbs and central cities played out in metropolitan areas across the country.

The Regional Economy

Compared to politics and race, less has been written in the academic literature about Atlanta's regional economy. But the city's entrepreneurial and pro-business culture both within and outside of the Black community is consistently emphasized by both academic and non-academic observers. Again, this is, after all, "the city too busy to hate."[57] Atlanta has been a core economic engine in the South since before the Civil War, when Sherman famously burned the city to the ground, in part because of its economic importance.

Atlanta's Black neighborhoods benefit from the strong regional economy. The city's unemployment rate is a paltry 3.2 percent, it is the home of Coca-Cola and Delta Airlines, and the metropolitan area is eighth in the country in the number of Fortune 1000 companies headquartered there.[58] This ranking is commensurate with Atlanta's metropolitan-area population ranking: in the South, the larger metros of Houston, Dallas, and Washington, D.C., have more Fortune 1000 companies (also in line with their population rankings).[59] However, the Atlanta region as a whole has the third-highest concentration of Fortune 500 companies in the nation behind New York and Houston.[60]

The center of Atlanta Black commerce, famously, is Auburn Avenue, which runs east of downtown Atlanta, and the center of the Sweet Auburn neighborhood. Auburn Avenue was so affluent and central to the Atlanta Black community historically that in 1956 *Fortune* magazine proclaimed it "the richest Negro street in the world."[61] Alonzo Herndon started off as a barber (serving only Whites) and then founded the Atlanta Life Insurance Company in 1905; eventually he became Atlanta's first Black millionaire. Home to Ebenezer Baptist Church, Martin Luther King Jr.'s childhood home, and the *Atlanta Daily World*, Auburn Avenue is not just a commercial center but a Black cultural center as well. The NAACP and the National Urban League have also had offices on Auburn Avenue.[62] On the other side of downtown is the Atlanta University Center, where the city's unparalleled concentration of HBCUs is found. Downtown Atlanta is therefore surrounded on two sides by a unique combination of Black Atlanta's intellectual, commercial, and cultural institutions.

There are at least two explanations for Atlanta's Black economic advancement. Grant describes Black Atlanta as an "independent communitarian economy."[63] He describes the entrepreneurial spirit of Atlanta's Black districts on Hunter Street and Auburn Avenue as intertwined with Black self-determination and a stabilizing influence on the community. In summarizing his interviews with Black Atlantans of various generations, he emphasizes how important it was to them that the community support Black-owned businesses. This priority is undoubtedly a feature of Black communities throughout the country, but in Atlanta's Black districts it is reinforced by a longer history and more capital than in most Black communities.

Cynthia Hewitt provides a more top-down explanation for Black Atlantans' success in the job market.[64] She notes that Blacks have managed to use an unusual amount of political clout to achieve Black concentration in relatively good jobs. Many of these jobs are in industries with connections to the local government and are obtained partly through what she calls "state-enforced inclusion" after "an extensive history of state-enforced exclusion."[65] Thus, in some job sectors in Atlanta, Black concentration bucks the norm of Black concentration in jobs typically being an indicator of low earnings and mediocre conditions. Black-concentrated jobs in Atlanta are still lower-paying than jobs in White-dominated industries, but that is not the case in some clusters of jobs—specifically, jobs close to local government, where Blacks wield more power than in the private sector.[66]

Kruse contrasts the deindustrialization of northern cities with less drastic changes in cities like Atlanta.[67] He argues that, on the one hand, Black and White workers in heavily industrial northern cities were more likely to work together and organize together in (eventually) desegregated labor unions. On the other hand, the disappearance of those industries fueled White flight and led to massive unemployment in central cities disproportionately occupied by Blacks. With its limited scale of industry, these forces were muted in Atlanta, but without deindustrialization as a problem, Kruse argues, the focus of attention was on desegregation, particularly in schools. In spite of this shift in attention toward desegregation (which had also prompted more fervent reactions in southern cities because of what Supreme Court decisions meant to the formal and informal ways that the color line was reinforced there), the comparison with northern cities is illuminating. Without the massive layoffs and employment declines in centrally located industries, Black neighborhoods in cities like Atlanta were less likely to be decimated by such layoffs. The cruel trajectory of Blacks moving to northern cities en masse, struggling to achieve equality in the workplace, and seeing huge numbers of low-skilled jobs leave just as they were gaining footholds in these industries, happened on a smaller scale in Atlanta.

For these reasons and others, the Atlanta regional economy is very strong, even if the central city has experienced some of the job losses that characterized most central cities in the late twentieth century. For better or worse, regional leaders embraced highway development in a way that helped Atlanta stand out as a logistics and warehousing center, further helped by the region's polycentric urban form. Coca-Cola is the oldest and most globally recognized Atlanta brand, but the United Parcel Service (UPS) and Delta Airlines are more indicative of the Atlanta region's dominance of the transportation and logistics sectors. Service jobs are generally far more prevalent than manufacturing ones, and the service sector is growing in the United States, while manufacturing is not. But as Fred Brooks notes, service jobs are low-paying.[68] He estimates that the five jobs with the most projected growth from 2001 to 2012 (he was writing in 2009) in Atlanta pay below the federal poverty line for a family of four.

Atlanta's Black neighborhood strength flows from its historical and contemporary strength in Black political power and intellectual leadership and its robust regional economy. Housing discrimination and income and wealth disadvantages for Black Atlantans have constrained that neighborhood strength, as in all other U.S. metros. Atlanta shares some of these features with the D.C. metro area, but there are important differences.

Chocolate City, Nation's Capital

Washington, D.C.'s unique relationship to state and federal government makes its historical, political, and economic context similarly unique among American cities. But there are some overlaps with Atlanta, which I will echo here rather than repeat in detail. Unlike Atlanta, Washington is regionally ambiguous—the census designates it as the South, and it shares many characteristics of a southern city, but in some ways D.C. is part of an East Coast mega-region that stretches up to Boston.

Like Atlanta, Washington was one of the first cities to have a large Black population, which has never consistently been lower than 25 percent, even going back to the early 1800s.[69] In 1900, Washington, D.C., had a higher Black share than any other city. Its population of more than eighty-six thousand Blacks was higher than the Black population of much larger New York City and roughly equivalent to Atlanta's Black population. As a result, a sizable educated Black elite has lived in Washington, D.C., for longer than Black elites in virtually every other American city, even Atlanta's, predating the Civil War.[70] Washington, D.C., also has one of the nation's best-known HBCUs in Howard University, and the smaller University of the District of Columbia is also located in the city. There are four HBCUs in Maryland, including Bowie State in Prince George's County and Coppin State and Morgan State in Baltimore. Another five HBCUs are farther away in Virginia but still accessible to the District. An additional similarity is that the two cities largely skipped the heavy manufacturing phase in the early to mid-twentieth century, so neither experienced the big decline in that sector.

Washington, D.C., like Atlanta, played an outsized role in the civil rights movement, but their roles were very different. Washington was the backdrop for congressional battles over civil rights legislation, Supreme Court arguments, and the March on Washington. Further, racial injustice in the capital city was a special stain on the image of a nation founded on the lofty ideals of equality, liberty, and freedom. While Atlanta provided high-level civil rights leadership, D.C. often provided the setting for major civil rights actions, most notably federal legislation and protest marches.

There are at least three significant differences in how Black neighborhoods in the D.C. and Atlanta metro areas developed. First, although the potential share of Black voters in Washington, D.C., was similar to the potential share of Black voters in Atlanta throughout much of the twentieth century, there was very little to vote for in the District. Second, the D.C. economy is heavily concentrated in federal jobs and related industries, although the twenty-first-century D.C. economy has diversified considerably. Third, while crime and the War on Drugs has plagued Black communities throughout the country, the flight of the Black middle class from Washington, D.C., and Baltimore had much to do with extreme problems with crime and violence in those cities.

An Atlanta-style community power structure never materialized in Washington, D.C., city politics in the mid-twentieth century because virtually no power structure was necessary. It is well known that D.C. has a peculiarly muted electoral voice. Visitors see the license plates that bemoan "Taxation Without Representation," but few know the history of why the District lacks representation, or that limits were placed on resident participation in municipal governance until relatively recently.

In the 1870s, the White power elite in Washington, D.C., chose to strip away their own control over city government in large part to stop Black voters from shaping that government. This would be the status quo for nearly a century. Black voters in Washington, D.C., had wielded political power even before the Fifteenth Amendment brought voting rights to Black men in 1870, influencing the mayoral election in 1868. Mayor Sayles J. Bowen was elected with Black help and appointed Blacks to positions in the fire and police departments.[71] However, the backlash was fierce—so fierce that the White power structure decided against a biracial democracy in favor of disenfranchising themselves and ceding control over city government to a congressionally appointed committee.

The territory that became Washington, D.C., was ceded by Maryland and Virginia in 1801; when that happened, residents learned that they no longer had representation in the national government. Congress, effectively playing the role of a state legislature governing the District, allowed the District's White male taxpayers to elect a city council.[72] In 1870, Whites who styled themselves reformers pushed back on Bowen's biracial coalition and convinced Congress to treat D.C. like a territorial government. This gave D.C.'s leader, Alexander Shepherd, broad authority over city growth and business.[73] Not only was Shepherd against Black suffrage, but like the nation's founders, he favored restricting voting rights to property owners. Shepherd overreached by going on a building spree that helped shape modern D.C. but left the city broke. Congress responded by breaking up the territorial government and replacing it with a system of three presidentially appointed city commissioners. This system ended home rule in Washington until the 1960s.

Through the twentieth century, Blacks organized politically through neighborhood and civic associations and churches, but nobody in the District was able to cast a meaningful vote until after President Lyndon Johnson obtained congressional approval to appoint Walter Washington mayor and name a majority-Black city council in 1967.[74] President Johnson made this move because political frustration among Black Washingtonians had reached a fever pitch. They were particularly dissatisfied with urban renewal, crumbling and failing schools, and police brutality. Swift demographic changes in the 1950s—the city went from 65 percent White to 54 percent Black during that decade—had led to rapidly rising poverty rates and declining city budgets.[75]

With poverty still rising and budgets becoming even more constrained in the 1970s, longtime Black activist Marion Barry was elected mayor in 1978. Barry was very successful at steering government contracts toward Black businesses (and his Black friends), but he faced a sea of challenges. The city had not yet fully formed a bureaucracy accountable to the mayor and council. The federal agencies that had governed the District for nearly a hundred years still served too many functions. But the biggest challenge was rising crime.

There were many causes of Washington, D.C.'s crime crisis in the 1970s and 1980s, but one significant factor was population loss that further concentrated poverty in the District. D.C. would lose population in every decade from 1950 to 2000, including nearly 120,000 people in the 1970s alone. Cash-strapped cities across the country were in the grip of rising heroin and later cocaine epidemics during this time, and cities experiencing substantial population losses were particularly vulnerable to rising crime and violence. Washington's crime problem and reputation as a high-crime city go back to at least the 1930s.[76] When crime rates rose throughout the country during the War on Drugs, Washington's rates were already high to begin with. By the 1980s, Washington's reputation as the nation's "murder capital" exceeded Detroit's reputation as a crime-ridden city. Although the moniker "murder capital" is undoubtedly racialized, it was also accurate. In 1991, D.C.'s homicide rate peaked at eighty per one hundred thousand residents—more than eight times the national average. The District's extreme problems with crime and violence hastened the flight of the Black middle class and contributed to the rapid establishment of the affluent Black neighborhoods clustered in Prince George's County.

The federal government heavily influenced the subsequent turnaround of Washington, D.C., on at least two fronts. First, in shaping Washington, D.C.'s urban and regional economy, the federal government set the stage for a globalized, post-industrial economic renaissance at the dawn of the twenty-first century. Second, the federal government stepped in when Marion Barry's patronage-plagued government went off the rails. In 1995, the federal government (again) took formal control over the city. Although this move clearly usurped DC residents' right to self-rule, which had been established only thirty years prior, it paved the way for a more technocratic style of governance that has helped usher in a new era of prosperity in the District.

This shift in governance has been complemented by unprecedented growth in the D.C. regional economy. There are many factors that have made the D.C. metro area home to some of the most affluent counties in the nation. A broad base of federal employment has always helped, and this sector has only grown its budgets and labor forces in recent decades. Increased outsourcing has further birthed and expanded private companies in the region, most (in)famously defense contractors, including Northrup Grumman, Lockheed Martin, and Raytheon. But what may have changed most dramatically in the last thirty years is the globalization of the U.S. economy and the unique position of the D.C. economy to take advantage of it.[77] The city is home to embassies representing the vast majority of the world's countries, and it has long been a tourist destination for foreign visitors. The federal government also has several agencies that oversee financial markets, making the region increasingly relevant (and wealthy) as financial industries occupy a larger share of global economic activity. The rapid economic growth in the region, improved D.C. governance, and reductions in crime have led to a dramatic turnaround in the city and surrounding area. But substantial economic and racial inequality has accompanied this turnaround, which has created the conditions for unequaled Black neighborhood gentrification—most obviously exemplified by the Shaw–U Street area.

Wrapping Up: Twenty-First-Century Black Meccas

Quantitative data are good at giving us an indication of what places have particular measurable characteristics, but they don't tell us how those characteristics came to be sorted across space. Data also efficiently describe average attributes of many places, but cannot dig deeply into any one place. Chapter 2 provided a summary of the typical forces that have concentrated disadvantage in Black neighborhoods. This chapter has traced the history of Black neighborhood development in the nation's two Black Meccas to better understand why Black neighborhoods are typically much more advantaged in those places. They are unique histories that offer some lessons for advancement in other metros.

Atlanta and Washington, D.C., share attributes that led to the concentration of the nation's Black middle class in these two metro areas. They were the two cities with the earliest critical mass of educated, wealthy, and free Black people. As a result, they were the first cities with the types of Black institutions necessary to promote Black advancement—HBCUs being one clear example in both cities. But political disenfranchisement in Washington contrasts sharply with the early informal political power of Atlanta's Black elite and the relatively early formal political power exercised by Black Atlantans, exemplified by Maynard Jackson, America's first big city Black mayor.

Both cities show the importance of a strong regional economy in making affluent Black neighborhoods possible. The rise of the Black middle class and its neighborhoods was more gradual in Atlanta, reflecting the earlier strength of its regional economy. The D.C. region's economy took off near the end of the twentieth century, solidifying the concentration of Black affluence, largely in Prince George's County. The success of the Black Meccas in Atlanta and Washington, D.C., suggests that the conditions that created them can be replicated elsewhere. Washington, D.C.'s ascendance is very recent and not wholly tied to long-standing demographics or industries. Other southern metro areas, such as Raleigh,

Dallas, and Houston, have experienced economic growth and strength similar to the D.C. and Atlanta metros. A growing Black population could create smaller-scale Black middle-class enclaves similar to those in the Black Meccas.

The study of growing southern metros is a necessary correction to the overwhelming northern bias of research on segregation and Black neighborhoods. D.C. and Atlanta in particular show a very different evolution of Black neighborhoods and political and economic power than is seen in the industrial North. Further, the industrial North is more representative of the twentieth-century past than the twenty-first-century present and future found in growing southern Black neighborhoods.

Chapter 8

How Do We Close the Gaps?

L.A. proved too much for the man
So, he's leaving the life he's come to know
—Gladys Knight and the Pips, "Midnight Train to Georgia," 1973

Black neighborhoods are the longest existing racial or ethnic enclaves in U.S. cities, having been ever present since the nineteenth century, when American urbanization began in earnest. The Black neighborhood also represents the greatest failures of U.S. urban policy, as these neighborhoods are persistently the most disadvantaged, both on average and at the extremes. Poverty, violence, and other indicators of disadvantage are not unique to Black neighborhoods, but they are most heavily concentrated in them.

In chapter 2, I reviewed the role of the state in creating the conditions for Black neighborhood disadvantage, which developed largely as a response to the Great Migration of millions of Blacks from the largely rural South to cities in the North (and later the West). Discrimination permeated virtually every aspect of urban life, including employment, education, policing, and voting. In housing, individuals and collectives discriminated against Black home-seekers in cities across the country. Federal, state, and local governments could have responded by pushing back against housing discrimination in the private market, but all available evidence suggests that pushback was tepid at best and overwhelmed by the discriminatory actions of these very governments.

The data presented in this book make clear that the gaps between Black neighborhoods and non-Black ones are substantial and have narrowed only slowly over time. But there is a lot of heterogeneity in Black neighborhoods, and particularly across metropolitan areas and even across regions. In the Midwest and smaller metros in the Northeast, Black neighborhood outcomes are worse, regardless of how they are measured. In many metropolitan areas of the South and West, Black neighborhood outcomes are stronger and more similar to outcomes in non-Black neighborhoods.

https://doi.org/10.7758/tjvh5404.1790

In models that look at the relative power of metropolitan-level and neighborhood-level characteristics in predicting Black neighborhood poverty rates, I find that income-generating and income-sorting processes at the metropolitan level are very important. It is not the case that a rising tide lifts all boats, but Black neighborhoods are much more likely to have lower poverty rates in high-income metros with lower income inequality. More manufacturing job shares are associated with lower Black poverty rates, suggesting that the loss of manufacturing jobs has contributed to Black neighborhood poverty. Segregation by income and race has weaker and more inconsistent correlations with Black neighborhood poverty. Metros with higher Black populations are also more likely to have lower-poverty Black neighborhoods. Neighborhood-level characteristics—high vacancy, unemployment, and female-headed household rates and lower educational attainment—are also strongly associated with Black neighborhood poverty, even controlling for metropolitan-level factors.

Within metropolitan areas, not surprisingly, Black neighborhood conditions in the suburbs are better than in central cities, and the gap is widening as more and more Black families relocate to the suburbs. I also find that neighborhood change is slow in Black neighborhoods. Rather than gentrification, stasis is the norm in Black neighborhoods. Of the Black neighborhoods with poverty rates 20 percent or higher in 1980 that remained Black neighborhoods in 2017, 86 percent still had poverty rates that high nearly forty years later. This all suggests that neighborhood-level interventions are unlikely to be very successful in the face of intransigent metro-level conditions and the persistence of Black neighborhood poverty.

There are success stories. Black neighborhoods in the Washington, D.C., and Atlanta metro areas have particularly high socioeconomic indicators, and other large southern metro areas are also doing well. Unfortunately, 20 percent poverty rates qualify as low for Black neighborhoods; Charlotte, Dallas, Raleigh, and Houston all boast average Black neighborhood poverty rates below that mark. These growing southern metros accounted for roughly 6 percent of the nation's total Black neighborhoods in the 2015–2019 ACS. Outside of the South, the nation's mega-regions have good indicators in Black neighborhoods. The New York, Los Angeles, and San Francisco metro areas are also locations where Black neighborhoods are stronger. Los Angeles and San Francisco have lost most of their Black neighborhoods, first owing to immigration (particularly Los Angeles) and now to rising rents. In high-cost metros in particular, low homeownership rates and rising rents are likely to make it difficult for Black neighborhoods to remain Black owing to the displacement of lower-income renters.

Given the substantial differences across metropolitan areas, policies at a higher level of geography than neighborhoods are more likely to be successful. Current policy interventions are narrowly targeted to neighborhoods, however, and rarely sustained over time.

In this chapter, I discuss why past and present policies have largely failed to remedy Black neighborhood disadvantage and offer a set of proposals that might be more successful. The policy debate on turning around neighborhood disadvantage has centered on identifying the right mix between people- and place-based investments, although most scholars and policymakers in this field by now recognize that both are essential.[1] However, given the substantial differences across metropolitan areas and regions and the persistent disparities between Blacks and other racial groups, policy needs to operate at higher levels of geography than just the neighborhood, while also addressing household-level disparities. There is a place for neighborhood-level investments, but these investments will continue to have limited reach if they are not accompanied by interventions to address disparities at the household and metropolitan levels.

Four Key Findings

I begin with four observations from the data presented in this book that shed light on the limits of neighborhood-based policy. First, the slow improvement in socioeconomic conditions in Black neighborhoods has tracked the slow improvement in such outcomes for Black people more broadly, even as those neighborhoods have become somewhat less racially concentrated. From 1980 to 2017, the average poverty rate of Black neighborhoods declined from 28 to 23 percent, which essentially mirrors the change over that time in Black household poverty rates (in the sample of metros in the book), which declined from 30 to 23 percent. Unemployment rates and educational characteristics have also changed for Black individuals and neighborhoods in similar ways. Homeownership rates are the main notable divergence: they slowly rose in Black neighborhoods but remained flat among Black individuals.

The second observation is that metropolitan-level differences are vast, reflecting the importance of regional economies. In the Peoria, Illinois, metropolitan area, there were ten Black census tracts in 2017. The unemployment rate in those neighborhoods ranged from 12 percent to 31 percent. The *average* Black census tract in the Nashville metro has an unemployment rate half as high (6 percent) as Peoria's most gainfully employed Black tract. Black people who wish to move to a Black neighborhood in Peoria with decent labor force outcomes are out of luck. Peoria's non-Black census tracts have a poverty rate of only 10 percent, compared to an astonishing 41 percent poverty rate in Black census tracts. Black people in Peoria could move to non-Black neighborhoods to surround themselves with greater incomes and opportunity. But these numbers suggest that there is something about Peoria that constrains opportunity for Black people regardless of where they reside. This was the case for the family of native son Richard Pryor, the comedian who infamously grew up in a brothel.

The third observation is that the characteristics of various metropolitan areas that appear to be associated with stronger Black neighborhood outcomes are often quite fundamental to those metropolitan areas. In other words, it is hard to replicate these conditions in other metros, if they don't already exist, because they have been this way for a long time. The widespread Black neighborhood disadvantage in midwestern metros and a handful of aging, smaller northeastern metros emphasizes the role of the economic geography of these places—and thus of their economic history. The characteristics that make Atlanta and Washington, D.C., centers of the Black middle class are also historical and difficult to replicate elsewhere. Each of these cities had Black political majorities as early as the 1960s, and neither region experienced the rapid deindustrialization common in northeastern and midwestern metros. More contemporarily, Atlanta and D.C. represent two of the most populous and affluent metropolitan areas in the South, a region that is growing economically and becoming the source of the country's most affluent Black neighborhoods.

Finally, the fourth observation is that the loud chorus around gentrification is overheated in Black neighborhoods, relative to the data. There is some evidence that gentrification has been increasingly prevalent in Black neighborhoods over the last twenty years, but the problem is growing slowly. A problem far more common than gentrification in Black neighborhoods is concentrated disadvantage. But as with most characteristics and trends, there is substantial variation across regions and metropolitan areas. Black neighborhoods are not only disappearing in the West but undergoing gentrification at nearly twice the rate of any other region. In the San Francisco–San Jose–Oakland metropolitan area, 25 percent of Black neighborhoods gentrified between 2000 and 2017, compared to 6 percent in the Detroit metro.

Existing Interventions in Black Neighborhoods

Despite the ubiquity and gravity of social and economic problems in urban Black neighborhoods since the Great Migration, policy interventions to address them have been inconsistent and uncoordinated. Three place-based policy areas are often pertinent to Black neighborhood outcomes: housing, economic development, and community development.[2] Because of the race-neutral nature of each of these policy areas (and U.S. social policy more broadly), very few interventions explicitly target Black neighborhoods. In each domain, neighborhood poverty rates and other economic indicators typically determine neighborhood eligibility for resources or policy. But a disproportionate number of Black neighborhoods qualify for such interventions because of their poor economic indicators. Thus, many of the housing, community development, and economic development policy interventions over the last fifty-plus years have been carried out in Black neighborhoods.

The legacy of housing discrimination and disparate outcomes in housing policy form the core mechanisms through which residential segregation shapes Black neighborhood disadvantage. Further, there is arguably much more activity in housing policy, as it pertains to reversing segregation and improving conditions in Black neighborhoods, so I begin and focus there.

Over the last fifty years, low-income housing policy has changed dramatically, shifting from public housing to a much greater reliance on housing vouchers and the Low-Income Housing Tax Credit. To the extent that public housing contributed to problems in Black neighborhoods, this shift should benefit those places. But public housing has generally been blamed for too many problems and not given sufficient credit as a solution, so the loss of affordable housing options through public housing redevelopment has at times outweighed the benefit of removing distressed and segregated public housing in Black neighborhoods.

The Housing Choice Voucher Program, the largest subsidy program to assist low-income households with the cost of rental housing, disproportionately locates residents in Black neighborhoods.[3] As a people-based subsidy, however, the program has a limited impact on Black neighborhoods. The voucher program does provide substantial revenue for landowners in Black neighborhoods and creates incentives to invest in housing in these neighborhoods. The residents who obtain vouchers benefit, as do the landlords. But many landlords reside outside of these communities, and there is evidence that the voucher program raises the cost of housing for people who do not have a voucher.[4] We don't know much about how the housing voucher program influences socioeconomic characteristics in neighborhoods—either the neighborhoods where renters use vouchers to remain or move into or the neighborhoods that renters use vouchers to leave. But we can probably be confident that the limited number of housing voucher households either entering or leaving any community means that the movement of these populations is having a limited effect on Black neighborhoods. Public housing, in contrast, provides a visible target that higher-income households often want to avoid, and in some places housing developments comprise entire neighborhoods on their own.

We do, however, know a lot about what happens to individuals who use vouchers to escape high-poverty (and often highly Black) neighborhoods. Matthew Desmond has credibly estimated that there is roughly one study for each of the 4,608 families that participated in the Moving to Opportunity for Fair Housing Demonstration Program.[5] MTO randomly assigned public housing tenants in five cities to one of three groups: (1) the experimental group, which was given a housing voucher that could only be used in low-poverty (rates less than 10 percent) neighborhoods; (2) the Section 8 group, which was given a housing voucher that could be used in any neighborhood; and (3) the control group, which was provided with no additional services. Sixty-one percent of the study sample households were headed by a Black adult, and the origin census tracts were 91 percent minority.[6] Therefore, we can apply many of the MTO findings to the experiences of Black people living in Black neighborhoods. MTO was largely a study of people who left Black public housing neighborhoods to move, in many cases, to other Black neighborhoods.

The voucher groups achieved better outcomes than the control group in several ways. Neighborhood and housing satisfaction increased, and adult mental and physical health outcomes improved. Long-term follow-ups detected better employment, earnings, and college attendance outcomes for youth participants as they aged into adulthood, particularly those who entered the program at an early age and spent a relatively long time in higher-opportunity neighborhoods.[7] But some outcomes were no different than they would have been without the vouchers, including adult employment and earnings, criminal involvement, and risk behaviors for adults and children. There are limitations to using a housing voucher program to move people out of disadvantaged neighborhoods and into better household outcomes.[8] A ticket out of a disadvantaged Black neighborhood is not sufficient to eliminate racial disparities in income, education, and other life outcomes. That is an incredibly high bar for a housing program to reach.

A formidable limitation to residential mobility is the White supremacist infrastructure that governs neighborhood and individual-level opportunity (much of which was covered in chapter 2). Most recently, David Imbroscio has critiqued the overemphasis on residential mobility for failing to acknowledge that opportunity follows whiteness and that efforts to nudge or incentivize moves into high-opportunity neighborhoods will never achieve the desired outcomes.[9] Imbroscio points out that White flight siphons opportunity away from central cities and into the suburbs, and that such opportunity returns to central cities when Whites return as gentrifiers. This is a delicate point, so I quote Imbroscio directly:

> In specific terms, concentrations of affluent Whites in privileged areas do not have (or possess) "opportunity," in the sense that, ontologically, it is characterized by the property of something that can be alienated or estranged from them. Rather they are—in essential terms—the "opportunity" itself. Simply put, in a society where affluent whiteness conveys massive privilege—and, indeed, outright supremacy—the reason affluent White areas are such depositories of opportunity is because they have a plethora of affluent and White people living in them.[10]

Imbroscio's solution is to focus more on the distribution of wealth (more on this later). Although the distribution of wealth is undoubtedly a source of spatial inequities by income, wealth, and race, a more ambitious attack on segregation is also warranted. Mobility programs that give small numbers of low-income households access to marginally better neighborhoods have two obvious limitations. First, they solve the neighborhood disadvantage problem for only the small fraction of people who obtain the golden ticket. Second, they do nothing to reduce the disparities between affluent and disadvantaged neighborhoods, and they clearly do not address the devaluation of Black neighborhoods in real estate markets and the public imagination. In fact, prioritizing mobility out of such neighborhoods can reaffirm that devaluation. While MTO's results suggest that crucial benefits can accrue to individual movers, narrowing the gaps between affluent and disadvantaged (often Black) neighborhoods and decoupling neighborhood whiteness from neighborhood opportunity require something different.

The Low-Income Housing Tax Credit program is now (along with housing vouchers) the other anchor of low-income rental housing subsidies. There are some ways that LIHTC can help reduce segregation and, potentially, Black neighborhood disadvantage. First, because LIHTC developments have a smaller footprint than public housing and tend to blend into neighborhoods, they are less likely to arouse stigma and negative perceptions of the surrounding neighborhood. As a replacement for public housing, LIHTC developments can reduce the devaluation of Black neighborhoods where public housing has been removed. Second, LIHTC developments are less likely to be located in high-poverty and racially concentrated neighborhoods than public housing.[11] The benefits of this are ambiguous, as some neighborhoods may feel the loss of housing investment and affordable housing stock. On the other hand, LIHTC housing in less-disadvantaged neighborhoods can give people more options for locating in higher-opportunity areas. Two additional aspects of LIHTC may benefit Black neighborhoods. First, there is potential for income mix built into the program, in that developers obtain funding from tax credits if they set aside a share of units for low-income tenants, so not all of the tenants in the development have to have low incomes.[12] Thus, LIHTC developments may be able to economically integrate poorer Black neighborhoods. Second, LIHTC funds (particularly the smaller 4 percent tax credit) are often deployed to rehabilitate distressed properties. This use of funds could buoy demand in Black neighborhoods that people avoid because of aging infrastructure and reverse decades of underinvestment. Most of the LIHTC program's integrative potential, however, has yet to be realized.[13] The empirical evidence suggests that LIHTC does little to exacerbate or mitigate concentrated poverty.[14] On the other hand, there is preliminary evidence that LIHTC does a little more to reduce racial segregation.[15]

In addition to the more direct effects on neighborhood demographics, LIHTC production may affect neighborhoods more indirectly, similar to how neighborhood investment or other forms of subsidized housing production affect a surrounding area. Research on these indirect effects finds mixed results. On the one hand, the LIHTC decreases neighborhood income and housing turnover, but on the other hand, it raises property values in more-distressed neighborhoods.[16] The overall effects might be rather small. Matthew Freedman and Tamara McGavock also find changes in neighborhood income composition, but those changes are not large enough to affect measures of concentrated poverty or racial segregation.[17] Freedman and Emily Owens find that LIHTC development contributes to lower levels of neighborhood violent crime but has no effect on property crime.[18] Several studies also find that LIHTC development crowds out private development, so we should expect somewhat muted effects on neighborhoods.[19] Because some of this development would have occurred anyway, LIHTC probably should not be compared to a counterfactual of zero development.

The third big change in housing policy concerns public housing demolition and redevelopment. Congress funded HOPE VI in 1993 as a HUD-administered grant program. HOPE VI funded local public housing authorities for the planning of demolition and revitalization of public housing; ultimately, HOPE VI contributed approximately $6.7 billion to the development of 262 sites in 34 states. Evidence for HOPE VI's effects on neighborhoods is provided by Coley and her colleagues and by Laura Tach and Allison Emory.[20] To begin, each paper provides evidence for just how concentrated HOPE VI spending was in Black neighborhoods. Coley and her colleagues look at 309 census tracts covering the vast majority of HOPE VI spending and estimate that those census tracts were, on average, 60 percent Black.[21] Tach and Emory estimate that the 1990 share Black for the 420 block groups with HOPE VI grantees was 66 percent.[22] In fact, there is a common concern that housing authorities intentionally demolished public housing in Black neighborhoods in order to make centrally located but racially segregated neighborhoods attractive to outside investment.[23]

HOPE VI is thus very relevant to Black neighborhoods. In theory, HOPE VI—and its successor, Choice Neighborhoods—can make some Black neighborhoods more attractive to renters, prospective homeowners, and investors by removing distressed public housing and reducing concentrated poverty and racial segregation. Tach and Emory find that HOPE VI neighborhoods did experience declines in poverty and share minority as a result of public housing redevelopment.[24] But confirming what many feared about HOPE VI investments, these neighborhood changes displaced significant numbers of low-income and minority residents.[25] In some ways, Coley and her colleagues update Tach and Emory's work in their finding that, five years after redevelopment was completed, poverty had decreased more in census tracts with HOPE VI developments than in matched comparison census tracts, by over two percentage points.[26] They do not find any effects on the racial composition of these census tracts, nor on the presence of services and amenities. Importantly, in a separate analysis of Black neighborhoods, they find that HOPE VI led to decreased poverty and increases in median income in these census tracts but did not change the racial composition. On the one hand, this is pretty good news—reducing concentrated poverty without displacing the Black population is a great outcome. On the other hand, these authors conclude, the changes in income and poverty characteristics probably stemmed from an influx of moderate-income families into HOPE VI neighborhoods and the displacement of at least some poor incumbent residents.

On the whole, recent housing policy has not been successful at turning around the fortunes of Black neighborhoods. Nor, in the case of housing vouchers, have they been a panacea for Black recipients who leave disadvantaged neighborhoods hoping to turn their fortunes around. HOPE VI helped spur innovation in public housing redevelopment in the form of the Choice Neighborhoods program. More recently, HUD has provided additional ways to merge public and private resources in the hope of revitalizing the public housing stock through the Rental Assistance Demonstration. But both programs are located in a small number of places with short-term financial commitments, so they are unlikely to be long-term solutions to concentrated disadvantage in Black neighborhoods. Further, the successes of HOPE VI came from removing distressed public housing, which is not in large supply in most Black neighborhoods.

These problems are indicative of Sharkey's critique that the United States has never had a durable urban policy.[27] U.S. urban policy interventions tend to be fleeting, and many are implemented in response to crisis. But the injustices and policy failures that produced urban inequality were decades in the making and therefore stabilizing the affected neighborhoods and their residents will require decades of a different kind of intervention. Durable investments are particularly important in Black neighborhoods. Chapter 5 showed (confirming research by Sharkey) that advantaged Black neighborhoods are far more likely than advantaged non-Black neighborhoods to be surrounded by disadvantaged neighborhoods. Given this, even advantaged Black neighborhoods have a tenuous grip on their higher status, as disinvestment and disrepair can bleed across borders.

Community and Economic Development

Housing has received the bulk of the attention, money, and research when it comes to neighborhood-based investments. And most of the research on housing has focused on policies to counteract segregation, largely by providing people a way out of disadvantaged (often Black) neighborhoods. Research and policy on community development and economic development, by contrast, are concerned with direct interventions in these neighborhoods, similar to scholarship on housing production (LIHTC, HOPE VI, and public housing). This smaller and more scattered body of research evaluates what investments in disadvantaged neighborhoods work. As in housing policy, these disadvantaged neighborhoods hold concentrations of various races and ethnicities, so the policies and research on them are not exclusively about Black neighborhoods. But the results give us a window into what can lead to more successful outcomes in Black neighborhoods.

Community development can be any process in which individuals and groups collectively organize to affect change in their communities. The desired changes commonly concern housing and economic development. In other words, a substantial amount of what we know about the effectiveness of localized housing interventions can be applied to community development policy and practice. But there is separate funding and programming for community development. The modern form of community development took shape in the 1960s—organically in many Black neighborhoods—as a response to concentrated disadvantage. These grassroots processes gained funding and institutional support through various Great Society programs. Since 1974, the federal government has funded such work with the Community Development Block Grant (CDBG). CDBG allows local communities and jurisdictions to apply for funding for a range of activities to benefit low-income people, prevent or eliminate blight, or address other urgent infrastructure or service needs. Using data from seventeen cities, Galster and his colleagues find that CDBG spending positively impacted home loans, mortgage approvals, and the number of businesses, suggesting that more spending can catalyze additional private investment in communities.[28] On the fortieth anniversary of the CDBG, William Rohe and Galster took a broader look at the accomplishments and shortcomings of the program, which disbursed about $130 billion from 1974 to 2014.[29] On the plus side, they note that CDBG streamlined several programs for different purposes into one block grant that communities could apply for, and that it provided a consistent source of funds for activities that rarely had consistent funding. On the negative side, waste and lack of transparency were problems, the neediest jurisdictions and individuals tended not to obtain CDBG funds, and there was no well-defined group of activities for which these funds were deemed appropriate (or inappropriate). Evaluations of community development efforts are challenging to do and have been sparse. As a result, we have little concrete data on whether and how community development has been effective.

One of the most dramatic improvements in U.S. urban life has been the decline in crime and violence since the early 1990s. In virtually every city in the nation, the crime rates of the 2010s were substantially below those of the 1990s. Crime started falling in different years in different cities, but the trend mostly began in the 1990s. Once it started falling in a given city, it essentially never stopped.[30] Crime and violence rates had the furthest to fall in Black neighborhoods, in many of which those declines were substantial. Unfortunately, these improvements were not universal in Black neighborhoods, and the neighborhoods where crime rates did not improve still have the highest rates of crime and violence in the country. Sharkey points to a wave of community mobilization—essentially community development—as deserving some of the credit for the historic turnaround.[31] In related work, Sharkey, Gerard Torrats-Espinosa, and Delaram Takyar amassed a national longitudinal dataset of nonprofit organizations that address neighborhood safety and local crime rates to test whether the former contributed to a decline in the latter.[32] They found that every ten additional organizations led to a 9 percent lower murder rate, a 6 percent lower violent crime rate, and a 4 percent lower property crime rate. There are many other causes of the crime decline, including policing improvements and increased technological surveillance (for better or worse). This is one example of community development appearing to have played an important role in a critical improvement to Black neighborhood life, but we still lack rigorous evidence of its broader efficacy.

Economic development policy has produced more rigorous scholarship, even if the policies implemented have been similarly fleeting. Many of these policies involve tax incentives that conveniently have cutoffs that allow us to assess the effects of these policies on neighborhood employment, income, and other economic outcomes. Enterprise zones are a broad category of neighborhood-based or local tax incentives that have been implemented through different programs in the United States. The federal Enterprise Community program was authorized in 1993, confusingly at the same time as the federal Empowerment Zone program was implemented. Each of these programs allows local governments to submit proposals to target incentives to communities with high unemployment and poverty rates.[33]

The California enterprise zone program offers some of the best opportunities to study the effects of such policies on Black neighborhoods because it geographically targets small areas. David Neumark and Jed Kolko ably summarize prior attempts to study enterprise zones and address many of the programs' shortcomings by exploiting the expansion of the original zones to create more reliable control areas.[34] They find no evidence that enterprise zones affect employment. On the other hand, Freedman found annual employment growth of 1 to 2 percent when he exploited a discontinuity in the selection criteria (poverty rates had to be 20 percent or higher, thus more likely affecting Black neighborhoods) to identify whether employment rates changed in Texas neighborhoods just above the cutoff more than they did in neighborhoods below the cutoff, after enterprise zone incentives were awarded.[35]

But these localized programs, even if they work, probably solve less important job problems. Spatial mismatch probably doesn't matter that much for Black unemployment.[36] The lack of jobs in and near Black neighborhoods matters less than the fact that Black people are less likely to be hired for those jobs regardless of whether or not they are nearby. This is evident from recent research on the New Market Tax Credit (NMTC) program; that study finds that a lot of the jobs created through this program went to people who lived outside of the targeted neighborhood.[37] So small declines in spatial mismatch in response to localized economic development incentives are unlikely to play a significant role. More worryingly, recent localized economic development incentives appear to be less effective than their predecessors. The Opportunity Zone program was created by Congress in 2017 to much suspicion about the high-wealth recipients of these tax breaks and questions about how those benefits were to trickle down to the residents of the target neighborhoods.[38] It is too early to definitively state the effects of this program, but the early evidence is not promising.[39]

Several major housing, community development, and economic development policies have been targeted at Black neighborhoods, with only mild success. These neighborhood-based investments have rarely been sustained over decades. More frequently, they have targeted a project or set of households for relatively brief periods of time.

Moving Forward on Three Pillars: Regional Focus, Inclusive Development, and Investing in People

Much is needed to eliminate the gap in socioeconomic conditions between Black and non-Black neighborhoods. I have narrowed the top priorities down to three pillars: regional focus, inclusive development, and invest in people.

Regional Focus

Rethink Mobility One of the most consistent findings in this book is how persistently poor the Black neighborhood outcomes are in the aging metropolitan areas of the Midwest and Northeast compared to the South and the West. The big caveat to the strong indicators in the West is that there are few Black neighborhoods in that region and their number is getting smaller. For a Black family that wishes to live in a stable Black neighborhood with high-income neighbors, there are many options in the South and very few elsewhere.

This is where a radical proposal by Charles Blow comes in. Blow's 2021 book *The Devil You Know* is a full-throated argument that Black people should move back to the South so that they can command electoral majorities and gain political power.[40] Blow notes that Black electoral majorities probably would have already formed in the South had the Great Migration never happened, as population majorities would have translated into electoral ones by now. Although Blow's proposition is smart and radical, I don't think that huge numbers of Black people will be motivated by electoral politics to make such a move. Barely a majority of people vote in our most highly publicized and hotly contested elections, and very few people move in order to make their vote matter more. Anticipating this latter point, Blow points to a precedent. In the 1960s, some on the left called for an electoral mobilization to Vermont. Blow estimates (without citation) that "between 1965 and 1975, 100,000 young, like-minded people would move to the state."[41] He credits such political mobility as the making of the political careers of Senators Patrick Leahy and Bernie Sanders.

I remain skeptical that electoral concerns can drive mass migration. While political refugees comprise substantial shares of the world's migrants, that is not what northern Blacks moving to the South would be. And while it is fine to advocate for these moves based on electoral concerns, absent flight from war or political persecution, economic opportunity is always a more compelling migratory motivator. Urban areas in the South (and the Black neighborhoods within them) offer Black people ample economic opportunities. Many of the country's fastest-growing metropolitan regions, by population and economics, are in the South.[42] Further, the most rapidly improving conditions in Black neighborhoods are clearly found in the South when we combine indicators of economic improvement with sheer numbers of Black neighborhoods. Black people have been moving back to the South in significant numbers since the 1970s, and this movement has been accelerating in recent years.[43] Atlanta, for example, overtook Chicago in 2010 as the city with the second-largest Black population (after New York). Blacks are likely to be making these moves for largely economic and cultural reasons. Black migrants returning to the South can expand their economic *and* political power when they move into existing southern Black neighborhoods.

It may be hard to see how public policy can influence moves across the country. There are things that government can do, but other sectors can play a role in nudging migration. The Great Migration grew from word of mouth but also in response to exhortations in Black newspapers such as the *Chicago Defender*. Blow emphasizes the intentional role that newspapers like (but especially) the *Defender* played in inspiring southern Blacks to leave for the North. Black social media as well as traditional media outlets can play a similar role in normalizing a return to the South and making a case for seeking opportunities in fast-growing southern regions such as Raleigh, Atlanta, and Dallas. Although much of this media infrastructure is, of course, located in places like New York, Black newspapers are numerous and thriving in Atlanta, which undoubtedly has a massive Black social and traditional media presence.

Would a southern government actively recruit Black people to move to its Black neighborhoods? The growing number of Black mayors—who govern fourteen of the largest fifty cities in the country—may think along those lines.[44] These include Atlanta, Baltimore, Dallas, Charlotte, Houston, and Washington, D.C., as well as several in the South outside the top fifty, such as Birmingham, Little Rock, and New Orleans. If, for better or worse, companies target specific demographics all the time, southern mayors can also sponsor ad campaigns promoting their cities to Black people and even spearhead local legislation that would provide financial incentives for locating in Black neighborhoods. Economic development programs can target Black neighborhoods in cities that provide tax breaks to entrepreneurs or other small business owners, and down payment assistance for first-time homebuyers might entice Black migrants from the North. In highly productive metropolitan areas in the South and elsewhere, it is essential to build enough homes to keep up with the pace of migration and broader population trends. If people move to these highly productive metros and we do not build enough housing, existing housing will become too expensive for many incumbent residents and make these migration patterns less attractive and feasible. Peter Ganong and Daniel Shoag have demonstrated that high housing costs in productive metros have deterred low-skilled workers from moving to them.[45]

Although regional mobility may seem like a much harder lift than encouraging mobility across neighborhoods within metropolitan areas, the potential for improving neighborhood location is actually higher when moving across regions. Moving within regions, a prospective job seeker is subject to the same labor market, and children are subject to the same schools unless their family moves across district boundaries.

Further, when people make regional moves rather than move within their own metropolitan area, they are more likely to make integrative moves; in other words, regional mobility is more likely to promote residential integration.[46] Although the focus of this book and my policy proposals is to improve conditions in Black neighborhoods, integration performs important functions as well. Black neighborhoods will continue to be devalued until a diverse population sees living in and visiting Black neighborhoods as normal. That cannot happen until a greater array of people know others who live there.

Whether or not local officials are likely to incentivize Black people to move South, some might wonder if Blacks will feel comfortable moving to the South, where racial lines have traditionally been more sharply drawn. But the post–Great Migration experiences of urban Black Americans outside of the South have largely been a massive struggle, and there is little promise of widespread Black advancement in these cities. The North-South gap in racial animosity toward Blacks has probably been overblown for quite some time. As far back as 1971, comedian and activist Dick Gregory observed: "Down South white folks don't care how close I get as long as I don't get too big. Up North white folks don't care how big I get as long as I don't get too close."[47] Accordingly, in the post–civil rights era, discrimination against Black Americans has probably differed between North and South not so much in degree as in kind. Blow emphasizes the role of police violence and everyday harassment through policies such as stop-and-frisk. The highest-profile and most systematic violations of Black rights by police have occurred in northern cities. Philando Castile and George Floyd were murdered in Minnesota's Twin Cities, Michael Brown in Ferguson, Missouri, Tamir Rice in Cleveland, and Laquan McDonald in Chicago. Southern police, of course, have blood on their hands as well—the killings of Breonna Taylor (Louisville) and Freddie Gray (Baltimore) are just two tragedies out of many—but the urban warfare and infringement on civil liberties brought by the War on Drugs has been acutely felt by Black communities in the North, with devastating consequences. And again, Blacks have been migrating to the South in substantial numbers over the past fifty years. They will continue to do so, and they should.

Invest in the Midwest The people-versus-place debate at the neighborhood level also takes place at the regional level. Even as I hope to draw attention to the logic of a reverse migration to the South, regional economic development is an active policy area where some radical proposals could help catalyze the midwestern (and some northeastern) economies that have been left behind by deindustrialization. These are the regions where Black neighborhoods are struggling the most, and simply moving all of their residents to the South is neither desirable nor feasible. Reducing economic inequality across regions by improving midwestern economic fortunes would dramatically improve Black neighborhood conditions.

State and municipal governments offer tax breaks, services (such as job training), and other incentives to attract businesses, influence their expansion, or stop them from leaving, closing, or downsizing. Much of the empirical evidence on these cross-jurisdictional competitions for business attention has been covered by Timothy Bartik and George Erickcek.[48] In short, sometimes these efforts are worth the government expenditure or tax loss, and sometimes they are not. But we can think bigger in this area. The first idea is to move some federal government functions to aging midwestern cities. Matthew Yglesias makes a case for making such a move, noting that while some government agencies are located in the Washington, D.C., area to facilitate access to Congress, there are undoubtedly many government employees and functions that do not require proximity.[49] The Centers for Disease Control and Prevention (CDC) in Atlanta is a good example of a major federal undertaking headquartered elsewhere. Perhaps not coincidentally, D.C. and Atlanta are the metro areas with the strongest Black neighborhood outcomes, demonstrating that a federal presence matters. Yglesias suggests that the National Institutes of Health (NIH) and its twenty thousand employees could leave Bethesda, Maryland, and relocate in Cleveland, among other potential destinations. A tell that spatial proximity is not entirely essential is the fact that so many federal agencies are already in suburban D.C.—not to mention the recent explosion in remote work spawned by the COVID-19 pandemic.

Yglesias further notes that the Midwest has some fundamental strengths that would complement a larger federal presence. The low cost of housing would be attractive to federal employees whose salaries are lower than in much of the private sector. But perhaps most importantly, there are world-class public universities in the Midwest that would not only collaborate with these agencies for the production of knowledge and policy innovation but also provide graduates seeking to stay local with federal employment options. Relatedly, such a collaboration would benefit even further if state governments in the Midwest reversed course and invested money in their public university systems to make existing campuses larger and open more satellite campuses. An enlarged state university system in Ohio would address high Black neighborhood poverty rates in Cleveland and Columbus. The University of Michigan was founded in Detroit in 1817 but now has only a small presence in the state's largest city. The recent turnaround of the area around Wayne State University in Detroit shows the important local role that a university can play. Additional investment by the state in this university and the University of Michigan system would pay big regional dividends that would most likely pull up Black and other disadvantaged neighborhoods. State university expansion in struggling midwestern and northeastern regions would exemplify the type of sustained, durable investments that have too often been lacking in economically declining cities and neighborhoods.

Another way to expand regional economic development and spur population growth in aging metropolitan areas in the Midwest and Northeast is to encourage immigrants to locate there. One of the key mechanisms for the decline of Black neighborhoods was the end of the Great Migration, which cut off a supply of housing demand, labor supply, and business development in these neighborhoods. Immigrants have been associated with neighborhood revitalization in recent decades.[50] Immigration to disadvantaged central-city neighborhoods is particularly associated with declines in violent crime, which is a major impediment to quality of life and demand for investment in Black neighborhoods.

One mechanism to nudge immigrants toward settlement in aging midwestern and northeastern metros is the "Heartland visa": place-based visas that would be issued to someone emigrating to the United States, incumbent on their location in a qualifying location.[51] Although increased immigration is desirable for a number of reasons, this proposal has less to do with aggregate immigration than with where immigrants settle. Immigrants are entering a broader set of metropolitan areas today than ever before, but they still tend to locate in traditional gateway destinations and other fast-growing metros and counties.[52] Adam Ozimek, Kenan Fikri, and John Lettieri suggest that directing immigrants to slow-growing metros would not just stem the tide against population loss and other demographic challenges in declining metros and counties but also help turn around their economic fortunes.[53] These authors are less concerned with disadvantaged urban neighborhoods than with the bad demographic trajectories of the broader geography of the Midwest and Northeast, where rising regional inequality has concentrated a growing share of the nation's economic output in a small group of metros. Such a visa program, however, would be likely to benefit some of the counties where Black neighborhoods are struggling, particularly in smaller cities in the Midwest. It could also be crafted to benefit counties where population may be rising but population growth is stagnant or falling. Such counties would encompass a larger set of cities and likely many struggling Black neighborhoods.

As with the people-versus-place debate at the neighborhood level, the answer at the regional level is probably "both." But policy is too dominated by interventions at the neighborhood scale. We need to think more about regions.

Inclusive Development

Integrate the Suburbs In addition to migrating to the South, all U.S. demographic groups have continued to suburbanize in recent decades. Blacks have been later in joining this trend than others, but since 2010 a slim majority of Blacks have been living in the suburbs of metropolitan areas.[54] Accordingly, in chapter 5 we saw that the share of Black neighborhoods in central cities has declined in each decade, and that one-third of Black neighborhoods are now located in suburban areas. Although concentrated poverty has grown steadily in the suburbs in recent years, poverty rates are, on average, nine percentage points lower in suburban Black neighborhoods than in central-city ones (27 to 18 percent).[55] Concentrated disadvantage in central-city Black neighborhoods is twice as high as in suburban Black neighborhoods. In fact, Black neighborhood poverty rates in central cities are unchanged since 1970. So while we don't know what would have happened had Black neighborhoods not increased in the suburbs, we do know that suburban Black poverty is lower and the trend is better, so this movement mechanically seems to have made the Black neighborhood poverty rate decline possible. Given this, efforts to open up suburban cities and neighborhoods to more housing, and more affordable housing, should provide Black households with more plentiful opportunities to locate in more advantaged neighborhoods.

One side of mobility to the suburbs is encouraging mobility through the housing voucher program. But the vast majority of Black renters do not participate in this program. The primary impediment to locating in higher-cost suburban neighborhoods (Black or otherwise) is exclusionary zoning. A lot of policy attention is being paid to this matter, in response to the broader housing affordability crisis afflicting many higher-cost metropolitan areas. This attention to exclusionary zoning builds on a significant body of research that makes clear that restrictive land use and zoning policies exacerbate segregation by income and race.[56]

Black neighborhoods in the suburbs are not the hottest battleground for fights over zoning and housing production. But Black suburban neighborhoods can and should avoid replicating the exclusionary policies of the past and present and allow more housing to be built there. More commonly, the battle is over increasing housing production in higher-income, often whiter suburbs (and similar neighborhoods within large cities). These battles are crucial not just for allowing people of various racial backgrounds and incomes access to a larger number of neighborhoods but also for relieving rent and gentrification pressures in Black neighborhoods. These pressures mount when housing supply constraints in exclusionary neighborhoods cause the unmet demand to spill over into other neighborhoods where housing is more plentiful. This is consistent with the rising rent pressures in central-city, often Black neighborhoods as higher-income and whiter populations increasingly locate in or remain in central cities, where traditionally Black neighborhoods are located. In chapter 6, we saw that even though only a small minority of Black neighborhoods are undergoing gentrification, there are some signs that gentrification in these neighborhoods is happening more frequently. There have been some rapid and high-profile changes in Black neighborhoods in recent decades. In Washington, D.C., the metro home to the strongest Black neighborhood indicators, the U Street neighborhood is entirely unrecognizable from just a generation ago. The famous Ben's Chili Bowl is one of only three remaining business on U Street from the neighborhood's days as a center of Black commerce.[57]

Opening up Black and non-Black suburban neighborhoods to more development provides Black renters and first-time homebuyers with more opportunities to locate in more advantaged places. If they locate in suburban Black neighborhoods, they are more likely to be in advantaged ones. Importantly, land use reforms are beginning to take hold in many parts of the country. Minneapolis, Oregon, and California, among other places, have undergone high-profile land use changes or passed state legislation to hold exclusionary jurisdictions accountable in their land use policies and housing production outcomes. In California, these reforms use state oversight to influence higher production in exclusionary cities and enforce fair housing outcomes in higher-opportunity neighborhoods. It is often counterintuitive to focus on housing policies outside of Black neighborhoods to improve conditions within them, but such a focus is sometimes necessary.

Knowing (and Getting) Our Price Although this book is about the geography of race and poverty, it's not just about where people live or where they don't. It is also about what resources people have at their disposal, what people do or do not own, and, crucially, how society and markets value people and their resources. Andre Perry, in his book *Know Your Price*, powerfully summarizes how Black life, talent, and assets are deeply undervalued in our country across several domains, including community and economic development, education, and health care.[58] Most relevant to Black neighborhoods is the devaluing of commercial and residential property owned (relatively rarely) by Black people. Perry, Rothwell, and Harshbarger find that homes in Black-majority neighborhoods are valued at 22 percent less than homes in neighborhoods where Blacks are not found, even controlling for differences in housing and neighborhood quality.[59] They estimate that homes in Black neighborhoods leave over $156 million in equity on the table, simply because of the race of the surrounding population. Junia Howell and Elizabeth Korver-Glenn find that neighborhood racial composition was actually more predictive of appraised home values in 2015 than in 1980, suggesting that the appraisal industry has become more racially discriminatory, not less.[60] In another report Perry, Rothwell, and Harshbarger find that this devaluation extends to commercial establishments.[61] Although Yelp reviews are just as high for businesses in Black-majority neighborhoods, their profits are much smaller and losses much higher. Businesses in these neighborhoods are probably providing the same level of quality as businesses in other neighborhoods, but the market discounts their quality because of the racial composition of the surrounding neighborhood. This research highlights not just that opportunity follows whiteness but that value follows whiteness (or more specifically, devaluation follows blackness).

Solving this problem requires solving racism. As Perry puts it, "There is nothing wrong with Black people that ending racism cannot solve."[62] But there are some promising approaches that can help revitalize Black neighborhoods. Given the low homeownership rates among Black households and in Black neighborhoods, automatically raising property values in these places could create problems by pricing out incumbent renters. Rapid rises in property values can even create problems for homeowners if property taxes rise at the same rate. Perry and Stuart Yasgur identify some burgeoning solutions that can hit the trifecta of revitalizing neighborhood assets, building access to ownership, and producing neighborhood growth while limiting displacement.[63]

The central challenge is well summarized by Bree Jones, CEO of Parity, an equitable development company located in West Baltimore, a longstanding Black community:

> A lot of historically Black communities will stay dormant for 20, 30, 40 years. There's no activity happening, and then suddenly, boom, gentrification. And then it's too late, and people get displaced. So we work in historically Black neighborhoods that still have zero housing development and develop them preemptively in a way that's community-led and creates ownership of the process, so we're actually strengthening the neighborhood against gentrification.[64]

Parity buys and flips entire blocks at a time in disadvantaged, predominantly Black West Baltimore neighborhoods. They take a collective economics approach, recruiting groups of homeowners to buy and move into the renovated properties and create a cohesive community.[65] Parity is one of three models that Perry and Yasgur summarize, all of which use strategies similar to community land trusts (CLTs).[66] CLTs are often proposed as solutions to rising rent, gentrification, and displacement pressures. They rely on collective ownership of the land while allowing for individual ownership of the properties on it.[67] There are not many successful examples of CLTs in the United States, but it is a frequently explored solution when communities wish to prioritize neighborhood preservation (of property, people, or both) over private profit.

Perry and Yasgur identify an interesting strategy being used in Seattle to leverage upzoning (when a city changes local zoning laws to allow increased density on one or many parcels) in single-family neighborhoods to create cooperative ownership of multifamily housing. An important consideration with upzoning is that it can increase the value of the land upzoned. Once developers can build and sell multiple lots or units on a parcel of land, that parcel becomes more valuable, all else equal, even if the per-unit price is lower (because multifamily housing is generally smaller and less expensive than single-family housing). Even for homeowners, rapid increases in land values can produce higher property tax bills. A company named Frolic works with homeowners who wish to stay in their neighborhoods to build more density on their lots and recruit prospective multifamily homeowners to buy the properties with low down payments and carrying costs. Like Parity, Frolic is a nonprofit, so with no profit margins to maximize, the company's services do not inflate the costs to the homeowners. Unlike Parity, Frolic does not rely on outside subsidies, so if successful, its business model may be more replicable in other markets where such subsidies are scarce.

Finally, Perry and Yasgur uncover a model in Tulsa, Oklahoma, called the Mixed Income Neighborhood Trust (MINT). Similar to Frolic, MINT provides renters with an equity stake in the project. And reflecting the name, MINT charges different rents to different tenants, so higher-income tenants cross-subsidize lower-income ones. Given the horrific end to Black Wall Street in the 1921 Tulsa massacre, successful, equitable development in Tulsa's twenty-first-century Black neighborhoods is a profound achievement.

In the United States, the deck is stacked against all four models—CLTs, Parity, Frolic, and MINT. The American housing system does not do well with forms of ownership and financing that deviate from the rent-or-own dichotomy. But this dichotomy is not serving urban home-seekers well, and we need to expand opportunities for nontraditional forms of ownership. CLTs can create permanently affordable housing through pooled resources in the form of a trust. Parity, an offshoot of the CLT model, leverages social connections to create a pool of buyers and an instant, connected neighborhood. If a revolution in zoning and land use occurs in the coming years—as is needed in particularly high-cost cities and metros—Frolic is a model that could leverage upzoning to radically expand housing opportunities through multifamily cooperatives. And MINT is a model for transitioning renters into homeowners and leveraging rising housing demand to cross-subsidize existing renters and keep rents affordable in gentrifying communities. Against the odds, these models are working, and many other examples are proliferating throughout the country. As lenders become more comfortable with these models, CLTs and related tools are likely to proliferate where community ownership is essential to protect renters and keep wealth in the neighborhood.

Invest in People

Although I find that Black neighborhoods are more racially diverse than ever, the socioeconomic disadvantage found in these neighborhoods is still a direct result of substantial racial disparities at the individual and household levels, such as in income, wealth, and education. Given 250 years of slavery and an additional 100 years of substantial enforced political and legal impediments to the economic advancement of Black Americans, it is no surprise that the racial wealth gap has persisted (and even grown, by some measures) over the last fifty years. These gaps, in addition to racist perceptions of Black neighborhoods, continue to keep these neighborhoods well behind other urban spaces.

The most obvious way to address persistent racial disparities and to right past wrongs is through reparations. Beginning in 1989, Representative John Conyers (D-MI) introduced the Commission to Study and Develop Reparations for African Americans Act.[68] Since Conyers's death in 2019, Representative Sheila Jackson Lee (D-TX) has picked up the mantle and kept reparations on the congressional agenda.

This bill, though it only asks for a *study* of reparations proposals, is not likely to go far in Congress. But reparations are an important framework for thinking about how much various levels of government could or might invest in Black Americans. Fortunately for Congress, reparations have already been studied, from the who and the why to the how much.

Given the nation's treatment of Black Americans, reparations are owed, and there is precedent. Germany provided reparations for Holocaust victims in the 1950s. Canada paid reparations to indigenous peoples forcibly removed from their homes and reeducated in Christian camps. Most relevantly, in 1988 the U.S. government provided reparations to people incarcerated in Japanese internment camps during World War II.[69] Although reparations are individual-level interventions, they would have profound effects on Black neighborhoods, so they are worth a brief discussion here.

Using a couple of assumptions and some arithmetic, we quickly see that the impact would be substantial. In calculating reparations owed, scholars often arrive at different estimates, which depend on how they value the loss of liberty and the shorter lives lived as a result of slavery, and whether or not they include Jim Crow and other discriminatory processes. Thomas Craemer estimates that the present-day dollar value of U.S. slave labor would vary from $5.9 to $14.2 trillion.[70] William Darity summarizes three reparations totals estimated by economists that vary from $9 billion to $6 trillion.[71] He then provides his own simple and elegant solution. In 1865, Union general William T. Sherman gathered with a group of Black ministers in Savannah, Georgia, to discuss their wishes for how Black people should live freely after the end of the Civil War.[72] The ministers proposed that Blacks should live separately, on their own land, so Sherman proposed, in Special Field Order 15, to set aside four hundred thousand acres of confiscated Confederate property and divide that land among former slaves. The field order specified that each household would receive no more than forty acres, and Sherman added some leftover U.S. Army mules to the equation. Thus was spawned the famous "40 acres and a mule" promise that was never fulfilled, largely because the slain President Lincoln's successor, Andrew Johnson, rescinded the order. Darity proposes that a price tag for reparations be based on the present-day value of the once-promised forty acres and a mule. He estimates that there were four million emancipated slaves at the end of the Civil War; given household size, that would have resulted in allocations of ten acres per individual. Ten acres would have been valued, on average at about $100. That would put the value of the land at that time at $400 million. The present value, including an assumed 5 percent in annual interest and 1 percent annual inflation, would be more than $1.3 trillion. For the thirty million descendants of slaves living today, that would amount to about $400,000 per person.

For every Black neighborhood, an infusion of $1.6 million for each Black family of four would obviously be a massive influx of wealth. The vast majority of Black renters could purchase the home they are renting, and most homeowners would be able to pay off their mortgages and perhaps buy the home down the street. Many Black individuals would choose to move up the neighborhood ladder and use that wealth to buy into higher-priced neighborhoods than where they now live. If enough households move out of these neighborhoods, it is possible that vacancies would rise and contribute to decline. But it is more likely that the elimination of the racial wealth gap through reparations of this magnitude would lead to so massive a shift in how Black neighborhoods are viewed that conditions in them would be substantially improved.

Several cities across the country have either implemented or studied reparations. The city of Evanston, Illinois, is disbursing payments to Black residents as a form of reparations. The city of Los Angeles convened a reparations commission in 2021 that appears close to recommendations that are likely to lead to a redistributive effort of some kind. In 2022, the L.A. County Board of Supervisors voted to seize Bruce's Beach, a Manhattan Beach property that was seized from the Bruce family in 1924. The Bruces, who were Black, owned a successful resort that was also taken from them. Nearly a hundred years later, their descendants now will receive hundreds of thousands per year from the county to lease the property, with the option to sell for up to $20 million.[73]

I fear that such well-intentioned local efforts to enact reparations can let the federal government off the hook, and it is the federal government with both the deepest pockets and the most expensive culpability. Unfortunately, reparations policy at the federal level is stuffed in a can that is likely to be perpetually kicked down the road.

At all levels of government, race-neutral strategies to redistribute income and wealth toward Black people are more politically feasible. The federal government could celebrate every birth of a U.S. baby by providing families with a "Baby Bond"—a federal bond whose dollar value is dependent on the wealth of the family. By distributing Baby Bonds inversely on the basis of household wealth, the federal government could narrow the Black-White wealth gap, because the bonds would be larger for Black families.[74] Down payment assistance and first-time homebuyer loan subsidies could be used to shrink the homeownership gap. Renter wealth creation funds could make this gap less important by allowing renters to build equity as they remain renters. Enterprise Community Partners has rolled out such a fund focused on LIHTC and Section 8 renters; that group estimates that it will provide returns to participants on the order of about 5 percent per year.[75]

Neighborhood-level interventions are often a drop in the bucket. Decades of investment directed elsewhere has left Black neighborhoods behind, and in neighborhoods located in cities with weak regional economies, sporadic public investment has them swimming against the tide. Turning around struggling regions requires a much bigger commitment, but neighborhoods are unlikely to become more affluent without such turnarounds.

Incentivizing immigrants to locate in those regions and shifting major public resources there, such as federal agencies and universities, can make it possible. The United States has never had a lasting urban agenda. Investing in aging, struggling metros would do much of that work. If that doesn't happen, people of all races are likely to continue to leave those metros. Black migrants can find relatively prosperous Black neighborhoods in the South.

Wrapping Up: Integration or Strengthening from Within

In the 1985 film *Back to the Future*, Marty McFly (would have been a good name for a hip-hop MC) travels back thirty years, remaining geographically fixed in his hometown of Hill Valley. He finds a young suburb slowly but surely developing farmland into housing. In an overstatement of thirty years of racial progress, he encounters Hill Valley's Black mayor cleaning floors in 1955.[76] If a community organizer from 1985 Crenshaw, Los Angeles, or D.C.'s Shaw–U Street sped ahead to 2024, they would encounter an entirely different racial diversity and built environment that suggested heretofore unprecedented investment. What would they think about racial progress in those communities? What *should* they think?

The answer to these questions gets to some of the most fundamental debates in urban governance and racial inequality. Uninfluenced by contemporary debates on community control, gentrification, or displacement, that time-traveling community organizer might think that decades of struggle had finally paid off, that deeply disadvantaged and hypersegregated Black neighborhoods had become more affluent and diverse. The organizer might be hopeful that a neighborhood's advantages were no longer tied to its racial composition.

Two facts complicate that conclusion. First, very few Black neighborhoods have changed as dramatically as Crenshaw or Shaw–U Street. Second, in the rare cases of such changes, they have not often been welcome.

On average, Black neighborhood poverty rates have dropped only four percentage points in nearly fifty years, and they are still double the poverty rates outside of those neighborhoods. During this same period, Black household poverty rates declined by twelve points. This is strong evidence that Black neighborhoods are still frequently neighborhoods of last resort. There is variation in Black neighborhood indicators, but that diversity is actually greater outside of Black neighborhoods. Selecting on neighborhood race constrains that variation. What variation does exist is largely regional. The Midwest and aging metros in the Northeast have much weaker Black neighborhood characteristics than in Black neighborhoods in the South and West, although those neighborhoods are disappearing in the West.

Housing markets are posing major challenges for Black neighborhood residents. Home values are rising more slowly than rents, and homeownership rates are still as low in Black neighborhoods (42 percent) as they were in 1970. Although first-time homebuyers have better options in these neighborhoods, existing homeowners have limited equity and renters are increasingly priced out. This gets to the second complicating factor. Although I find that gentrification is relatively rare in Black neighborhoods—even in comparison to other lower-income neighborhoods—gentrification is slowly increasing. And Shaw–U Street is proof not only that an established yet low-income Black neighborhood can become one of the hottest neighborhoods in a very affluent city but also that the vast majority of Black renters there will subsequently be priced out.

The appropriate responses to these challenges depend on what Black people and Black neighborhood residents want. There is evidence that Black people want to live in integrated neighborhoods with significant shares of fellow Blacks. As noted in chapter 1, Camille Zubrinsky Charles's research finds that Blacks prefer neighborhoods where they comprise a majority; very few Blacks want to live in all-Black neighborhoods. Unfortunately, Black neighborhoods are often virtually all-Black, or in recent decades, virtually all–Black and Brown.

In segregation research and policy, neighborhoods with 50 to 75 percent Black shares are typically considered segregated. Given that Blacks prefer such a share, perhaps these neighborhoods should not be considered segregated. Or perhaps integration should not be the only answer. Black people desire neighborhoods of their own. Only some Black people prefer to pursue integration by moving to neighborhoods where they comprise a minority. Integration from within is also not an easy answer, as people rightfully mourn the loss of space and culture in places like Crenshaw, Shaw–U Street, Fort Greene, Bayview–Hunters Point, and the Old Fourth Ward. Further, gentrification has not been found to be a credible path to integration.[77]

Even though Black Americans constitute a smaller share of the non-White population than ever before, the study of Black neighborhood life is still essential. Black neighborhoods hold promise and opportunity yet continue to be the sites of many of the gravest injustices in urban America. As I write, the city of Memphis is reeling from the death of Tyre Nichols, who died of his injuries three days after being repeatedly beaten by police. Nichols was murdered at the intersection of Raines Road and Ross Road in Memphis, where the population of the surrounding area ranges from 70 to 99 percent Black. Every major city in the country has the blood of a Tyre Nichols on its hands, not just through the higher-profile cases of police brutality that are caught on body cameras and smartphones, but through the everyday violence that claims Black lives in their neighborhoods. The stakes are high.

Notes

Chapter 1: Introduction

1. Smith 2021.
2. Martin 2023.
3. Moore 1992; *United States v. Yonkers Board of Education*, 837 F.2d 1181 (2d Cir. 1987).
4. The fight over desegregation in Westchester County was not resolved by the dispersal of public housing in Yonkers. Further, scholars projected at the time that the pace of housing production would not meaningfully reduce segregation in the city (Galster and Keeney 1993). Yonkers is in the top half of large U.S. cities by most measures of segregation (Othering & Belonging Institute. 2020).
5. Simmons and Fontaine 2002, 16.
6. The title of this book is drawn from a 2003 DMX song of the same name that would be his last major hit. The first verse is nothing but a litany of homophobic and transphobic statements, likely directed at contemporary artist Ja Rule. My use of the title is not an endorsement of DMX's message, which I strongly condemn.
7. Martin 2023.
8. Jencks and Phillips 2011.
9. Nellis 2016.
10. Krivo, Peterson, and Kuhl 2009.
11. Peterson and Krivo 2005.
12. DeSilver 2013.
13. Aliprantis and Carroll 2019.
14. Choi et al. 2019.
15. Ibid.
16. Wilson 1987.
17. Perry, Rothwell, and Harshbarger 2018, 2020.
18. Charles 2003.
19. Charles 2000.
20. Charles 2001.
21. A foundational example is St. Clair Drake and Horace Cayton's *Black Metropolis* (1945). Other early examples include Kenneth Clark's study of Harlem, *Dark Ghetto* (1965), works on the Pruitt-Igoe projects in St. Louis (Rainwater 1970), and studies of Black neighborhoods in Washington, D.C. (Hannerz 1970; Liebow 1967). Elijah Anderson's *Streetwise* (1990) and *Code of the Street* (1999) are also influential, the latter set in Philadelphia. More recently, sociologist Sudhir Venkatesh (2000, 2006, 2008) published three ethnographies centered in Chicago and focusing on gang relations, the drug

https://doi.org/10.7758/tjvh5404.4793

trade, the underground/informal economy, and sex work. Deviating from the focus on deficits in Black neighborhoods, Mary Pattillo has examined the Black middle class in the South Side of Chicago in *Black Picket Fences* (1999) and the black-led revitalization/gentrification of a historically disadvantaged neighborhood, also in the South Side (Pattillo 2007). Related is the work (also primarily in Chicago) of Robert J. Chaskin and Mark L. Joseph (2015), who examine the intentional development of mixed-income communities to replace deteriorating public housing.

In the twenty-first century, gentrification and displacement dominate conversations about urban America and are prominent in recent scholarship on Black neighborhoods. Lance Freeman's *There Goes the 'Hood: Views of Gentrification from the Ground Up* (2006) looks at two traditionally Black neighborhoods—New York City's Clinton Hill and Harlem—from the point of view of those experiencing racial and economic neighborhood change. Derek Hyra (2008) takes a comparative approach to study urban revitalization through public programs—chiefly empowerment zones and public housing demolition—in Chicago (Bronzeville) and New York City (Harlem), two frequent sites of ethnography on Black neighborhoods. More recently, Hyra explicitly examined gentrification in rapidly changing (and historically Black) Washington, D.C., in his book *Race, Class, and Politics in the Cappuccino City* (2017).

22. Lieberson 1981.
23. Cashin 2021.
24. Grant 2022; Hobson 2017.
25. Two exceptions: chapter 2 covers the genesis of Motown in relation to the Great Migration, and chapter 6 examines go-go music, the heart of D.C.'s Black music culture.
26. Hunter and Robinson 2018.
27. Ibid., 3.
28. Eichler 2010.

Chapter 2: The Role of the State in Black Neighborhood Disadvantage

1. This section draws heavily from two sources: Nelson George's *Where Did Our Love Go: The Rise and Fall of the Motown Sound* (George 2007) and Berry Gordy Jr.'s autobiography, *To Be Loved: The Music, The Magic, The Memories of Motown* (Gordy 1994).
2. Also deserving credit are the Holland-Dozier-Holland writing and production team and the in-house studio musicians, the Funk Brothers.
3. Gordy 1994, 190.
4. George 2007, 51.
5. Rothstein 2017; Freeman 2019; Wilkerson 2010; Freund 2010.
6. *Plessy v. Ferguson*, 163 U.S. 537 (1896).
7. Freeman 2019.
8. Sander, Kucheva, and Zasloff 2018, 106.
9. In emphasizing that government inaction in the face of housing discrimination is not distinct from government-produced segregation, Rothstein (2017,

ch. 11, part VI) essentially flattens the long-held distinction between de jure and de facto segregation: "Actions of government in housing cannot be neutral about segregation. They will either exacerbate or reverse it."

10. *Brown v. Board of Education of Topeka*, 347 U.S. 483 (1954).
11. For example, Boustan 2010; Tolnay 2003; Wilkerson 2010.
12. Wilkerson 2010.
13. Cutler, Glaeser, and Vigdor 1999; Lieberson 1981; Massey 2015.
14. Recent work by John Logan, Weiwei Zhang, and Miao David Chunyu (2015) calls some of this claim into question by showing that some of the Black-White "integration" observed in early studies on census tract–level segregation reflected the presence of Blacks in servants' quarters. In such cases, Blacks and Whites may have lived in the same neighborhoods, but under a very strict social and economic order.
15. Jones-Correa 2000.
16. Tuttle 1970. *Buchanan v. Warley*, 245 U.S. 60 (1917), struck down laws that explicitly carved up cities into racial territories. These laws proliferated as Blacks urbanized, primarily in the South. In this case, Louisville, Kentucky, had a law that was sweeping and straightforward: on a majority-White block, an owner could not sell to Blacks, and on a block that was majority-Black, an owner could not sell to Whites (Fischel 2015). The nature of the decision had much more to do with the protection of property rights than the defense of civil rights; in fact, legal scholars often emphasize *Buchanan*'s lack of relevance to racial jurisprudence (Ely 1998).
17. Jones-Correa 2000.
18. Slater 2021.
19. Silver 1991.
20. Ibid., 193.
21. Silver 1991. Richmond tried to keep racial zoning well after *Buchanan* with some imaginative policymaking (Rothstein 2017). The state of Virginia banned interracial marriage in 1924. Richmond then passed an ordinance prohibiting anyone from living on a street where they were not eligible to marry a majority of its residents. The Supreme Court rejected this creatively depraved reasoning in 1930. Virginia residents would still be unable to marry those of another race until the interracial marriage ban was overturned over four decades later in the *Loving v. Virginia* decision.
22. Rothstein 2017.
23. Hirt 2015.
24. *Village of Euclid v. Ambler Realty Co.*, 272 U.S. 365 (1926).
25. Ibid.
26. Fischel 2015.
27. *Shelley v. Kraemer*, 334 U.S. 1 (1948).
28. Hirt 2015.
29. Sahn 2021.
30. Shertzer, Twinam, and Walsh 2016.
31. Shertzer, Twinam, and Walsh 2018.
32. For example, Lens and Monkkonen 2016; Pendall 2000; Rothwell and Massey 2009; Rothwell and Massey 2010.
33. Logan, Zhang, and Chunyu 2015.

34. The FHLBB was created as part of the Federal Home Loan Bank System to stabilize the community lending institutions that had been devastated by the foreclosure crisis caused by the Great Depression.
35. Crossney and Bartelt 2005; Harriss 1951.
36. Crossney and Bartelt 2005; Jackson 1987.
37. Crossney and Bartelt 2005; Jackson 1987.
38. Coates 2014.
39. Gross 2017; Reft 2017.
40. Rothstein 2017.
41. "HOLC also initiated and institutionalized the practice of 'redlining'" (Massey and Denton 1993, 51). "Real estate appraisers employed by HOLC developed the practice we know as redlining, wherein loans are not granted in portions of the city classified as physically or economically deteriorated or in neighborhoods inhabited by Afro-Americans or ethnics" (Ebner 1985, 379).
42. Jackson 1987, 200.
43. Freeman 2019; Sander, Kucheva, and Zasloff 2018.
44. Aaronson, Hartley, and Mazumder 2021.
45. Woods 2012.
46. Hillier 2003.
47. Fishback et al. 2021.
48. Michney and Winling 2020.
49. Aaronson, Hartley, and Mazumder 2021.
50. Faber 2020.
51. Michney and Winling 2020.
52. Jackson 1987, 203.
53. Jackson 1987.
54. Federal Housing Administration 1938, 110.
55. Whittemore 2013.
56. Sander, Kucheva, and Zasloff 2018.
57. Fishback et al. 2021, 3.
58. Ebner 1985, 379.
59. Mitchell 2018; Sugrue 1996.
60. Jackson (1987) notes the massive disparity in the amount of mortgage insurance sold outside of central cities and in newer suburbs from the FHA's inception into the 1960s. Jackson attributes this disparity to the FHA's favoring of single-family construction and its stinginess in giving out loans for rehabilitation (often making it cheaper to buy a new home outright), as well as the underwriting criteria's overwhelming preference for the all-White suburban subdivisions.
61. Suzanne Mettler (2005, 102) states that, "more than any other feature of the GI Bill, the loan program was vulnerable to racism because it required African American veterans to pass through a gauntlet of local banks that were often unwilling to make loans to them." Mettler cites data from an *Ebony* magazine finding that of 3,229 loans backed by the Veterans' Administration in Mississippi, only two went to Blacks. Although banks in Mississippi were surely more discriminatory than those servicing urban neighborhoods in the rest of the country, it can be assumed that discrimination was still pervasive.

The federal government's reliance on local governments to carry out the provisions of the GI Bill (Katznelson 2005) mirrored a hands-off approach to housing segregation that allowed it to grow and solidify for decades.

62. Jackson 1987.
63. Rothstein 2017, 17.
64. Sander, Kucheva, and Zasloff 2018.
65. Sander, Kucheva, and Zasloff (2018, 90–91)—who are particularly skeptical of the role of public housing in the production of segregated cities—describe a stark scene in Chicago: "a two-and-a-half-mile line of harsh, uniform, high-rise public projects with 100 percent black occupancy stretching along the east side of the twelve-lane Dan Ryan Freeway on Chicago's South Side, with a series of predominantly white ethnic neighborhoods lining the west side of the freeway. In Chicago, the 'family' public housing program was almost all occupied by African-Americans; 'elderly' public housing was predominantly white, and the neighborhood locations of each type of housing consistently underlined this difference."
66. Housing Act of 1937, Pub.L. 75-412, 50 Stat. 888 (enacted September 1, 1937).
67. There is debate over whether the Housing Act of 1937 set the stage for public housing's many challenges over subsequent decades (Hunt 2005). A common telling of the story is that compromises set up public housing to eventually fail, and that the progressive coalition was split over the prioritization of slum clearance versus a broader commitment to rental housing supports of the type that existed in Europe at the time (and still do today) (Hunt 2005; Hoffman 2000).

    In the earlier years of the New Deal, the Public Works Administration (PWA) constructed a small amount of public housing in concert with infrastructure projects, but that was temporary. Rothstein (2017) provides examples in several cities of PWA housing that was built in integrated neighborhoods but then set aside for the predominant racial group in the area, pushing some communities toward segregation. More damning, Secretary of the Interior (the agency in charge of the PWA) Harold Ickes, former president of the Chicago NAACP, mandated a neighborhood composition rule, dictating that federal housing had to house the predominant racial group in the neighborhood in which it was sited. Prior to the PWA, the government had constructed temporary housing to support World War I efforts.
68. Hunt 2009.
69. Freeman 2019.
70. Rothstein 2017, 23.
71. Freeman 2019, 87.
72. Orlebeke 2000, 489.
73. Hunt 2009.
74. Bauman, Hummon, and Muller 1991.
75. Bickford and Massey 1991.
76. Sugrue 1996.
77. Ibid., 74.
78. Souza Briggs, Darden, and Aidala 1999; Massey et al. 2013; Roisman 2007; Rosenbaum 1995.

79. Freeman 2019; Rothstein 2017.
80. Sander, Kucheva, and Zasloff 2018.
81. Hoffman 2000.
82. Sander, Kucheva, and Zasloff 2018.
83. Nall 2015.
84. Rather, the concerns were both familiar to twenty-first-century observers (road safety and traffic) and quite unfamiliar (the importance of being able to flee a major city under atomic attack) (Jackson 1987).
85. Rusk 2010.
86. Avila 2014, 23.
87. Sugrue 1996.
88. Bayor 1996.
89. Kruse 2005.
90. Sugrue 1996.
91. Silver 1984.
92. Schwarzer 2021.
93. Binoy 2022.
94. Baum-Snow 2007.
95. The 1949 Housing Act was a major catalyst for slum clearance and urban redevelopment. William Collins and Katharine Shester (2013) estimate that the 1949 act and subsequent reauthorizations led to over 2,100 urban renewal projects using roughly $53 billion (2009 dollars) through 1974. As with highways and public housing, much of the general understanding of urban renewal comes from case studies that are often not representative of what is typical, perhaps because they are egregious and/or high-profile. By examining all cities with a population greater than 25,000 in 1950 and 1980, Collins and Shester look at nearly all renewal projects. Using these data, they estimate that the projects had cleared over 400,000 housing units, displacing over 300,000 families, and they quote HUD estimates that approximately 54 percent of those families were non-White. Besides removing blight and replacing decrepit housing with something newer, the projects also focused on broader planning and code enforcement. They often, but not always, employed eminent domain to obtain land and property. Jon Teaford (2000) notes the policy drift of urban renewal spending: the initial goals of clearing out substandard housing morphed so much that hospitals, universities, and corporate entities were gobbling up renewal funding by the 1960s. This shift helped turn advocates for the poor against urban renewal spending. The costs of slum clearance, they concluded, were disproportionately borne by low-income families, who realized only limited benefits through affordable housing production and the like.

    "Slum clearance," though a pejorative phrase, was commonly used at the time and describes something distinct from "urban renewal" or the more commonly accepted "urban redevelopment." The latter phrases refer to new land uses or physical structures. "Slum clearance" is more specifically the removal of housing deemed to be substandard or unfit for habitation. "Urban renewal" is also a controversial phrase. James Baldwin (Karjanen 2023, 147) famously renamed it "Negro removal"; less explosively, the term is more likely to be used to describe bygone practices that have been rethought rather than contemporary planning or development policies.

96. Rothstein 2017, 128.
97. Specifically, Collins and Shester 2013 use state laws that enable urban renewal programs as instrumental variables to deal with omitted variable bias.
98. Hartman 1966.
99. Teaford 2000; Wilson 1966.
100. Massey 2015, 574.
101. Freemark, Steil, and Thelen 2020.
102. Hirsch 1983 (Chicago); Kruse 2005 (Atlanta); Sugrue 1996 (Detroit).
103. Sander, Kucheva, and Zasloff 2018, 104.
104. Freeman 2019.
105. Ibid.
106. National Advisory Commission on Civil Disorders 1968, 158.
107. Leovy and Sayers 2015.
108. Galster 2019b, 174.
109. See Ellen and Turner 1997; Galster 2019a; Galster 2019b; Sampson 2012; Sharkey and Faber 2014.
110. A lot of what we know comes from the Moving to Opportunity (MTO) for Fair Housing Demonstration, widely considered a groundbreaking study because it used random assignment to study how neighborhood affects a wide range of outcomes. MTO randomly assigned over 4,600 families from public housing developments in five cities (Baltimore, Boston, Chicago, Los Angeles, and New York) to three groups: one that received a housing voucher to be used in any neighborhood, one that received a housing voucher to be used only in a low-poverty neighborhood, and a control group that would not receive a voucher and had the option to remain in public housing. Over 60 percent of participants in all groups were Black, and over 90 percent of the residents of the neighborhoods where they lived at baseline were minorities (Sanbonmatsu et al. 2011). MTO thus tells us about the effects of living in racially segregated neighborhoods, but more directly it tests the effects of moving to lower-poverty neighborhoods, as that was the tested intervention.

    Although the scores of MTO studies suggest that moving to lower-poverty neighborhood environments is not a cure-all, there are some critical benefits to it. Participants used housing vouchers to move to lower-crime neighborhoods where they were more satisfied, and some adult mental and physical health outcomes improved (Sanbonmatsu et al. 2011). Youth mental health and risk behaviors were a little worse for boys but better for girls. An important conclusion is that the length of time spent living in a high-poverty, segregated environment—or the "dosage effect"—really seems to matter. Adults did not have better employment outcomes, perhaps because the meaningful effects accrue from growing up in low-poverty neighborhoods. But research that identifies children who entered MTO earlier in life (and spent more time in lower-poverty neighborhoods) finds that they earn more in adulthood and are more likely to attend and graduate from college (Chetty, Hendren, and Katz 2016).

    Several other studies benefit from experimental-like conditions to the point of being able to tell us how and when neighborhoods matter. Eric Chyn (2018) tracked locations and outcomes of children who were forced out of Chicago's public housing projects in the 1990s via lottery. He found substantial benefits to leaving behind some of Chicago's most-disadvantaged neighborhoods. Three years after their homes were demolished, displaced families lived in neighborhoods with 25 percent lower poverty and 23 percent less violent crime than the neighborhoods of those who stayed behind in public housing that was not demolished. Children who were forced to move were 9 percent more likely to be employed as adults and had 16 percent higher annual earnings than those who remained in public housing. This contradicts an earlier study by Brian Jacob (2004), who finds that students who were affected by demolitions, also in Chicago, did no worse or better than those who remained in public housing.

At least two studies use waitlists for housing vouchers (Jacob, Ludwig, and Miller 2013) or scattered-site public housing (Galster et al. 2016) to reduce the role of selection bias, as there was an element of randomness in how people were placed on or left the waiting list, and thus where they ultimately moved. Jacob and colleagues (2013) found that receiving a voucher dramatically reduced the poverty rates where the recipients lived and led to lower mortality rates for female children. George Galster and his colleagues (2016) found that living in neighborhoods with less disadvantage, higher occupational prestige, and a lower share of Black residents made it less likely that secondary school students whose families were recipients of housing assistance would drop out or repeat a grade.

Looking beyond MTO at this broader set of studies makes it clear that more than just a neighborhood's poverty rates matters. In fact, the predecessor to MTO as a program designed to use housing vouchers to move public housing residents out of disadvantaged neighborhoods, Gautreaux in Chicago, provided housing options in neighborhoods that were either racially integrated or majority-White. Dorothy Gautreaux was a community organizer and resident of public housing administered by the Chicago Housing Authority who successfully sued the Housing Authority for intentionally segregating Chicago's public housing developments (Keels et al. 2005). The Gautreaux program was a remedy, ordered by the courts, through which Black families living in segregated public housing (in overwhelmingly Black neighborhoods) would be provided with housing opportunities in majority-White neighborhoods, often in the suburbs. The positive outcomes for Gautreaux participants included higher high school graduation rates for children, better employment and earnings outcomes for parents, persistently better living environments long after the program was over, and more. These findings convinced many observers that predominantly Black and high-poverty neighborhoods were major factors in the persistence of widespread racial disparities in the United States (Keels et al. 2005).

Gautreaux was designed to remedy racial segregation in 1970s Chicago—a time and place where public housing developments were virtually all in Black neighborhoods and those Black neighborhoods were severely disadvantaged across every meaningful metric. But Black neighborhoods are no longer uniformly disadvantaged, meaning that today a neighborhood's share Black is not a good proxy for disadvantage. Poverty is most commonly used as such a proxy, and a lot of ink has been spilled (Lens 2015; Turner et al. 2011) on why more expansive neighborhood measures are necessary. But we do have strong evidence that poverty rates are a key ingredient in how neighborhoods affect people's lives. Further, it is unfortunately likely that poverty rates are strongly correlated with a host of other ingredients. These correlations are probably strongest with other socioeconomic features of neighborhood populations such as race, household composition, educational attainment, and employment. But poverty probably also strongly correlates with structural characteristics of neighborhoods that constrain or facilitate opportunity, such as job accessibility, school quality, environmental quality, and public safety.

111. Freeman 2019, 69.
112. After the Hart-Cellar Act of 1965 imposed country quotas, undocumented immigration from Mexico and Central American countries rose significantly (Massey 2013). The rapid increase in immigrants from these countries, as well as from China and Southeast Asia (due in no small part to the wars waged by the United States in those countries), greatly diversified urban neighborhoods that had been mostly White or Black.

Chapter 3: The State of Black Neighborhoods, 1970–2017

1. Caro 1974.
2. "Rap" and "hip-hop" are often used interchangeably as a musical genre name. "Hip-hop" commonly refers to the broader culture that inspires and is inspired by the music. Afrika Bambaataa and Fred Braithwaite have been credited with the term to describe MC-ing, DJ-ing, graffiti writing, and breakdancing (Charnas 2011).
3. Chang 2005.
4. Combined statistical areas are defined by the U.S. Office of Management and Budget as the larger areas that include metropolitan statistical areas and micropolitan statistical areas. Core-based statistical areas can either stand alone or be included in a CSA. For more information, see Executive Office of the President of the United States 2020.
5. Openshaw and Taylor 1979; Reardon and O'Sullivan 2004; Wong 2004.
6. Mock 2016.
7. If the tract is in a CSA that meets the criteria, it is included even if it is in a CBSA that does not meet the criteria.
8. An important caveat, and a limitation to any research that uses census tract data as far back as 1970 (and to a lesser extent 1980), is that the U.S. Census Bureau did not "tract" the entire country at the same time. Census tracts change over time, and that is why I use the weights from the Longitudinal Tract Data Base (Logan, Xu, and Stults 2014) for this study. But in some metropolitan areas, the census had not identified census tracts at all (or did for very little of the area). Thus, there is no way to identify whether or not a neighborhood is Black because there is no neighborhood at all.
9. Comandon 2020; Ellis et al. 2018; Holloway, Wright, and Ellis 2012; Wright et al. 2018.

10. Some of the convergence between Black and non-Black neighborhoods might be due to increased racial and ethnic diversity in both types of neighborhoods. In 1970, the average non-Black neighborhood was 94 percent White. We know that this is probably an overestimate, because we did not ask about Hispanic or Latino ethnicity. But by 1980, when we did begin tabulating Hispanic or Latino ethnicity, the share non-Hispanic White was still 85 percent. By the 2015–2019 ACS, that share was down to 62 percent. This might mean that some of the convergence was due to this diversification, as less-advantaged Asian and Hispanic or Latino (and Black) households are more likely to live in non-Black neighborhoods. Later in the book, I provide substantial evidence that a lot of the improvement in Black neighborhoods is a result of a growing number of Black middle-class neighborhoods and some socioeconomic diversification of Black neighborhoods that we might term gentrification. This latter trend sheds light on the diversification within Black neighborhoods. The share White has essentially stayed flat since 1970, fluctuating only between 14 and 18 percent. But the share Hispanic or Latino has gone from less than 6 percent in 1980 to almost 12 percent in Black neighborhoods, and while the share Asian is still just under 3 percent, it was less than 1 percent in 1970 and 1980. So Black neighborhoods have racially diversified in similar ways as non-Black neighborhoods, making these comparisons similarly relevant over time.
11. You could also make a case for using a relative definition of a Black neighborhood. In cities or metropolitan areas with small Black populations, there may be neighborhoods with a much higher share of Blacks than in the overall population, and those neighborhoods may be considered Black by the local population, even if Blacks are not the largest group. This could justify defining a Black neighborhood according to its share relative to the surrounding area. However, that would undoubtedly pull in many neighborhoods with very low shares of Black residents, particularly since my sample includes a large number of metropolitan areas, some with a small Black population.
12. This chapter examines neighborhoods as a series of cross-sections. For example, table 3.1 shows poverty rates for Black neighborhoods in each year, regardless of whether those neighborhoods remained Black in subsequent years (or whether they were Black neighborhoods in the past). The sample of neighborhoods—and their locations across the country—changed over time. So table 3.1 and similar tables throughout this chapter should not be viewed as examining changes over time in a consistent sample of neighborhoods. Chapter 6 will examine neighborhoods that both remained Black and lost their Black status, and the trajectories of such neighborhoods over time.
13. Non-Black census tracts are those where Blacks do not constitute a plurality.
14. The dramatic change in urban America's racial composition is important context for changes in Black neighborhoods over time and for how we compare them to other neighborhoods. Particularly in using a plurality, the share Black in these neighborhoods has declined considerably over time. On the other side of the coin, non-Black neighborhoods have become substantially less White. Hispanics and Latinos are the fastest-growing group in both types of neighborhood. Thus, some of these changes offset each other. Appendix table A.3.2 shows that we arrive at similar conclusions about

limited progress for Black neighborhoods when we compare to White-, Asian-, and Hispanic-plurality neighborhoods separately.

Conceptually, this book is about Black neighborhoods, however they are composed, with some comparisons to the rest of the country's urban neighborhoods. Although I care *why* Black neighborhoods have better or worse outcomes, changes in racial composition are just one explanatory variable. If those changes play a role in improving (or worsening) conditions, what is important is that the conditions in the neighborhood changed. This is different than looking at the changes in the Black population's exposure to various neighborhood outcomes. My unit of analysis is the neighborhood, not the individual. For reference, appendix table A.3.3 provides poverty exposure rates for Black individuals within and outside of Black-plurality, Black-majority and Black-dominant neighborhoods.

15. Scholars have constructed and analyzed many such indices over the years. An early and similar example comes from Erol Ricketts and Isabel Sawhill (1988), who consider a census tract to be "underclass" if it is one standard deviation above the U.S. mean on each of the following indicators: high school dropouts, male unemployment, welfare recipients, and female-headed households. More recently, Patrick Sharkey (2014) created an index of disadvantage with slightly different variables: welfare receipt, poverty, unemployment, female-headed households, and the percent of residents under age eighteen.

To construct the index, I calculate Z-scores of each variable and measure the number of standard deviations that each observation (census tract) is from the mean of all census tracts in that year, setting the mean at zero. I then average the five Z-scores (after flipping the sign on median income, so that more income will be negative). For example, there is a Black census tract in Chicago with the following Z-scores for the five variables, and the resulting disadvantage index in 2017:

Poverty Rate Z-score	No High School Degree Z-score	Unemployment Rate Z-score	Female Household Head Z-score	Median Household Income Z-score (−1)	Disadvantage Index
1.61	1.76	4.18	3.32	1.47	2.47

This census tract is considerably disadvantaged. Again, Z-scores standardize the variables in like units by measuring the number of standard deviations from the mean of that variable. Thus, the poverty rate in this example tract is 1.6 standard deviations above the mean of 12.9 percent, putting it at about 30 percent (12.9 + 1.6 times the standard deviation of 10.7). The share of female-headed households, which grew considerably over time across the country but started from a much higher baseline in Black census tracts in 1970, is over three standard deviations higher in this census tract. In this census tract, about 70 percent of households are female-headed, which is considerably higher than the Black census tract average of 42 percent.

16. Non-Black tracts make up a greater share of the total, which is how both types of tract can become less disadvantaged over time.
17. Duncan and Duncan 1957; Freeman 2019; Sander, Kucheva, and Zasloff 2018; Spear 1967.
18. Kain and Quigley 1972.
19. The correlation between the share rental housing and share multi-family housing in 2017 was very high: 0.78.
20. Manville, Monkkonen, and Lens 2020.
21. These age measures are based on the number of years since the median-aged housing unit was built. For example, if the median housing unit was built in 1950 in a neighborhood described in the 1970 census, that median housing unit would be built in 1970 in the 2010 census. Thus, the median housing unit would be twenty years old in 1970 and 40 years old in 2010 (as an example). With much more recent housing production, the median housing unit would be either not as old or the same age as the median used to be years ago.
22. As summarized recently by Junia Howell and Elizabeth Korver-Glenn (2021), there are at least four definitions of home value: appraised values by private assessors, typically for mortgages; market values (what people have paid or are willing to pay); appraised values by public assessors for taxation; and self-reported values in surveys such as the census. There is a strong correlation between these values, though naturally some variation. The census and ACS report median values for census tracts, but also home values and rents in several dollar bands.
23. Perry, Rothwell, and Harshbarger 2018.
24. Raymond, Wang, and Immergluck 2016.
25. Sander, Kucheva, and Zasloff 2018.
26. Ibid.

Chapter 4: Where Black Neighborhoods Thrive and Where They Struggle

1. Biggie Smalls's killers are unknown, and the case for East Coast rap involvement in Tupac's killing is complicated. The one living suspect in the crime, Duane Davis, has stated in interviews that he was hired by Combs to kill Tupac. But there is also a simpler explanation. Earlier in the evening, Tupac and his entourage assaulted Davis's nephew, Orlando Anderson, a member of the Crips (a Death Row rival given the label's strong ties to the Bloods). Anderson and Davis could have been retaliating for this assault, or the Combs connection could be real (Courtneyb 2024; Yamat and Ritter 2023).
2. Those labels were Swishahouse in Houston; Cash Money Records and No Limit Records in New Orleans; and LaFace Records, Organized Noise Productions, and So So Def Recordings in Atlanta.
3. Long before Snoop Dogg was a ubiquitous pitchman and American cultural icon, he was a member of the Crips. He is merely the most famous of a long line of gang-involved rap artists.
4. Stuart 2020.
5. The connections between race, crime, and urban disadvantage in Chicago go much further back, of course. St. Clair Drake and Horace Cayton wrote

about this in their seminal book *Black Metropolis,* set in Chicago in 1945. More recently, Rashad Shabazz, in *Spatializing Blackness,* traces the development of the modern police department to late nineteenth-century Chicago fears of miscegenation. According to Shabazz, modern policing was effectively invented as a response to vice districts and the race mixing that had become frequent in those districts, at times located outside of Chicago's Black belt. He also connects housing to Black male criminality in Chicago, as the small geography of where they lived relative to the fast-growing size of the population meant that many of them were confined to kitchenettes—one-room apartments with a small icebox and a cooktop. Shabazz makes the case that the kitchenette amplified Black male violence and criminality owing to the stress of living there and the tendency for men to escape the space constraints without anything in particular to do. This is ironic, since the perception of Black male criminality contributed to Black families being restricted to kitchenettes in the first place.

6. Parkway Gardens is part of the Greater Grand Crossing community area, but that area is entirely broken up by Interstates 90 and 94. Chicago's community areas predate these freeways by a few decades.
7. Office of Policy Development and Research 2014.
8. Main 2014.
9. *Chicago Tribune* 2004.
10. For the tenuous links, see Rosin (2008), and for a rebuttal, see Ellen, Lens, and O'Regan 2012.
11. Popkin et al. 2012.
12. Stuart 2020. MF Doom and Mr. Fantastik warned of this behavior in their 2004 song "Rapp Snitch Knishes." "Rap snitches, telling all they business. Sit in the court to be their own star witness."
13. Anderson 1990, 1999; Drake and Cayton 1945; Hirsch 1983; Hyra 2008; Sugrue 1996; Wilson 1987, 1996.
14. Massey and Denton 1993 (racial segregation); Wilson 1996 (central-city joblessness); Jargowsky 1997 (metropolitan income generation and sorting processes).
15. Wilson 1987, 1996.
16. The southern population is less urban than populations in the Northeast and Midwest, but as Akira Rodriguez (2021) highlights, the South did experience two periods of significant urbanization. While the Great Migration to the North was underway from 1880 to 1940, the remaining southern population went from 9 to 35 percent urban. (The nation as a whole went from 25 to 54 percent urban during that span.) The second period of southern urbanization was during the rise of the Sunbelt from 1940 to 1970.
17. Lloyd 2012; Ross, Sjoquist, and Wooten 2009.
18. Falk, Hunt, and Hunt 2004; Frey 2014b.
19. Pattillo 2005.
20. Wilson 1987.
21. Freeman 2019.
22. One of a countless number of fun connections between the Great Migration and hip-hop is that in 1947 a woman named Alice Faye Williams was born in Lumberton, North Carolina. At the age of twelve, she moved to the South

Bronx, the birthplace of hip-hop. She would eventually change her name to Afeni Shakur and give birth to a boy who would come to be known as Tupac.

23. Lacy 2007; Pattillo 2005; Sharkey 2014.
24. For this purpose I calculated the top quartile using home value thresholds for the surrounding metropolitan area, given substantial differences in value across metros.
25. Jargowsky 1997.
26. Galster and Mincy 1993; Galster, Mincy, and Tobin 1997; Galster et al. 2003.
27. Although I begin with 172 metropolitan areas, I lose a lot of observations because some metropolitan areas had no Black neighborhoods in some or all years. To reduce the potential for outlier Black neighborhoods to impact the results, I further restrict the models to include only CSA/CBSA-years for which the CSA/CBSA had at least ten Black census tracts. That reduces the analytic sample to between 400 and 454 (depending on the model) from a possible 1,032. From 2000 on, there have been 86 CSAs/CBSAs with at least ten Black census tracts.
28. In the last model that includes information on the share of Hispanics in and outside of Black neighborhoods, I use 1980 as the reference year.
29. I have also run these models for each year individually. Statistical power is considerably lower, but the results are very consistent with those reported in table 4.5.
30. Galster and Mincy 1993; Galster et al. 2003; Jargowsky 1997.
31. Galster and Mincy 1993.
32. Galster et al. 2003.
33. Galster 2019a, 2019b.
34. Boustan and Margo 2009.
35. For all variables, I first calculate the eightieth and twentieth percentile values for each CSA/CBSA, then average across CSAs/CBSAs, weighting by the number of Black tracts within every CSA/CBSA. These are thus measures of within-CSA/CBSA inequality.

Chapter 5: Race and Space

1. Author's tabulation of US2010 Longitudinal Tract Database (Logan, Xu, and Stults 2014).
2. Farley 1970.
3. Jennings and Esquivel 2015.
4. Tickner 2017; Williams 2010.
5. Hall 2015.
6. The Beach Boys' catalog is filled with songs about cars and cruising, such as "I Get Around," "Fun, Fun, Fun," and "409."
7. Public Enemy's Chuck D rapped about his Oldsmobile 98 in 1987, which makes sense given that the group was based in Long Island, New York.
8. Charnas 2011; Kelley 1994.
9. "Gangsta rap" has long been a loaded and controversial phrase, most obviously because it has been overused in its application to artists who have neither criminal connections nor criminally focused lyrical content. Black men

more generally have been stereotyped as having gang affiliations. I try to use the phrase sparingly, and only where it applies.

10. Kelley 1994.
11. Alonso 2010.
12. Kelley 1994; Quinn 2005.
13. Einhorn and Lewis 2021.
14. Sharkey 2014.
15. Kneebone and Holmes 2016.
16. Sander, Kucheva, and Zasloff 2018. "Racial tipping" refers to the dynamic—studied and identified in the latter half in the twentieth century—of White neighborhoods rapidly transitioning to Black ones after they become integrated. Early research on tipping is most closely associated with Thomas Schelling (1971).
17. Sander, Kucheva, and Zasloff 2018.
18. Charles 2000.
19. Galster 2019b, 21.
20. Openshaw and Taylor 1979; Reardon and O'Sullivan 2004; Wong 2004.
21. Reardon and O'Sullivan 2004.
22. Ibid.
23. Charles 2000; Sander, Kucheva, and Zasloff 2018; Schelling 1971.
24. Guerrieri, Hartley, and Hurst 2013.
25. Less than 1 percent of tracts border only one other tract. About 75 percent of tracts border between five and eight other tracts, and about 5 percent of tracts border more than ten.
26. Categories 2, 3, and 4 are not mutually exclusive with one another, nor are categories 6, 7, and 8.
27. Ellen 2000; Wright et al. 2018.
28. The LSAD variable only pertains to the census tract's location in the 2010 census, so I backfill those locations in previous years and count a census tract as city or suburb in the 2015–2019 ACS according to its status in 2010. This relies on an imperfect assumption that central-city versus suburban location does not vary over time for specific tracts. It appears to make the variation over time a little lower than we would expect. The LSAD variable indicates whether the tract is part of a city or whether it is part of a census-designated place or a census-designated place that is not a city. I considered this potentially too broad a definition of a "central city" because there are a lot of relatively large suburbs that the census may consider a census-designated place. However, some people might dispute whether such a place is a city or a suburb. For instance, what is Mesa, Arizona, or Long Beach, California? Such is the nature of the term "suburb." I tighten this definition of central city by also referring to the variable in the census that indicates whether the city is the principal city in the CBSA. So a census tract must be located in a city according to the LSAD variable *and* the principal city according to the latter variable to be considered in the central city; all other tracts are in the "suburbs."
29. Holian 2019. For tracts located in CSAs that are comprised of multiple CBSAs, I estimate a central point for each CBSA and measure the distance of each tract in those CBSAs to that CBSA-specific point. For example,

the San Francisco–Oakland–San Jose CSA is comprised of three CBSAs—San Francisco, Oakland, and San Jose. For this CSA and others like it, I identify three central points, not one, to account for polycentric CSAs where there are likely to be clusters of Black neighborhoods organized (typically) around multiple central areas.

30. More specifically, it is a Black population–weighted average distance from each census tract to the central point.
31. Moran's I measures spatial autocorrelation, or the extent to which neighboring geographic units share characteristics according to the included variables (Anselin 1995; Chung and Brown 2007). An advantage of Moran's I is its ease of interpretation: values range from –1 (denoting random dispersion of a variable across space) to 1 (total dependency across space).
32. The difference in spatial correlation between percent Black and Black neighborhoods reflects differences between using binary (Black neighborhood) and continuous (percent Black) variables. Using a continuous input variable is more likely to produce higher levels of spatial autocorrelation, because changes across census tract borders are smoother. For example, a Black census tract might be 33 percent Black and neighbor a non-Black census tract that is 30 percent Black. The difference between 33 and 30 percent is much less consequential for spatial autocorrelation than the difference between 1 (Black census tract) and 0 (non-Black census tract).
33. Jargowsky 1997.
34. Sharkey 2014.
35. There are many ways to weight the characteristics of bordering tracts. Following Sharkey (2014), I use the "queen criterion," which weighs all border tracts equally, regardless of the length of the shared border, the distance between tract centroids, or the number of census tracts bordered.
36. Sharkey 2014.

Chapter 6: Trajectories of Neighborhood Change

1. Concurrent with the rise of hip-hop outside of D.C., and the rise of go-go within it, was a robust punk scene in the nation's capital. Minor Threat, Fugazi, and Bad Brains were all major figures in U.S. punk. Bad Brains, the most consequential Black punk band of all time, incorporated funk and reggae. Rolling Stone (very credibly) called them "the mother of all Black hard-rock bands" (Harrington 1995).
2. When I first intentionally listened to go-go in recent years, it reminded me of a song from my childhood called "Da Butt." My ear turned out to be accurate: this song was semifamously the main hit in go-go recording history, owing to its use in Spike Lee's film *School Daze*.
3. Lornell and Stephenson 2010.
4. Hopkinson 2012, 153–54.
5. Ruble 2010.
6. Hopkinson 2012.
7. Ibid.
8. Hyra 2017; Summers 2021.
9. Kolko 2016.

10. Kolko 2021.
11. Hwang and Lin 2016, 10.
12. Hwang and Lin 2016.
13. Hwang and Sampson 2014.
14. Stancil 2019.
15. Ellen, Horn, and Reed 2019 (lower crime rates); Couture and Handbury 2017; Hwang and Lin 2016 (restaurants and nightlife).
16. This is the number among the CSAs/CBSAs in the sample after census tracts with fewer than 200 people at any point have been removed. There are 3,325 with those tracts included.
17. Schelling 1971.
18. Ellen 2000.
19. Ellis et al. 2018; Holloway, Wright, and Ellis 2012; Wright et al. 2018.
20. Holloway, Wright, and Ellis 2012.
21. Wright et al. 2018.
22. Needless to say, immigration has brought profound changes to Black neighborhoods, as is particularly clear in regions such as Los Angeles. These changes have been covered by others, including Pastor et al. (2016). It is important to note that much of this change is due not only to moves by immigrants but also to native-born Latinos as well. Across the country, only about 14 percent of those living in Black tracts are foreign-born, which is very similar to the share in non-Black tracts (16 percent). The trends in Black and non-Black tracts have largely tracked each other over time, growing steadily from lows in 1970, when only 3 percent of Black neighborhood residents were foreign-born. A share of only 14 percent suggests that Black neighborhoods are not particularly likely to be gateway destinations for incoming immigrants. However, the vast majority of Blacks are native-born, and the average share of Blacks in Black-plurality neighborhoods is strikingly high—66 percent in the 2015–2019 ACS. That does not leave a lot of room for immigrants to appear in the data, with the important caveat that there are many Black-plurality neighborhoods where many in the Black population itself were born outside the United States, such as Flatbush in New York City and Little Haiti in Miami. So while the share of foreign-born is a little lower in Black tracts, and the growth over time has been largely consistent with the rate of growth in the full sample of tracts, the foreign-born presence in Black neighborhoods may be artificially low, given the way these neighborhoods are defined.
23. For example, Ellen, Horn, and Reed 2019; Hwang and Lin 2016.
24. Baum-Snow and Hartley 2020; Hwang and Lin 2016.
25. On the other hand, this measure inevitably obscures some trends. For example, rent may increase across a metropolitan area and such increases may be hidden in low-income areas, where they are more acutely felt.
26. Baum-Snow and Hartley 2020; Hwang and Lin 2016.
27. Hwang and Sampson 2014.
28. Guerrieri, Hartley, and Hurst 2013.
29. Baum-Snow and Hartley 2020, and Edlund, Machado, and Sviatschi 2015 (job access); Zheng and Kahn 2013 (investments in amenities); Hicks and Lens 2022 (charter schools); Hwang and Lin 2016 (consumption amenities); Ellen, Horn, and Reed 2019 (falling crime rates).

30. Smith 1979.
31. Cullen and Levitt 1999 (White flight); Ellen and O'Regan 2010 (decline in crime rates); Ellen, Horn, and Reed 2019 (gentrification).
32. Ellen and Torrats-Espinosa 2019.

Chapter 7: The Rise of Black Middle-Class Neighborhoods in Washington, D.C., and Atlanta

1. French 2017.
2. Joe Coscarelli (2022, xiv, xv) goes so far as to say: "Their experiences—[Lil'] Baby's experience—growing up rough in the city of Atlanta had somehow become national youth culture, their music the dominant lens through which a neglected humanity was partially understood, all while serving as America's principal artistic illustration of both crushing poverty and absurd, unexpected wealth." And "Lady Gaga, Beyoncé, Miley Cyrus and Ariana Grande mined trap's rhythms and its slang; Super Bowl commercials tapped its talent; and suburban teenagers everywhere adhered to its sleek and loud designer dress code."
3. In Atlanta slang (now global), homes where drug deals go down are called "trap houses" (Sizemore 2019).
4. The Migos disbanded after one of the three members, Takeoff, was murdered in Houston in 2022.
5. T.I. has been referred to as the "Jay-Z of the South" by such credible observers as super-producer Pharrell Williams.
6. Grem 2006.
7. There is nothing entirely new in music. Before trap, the TR-808 high-hat sound helped produce at least two other rap subgenres: crunk in Memphis and bounce in New Orleans. Trap is just far more widely known. Out of New Orleans, Juvenile's "Back That Azz Up" (1998), a clear example of the sound, was a massive hit (Sizemore 2019).
8. Not only did Outkast make five highly acclaimed albums, but the single "Hey Ya," while not exactly rap, was a number-one hit and sits at number ten in *Rolling Stone*'s (2024) greatest songs of all time.
9. Grem 2006.
10. Coscarelli 2022.
11. Ibid., 22. Some of the neighborhood demographics that Dupri noticed resulted from White flight. If Whites had not left Atlanta in such large numbers, there might be more White neighborhoods within the city limits.
12. In the 1870s, Washington, D.C., leaders chose to cede power over the city to a federal board of commissioners, in part to neutralize the power of the sizable Black voting population in the city. D.C. residents were not able to vote again for president until the 1964 election, and the first mayor of D.C. was elected in 1973.
13. Note that the Washington, D.C., CSA, which we use as the unit of analysis in comparing metropolitan-level indicators, includes the city of Baltimore and its surrounding area. Given the high levels of disadvantage in Black

neighborhoods in Baltimore, it is particularly notable that Black neighborhood advantage is so high in the D.C. metropolitan area, given the Maryland city's inclusion.

14. Coscarelli 2022.
15. Raymond, Wang, and Immergluck (2016) find that housing in Atlanta's Black neighborhoods recovered slowly from the Great Recession. This finding is an important reminder that even if Black neighborhood indicators are better in Atlanta than in most places, they are still not nearly as good as in non-Black Atlanta neighborhoods.
16. Allums, Markley, and Hafley 2022; Lacy 2007.
17. Only the Boston, Los Angeles, and San Francisco–Oakland–San Jose metro areas had fewer than a hundred Black census tracts in 2017. San Francisco–Oakland–San Jose had the least, at thirty-six.
18. Greene 1999.
19. University of Maryland 2022.
20. Lacy 2007.
21. In 1980, census tract median income had to be above $73,000 to be in the top quartile. In 2017, it had to be above $90,000 (all figures in 2012 dollars).
22. Van Dam 2022.
23. Ross, Sjoquist, and Wooten 2009.
24. Rodriguez 2021.
25. Gibson and Jung 2005.
26. Kruse 2005.
27. Bayor 1996.
28. Kruse 2005.
29. *Smith v. Allwright*, 321 U.S. 649 (1944).
30. Kruse 2005.
31. Bayor 1996.
32. Ibid.; Kruse 2005.
33. Hunter 1953.
34. Hobson 2017.
35. Rodriguez 2021.
36. The nation's first public housing development was located in Atlanta, but it was for Whites only. Many subsequent developments housed Blacks.
37. Rodriguez 2021.
38. Hobson 2017.
39. Bayor 1996; Hobson 2017; Hunter 1953; Rodriguez 2021.
40. Grant 2022.
41. Teel 1989.
42. Ibid.
43. Hein 1972; Teel 1989.
44. Kruse 2005.
45. Hatfield 2021.
46. *Buchanan v. Warley*, 245 U.S. 60 (1917).
47. Slater 2021.
48. *Shelley v. Kraemer*, 334 U.S. 1 (1948).
49. Bayor 1996; Kruse 2005.
50. Kruse 2005.

51. Ibid.
52. Bayor 1996; Kruse 2005.
53. Kruse 2005, 78–79.
54. Ibid., 79.
55. *Brown v. Board of Education of Topeka*, 347 U.S. 483 (1954).
56. Kruse 2005.
57. Hein 1972; Kruse 2005.
58. U.S. Bureau of Labor Statistics 2022.
59. Proximity One 2016.
60. Ross, Sjoquist, and Wooten 2009.
61. Hatfield 2020.
62. Ibid.
63. Grant 2022, 8.
64. Hewitt 2004.
65. Ibid., 319.
66. Hewitt (2004, 323) explains that once the Jackson administration took over, the city's Equal Employment Opportunity (EEO) and Equal Business Opportunity (EBO) offices were given considerable power to begin enforcing economic inclusion for Black Atlantans: "Atlanta became first among U.S. cities in enacting what can now be seen as the archetypal pattern of desegregation: change spreading from working-class positions, to elite positions, and then to opportunities for profit from business ownership." By 1988, over 40 percent of minority-owned firms in the EBO program were in construction, architecture, and engineering, sectors with a clear reliance on local government spending, particularly through large infrastructure projects at Hartsfield-Jackson Atlanta International Airport and the Georgia Dome.
67. Kruse 2005.
68. Brooks 2009.
69. U.S. Census Bureau 2002.
70. Musgrove and Asch 2017.
71. Ibid.
72. Pearlman 2019.
73. Musgrove and Asch 2017.
74. Hyra 2017.
75. Musgrove and Asch 2017.
76. Price 1989.
77. Hyra 2017.

Chapter 8: How Do We Close the Gaps?

1. Turner 2017.
2. Although these policies operate most directly at the individual or federal level, social welfare, labor, and macroeconomic policies are also extremely important to Black neighborhood outcomes owing to their effects on Black employment and income and the role of the social safety net. Education

policy is also extremely important, and much of education policy is indeed local. But public education policy is not exactly place-based, and variation in schooling resources across neighborhoods has its roots in inequalities by race and income in housing, employment, and other policy outcomes.

3. Lens, Ellen, and O'Regan 2011; Schwartz, McClure, and Taghavi 2016.
4. Collinson and Ganong 2018.
5. Desmond 2016, 293.
6. Sanbonmatsu et al. 2011.
7. Chetty, Hendren, and Katz 2016.
8. The Creating Moves to Opportunity (CMTO) project is an ongoing experiment in Seattle–King County, Washington, to apply lessons learned from MTO to further improve the design of housing voucher programs. There should be much to learn from its ongoing evaluations of the effects of mobility on life outcomes.
9. Imbroscio 2023.
10. Ibid., 772.
11. Ellen, Horn, and O'Regan 2016; Lens, Ellen, and O'Regan 2011.
12. LIHTC developments must set aside either 40 percent of their units to be affordable to those who earn 60 percent (or less) of the area median income (AMI) or 20 percent of units to those earning 50 percent of AMI.
13. Kuai 2023.
14. Ellen, Horn, and O'Regan 2016.
15. Horn and O'Regan 2011.
16. Baum-Snow and Marion 2009.
17. Freedman and McGavock 2015.
18. Freedman and Owens 2011.
19. Baum-Snow and Marion 2009; Eriksen and Rosenthal 2010; Freedman and McGavock 2015.
20. Coley et al. 2023; Tach and Emory 2017.
21. Coley et al. 2023.
22. Tach and Emory 2017.
23. Goetz 2011, 2013.
24. Tach and Emory 2017.
25. Slater 2008.
26. Coley et al. 2023.
27. Sharkey 2013.
28. Galster et al. 2004.
29. Rohe and Galster 2014.
30. Until, that is, about 2020. The COVID-19 crisis, combined with inflamed tensions between police agencies in the communities they serve, brought this positive trend to a halt. In some cities, crime and violence rates have risen in the last few years, but cities are generally still far safer than they were at the beginning of the crime decline.
31. Sharkey 2018.
32. Sharkey, Torrats-Espinosa, and Takyar 2017.
33. Neumark and Simpson 2015.
34. Neumark and Kolko 2010.

35. Freedman 2013.
36. Neumark and Simpson 2015.
37. Freedman 2015.
38. Wessel 2021.
39. Freedman, Khanna, and Neumark 2021.
40. Blow 2021.
41. Ibid., 38.
42. Frey 2014a (population); Fernandez 2022 (economics).
43. Felton, Harden, and Schaul 2022; Frey 2022.
44. Booker 2022.
45. Ganong and Shoag 2017.
46. Sander, Kucheva, and Zasloff 2018.
47. Garcia-Navarro and James 2017.
48. Bartik and Erickcek 2014.
49. Yglesias 2016.
50. Ramey 2013; Sandoval-Strausz 2019.
51. Ozimek, Fikri, and Lettieri 2019.
52. Lichter and Johnson 2009; Wilson and Svajlenka 2014.
53. Ozimek, Fikri, and Lettieri 2019.
54. Frey 2014a.
55. Kneebone 2017.
56. Lens and Monkkonen 2016; Pendall 2000; Rothwell and Massey 2010 (income); Rothwell and Massey 2009 (race).
57. Ruble 2010.
58. Perry 2020.
59. Perry, Rothwell, and Harshbarger 2018.
60. Howell and Korver-Glenn 2021.
61. Perry, Rothwell, and Harshbarger 2020.
62. Perry 2020, 9.
63. Perry and Yasgur 2022.
64. Ibid., 7.
65. I interpret Perry and Yasgur's phrasing "collective economics" to be at least a step further than cooperative ownership of land and property. "Collective economics" is probably akin to "group economics" (a concept with a significant history in Black struggle) to describe a collective pooling together of resources to buy or produce something that they would not be able to afford as individuals (Nembhard 2015). Group economics in this context goes beyond just the housing cooperative and focuses on keeping the money in the broader Black community through hiring Black people and contracting with or soliciting Black businesses.
66. Perry and Yasgur 2022.
67. Meehan 2014.
68. Jackson Lee 2021.
69. Darity 2008; Darity and Mullen 2020.
70. Craemer 2015.
71. Darity 2008.
72. McCammon 2015.
73. Chappell 2023.

74. Hamilton and Darity 2010.
75. Salmon 2022.
76. There is also an infuriating moment in the movie's climax where it is implied that McFly's 1985-influenced guitar shredding contributed to Chuck Berry's development of a "new sound." I'll assume that the writers thought this gag was innocent and funny, but it is extremely problematic in the context of race and the actual evolution of rock and roll.
77. Ellen and Torrats-Espinosa 2019.

References

Aaronson, Daniel, Daniel Hartley, and Bhashkar Mazumder. 2021. "The Effects of the 1930s HOLC 'Redlining' Maps." *American Economic Journal: Economic Policy* 13(4, November): 355–92. https://doi.org/10.1257/pol.20190414.

Aliprantis, Dionissi, and Daniel R. Carroll. 2019. "What Is Behind the Persistence of the Racial Wealth Gap?" *Economic Commentary* 2019-03 (February 28). https://doi.org/10.26509/frbc-ec-201903.

Allums, Coleman A., Scott N. Markley, and Taylor J. Hafley. 2022. "'A Better Place to Be'? Black Mecca, White Democracy, and the Contradictions of Neoliberal Cityhood in Atlanta's Black Suburbs." *Journal of Urban Affairs* 44(6): 793–807. https://doi.org/10.1080/07352166.2020.1854612.

Alonso, Alex. 2010. "Out of the Void: Street Gangs in Los Angeles." In *Black Los Angeles: American Dreams and Racial Realities*, edited by Darnell M. Hunt and Ana-Christina Ramón. New York: New York University Press.

Anderson, Elijah. 1990. *Streetwise: Race, Class, and Change in an Urban Community.* Chicago: University of Chicago Press.

———. 1999. *Code of the Street: Decency, Violence, and the Moral Life of the Inner City.* New York: W. W. Norton & Company.

Anselin, Luc. 1995. "Local Indicators of Spatial Association—LISA." *Geographical Analysis* 27(2): 93–115. https://doi.org/10.1111/j.1538-4632.1995.tb00338.x.

Avila, Eric. 2014. *The Folklore of the Freeway: Race and Revolt in the Modernist City.* Minneapolis: University of Minnesota Press.

Bartik, Timothy J., and George Erickcek. 2014. "Simulating the Effects of the Tax Credit Program of the Michigan Economic Growth Authority on Job Creation and Fiscal Benefits." *Economic Development Quarterly* 28(4): 314–27. https://doi.org/10.1177/0891242414548893.

Bauman, John F., Norman P. Hummon, and Edward K. Muller. 1991. "Public Housing, Isolation, and the Urban Underclass: Philadelphia's Richard Allen Homes, 1941–1965." *Journal of Urban History* 17(3): 264–92. https://doi.org/10.1177/009614429101700302.

Baum-Snow, Nathaniel. 2007. "Did Highways Cause Suburbanization?" *Quarterly Journal of Economics* 122(2, May): 775–805. https://doi.org/10.1162/qjec.122.2.775.

Baum-Snow, Nathaniel, and Daniel Hartley. 2020. "Accounting for Central Neighborhood Change, 1980–2010." *Journal of Urban Economics* 117(May): 103228. https://doi.org/10.1016/j.jue.2019.103228.

Baum-Snow, Nathaniel, and Justin Marion. 2009. "The Effects of Low Income Housing Tax Credit Developments on Neighborhoods." *Journal of Public Economics* 93(5, June): 654–66. https://doi.org/10.1016/j.jpubeco.2009.01.001.

Bayor, Ronald H. 1996. *Race and the Shaping of Twentieth-Century Atlanta.* Chapel Hill: University of North Carolina Press.

Bickford, Adam, and Douglas S. Massey. 1991. "Segregation in the Second Ghetto: Racial and Ethnic Segregation in American Public Housing, 1977." *Social Forces* 69(4, June): 1011–36. https://doi.org/10.1093/sf/69.4.1011.

Binoy, Parvathy. 2022. "Remembering Rondo: Black Counter-Memory and Collective Practices of Place-Making in Saint Paul's Historic Black Neighborhood." *Geoforum* 133(July): 32–42. https://doi.org/10.1016/j.geoforum.2022.04.014.

Blow, Charles M. 2021. *The Devil You Know: A Black Power Manifesto.* New York: HarperCollins.

Booker, Brakkton. 2022. "Black Mayors Will Lead America's Largest Cities." *Politico,* November 22. https://www.politico.com/newsletters/the-recast/2022/11/22/karen-bass-black-mayors-largest-cities-00070490.

Boustan, Leah Platt. 2010. "Was Postwar Suburbanization 'White Flight'? Evidence from the Black Migration." *Quarterly Journal of Economics* 125(1, February): 417–43. https://doi.org/10.1162/qjec.2010.125.1.417.

Boustan, Leah Platt, and Robert A. Margo. 2009. "Race, Segregation, and Postal Employment: New Evidence on Spatial Mismatch." *Journal of Urban Economics* 65(1): 1–10. https://doi.org/10.1016/j.jue.2008.08.002.

Brooks, Fred. 2009. "Recent Trends and Future Prospects for Low Income Working Families in Atlanta." In *Past Trends and Future Prospects of the American City: The Dynamics of Atlanta,* edited by David L. Sjoquist. Lanham, Md.: Rowman & Littlefield.

Caro, Robert. 1974. *The Power Broker: Robert Moses and the Fall of New York.* New York: Alfred A. Knopf.

Cashin, Sheryll. 2021. *White Space, Black Hood: Opportunity Hoarding and Segregation in the Age of Inequality.* Boston: Beacon Press.

Chang, Jeff. 2005. *Can't Stop, Won't Stop: A History of the Hip-Hop Generation.* New York: St. Martin's Press.

Chappell, Bill. 2023. "The Black Family Who Won the Return of Bruce's Beach Will Sell It Back to L.A. County." NPR, January 4. https://www.npr.org/2023/01/04/1146879302/bruces-beach-la-county-california.

Charles, Camille Zubrinsky. 2000. "Neighborhood Racial-Composition Preferences: Evidence from a Multiethnic Metropolis." *Social Problems* 47(3, August 1): 379–407. https://doi.org/10.2307/3097236.

———. 2001. "Processes of Racial Residential Segregation." In *Urban Inequality: Evidence from Four Cities,* edited by Alice O'Connor, Chris Tilly, and Lawrence Bobo. New York: Russell Sage Foundation.

———. 2003. "The Dynamics of Racial Residential Segregation." *Annual Review of Sociology* 29(1): 167–207. https://doi.org/10.1146/annurev.soc.29.010202.100002.

Charnas, Dan. 2011. *The Big Payback: The History of the Business of Hip-Hop.* New York: Penguin.

Chaskin, R. J., and M. L. Joseph. 2015. *Integrating the Inner City: The Promise and Perils of Mixed-Income Public Housing Transformation.* Chicago: University of Chicago Press.

Chetty, Raj, Nathaniel Hendren, and Lawrence F. Katz. 2016. "The Effects of Exposure to Better Neighborhoods on Children: New Evidence from the Moving to Opportunity Experiment." *American Economic Review* 106(4, April): 855–902. https://doi.org/10.1257/aer.20150572.

Chicago Tribune. 2004. "U.S. Hits Drug Empire." *Chicago Tribune*, May 14. https://www.chicagotribune.com/2004/05/14/us-hits-drug-empire/.

Choi, Jung Hyun, Alanna McCargo, Michael Neal, Laurie Goodman, and Caitlin Young. 2019. "Explaining the Black-White Homeownership Gap: A Closer Look at Disparities across Local Markets." Urban Institute, October 10. https://www.urban.org/research/publication/explaining-black-white-homeownership-gap-closer-look-disparities-across-local-markets.

Chung, Su-Yeul, and Lawrence A. Brown. 2007."Racial/Ethnic Residential Sorting in Spatial Context: Testing the Explanatory Frameworks." *Urban Geography* 28(4): 312–39. https://doi.org/10.2747/0272-3638.28.4.312.

Chyn, Eric. 2018. "Moved to Opportunity: The Long-Run Effects of Public Housing Demolition on Children." *American Economic Review* 108(10): 3028–56. https://doi.org/10.1257/aer.20161352

City Survey Files, 1935–1940, at the National Archives. https://dsl.richmond.edu/panorama/redlining/data/CA-LosAngeles#cityData.

Clark, Kenneth B. 1965. *Dark Ghetto: Dilemmas of Social Power*. New York: Harper & Row.

Coates, Ta-Nehisi. 2014. "The Case for Reparations." *Atlantic*, May 22. https://www.theatlantic.com/magazine/archive/2014/06/the-case-for-reparations/361631/.

Coley, Rebekah Levine, Bryn Spielvogel, Dabin Hwang, Joshua Lown, and Samantha Teixeira. 2023. "Did HOPE VI Move Communities to Opportunity? How Public Housing Redevelopment Affected Neighborhood Poverty, Racial Composition, and Resources, 1990–2016." *Housing Policy Debate* 33(4): 909–40. https://doi.org/10.1080/10511482.2022.2121614.

Collins, William J., and Katharine L. Shester. 2013. "Slum Clearance and Urban Renewal in the United States." *American Economic Journal: Applied Economics* 5(1, January): 239–73. https://doi.org/10.1257/app.5.1.239.

Collinson, Robert, and Peter Ganong. 2018. "How Do Changes in Housing Voucher Design Affect Rent and Neighborhood Quality?" *American Economic Journal: Economic Policy* 10(2): 62–89. https://doi.org/10.1257/pol.20150176.

Comandon, Andre Robert. 2020. "Ethnoracial Diversification at the Edges of Exclusion." PhD diss., University of California–Los Angeles. https://www.proquest.com/docview/2455606599/abstract/5ACD04C850E04ADDPQ/1.

Coscarelli, Joe. 2022. *Rap Capital: An Atlanta Story*. New York: Simon & Schuster.

Courtneyb. 2024. "Explosive Audio Submitted as Evidence Alleges Diddy's Involvement in Tupac Shakur's Murder." *The Source*, January 16. https://thesource.com/2024/01/16/explosive-audio-submitted-as-evidence-alleges-diddys-involvement-in-tupac-shakurs-murder/, https://thesource.com/2024/01/16/explosive-audio-submitted-as-evidence-alleges-diddys-involvement-in-tupac-shakurs-murder/.

Couture, Victor, and Jessie Handbury. 2017. "Urban Revival in America, 2000 to 2010." Working Paper 24084. National Bureau of Economic Research, November. https://doi.org/10.3386/w24084.

Craemer, Thomas. 2015. "Estimating Slavery Reparations: Present Value Comparisons of Historical Multigenerational Reparations Policies." *Social Science Quarterly* 96(2, June): 639–55. https://doi.org/10.1111/ssqu.12151.

Crossney, Kristen B., and David W. Bartelt. 2005. "The Legacy of the Home Owners' Loan Corporation." *Housing Policy Debate* 16(3/4): 547–74. https://doi.org/10.1080/10511482.2005.9521555.

Cullen, Julie Berry, and Steven D. Levitt. 1999. "Crime, Urban Flight, and the Consequences for Cities." *Review of Economics and Statistics* 81(2): 159–69. https://doi.org/10.1162/003465399558030.

Cutler, David M., Edward L. Glaeser, and Jacob L. Vigdor. 1999. "The Rise and Decline of the American Ghetto." *Journal of Political Economy* 107(3): 455–506. https://doi.org/10.1086/250069.

Darity, William, Jr. 2008. "Forty Acres and a Mule in the 21st Century." *Social Science Quarterly* 89(3, September): 656–64. https://doi.org/10.1111/j.1540-6237.2008.00555.x.

Darity, William A., Jr., and A. Kirsten Mullen. 2020. *From Here to Equality: Reparations for Black Americans in the Twenty-First Century.* Chapel Hill: University of North Carolina Press.

DeSilver, Drew. 2013. "Black Unemployment Rate Is Consistently Twice That of Whites." Pew Research Center, August 21. https://www.pewresearch.org/fact-tank/2013/08/21/through-good-times-and-bad-black-unemployment-is-consistently-double-that-of-whites/.

Desmond, Matthew. 2016. *Evicted: Poverty and Profit in the American City.* New York: Crown Publishers.

Drake, St. Clair, and Horace R. Cayton. 1945. *Black Metropolis: A Study of Negro Life in a Northern City.* Chicago: University of Chicago Press.

Duncan, Otis Dudley, and Beverly Duncan. 1957. *The Negro Population of Chicago: A Study of Residential Succession.* Chicago: University of Chicago Press.

Ebner, Michael H.1985. "Re-Reading Suburban America: Urban Population Deconcentration, 1810-1980." *American Quarterly* 37(3): 368–81. https://doi.org/10.2307/2712663.

Edlund, Lena, Cecilia Machado, and Maria Micaela Sviatschi. 2015. "Gentrification and the Rising Returns to Skill." Working Paper 21729. National Bureau of Economic Research, November. https://doi.org/10.3386/w21729.

Eichler, Alex. 2010. "Rap Isn't 'Black America's CNN.'" *Atlantic,* October 12. https://www.theatlantic.com/culture/archive/2010/10/rap-isn-t-black-america-s-cnn/339862/.

Einhorn, Erin, and Olivia Lewis. 2021. "Detroit Segregation Wall Still Stands, a Stark Reminder of Racial Divisions." *NBC News,* July 19. https://www.nbcnews.com/specials/detroit-segregation-wall/.

Ellen, Ingrid Gould. 2000. *Sharing America's Neighborhoods: The Prospects for Stable Racial Integration.* Cambridge, Mass.: Harvard University Press.

Ellen, Ingrid G., Keren M. Horn, and Katherine M. O'Regan. 2016. "Poverty Concentration and the Low Income Housing Tax Credit: Effects of Siting and Tenant Composition." *Journal of Housing Economics* 34(December): 49–59. https://doi.org/10.1016/j.jhe.2016.08.001.

Ellen, Ingrid Gould, Keren Mertens Horn, and Davin Reed. 2019. "Has Falling Crime Invited Gentrification?" *Journal of Housing Economics* 46(December): 101636. https://doi.org/10.1016/j.jhe.2019.101636.

Ellen, Ingrid Gould, Michael C. Lens, and Katherine O'Regan. 2012. "American Murder Mystery Revisited: Do Housing Voucher Households Cause Crime?" *Housing Policy Debate* 22(4): 551–72. https://doi.org/10.1080/10511482.2012.697913.

Ellen, Ingrid Gould, and Katherine O'Regan. 2010. "Crime and Urban Flight Revisited: The Effect of the 1990s Drop in Crime on Cities." *Journal of Urban Economics* 68(3, November): 247–59. https://doi.org/10.1016/j.jue.2010.05.002.

Ellen, Ingrid Gould, and Gerard Torrats-Espinosa. 2019. "Gentrification and Fair Housing: Does Gentrification Further Integration?" *Housing Policy Debate* 29(5): 835–51. https://doi.org/10.1080/10511482.2018.1524440.

Ellen, Ingrid Gould, and Margery Austin Turner. 1997. "Does Neighborhood Matter? Assessing Recent Evidence." *Housing Policy Debate* 8(4): 833–66. https://doi.org/10.1080/10511482.1997.9521280.

Ellis, Mark, Richard Wright, Lee Fiorio, and Steven Holloway. 2018. "Predicting Neighborhood Racial Change in Large U.S. Metropolitan Areas, 1990–2010." *Environment and Planning B: Urban Analytics and City Science* 45(6): 1022–37. https://doi.org/10.1177/2399808317744558.

Ely, James W., Jr. 1998. "Reflections on Buchanan v. Warley Property Rights, and Race Colloquium: Rethinking Buchanan v. Warley." *Vanderbilt Law Review* 51(4): 953–74.

Eriksen, Michael D., and Stuart S. Rosenthal. 2010. "Crowd Out Effects of Place-Based Subsidized Rental Housing: New Evidence from the LIHTC Program." *Journal of Public Economics* 94(11/12): 953–66. https://doi.org/10.1016/j.jpubeco.2010.07.002.

Executive Office of the President of the United States. 2020. "OMB Bulletin 20101: Revised Delineations of Metropolitan Statistical Areas, Micropolitan Statistical Areas, and Combined Statistical Areas, and Guidance on Uses of the Delineations of These Areas." Office of Management and Budget, March 6. https://www.whitehouse.gov/wp-content/uploads/2020/03/Bulletin-20-01.pdf.

Faber, Jacob W. 2020. "We Built This: Consequences of New Deal Era Intervention in America's Racial Geography." *American Sociological Review* 85(5): 739–75. https://doi.org/10.1177/0003122420948464.

Falk, William W., Larry L. Hunt, and Matthew O. Hunt. 2004. "Return Migrations of African-Americans to the South: Reclaiming a Land of Promise, Going Home, or Both?" *Rural Sociology* 69(4): 490–509. https://doi.org/10.1526/0036011042722831.

Farley, Reynolds. 1970. "The Changing Distribution of Negroes within Metropolitan Areas: The Emergence of Black Suburbs." *American Journal of Sociology* 75(4, pt. 1): 512–29. https://doi.org/10.1086/224873.

Federal Housing Administration. 1938. *Underwriting Manual: Underwriting and Valuation Procedure under Title II of the National Housing Act.* Washington: U.S. Government Printing Office. https://www.huduser.gov/portal/publications/Federal-Housing-Administration-Underwriting-Manual.html.

Felton, Emmanuel, John D. Harden, and Kevin Schaul. 2022. "Still Looking for a 'Black Mecca,' the New Great Migration." *Washington Post*, January 14. https://www.washingtonpost.com/nation/2022/01/14/black-migration-south/.

Fernandez, Celia. 2022. "10 U.S. Cities That Are Growing the Fastest—and New York City Isn't One of Them." CNBC, November 9. https://www.cnbc.com/2022/11/09/fastest-growing-us-cities-kenan-institute.html.

Fischel, William A. 2015. *Zoning Rules! The Economics of Land Use Regulation.* Cambridge, Mass.: Lincoln Institute of Land Policy.

Fishback, Price V., Jonathan Rose, Kenneth A. Snowden, and Thomas Storrs. 2021. "New Evidence on Redlining by Federal Housing Programs in the 1930s." Working Paper 29244. National Bureau of Economic Research, September. https://doi.org/10.3386/w29244.

Freedman, Matthew. 2013. "Targeted Business Incentives and Local Labor Markets." *Journal of Human Resources* 48(2, March): 311–44. https://doi.org/10.3368/jhr.48.2.311.

———. 2015. "Place-Based Programs and the Geographic Dispersion of Employment." *Regional Science and Urban Economics* 53(July): 1–19. https://doi.org/10.1016/j.regsciurbeco.2015.04.002.

Freedman, Matthew, Shantanu Khanna, and David Neumark. 2021. "JUE Insight: The Impacts of Opportunity Zones on Zone Residents." *Journal of Urban Economics* 133(January): 103407. https://doi.org/10.1016/j.jue.2021.103407.

Freedman, Matthew, and Tamara McGavock. 2015. "Low-Income Housing Development, Poverty Concentration, and Neighborhood Inequality." *Journal of Policy Analysis and Management* 34(4, Fall): 805–34. https://doi.org/10.1002/pam.21856.

Freedman, Matthew, and Emily G. Owens. 2011. "Low-Income Housing Development and Crime." *Journal of Urban Economics* 70(2/3): 115–31. https://doi.org/10.1016/j.jue.2011.04.001.

Freeman, Lance. 2006. *There Goes the 'Hood: Views of Gentrification from the Ground Up*. Philadelphia: Temple University Press.

———. 2019. *A Haven and a Hell: The Ghetto in Black America.* New York: Columbia University Press.

Freemark, Yonah, Justin Steil, and Kathleen Thelen. 2020. "Varieties of Urbanism: A Comparative View of Inequality and the Dual Dimensions of Metropolitan Fragmentation." *Politics and Society* 48(2): 235–74. https://doi.org/10.1177/0032329220908966.

French, Kenneth. 2017. "Geography of American Rap: Rap Diffusion and Rap Centers." *GeoJournal* 82(2): 259–72. https://doi.org/10.1007/s10708-015-9681-z.

Freund, David M. P. 2010. *Colored Property: State Policy and White Racial Politics in Suburban America.* Chicago: University of Chicago Press.

Frey, William H. 2014a. *Diversity Explosion: How New Racial Demographics Are Remaking America.* Washington, D.C.: Brookings Institution Press.

———. 2014b. "The New Great Migration: Black Americans' Return to the South, 1965–2000." Brookings, May 1. https://www.brookings.edu/research/the-new-great-migration-black-americans-return-to-the-south-1965-2000/.

———. 2022. "A 'New Great Migration' Is Bringing Black Americans Back to the South." Brookings, September 12. https://www.brookings.edu/research/a-new-great-migration-is-bringing-black-americans-back-to-the-south/.

Galster, George C. 2019a. "Neighborhoods and National Housing Policy: Toward Circumscribed, Neighborhood-Sensitive Reforms." *Housing Policy Debate* 29(1): 217–31. https://doi.org/10.1080/10511482.2018.1452044.

———. 2019b. *Making Our Neighborhoods, Making Our Selves.* Chicago: University of Chicago Press.

Galster, George, and Heather Keeney. 1993. "Subsidized Housing and Racial Change in Yonkers, New York." *Journal of the American Planning Association* 59(2): 172–81. https://doi.org/10.1080/01944369308975866.

Galster, George C., and Ronald B. Mincy. 1993. "Understanding the Changing Fortunes of Metropolitan Neighborhoods, 1980 to 1990." *Housing Policy Debate* 4(3): 303–52. https://doi.org/10.1080/10511482.1993.9521136.

Galster, George, Ronald Mincy, and Mitchell Tobin. 1997. "The Disparate Racial Neighborhood Impacts of Metropolitan Economic Restructuring." *Urban Affairs Review* 32(6): 797–824. https://doi.org/10.1177/107808749703200603.

Galster, George C., Roberto G. Quercia, Alvaro Cortes, and Ron Malega. 2003. "The Fortunes of Poor Neighborhoods." *Urban Affairs Review* 39(2): 205–27. https://doi.org/10.1177/1078087403254493.

Galster, George, Christopher Walker, Christopher Hayes, Patrick Boxall, and Jennifer Johnson. 2004. "Measuring the Impact of Community Development Block Grant Spending on Urban Neighborhoods." *Housing Policy Debate* 15(4): 903–34. https://doi.org/10.1080/10511482.2004.9521526.

Galster, George, Anna Santiago, Lisa Stack, and Jackie Cutsinger. 2016. "Neighborhood Effects on Secondary School Performance of Latino and African American Youth: Evidence from a Natural Experiment in Denver." *Journal of Urban Economics* 93(May): 30–48. https://doi.org/10.1016/j.jue.2016.02.004.

Ganong, Peter, and Daniel Shoag. 2017. "Why Has Regional Income Convergence in the U.S. Declined?" *Journal of Urban Economics* 102(November): 76–90. https://doi.org/10.1016/j.jue.2017.07.002.

Garcia-Navarro, Lulu, and Marlon James. 2017. "A Writer on Being a Black Man in Minnesota." *Weekend Edition*, NPR, June 25. https://www.npr.org/2017/06/25/534286511/a-writer-on-being-a-black-man-in-minnesota.

George, Nelson. 2007. *Where Did Our Love Go? The Rise and Fall of the Motown Sound.* New York: St. Martin's Press. (Originally published in 1986.)

Gibson, Campbell, and Kay Jung. 2005. "Historical Census Statistics on Population Totals by Race, 1790 to 1990, and by Hispanic Origin, 1970 to 1990, for Large Cities and Other Urban Places in the United States." U.S. Census Bureau, February. https://www.census.gov/library/working-papers/2005/demo/POP-twps0076.html.

Goetz, Edward. 2011. "Gentrification in Black and White: The Racial Impact of Public Housing Demolition in American Cities." *Urban Studies* 48(8): 1581–1604. https://doi.org/10.1177/0042098010375323.

———. 2013. *New Deal Ruins: Race, Economic Justice, and Public Housing Policy.* Ithaca, N.Y.: Cornell University Press.

Gordy, Berry. 1994. *To Be Loved: The Music, the Magic, the Memories of Motown.* New York: Warner Books.

Grant, Jonathan. 2022. "Keys to the City: Race, Place and Class in America's Black Mecca." *International Journal of Qualitative Studies in Education* 36(5): 738–58. https://doi.org/10.1080/09518398.2022.2025487.

Greene, Marcia Slacum. 1999. "Moving In and Moving Up, Blacks Transform a County." *Washington Post*, November 22. https://www.washingtonpost.com/archive/politics/1999/11/22/moving-in-and-moving-up-blacks-transform-a-county/46a7d8ca-4bf1-4049-835f-e7445bba86cb/.

Grem, Darren E. 2006. "'The South Got Something to Say': Atlanta's Dirty South and the Southernization of Hip-Hop America." *Southern Cultures* 12(4): 55–73.

Gross, Terry. 2017. "A 'Forgotten History' of How the U.S. Government Segregated America." *Fresh Air*, NPR, May 3. https://www.npr.org/2017/05/03/526655831/a-forgotten-history-of-how-the-u-s-government-segregated-america.

Guerrieri, Veronica, Daniel Hartley, and Erik Hurst. 2013. "Endogenous Gentrification and Housing Price Dynamics." *Journal of Public Economics* 100(April): 45–60. https://doi.org/10.1016/j.jpubeco.2013.02.001.

Hall, Stephanie. 2015. "The Folklore and Folksong of Trains in America, Part Two." Library of Congress, Folklife Today: American Folklife Center and Veterans History Project, August 19. https://blogs.loc.gov/folklife/2015/08/folklore-of-trains-in-usa-part-two/.

Hamilton, Darrick, and William Darity Jr. 2010. "Can 'Baby Bonds' Eliminate the Racial Wealth Gap in Putative Post-Racial America?" *Review of Black Political Economy* 37(3–4): 207–16. https://doi.org/10.1007/s12114-010-9063-1.

Hannerz, Ulf. 1970. *Soulside: Inquiries into Ghetto Culture and Community*. Chicago: University of Chicago Press.

Harrington, Richard. 1995. "Lame Brains." *Washington Post*, July 30. https://www.washingtonpost.com/archive/lifestyle/style/1995/07/30/lame-brains/c4f7c02c-6e33-4a15-ba1a-5c1e2a01a4ad/.

Harriss, C. Lowell. 1951. *History and Policies of the Home Owners' Loan Corporation*. National Bureau of Economic Research, January. https://www.nber.org/books-and-chapters/history-and-policies-home-owners-loan-corporation.

Hartman, Chester W. 1966. "The Housing of Relocated Families." In *Urban Renewal: The Record and the Controversy*, edited by James Q. Wilson. Cambridge, Mass.: MIT Press.

Hatfield, Edward A. 2020. "Auburn Avenue." *New Georgia Encyclopedia*, September. https://www.georgiaencyclopedia.org/articles/counties-cities-neighborhoods/auburn-avenue-sweet-auburn/.

———. 2021. "Columbians." *New Georgia Encyclopedia*, May. https://www.georgiaencyclopedia.org/articles/history-archaeology/columbians/.

Hein, Virginia H. 1972. "The Image of 'A City Too Busy to Hate': Atlanta in the 1960s." *Phylon (1960–)* 33(3): 205–21. https://doi.org/10.2307/273521.

Hewitt, Cynthia M. 2004. "African-American Concentration in Jobs: The Political Economy of Job Segregation and Contestation in Atlanta." *Urban Affairs Review* 39(3): 318–41. https://doi.org/10.1177/1078087403253416.

Hicks, Brock, and Michael C. Lens. 2022. "Incoming! Spatial Enrollment Competition between Charter Schools and Traditional Public Schools." *Education and Urban Society* (September): 00131245221106708. https://doi.org/10.1177/00131245221106708.

Hillier, Amy E. 2003. "Redlining and the Home Owners' Loan Corporation." *Journal of Urban History* 29(4): 394–420. https://doi.org/10.1177/0096144203029004002.

Hirsch, Arnold R. 1983. *Making the Second Ghetto: Race and Housing in Chicago 1940–1960*. Chicago: University of Chicago Press.

Hirt, Sonia A. 2015. *Zoned in the USA: The Origins and Implications of American Land-Use Regulation*. Ithaca, N.Y.: Cornell University Press.

Hobson, Maurice J. 2017. *The Legend of the Black Mecca: Politics and Class in the Making of Modern Atlanta*. Chapel Hill: University of North Carolina Press.

Hoffman, Alexander von. 2000. "A Study in Contradictions: The Origins and Legacy of the Housing Act of 1949." *Housing Policy Debate* 11(2): 299–326. https://doi.org/10.1080/10511482.2000.9521370.

Holian, Matthew J. 2019. "Where Is the City's Center? Five Measures of Central Location." *Cityscape* 21(2): 213–26.

Holloway, Steven R., Richard Wright, and Mark Ellis. 2012. "The Racially Fragmented City? Neighborhood Racial Segregation and Diversity Jointly Considered." *The Professional Geographer* 64(1): 63–82. https://doi.org/10.1080/00330124.2011.585080.

Hopkinson, Natalie. 2012. *Go-Go Live: The Musical Life and Death of a Chocolate City*. Durham, N.C.: Duke University Press.

Horn, Keren M., and Katherine M. O'Regan. 2011. "The Low Income Housing Tax Credit and Racial Segregation." *Housing Policy Debate* 21(3): 443–73. https://doi.org/10.1080/10511482.2011.591536.

Howell, Junia, and Elizabeth Korver-Glenn. 2021. "The Increasing Effect of Neighborhood Racial Composition on Housing Values, 1980–2015." *Social Problems* 68(4, November): 1051–71. https://doi.org/10.1093/socpro/spaa033.

Hunt, D. Bradford. 2005. "Was the 1937 U.S. Housing Act a Pyrrhic Victory?" *Journal of Planning History* 4(3): 195–221. https://doi.org/10.1177/1538513205278372.

———. 2009. *Blueprint for Disaster: The Unraveling of Chicago Public Housing*. Chicago: University of Chicago Press.

Hunter, Floyd. 1953. *Community Power Structure: A Study of Decision Makers*. Chapel Hill: University of North Carolina Press.

Hunter, Marcus Anthony, and Zandria F. Robinson. 2018. *Chocolate Cities: The Black Map of American Life*. Berkeley: University of California Press.

Hwang, Jackelyn, and Jeffrey Lin. 2016. "What Have We Learned about the Causes of Recent Gentrification?" *Cityscape* 18(3): 9–26.

Hwang, Jackelyn, and Robert J. Sampson. 2014. "Divergent Pathways of Gentrification: Racial Inequality and the Social Order of Renewal in Chicago Neighborhoods." *American Sociological Review* 79(4): 726–51. https://doi.org/10.1177/0003122414535774.

Hyra, Derek S. 2008. *The New Urban Renewal: The Economic Transformation of Harlem and Bronzeville*. Chicago: University of Chicago Press.

———. 2017. *Race, Class, and Politics in the Cappuccino City*. Chicago: University of Chicago Press.

Imbroscio, David. 2023. "Beyond Opportunity Hoarding: Interrogating Its Limits as an Account of Urban Inequalities." *Housing Policy Debate* 33(4): 770–88. https://doi.org/10.1080/10511482.2023.2173979.

Jackson, Kenneth T. 1987. *Crabgrass Frontier: The Suburbanization of the United States*. New York: Oxford University Press.

Jackson Lee, Sheila. 2021. "H.R.40—117th Congress (2021–2022): Commission to Study and Develop Reparation Proposals for African Americans Act." U.S. House of Representatives, April 14. https://www.congress.gov/bill/117th-congress/house-bill/40.

Jacob, Brian A. 2004. "Public Housing, Housing Vouchers, and Student Achievement: Evidence from Public Housing Demolitions in Chicago." *American Economic Review* 94(1): 233–58. https://doi.org/10.1257/000282804322970788.

Jacob, Brian A., Jens Ludwig, and Douglas L. Miller. 2013. "The Effects of Housing and Neighborhood Conditions on Child Mortality." *Journal of Health Economics* 32(1): 195–206. https://doi.org/10.1016/j.jhealeco.2012.10.008.

Jargowsky, Paul A. 1997. *Poverty and Place: Ghettos, Barrios, and the American City*. New York: Russell Sage Foundation.

Jencks, Christopher, and Meredith Phillips. 2011. *The Black-White Test Score Gap.* Washington, D.C.: Brookings Institution Press.

Jennings, Angel, and Paloma Esquivel. 2015. "'Straight Outta' a Different Compton: City Says Much Has Changed in 25 Years." *Los Angeles Times*, August 15. https://www.latimes.com/local/california/la-me-0815-compton-image-20150815-story.html.

Jones-Correa, Michael. 2000. "The Origins and Diffusion of Racial Restrictive Covenants." *Political Science Quarterly* 115(4, Winter): 541–68. https://doi.org/10.2307/2657609.

Kain, John F., and John M. Quigley. 1972. "Housing Market Discrimination, Home-Ownership, and Savings Behavior." *American Economic Review* 62(3): 263–77.

Karjanen, David. 2023. "The Long Catalog of Horrors: Racial Capitalism from Slavery to Mass Incarceration." *American Studies* 62(1): 123–59.

Katznelson, Ira. 2005. *When Affirmative Action Was White: An Untold History of Racial Inequality in Twentieth-Century America.* New York: W. W. Norton.

Keels, Micere, Greg J. Duncan, Stefanie Deluca, Ruby Mendenhall, and James Rosenbaum. 2005. "Fifteen Years Later: Can Residential Mobility Programs Provide a Long-Term Escape from Neighborhood Segregation, Crime, and Poverty." *Demography* 42(1): 51–73. https://doi.org/10.1353/dem.2005.0005.

Kelley, Robin D. G. 1994. *Race Rebels: Culture, Politics, and the Black Working Class.* New York: Free Press.

Kneebone, Elizabeth. 2017. "The Changing Geography of U.S. Poverty." Brookings, February 15. https://www.brookings.edu/testimonies/the-changing-geography-of-us-poverty/.

Kneebone, Elizabeth, and Natalie Holmes. 2016. "U.S. Concentrated Poverty in the Wake of the Great Recession." Brookings, March 31. https://www.brookings.edu/research/u-s-concentrated-poverty-in-the-wake-of-the-great-recession/.

Kolko, Jed. 2016. "Urban Revival? Not for Most Americans." Jed Kolko (blog), March 30. http://jedkolko.com/2016/03/30/urban-revival-not-for-most-americans/.

———. 2021. "The Downtown Decade: U.S. Population Density Rose in the 2010s." *New York Times*, September 1. https://www.nytimes.com/2021/09/01/upshot/the-downtown-decade-us-population-density-rose-in-the-2010s.html.

Krivo, Lauren J., Ruth D. Peterson, and Danielle C. Kuhl. 2009. "Segregation, Racial Structure, and Neighborhood Violent Crime." *American Journal of Sociology* 114(6, May): 1765–1802. https://doi.org/10.1086/597285.

Kruse, Kevin Michael. 2005. *White Flight: Atlanta and the Making of Modern Conservatism.* Princeton, N.J.: Princeton University Press.

Kuai, Yiwen. 2023. "A Missed Opportunity? The 4% Low-Income Housing Tax Credit Program." *Housing Policy Debate* 34(3): 1–24. https://doi.org/10.1080/10511482.2023.2180651.

Lacy, Karyn R. 2007. *Blue-Chip Black: Race, Class, and Status in the New Black Middle Class.* Berkeley: University of California Press.

Lens, Michael C. 2015. "Measuring the Geography of Opportunity." *Progress in Human Geography* (December). https://doi.org/10.1177/0309132515618104.

Lens, Michael C., Ingrid Gould Ellen, and Katherine O'Regan. 2011. "Do Vouchers Help Low-Income Households Live in Safer Neighborhoods? Evidence on the Housing Choice Voucher Program." *Cityscape* 13(3): 135–59.

Lens, Michael C., and Paavo Monkkonen. 2016. "Do Strict Land Use Regulations Make Metropolitan Areas More Segregated by Income?" *Journal of the American Planning Association* 82(1): 6–21. https://doi.org/10.1080/01944363.2015.1111163.

Leovy, Jill, and Dorothy L. Sayers. 2015. *Ghettoside: A True Story of Murder in America.* New York: Random House.

Lichter, Daniel T., and Kenneth M. Johnson. 2009. "Immigrant Gateways and Hispanic Migration to New Destinations." *International Migration Review* 43(3): 496–518. https://doi.org/10.1111/j.1747-7379.2009.00775.x.

Lieberson, Stanley. 1981. *A Piece of the Pie: Blacks and White Immigrants since 1880.* Berkeley: University of California Press.

Liebow, Elliot. 1967. *Tally's Corner: A Study of Negro Streetcorner Men.* Boston, Little, Brown & Co.

Lloyd, Richard. 2012. "Urbanization and the Southern United States." *Annual Review of Sociology* 38(1, August): 483–506. https://doi.org/10.1146/annurev-soc-071811-145540.

Logan, John R., Zengwang Xu, and Brian J. Stults. 2014. "Interpolating U.S. Decennial Census Tract Data from as Early as 1970 to 2010: A Longitudinal Tract Database." *Professional Geographer* 66(3): 412–20. https://doi.org/10.1080/00330124.2014.905156.

Logan, John R., Weiwei Zhang, and Miao David Chunyu. 2015. "Emergent Ghettos: Black Neighborhoods in New York and Chicago, 1880–1940." *American Journal of Sociology* 120(4, January): 1055–94. https://doi.org/10.1086/680680.

Lornell, Kip, and Charles C. Stephenson Jr. 2010. *The Beat: Go-Go Music from Washington, D.C.* Jackson: University Press of Mississippi.

Main, Frank. 2014. "The Most Dangerous Block in Chicago, Once Home to Michelle Obama: 'O Block.'" *Chicago Sun-Times*, November 2. https://chicago.suntimes.com/2014/11/2/18458059/o-block-most-dangerous-block-in-chicago-michelle-obama-chief-keef-parkway-gardens-south-king-drive.

Manville, Michael, Paavo Monkkonen, and Michael Lens. 2020. "It's Time to End Single-Family Zoning." *Journal of the American Planning Association* 86(1): 106–12. https://doi.org/10.1080/01944363.2019.1651216.

Martin, Bradford. 2023. "'This Country Is Done': Fair Housing Discourse in Suburban Westchester." *Journal of Contemporary History* 58(4, May): 00220094231178700. https://doi.org/10.1177/00220094231178700.

Massey, Douglas S. 2013. "America's Immigration Policy Fiasco: Learning from Past Mistakes." *Daedalus* 142(3): 5–15. https://doi.org/10.1162/DAED_a_00215.

———. 2015. "The Legacy of the 1968 Fair Housing Act." *Sociological Forum* 30(S1, June): 571–88. https://doi.org/10.1111/socf.12178.

Massey, Douglas S., Len Albright, Rebecca Casciano, Elizabeth Derickson, and David N. Kinsey. 2013. *Climbing Mount Laurel: The Struggle for Affordable Housing and Social Mobility in an American Suburb.* Princeton, N.J.: Princeton University Press.

Massey, Douglas S., and Nancy A. Denton. 1993. *American Apartheid: Segregation and the Making of the Underclass.* Cambridge, Mass.: Harvard University Press.

McCammon, Sarah. 2015. "The Story behind '40 Acres and a Mule.'" *All Things Considered*, NPR, January 12. https://www.npr.org/sections/codeswitch/2015/01/12/376781165/the-story-behind-40-acres-and-a-mule.

Meehan, James. 2014. "Reinventing Real Estate: The Community Land Trust as a Social Invention in Affordable Housing." *Journal of Applied Social Science* 8(2): 113–33. https://doi.org/10.1177/1936724413497480.

Mettler, Suzanne. 2005. *Soldiers to Citizens: The G.I. Bill and the Making of the Greatest Generation*. New York: Oxford University Press.

Michney, Todd M., and LaDale Winling. 2020. "New Perspectives on New Deal Housing Policy: Explicating and Mapping HOLC Loans to African Americans." *Journal of Urban History* 46(1): 150–80. https://doi.org/10.1177/0096144218819429.

Mitchell, Scott A. 2018. "Spaces of Emergent Memory: Detroit's 8 Mile Wall and Public Memories of Civil Rights Injustice." *Communication and Critical/Cultural Studies* 15(3): 197–212. https://doi.org/10.1080/14791420.2018.1500699.

Mock, Brentin. 2016. "Half of Wisconsin's Black Neighborhoods Are Jails." *Bloomberg*, August 9. https://www.bloomberg.com/news/articles/2016-08-09/half-of-wisconsin-s-black-neighborhoods-are-jails.

Moore, Edward E. 1992. "United States v. Yonkers Board of Education, 837 F.2d 1181 (2d Cir. 1987)." *The Urban Lawyer* 24(3): 597–601.

Musgrove, George Derek, and Chris Myers Asch. 2017. *Chocolate City: A History of Race and Democracy in the Nation's Capital*. Chapel Hill: University of North Carolina Press.

Nall, Clayton. 2015. "The Political Consequences of Spatial Policies: How Interstate Highways Facilitated Geographic Polarization." *Journal of Politics* 77(2): 394–406. https://doi.org/10.1086/679597.

National Advisory Commission on Civil Disorders (Kerner Commission). 1968. *Report of the National Advisory Commission on Civil Disorders*. NCJ 8073. Washington: U.S. Department of Justice. https://www.ojp.gov/ncjrs/virtual-library/abstracts/national-advisory-commission-civil-disorders-report.

Nellis, Ashley. 2016. "The Color of Justice: Racial and Ethnic Disparity in State Prisons." The Sentencing Project, June 14. https://www.sentencingproject.org/publications/color-of-justice-racial-and-ethnic-disparity-in-state-prisons/.

Nembhard, Jessica Gordon. 2015. *Collective Courage: A History of African American Cooperative Economic Thought and Practice*. University Park: Penn State University Press.

Neumark, David, and Jed Kolko. 2010. "Do Enterprise Zones Create Jobs? Evidence from California's Enterprise Zone Program." *Journal of Urban Economics* 68(1): 1–19. https://doi.org/10.1016/j.jue.2010.01.002.

Neumark, David, and Helen Simpson. 2015. "Chapter 18: Place-Based Policies." *Handbook of Regional and Urban Economics* (edited by Gilles Duranton, J. Vernon Henderson, and William C. Strange) 5: 1197–1287. https://doi.org/10.1016/B978-0-444-59531-7.00018-1.

Office of Policy Development and Research (PD&R). 2014. "Preserving Affordable Housing at Parkway Gardens in Chicago." U.S. Department of Housing and Urban Development, PD&R, June 17. https://www.huduser.gov/portal/pdredge/pdr_edge_inpractice_061614.html.

Openshaw, Stan, and Peter J. Taylor. 1979. "A Million or So Correlation Coefficients: Three Experiments on the Modifiable Areal Unit Problem." In *Statistical Applications in the Spatial Sciences*, edited by Neil Wrigley. London: Pion.

Orlebeke, Charles J. 2000. "The Evolution of Low-Income Housing Policy, 1949 to 1999." *Housing Policy Debate* 11(2): 489–520. https://doi.org/10.1080/10511482.2000.9521375.

Othering & Belonging Institute. 2020. "Most to Least Segregated Cities in 2020." University of California–Berkeley, Othering & Belonging Institute. https://belonging.berkeley.edu/most-least-segregated-cities-in-2020 (accessed December 7, 2023).

Ozimek, Adam, Kenan Fikri, and John Lettieri. 2019. "From Managing Decline to Building the Future: Could a Heartland Visa Help Struggling Regions?" Economic Innovation Group, April 4. https://eig.org/wp-content/uploads/2019/04/Heartland-Visas-Report.pdf.

Pastor, Manuel, Pierrette Hondagneu-Sotelo, Alejandro Sanchez-Lopez, Pamela Stephens, Vanessa Carter, and Walter Thompson-Hernandez. 2016. "Roots Raíces: Latino Engagement, Place Identities, and Shared Futures in South Los Angeles." Los Angeles, Calif.: Center for the Study of Immigrant Integration (CSII) at USC. http://dornsifelive.usc.edu/csii/roots-raices-south-la.

Pattillo, Mary. 1999. *Black Picket Fences: Privilege and Peril among the Black Middle Class.* Chicago: University of Chicago Press.

———. 2005. "Black Middle-Class Neighborhoods." *Annual Review of Sociology* 31(1, August): 305–29. https://doi.org/10.1146/annurev.soc.29.010202.095956.

———. 2007. *Black on the Block: The Politics of Race and Class in the City.* Chicago: University of Chicago Press.

Pearlman, Lauren. 2019. *Democracy's Capital: Black Political Power in Washington, D.C., 1960s–1970s.* Chapel Hill: University of North Carolina Press.

Pendall, Rolf. 2000. "Local Land Use Regulation and the Chain of Exclusion." *Journal of the American Planning Association* 66(2): 125–42. https://doi.org/10.1080/01944360008976094.

Perry, Andre M. 2020. *Know Your Price: Valuing Black Lives and Property in America's Black Cities.* Washington, D.C.: Brookings Institution Press.

Perry, Andre M., Jonathan T. Rothwell, and David Harshbarger. 2018. "The Devaluation of Assets in Black Neighborhoods." Brookings, November 27. https://www.brookings.edu/research/devaluation-of-assets-in-black-neighborhoods/.

———. 2020. "Five-Star Reviews, One-Star Profits: The Devaluation of Businesses in Black Communities." Brookings, February 18. https://www.brookings.edu/research/five-star-reviews-one-star-profits-the-devaluation-of-businesses-in-black-communities/.

Perry, Andre M., and Stuart Yasgur. 2022. "Redesigning the Housing Market to Build an Architecture of Equality." Brookings, April 27. https://www.brookings.edu/2022/04/27/redesigning-the-housing-market-to-build-an-architecture-of-equality/.

Peterson, Ruth D., and Lauren J. Krivo. 2005. "Macrostructural Analyses of Race, Ethnicity, and Violent Crime: Recent Lessons and New Directions for Research." *Annual Review of Sociology* 31: 331–56.

Popkin, Susan J., Michael J. Rich, Leah Hendey, Chris Hayes, Joe Parilla, and George Galster. 2012. "Public Housing Transformation and Crime: Making the Case for Responsible Relocation." *Cityscape* 14(3): 137–60.

Price, Debbie M. 1989. "'Murder Capital' Label Has Long Stalked D.C." *Washington Post*, April 4. https://www.washingtonpost.com/archive/politics/1989/04/04/murder-capital-label-has-long-stalked-dc/06a3c715-5888-4c26-b6c7-64ef290b305d/.

Proximity One. 2016. "Metropolitan Areas and Fortune 1000 Companies" (based on 2016 data). http://proximityone.com/metros_fortune1000.htm.

Quinn, Eithne. 2005. *Nuthin' but a "G" Thang: The Culture and Commerce of Gangsta Rap*. New York: Columbia University Press.

Rainwater, Lee. 1970. *Behind Ghetto Walls: Black Families in a Federal Slum*. New York: Routledge.

Ramey, David M. 2013. "Immigrant Revitalization and Neighborhood Violent Crime in Established and New Destination Cities." *Social Forces* 92(2, December): 597–629. https://doi.org/10.1093/sf/sot085.

Raymond, Elora, Kyungsoon Wang, and Dan Immergluck. 2016. "Race and Uneven Recovery: Neighborhood Home Value Trajectories in Atlanta before and after the Housing Crisis." *Housing Studies* 31(3): 324–39. https://doi.org/10.1080/02673037.2015.1080821.

Reardon, Sean F., and David O'Sullivan. 2004. "Measures of Spatial Segregation." *Sociological Methodology* 34(1): 121–62. https://doi.org/10.1111/j.0081-1750.2004.00150.x.

Reft, Ryan. 2017. "Segregation in the City of Angels: A 1939 Map of Housing Inequality in L.A." KCET, PBS SoCal, November 14. https://www.kcet.org/shows/lost-la/segregation-in-the-city-of-angels-a-1939-map-of-housing-inequality-in-la.

Ricketts, Erol R., and Isabel V. Sawhill. 1988. "Defining and Measuring the Underclass." *Journal of Policy Analysis and Management* 7(2, Winter): 316–25. https://doi.org/10.2307/3323831.

Rodriguez, Akira Drake. 2021. *Diverging Space for Deviants: The Politics of Atlanta's Public Housing*. Athens: University of Georgia Press.

Rohe, William M., and George C. Galster. 2014. "The Community Development Block Grant Program Turns 40: Proposals for Program Expansion and Reform." *Housing Policy Debate* 24(1): 3–13. https://doi.org/10.1080/10511482.2013.865973.

Roisman, Florence Wagman. 2007. "Affirmatively Furthering Fair Housing in Regional Housing Markets: The Baltimore Public Housing Desegregation Litigation." *Wake Forest Law Review* 42(2): 333–92.

Rolling Stone. 2024. "The 500 Greatest Songs of All Time." *Rolling Stone*, February 16. https://www.rollingstone.com/music/music-lists/best-songs-of-all-time-1224767/.

Rosenbaum, James E. 1995. "Changing the Geography of Opportunity by Expanding Residential Choice: Lessons from the Gautreaux Program." *Housing Policy Debate* 6(1): 231–69. https://doi.org/10.1080/10511482.1995.9521186.

Rosin, Hanna. 2008. "American Murder Mystery." *Atlantic* (July/August). https://www.theatlantic.com/magazine/archive/2008/07/american-murder-mystery/306872/.

Ross, Glenwood, David L. Sjoquist, and Matthew Wooten. 2009. "Tracking the Economy of the City of Atlanta: Past Trends and Future Prospects." In *Past Trends and Future Prospects of the American City: The Dynamics of Atlanta*, edited by David L. Sjoquist. Lanham, Md.: Rowman & Littlefield.

Rothstein, Richard. 2017. *The Color of Law: A Forgotten History of How Our Government Segregated America*. New York: Liveright Publishing.

Rothwell, Jonathan, and Douglas S. Massey. 2009. "The Effect of Density Zoning on Racial Segregation in U.S. Urban Areas." *Urban Affairs Review* 44(6): 779–806. https://doi.org/10.1177/1078087409334163.

———. 2010. "Density Zoning and Class Segregation in U.S. Metropolitan Areas." *Social Science Quarterly* 91(5, December): 1123–43. https://doi.org/10.1111/j.1540-6237.2010.00724.x.

Ruble, Blair A. 2010. *Washington's U Street: A Biography*. Washington, D.C.: Woodrow Wilson Center Press.

Rusk, David. 2010. *Inside Game/Outside Game: Winning Strategies for Saving Urban America*. Washington, D.C.: Brookings Institution Press.

Sahn, Alexander. 2021. "Racial Diversity and Exclusionary Zoning: Evidence from the Great Migration." Lecture delivered at Princeton School of Public and International Affairs, October 7. https://spia.princeton.edu/events/racial-diversity-and-exclusionary-zoning-evidence-great-migration.

Salmon, Felix. 2022. "A Plan for Getting Housing Wealth to Renters." *Axios*, October 12. https://www.axios.com/2022/10/12/housing-wealth-renters.

Sampson, Robert J. 2012. *Great American City: Chicago and the Enduring Neighborhood Effect*. Chicago: University of Chicago Press.

Sanbonmatsu, Lisa, Lawrence F. Katz, Jens Ludwig, Lisa A. Gennetian, Greg J. Duncan, Ronald C. Kessler, Emma Adam, Thomas W. McDade, and Stacy Tessler Lindau. 2011. "Moving to Opportunity for Fair Housing Demonstration Program—Final Impacts Evaluation." Washington: U.S. Department of Housing and Urban Development. https://www.huduser.gov/portal/publications/pubasst/MTOFHD.html.

Sander, Richard H., Yana Kucheva, and Jonathan M. Zasloff. 2018. *Moving toward Integration: The Past and Future of Fair Housing*. Cambridge, Mass.: Harvard University Press.

Sandoval-Strausz, A. K. 2019. *Barrio America: How Latino Immigrants Saved the American City*. New York: Basic Books.

Schelling, Thomas C. 1971. "Dynamic Models of Segregation." *Journal of Mathematical Sociology* 1(2): 143–86. https://doi.org/10.1080/0022250X.1971.9989794.

Schwartz, Alex, Kirk McClure, and Lydia B. Taghavi. 2016. "Vouchers and Neighborhood Distress: The Unrealized Potential for Families with Housing Choice Vouchers to Reside in Neighborhoods with Low Levels of Distress." *Cityscape* 18(3): 207–28.

Schwarzer, Mitchell. 2021. *Hella Town: Oakland's History of Development and Disruption*. Berkeley: University of California Press.

Shabazz, Rashad. 2015. *Spatializing Blackness: Architectures of Confinement and Black Masculinity in Chicago*. Chicago: University of Illinois Press.

Sharkey, Patrick. 2013. *Stuck in Place: Urban Neighborhoods and the End of Progress toward Racial Equality*. Chicago: University of Chicago Press.

———. 2014. "Spatial Segmentation and the Black Middle Class." *American Journal of Sociology* 119(4): 903–54. https://doi.org/10.1086/674561.

———. 2018. *Uneasy Peace: The Great Crime Decline, the Renewal of City Life, and the Next War on Violence*. New York: W. W. Norton & Co.

Sharkey, Patrick, and Jacob W. Faber. 2014. "Where, When, Why, and for Whom Do Residential Contexts Matter? Moving Away from the Dichotomous Understanding of Neighborhood Effects." *Annual Review of Sociology* 40(1, July): 559–79. https://doi.org/10.1146/annurev-soc-071913-043350.

Sharkey, Patrick, Gerard Torrats-Espinosa, and Delaram Takyar. 2017. "Community and the Crime Decline: The Causal Effect of Local Nonprofits on Violent Crime." *American Sociological Review* 82(6): 1214–40. https://doi.org/10.1177/0003122417736289.

Shertzer, Allison, Tate Twinam, and Randall P. Walsh. 2016. "Race, Ethnicity, and Discriminatory Zoning." *American Economic Journal: Applied Economics* 8(3, July): 217–46. https://doi.org/10.1257/app.20140430.

———. 2018. "Zoning and the Economic Geography of Cities." *Journal of Urban Economics* 105(C, May): 20–39. https://doi.org/10.1016/j.jue.2018.01.006.

Silver, Christopher. 1984. *Twentieth-Century Richmond: Planning, Politics, and Race.* Knoxville: University of Tennessee Press.

———. 1991. "The Racial Origins of Zoning: Southern Cities from 1910–40." *Planning Perspectives* 6(2): 189–205. https://doi.org/10.1080/02665439108725726.

Simmons, Earl, and Smokey D. Fontaine. 2002. *E.A.R.L.: The Autobiography of DMX.* Medford, N.J.: Plexus.

Sizemore, Judy. 2019. "How Trap Music Took Over." PBS LearningMedia, Sound Field. https://www.pbslearningmedia.org/resource/how-trap-music-took-over-video/sound-field/.

Slater, Gene. 2021. *Freedom to Discriminate: How Realtors Conspired to Segregate Housing and Divide America.* Berkeley, Calif.: Heyday.

Slater, Tom. 2008. "'A Literal Necessity to Be Re-Placed': A Rejoinder to the Gentrification Debate." *International Journal of Urban and Regional Research* 32(1, March): 212–23. https://doi.org/10.1111/j.1468-2427.2008.00781.x.

Smith, Harrison. 2021. "DMX, Chart-Topping Rapper with Gruff Voice and Hardscrabble Life, Dies at 50." *Washington Post,* April 10, 2021. https://www.washingtonpost.com/local/obituaries/rapper-dmx-dead/2021/04/09/89509a0e-9618-11eb-962b-78c1d8228819_story.html.

Smith, Neil. 1979. "Toward a Theory of Gentrification: A Back to the City Movement by Capital, Not People." *Journal of the American Planning Association* 45(4): 538–48. https://doi.org/10.1080/01944367908977002.

Souza Briggs, Xavier de, Joe T. Darden, and Angela Aidala. 1999. "In the Wake of Desegregation." *Journal of the American Planning Association* 65(1): 27–49. https://doi.org/10.1080/01944369908976032.

Spear, Allan H. 1967. *Black Chicago: The Making of a Negro Ghetto, 1890–1920.* Chicago: University of Chicago Press.

Stancil, William. 2019. "American Neighborhood Change in the 21st Century." University of Minnesota Law School, Institute on Metropolitan Opportunity, April. https://www.law.umn.edu/sites/law.umn.edu/files/metro-files/american_neighborhood_change_in_the_21st_century_-_full_report_-_4-1-2019.pdf.

Stuart, Forrest. 2020. *Ballad of the Bullet: Gangs, Drill Music, and the Power of Online Infamy.* Princeton, N.J.: Princeton University Press.

Sugrue, Thomas J. 1996. *The Origins of the Urban Crisis: Race and Inequality in Postwar Detroit,* updated edition. Princeton, N.J.: Princeton University Press.

Summers, Brandi Thompson. 2021. "Reclaiming the Chocolate City: Soundscapes of Gentrification and Resistance in Washington, D.C." *Environment and Planning D: Society and Space* 39(1): 30–46. https://doi.org/10.1177/0263775820978242.

Tach, Laura, and Allison Dwyer Emory. 2017. "Public Housing Redevelopment, Neighborhood Change, and the Restructuring of Urban Inequality." *American Journal of Sociology* 123(3, November): 686–739. https://doi.org/10.1086/695468.

Teaford, Jon C. 2000. "Urban Renewal and Its Aftermath." *Housing Policy Debate* 11(2): 443–65. https://doi.org/10.1080/10511482.2000.9521373.

Teel, Leonard Ray. 1989. "W. A. Scott and the Atlanta *World.*" *American Journalism* 6(3): 158–78. https://doi.org/10.1080/08821127.1989.10731195.

Tickner, Quincey. 2017. "HBO's 'The Defiant Ones' Shows How L.A.'s Legendary Traffic Helped Form Dr. Dre." Quartz, July 18. https://qz.com/1029794/hbos-the-defiant-ones-shows-how-las-legendary-traffic-helped-form-dr-dre.

Tolnay, Stewart E. 2003. "The African American 'Great Migration' and Beyond." *Annual Review of Sociology* 29(1, August): 209–32. https://doi.org/10.1146/annurev.soc.29.010202.100009.

Turner, Margery Austin. 2017. "Beyond People versus Place: A Place-Conscious Framework for Investing in Housing and Neighborhoods." *Housing Policy Debate* 27(2): 306–14. https://doi.org/10.1080/10511482.2016.1164739.

Turner, Margery Austin, Jennifer Comey, Daniel Kuehn, and Austin Nichols. 2011. "Helping Poor Families Gain and Sustain Access to High-Opportunity Neighborhoods." Washington, D.C.: The Urban Institute. https://www.urban.org/sites/default/files/publication/26731/412455-Helping-Poor-Families-Gain-and-Sustain-Access-to-High-Opportunity-Neighborhoods.PDF.

Tuttle, William M., Jr. 1970. "Contested Neighborhoods and Racial Violence: Prelude to the Chicago Riot of 1919." *Journal of Negro History* 55(4, October): 266–88. https://doi.org/10.2307/2716173.

University of Maryland. 2022. "University of Maryland Reports." Office of Institutional Research, Planning, and Assessment. https://reports.umd.edu/tableaupublic/1813.

U.S. Bureau of Labor Statistics (BLS). 2022. "Economy at a Glance: Atlanta–Sandy Springs–Marietta, GA." BLS, May. https://www.bls.gov/eag/eag.ga_atlanta_msa.htm.

U.S. Census Bureau. 2002. "Table 23: District of Columbia—Race and Hispanic Origin: 1800–1990." Washington, D.C. https://www2.census.gov/library/working-papers/2002/demo/pop-twps0056/table23.pdf.

———. 2019. "American Community Survey." Washington, D.C. https://data.census.gov/advanced?g=010XX00US$1400000&y=2019&d=ACS%205-Year%20Estimates%20Detailed%20Tables.

Van Dam, Andrew. 2022. "Analysis: Is Prince George's Still the Richest Majority-Black County in America?" *Washington Post*, June 29. https://www.washingtonpost.com/business/2022/06/29/dept-of-data-prince-georges-richest-black-county/.

Venkatesh, Sudhir. 2000. *American Project: The Rise and Fall of a Modern Ghetto.* Cambridge, Mass.: Harvard University Press.

———. 2006. *Off the Books: The Underground Economy of the Urban Poor.* Cambridge, Mass.: Harvard University Press.

———. 2008. *Gang Leader for a Day: A Rogue Sociologist Takes to the Streets.* New York: Penguin Press.

Wessel, David. 2021. *Only the Rich Can Play: How Washington Works in the New Gilded Age.* New York: PublicAffairs.

Whittemore, Andrew H. 2013. "How the Federal Government Zoned America: The Federal Housing Administration and Zoning." *Journal of Urban History* 39(4): 620–42. https://doi.org/10.1177/0096144212470245.

Wilkerson, Isabel. 2010. *The Warmth of Other Suns: The Epic Story of America's Great Migration.* New York: Random House.

Williams, Justin. 2010. "'You Never Been on a Ride Like This Befo': Los Angeles, Automotive Listening, and Dr. Dre's 'G-Funk.'" *Popular Music History* 4(2): 160–76. https://doi.org/10.1558/pomh.v4i2.160.

Wilson, James Q., ed. 1966. *Urban Renewal: The Record and the Controversy.* Cambridge, Mass.: MIT Press.

Wilson, Jill H., and Nicole Prchal Svajlenka. 2014. "Immigrants Continue to Disperse, with Fastest Growth in the Suburbs." Brookings, October 29. https://www.brookings.edu/research/immigrants-continue-to-disperse-with-fastest-growth-in-the-suburbs/.

Wilson, William Julius. 1987. *The Truly Disadvantaged: The Inner City, the Underclass, and Public Policy,* 2nd ed. Chicago: University of Chicago Press.

———. 1996. *When Work Disappears: The World of the New Urban Poor.* New York: Knopf Doubleday Publishing Group.

Wong, David W. S. 2004. "The Modifiable Areal Unit Problem (MAUP)." In *WorldMinds: Geographical Perspectives on 100 Problems: Commemorating the 100th Anniversary of the Association of American Geographers 1904–2004,* edited by Donald G. Janelle, Barney Warf, and Kathy Hansen. Dordrecht: Springer Netherlands.

Woods, Louis Lee. 2012. "The Federal Home Loan Bank Board, Redlining, and the National Proliferation of Racial Lending Discrimination, 1921–1950." *Journal of Urban History* 38(6): 1036–59. https://doi.org/10.1177/0096144211435126.

Wright, Richard, Mark Ellis, Steven R. Holloway, and Gemma Catney. 2018. "The Instability of Highly Racially Diverse Residential Neighborhoods in the United States." *Sociology of Race and Ethnicity* 6(3, December). https://doi.org/10.1177/2332649218819168.

Yamat, Rio, and Ken Ritter. 2023. "Last Living Suspect in 1996 Drive-by Shooting of Tupac Shakur Indicted in Las Vegas on Murder Charge." *AP News,* September 29. https://apnews.com/article/tupac-shakur-killing-duane-keefe-davis-vegas-3f7050c2a68813d86a96b96fbb3f1d1a.

Yglesias, Matthew. 2016. "Let's Relocate a Bunch of Government Agencies to the Midwest." *Vox,* December 9. https://www.vox.com/new-money/2016/12/9/13881712/move-government-to-midwest.

Zheng, Siqi, and Matthew E. Kahn. 2013. "Does Government Investment in Local Public Goods Spur Gentrification? Evidence from Beijing." *Real Estate Economics* 41 (1): 1–28. https://doi.org/10.1111/j.1540-6229.2012.00339.x.

Index

Tables and figures are listed in **boldface**.